The Adoption of E-commerce in SMEs

Robert MacGregor

The Adoption of E-commerce in SMEs

The Role of Strategic Alliances

VDM Verlag Dr. Müller

Imprint

Bibliographic information by the German National Library: The German National Library lists this publication at the German National Bibliography; detailed bibliographic information is available on the Internet at http://dnb.d-nb.de.
    Any brand names and product names mentioned in this book are subject to trademark, brand or patent protection and are trademarks or registered trademarks of their respective holders. The use of brand names, product names, common names, trade names, product descriptions etc. even without a particular marking in this works is in no way to be construed to mean that such names may be regarded as unrestricted in respect of trademark and brand protection legislation and could thus be used by anyone.

Cover image: www.purestockx.com

Publisher:
VDM Verlag Dr. Müller Aktiengesellschaft & Co. KG , Dudweiler Landstr. 125 a, 66123 Saarbrücken, Germany,
Phone +49 681 9100-698, Fax +49 681 9100-988,
Email: info@vdm-verlag.de

Zugl.: Wollongong University 2004

Produced in USA and UK by:
Lightning Source Inc., La Vergne, Tennessee, USA
Lightning Source UK Ltd., Milton Keynes, UK
BookSurge LLC, 5341 Dorchester Road, Suite 16, North Charleston, SC 29418, USA

ISBN: 978-3-639-04673-1

ACKNOWLEDGEMENTS

I would like to acknowledge several people who have helped me in the preparation of this thesis.

Firstly, I would like to thank Sten Carlsson and Monika Magnusson for distributing the questionnaire in Sweden and supplying the data for analysis.

Secondly, to my PhD supervisor, Dr Peter Hyland, without whom this thesis would never have been finished. Peter provided detailed critical analysis of my study and his criticisms and advice have always been helpful and justified. Peter's attention to detail has improved the study immeasurably.

Thirdly, to my partner, Connie, who has been a constant source of encouragement in the preparation of this study. She has listened to my complaints and my endless discussions of data and statistics and still continued to smile.

I'd like to thank John Ferguson for the photograph.

Finally to my colleagues that have showed an interest in this work when my own interest was somewhat flagging. I thank them too.

TABLE OF CONTENTS

LIST OF TABLES

LIST OF FIGURES

Chapter 1
Introduction

1.1 Background

The past 5 years has seen a 'push' by many governments, in both developed and developing countries, for businesses to become 'wired to the digital marketplace' (Martin & Matlay 2001). In the UK, a campaign intended to 'make the internet work for everyone' was developed (Blair 2000). The European union developed 2 sets of policies, the first suggesting that individuals should become 'online and digitally literate' (European Community 1999), followed by a second to 'quickly exploit the opportunities of the new economy and particularly the internet' (European Community 2000). In Australia successful involvement in electronic commerce (E-commerce) is seen as a key to business survival (National Office of the Information Economy 1998), while in China, the government has begun supplying substantial quantities of information and strategies to its many SME operators.

These government initiatives have been directed both at the large business community as well as the SME sector. The initiatives are normally threefold, with some variation in approach to suit the large business or SME groups. For the large business sector, the first of these initiatives centres on the notion of downsizing by means of outsourcing the less important functions and for the large businesses to network with these outsourcers, as required. The second initiative provides a plethora of advantages obtainable through the adoption and use of E-commerce, including statements from business managers in similar businesses. The final initiative centres on a series of strategies that will enable the business to become 'wired to the marketplace', thus achieving the goals of E-commerce.

For the SME sector, similar initiatives are proposed. While large business is encouraged to outsource, SMEs are being encouraged to develop small business strategic alliances (networks), thus becoming able to compete with their larger counterparts. As with large businesses, a variety of benefits are presented, followed by a set of strategies to enable the SMEs that are part of a small business strategic alliance to adopt and use E-commerce.

These government initiatives have received criticism both in their applicability to large business as well as to the SME sector. One of these criticisms is the use of 'step-wise' models as a guide to E-commerce adoption (Martin & Matlay 2001, Culkin & Smith 2000, Fallon & Moran 2000). Other criticisms include the use of pre-E-commerce criteria in an E-commerce environment (MacGregor et al 1998) and the view that all businesses fit into homogeneous categories where there is little real difference between large businesses and SMEs (Schuknecht & Perez-Esteve 1999, Matlay & Fletcher 2000, Keniry et al 2003). These criticisms are particularly relevant to smaller businesses. As such, this current study concentrates on the SME sector only.

The first of the government initiatives, aimed at the SME sector, involves the development of small business strategic alliances, such that member SMEs can more adequately compete with large businesses. While this initiative has a number of advocates who suggest that small business strategic alliances provide much needed technical and marketing information (see Jarrat 1998, Copp & Ivy 2001, Tetteh & Burn 2001, O'Donnell et al 2001), a number of criticisms have been leveled at this initiative:

- The development of small business strategic alliances is based on the supposition that SMEs are really "small, large businesses" (Westhead & Storey 1996, Martin & Matlay 2001, MacGregor 2004).

1

- The model of a small business strategic alliance ignores business characteristics such as business size, business age, business sector, geographic location and replaces these with the notion that all SMEs are intent on gaining a global market share (Donckels & Lambrecht 1997, Martin & Matlay 2001, Culkin & Smith 2000).
- The decision to join a small business strategic alliance may not necessarily be based on attempts to reach a wider market or, indeed, to adopt E-commerce (Dennis 2000, Copp & Ivy 2001).

These criticisms are particularly pertinent to those SMEs that are located in regional areas and have chosen a regional focus, rather than a global market focus.

The role of small business strategic alliances remains unclear because no rigorous study has been carried out comparing the adoption of E-commerce by SMEs that are part of a strategic alliance and SMEs that are not.

The second government initiative, aimed at the SME sector details benefits that can be derived through E-commerce adoption and use. Many studies, of both large business and the SME sector, suggest that E-commerce adoption and use can provide a variety of benefits. These include:

- Increased competitiveness
- Development of buyer/seller relationships
- Reduced production costs
- Reduced inventory overheads

While some of these benefits have been achieved by the SME sector, a number of critics (Martin & Matlay 2001, Culkin & Smith 2000) suggest that research examining these benefits presupposes that the SME sector operates in the same manner as the large business sector, raising the question as to whether many of the benefits are necessarily applicable to the SME sector as a whole.

Some of the characteristics that are typical of SMEs are also, in fact, constraints faced by the SME. For example, SMEs have fewer resources and expertise available to them (Blili & Raymond, 1993; Cragg & King, 1993) and have less control over their external environment (Hill & Stewart, 2000; Westhead & Storey, 1996). These constraints limit the expansion and growth opportunities of SMEs, including the adoption and use of E-commerce technologies. Research (Larsson et al 2003, Keniry et al 2003) has shown that SMEs in regional areas are particularly susceptible to the constraints faced by the SME sector.

SMEs located in regional areas are affected by circumstances inherent to their location. Regional areas are defined as geographical areas located outside metropolitan centres. The Australian Bureau of Statistics (2001) classifies regional areas into inner and outer regions, remote and very remote areas. Determining the classification of a region is based on a formula that primarily relies on the measures of proximity to services in terms of physical distance, and population size.

Regional areas are of particular interest to governments because they are often characterised by high unemployment rates (Larsson et al, 2003), a shortage of skilled people, limited access to resources and a lack of infrastructure (Keniry et al, 2003). Yet, at the same time, businesses located in regional areas in Australia contribute 50% of the national export income (Keniry et al, 2003). This implies that SMEs have the potential to play a major role in developing regional areas. This potential has not gone unnoticed by government organisations. The European Union views SMEs as a catalyst for regional development (Europa, 2003). In 2001, the Swedish Parliament passed legislation that resulted in the creation of Regional Development Councils (Johansson, 2003). The Councils have a mandate to promote a positive business climate and sustainable growth in their respective regions. SMEs have been earmarked as playing an important role in promoting growth because they are seen as a key source of jobs and employment prospects (Keniry et al, 2003; Larssen et al, 2003). To encourage growth and development in regional areas, government organisations have been heavily promoting the adoption of information and communication technology (ICT), particularly E-commerce, by SMEs.

Rather than remote and rural areas (which are sparsely populated), this current study focuses on inner and outer regional areas (which are more urbanised). As such, the definition of regional areas would normally have at least one large business industry, would have a population of not less than 50,000 people, would have a viable tertiary education facility and would have government infrastructures to support both businesses and individuals (The Australian Bureau of Statistics 2001).

The third government initiative does not distinguish the large business sector from the SME sector. In both cases, a linear model of E-commerce adoption is proposed beginning with simple email, progressing through website development, E-commerce, and finally transforming the organisation.

A number of authors have not only questioned the similarities between SMEs and large businesses, but have questioned the adoption model itself. Among the criticisms directed, primarily, at the appropriateness of the model to the SME sector are the following:

- The model fails to account for the specific nature of SMEs (Culkin & Smith 2000, Martin & Matlay 2001)
- The model appears to put planning as the last step, rather than as the first step in E-commerce adoption (Tetteh & Burn 2001).
- The model is based on pre-E-commerce adoption techniques, many of which are inappropriate for the E-commerce environment (Fuller 2000).
- Not all SMEs will begin the adoption process at the same stage (Fletcher 2000).

The primary focus of this study is the role of strategic alliances in the adoption of E-commerce in SMEs. The role of strategic alliances in the small business sector is not a new one. Studies by Jorde & Teece (1989), Datta (1988), Gibb (1993), Golden & Dollinger (1993) have shown that strategic alliances can provide their small business members with a number of advantages over stand-alone organizations. These include reduction in financial risks, access to technical knowledge, information to assist market penetration and improvement in internal efficiency. The advent of E-commerce has given rise to a 'new wave' of research advocating the importance of strategic alliances (Overby & Min 2000), Schindehutte & Morris 2001)

For the purposes of this research, we can define an alliance as an 'interconnected set of member businesses moving towards an agreed set of objectives' (Dennis 2000, Yeung 1994) (see Section 2.7).

What emerges from the literature are diametrically different views of E-commerce adoption by SMEs, particularly those in urbanized regional areas. What is lacking in the literature to date is a rigorous analysis of:

- Whether or not small business strategic alliances assist regional SMEs to adopt E-commerce
- What prompt SMEs to join a small business strategic alliance
- Whether or not small business strategic alliances assist specific groups of the regional SME sector to adopt E-commerce
- Whether business characteristics that may be associated with the adoption process of E-commerce, are associated differently depending on whether the SME is part of a small business strategic alliance or not.

In addressing these issues, the current research contributes to a better understanding of SME adoption and use of E-commerce. In particular, the research clarifies the role of small business strategic alliances in the adoption process.

1.2 Purpose of the study

It was observed in Section 1.1 that there are a number of questions concerning the process of adoption and use of E-commerce by regional SMEs. As already stated, many of the government initiatives aimed at the SME sector begin by promoting the development of small business strategic alliances such that member SMEs can compete with large businesses. Not only do these initiatives ignore many of the findings of the research into the SME sector, but there have been no rigorous studies comparing the influence of membership or non-membership of small business strategic alliances on E-commerce adoption and use.The primary purpose, then, of this study is to examine the role of small business strategic alliances in E-commerce adoption and use. To this end, this study compares the adoption and use of E-commerce by SMEs that are members of a small business strategic alliance with the adoption and use of E-commerce by those that have decided to remain outside such an arrangement.

Recent research concerning E-commerce adoption by the SME sector has identified a number of business characteristics that appear to affect the decision to adopt/not adopt E-commerce. These business characteristics include business age (Donckels & Lambrecht 1997), business size (Fallon & Moran 2000, Donckels & Lambrecht 1997), business sector (Riquelme 2002), market focus (Blackburn & Athayde 2000) and level of IT skill (O'Donnell et al 2001). A more detailed discussion of these studies will be presented in Chapter 2 (see Section 2.6.5). It would be useful, then, to look at how these business characteristics affect membership of a small business strategic alliance, how these business characteristics affect E-commerce adoption itself and to examine whether there is any relationship between these business characteristics and membership of a small business strategic alliance in the E-commerce adoption process. Consequently, the current study proposes four major research goals:

> **Goal 1** To determine whether decisions to become a member of a small business strategic alliance is associated with the business characteristics (business age, business size, business sector, market focus and level of IT skill)
>
> **Goal 2** To determine whether membership of a small business strategic alliance is associated with perceptions of adoption factors (barriers to adoption, criteria for adoption, benefits of adoption or disadvantages of adoption) of E-commerce technologies

4

Goal 3 To determine whether membership of a small business strategic alliance is associated with perceptions of adoption factors (barriers to adoption, criteria for adoption, benefits of adoption or disadvantages of adoption) of E-commerce technologies, for particular groups of the SME sector

Goal 4 To determine whether business characteristics (business age, business size, business sector, market focus and level of IT skill) impinge differently on perceptions of adoption factors (barriers to adoption, criteria for adoption, benefits of adoption or disadvantages of adoption) of E-commerce technologies, depending on whether the SME is a member of a small business strategic alliance or not.

1.3 Significance of the Study

This study examines the role of small business strategic alliances in the adoption and use of E-commerce in regional SMEs. While there is a strong advocacy at the government level for the uptake of E-commerce by the SME sector, the role of small business strategic alliances in this process is not well understood. Furthermore, there is a realization by many governments that regional SMEs have fallen behind their city counterparts. As such, the study is significant to three groups:

Government bodies promoting E-commerce adoption by SMEs in regional areas,
SMEs that are considering the uptake of E-commerce and
Information Systems (IS) researchers.

A number of business characteristics have been associated with the type and level of E-commerce adoption. These business characteristics include business age, business size, business sector, market focus and level of IT skill. While the development of small business strategic alliances has been put forward as a necessary step for SMEs to adopt E-commerce, there has been no study to determine whether these business characteristics are, in any way, associated with membership of a small business strategic alliance. This analysis would be of benefit to both government and IS researchers in determining whether small business strategic alliances are applicable to SMEs or only certain groups within the SME sector.

The development of small business strategic alliances has both its advocates and its critics. Despite these different points of view, no rigorous study comparing regional SMEs that are part of a small business strategic alliance and regional SMEs that are not has been carried out. This study provides a comparison of these two groups for two sets of regional SMEs, one in Sweden, the other in Australia. The study compares membership/non-membership of a small business strategic alliance across two regional populations, and examines the role of a small business strategic alliance across sub groups (particular business ages, business sizes, business sectors, market focuses, IT skill levels).

Finally the use of two respondent samples, one in Sweden, the other in Australia provides a comparative study of E-commerce adoption and use and the role of small business strategic alliances for two population groups. The results will provide valuable insights into cultural differences between the two regional sample groups.

5

1.4 Scope of the study

The study aims to understand the role of small business strategic alliances in the adoption of E-commerce in regional SMEs and the business characteristics (business ages, business sizes, sectors, market focuses, IT skill levels) that influence that role. The comparison of members and non-members of small business strategic alliances in two regional SME centres, in Sweden and Australia, realizes these aims.

Government initiatives to promote E-commerce adoption have been criticized because they fail to fully understand the nature of SMEs, they use pre-E-commerce adoption techniques and they are unclear as to the role and purpose of small business strategic alliances for regional SMEs. Consequently, the literature review addresses the research surrounding these three issues.

A questionnaire that includes the business characteristics (business age, business size, business sector, market focus and level of IT skill), together with adoption factors (barriers to adoption, criteria for adoption, benefits of adoption or disadvantages of adoption) of E-commerce technologies, is constructed.

The questionnaire is validated through interviews with SMEs to determine the applicability and completeness of the lists of criteria, barriers, benefits and disadvantages derived from E-commerce adoption.

Identification of suitable regional centres through which the questionnaire may be applied is undertaken.

Results of the questionnaire could serve many purposes, but in this study it is carried out for five reasons. These are:

- To determine whether decisions to become a member of a small business strategic alliance is associated with business characteristics (business age, business size, business sector, market focus and level of IT skill)
- To determine whether membership of a small business strategic alliance is associated with perceptions of adoption factors (barriers to adoption, criteria for adoption, benefits of adoption or disadvantages of adoption) of E-commerce technologies
- To determine whether membership of a small business strategic alliance is associated with perceptions of adoption factors (barriers to adoption, criteria for adoption, benefits of adoption or disadvantages of adoption) of E-commerce technologies for particular groups of the SME sector
- To determine whether business characteristics (business age, business size, business sector, market focus and level of IT skill) impinge differently on perceptions of adoption factors (barriers to adoption, criteria for adoption, benefits of adoption or disadvantages of adoption) of E-commerce technologies, depending on whether the SME is a member of a small business strategic alliance or not.
- To determine if there are differences in the perception of adoption factors (barriers to adoption, criteria for adoption, benefits of adoption or disadvantages of adoption) of E-commerce technologies between respondents from Swedish regional SMEs and respondents from Australian regional SMEs

A number of theoretical frameworks were examined, including the Technology Acceptance Model (TAM), Diffusion of Innovation Theory and the use of Grounded Theory approaches.

The Technology Acceptance Model, while focusing on the use of specific technology, presupposes measurement of perceived usefulness and ease of use (Davis 1989). As this study's focus is on the role of small business strategic alliances in the adoption of E-commerce, the TAM model was rejected as a possible research framework. The use of Grounded Theory approach (see Glaser 1992) was considered as there were no overriding hypotheses being examined. However, as several of the study's aims required the examination of the data in a 'non-holistic' manner, this approach was rejected. Finally the Diffusion of Innovation Theory (see Clarke 1994) was examined. While it may be argued that E-commerce is a new technology, the existence of small business strategic alliances are existing structures (Jorde & Teece 1989, Datta 1988, Gibb 1993) and as such this framework was rejected.

A number of previous studies (Teo & Tan 1998, Kinder 2000, Shiels et al 2003, Daniel 2003), examining the role of business characteristics in the adoption/non-adoption of E-commerce by SMEs were examined. In all cases the authors expressed the view that no framework adequately suited their approach and that they were developing models from quantitative analyses. As this current study aims to provide the foundation of a model for the role of strategic alliances in E-commerce adoption in SMEs, a similar viewpoint will be adopted in this study.

1.5 Overview of the Study

This study was carried out in four broad phases:
1. A review of the literature including:
   - A detailed background to the study
   - The nature of pre-E-commerce acquisition and use of IT by SMEs and the business characteristics affecting acquisition and use
   - The adoption and use of E-commerce by SMEs and the business characteristics affecting acquisition and use
   - The role of small business strategic alliances and their use in the adoption and use of E-commerce by SMEs

2. Development of a questionnaire
   As part of the literature review, an appropriate set of adoption factors (barriers to adoption, criteria for adoption, benefits of adoption or disadvantages of adoption) of E-commerce technologies was selected, together with the business characteristics that may be associated with their applicability (business age, business size, business sector, market focus and level of IT skill).

3. Evaluation of the questionnaire
   The questionnaire was initially evaluated through six interview case studies (see Appendix 8) to determine the applicability and completeness of the list of adoption factors (barriers to adoption, criteria for adoption, benefits of adoption or disadvantages of adoption) of E-commerce technologies.

4. Identification of suitable regional centres.
   This study focuses on the role of small business strategic alliances in regional SMEs. The Australian Bureau of statistics (2001) classifies regional areas into

inner and outer regions, Determination is based on a formula that primarily relies on population size and proximity to services (in terms of physical distance). A similar classification exists for Sweden, however a number of studies (Klofsten 2000, Barry et al 2003, Kjellberg et al 1998, Gibbons-Wood & Lange 2000 and Filho et al 2000) suggest that proximity to services should include a full range of educational facilities. As such, a number of criteria were developed. Since the study is focused on regional SMEs, the location must be an urban regional area, and not a major/capital city or rural area. As the study is quantitative in nature, locations must have a large number of SMEs within the region. As the study will examine business characteristics such as business size, age, sector and market focus, the business community must represent a cross-section of business ages, business sizes, sectors and market foci. As the study is examining the role of small business strategic alliances in E-commerce adoption, a viable government initiated Chamber of Commerce must exist and be well patronised by the small business community. In line with the findings of Klofsten (2000), Barry et al (2003), Kjellberg et al (1998), Gibbons-Wood & Lange (2000) and Filho et al (2000), the location should have the full range of educational facilities (including a university). In order to attempt comparisons of the two locations, locations must have the same financial classification. This classification was based on those published by the World Bank Group and the Organisation for Economic Cooperation and Development (OECD).

5. Administration of the questionnaire
The questionnaire was administered to regional SMEs in Karlstad, Sweden and Wollongong, Australia. Respondents were asked to rate the applicability of adoption factors (barriers to adoption, criteria for adoption, benefits of adoption or disadvantages of adoption) of E-commerce technologies to their own situation. Data was also gathered on business characteristics (business age, business size, business sector, market focus and level of IT skill) as well as membership/non-membership of a small business strategic alliance.

1.6 Organisation of the Study

Having provided an overview of the problems being addressed in this study, the remainder is organized as follows.

Chapter 2 presents a detailed background for the study and uses this background to structure and review the literature surrounding the main issues of concern in this study. The main issues include the nature of SMEs, pre-E-commerce acquisition and use of IT by SMEs, business characteristics affecting pre-E-commerce acquisition and use of IT by SMEs, E-commerce acquisition and use by SMEs, business characteristics affecting E-commerce acquisition and use by SMEs and the role of small business strategic alliances in the acquisition and use of E-commerce by SMEs. This chapter demonstrates that the current study is based on a significant body of previous research and further clarifies the problems being addressed in the current study.

8

Chapter 3 provides a discussion of the approach used in this study. This is followed by a description of the methods and procedures used in the study, including the development and testing of the questionnaire, the choice and evaluation of locations used in the study, and the procedures for statistically analyzing the data derived from the study.

Having described the method and procedures used throughout this study, the next two chapters present the results derived from the questionnaire. **Chapter 4** presents the findings from administering the questionnaire in Karlstad, Sweden.

Chapter 5 presents the findings from administering the questionnaire in Wollongong, Australia. The chapter also presents comparisons of the ratings of criteria, barriers, benefits or disadvantages derived from E-commerce adoption by regional SMEs, between Sweden and Australia.

The statistical analysis reported in Chapters 4 and 5 presents a view of the data gathered from administering the questionnaire in Sweden and Australia. **Chapter 6** provides an interpretive analysis of the data. This chapter examines, in detail, the data gathered from Sweden and Australia separately, before providing comparisons and contrasts between the two locations.

The final chapter, **Chapter 7**, draws together the important findings and conclusions of the study, identifies the limitations of the study and suggests future directions for research arising from the study.

1.7 Conclusion

This chapter presents an overview of the problem domain and has identified a number of key elements that need to be addressed, the following chapter presents a review of the literature concerning:

- A detailed background to the study
- The nature of pre-E-commerce acquisition and use of IT by SMEs and the factors affecting acquisition and use
- The adoption and use of E-commerce by SMEs and the business characteristics affecting acquisition and use
- The role of small business strategic alliances and their use in the adoption and use of E-commerce by SMEs

Chapter 2
Review of the Relevant Literature
2.1 Introduction

The previous chapter began by briefly describing a number of government initiatives designed to stimulate the acquisition and use of E-commerce by the SME sector and suggested that those initiatives were based on questionable beliefs concerning the nature of SMEs. As a background to the present study, this chapter begins by examining those government initiatives.

2.2 Background to the present study

As stated in the previous chapter, government initiatives directed towards encouraging the SME sector to adopt E-commerce (Blair 2000, NOIE 1998, European Commission 2000) have 3 common components. These are:
- A detailed set of benefits that might be achievable through E-commerce adoption.
- A series of strategies that will enable SMEs to become 'wired to the marketplace' thus achieving the benefits of E-commerce adoption
- A set of suggestions for the development of small business strategic alliances with the view to be more able to compete with large business.

While this study, in no way attempts to use these three components as a framework for classification, it is important to consider each component separately.

2.2.1 Benefits of E-commerce to SMEs

The first component used by government offerings is the notion of benefits that can be derived from E-commerce adoption and use. Recent literature abounds with studies examining the benefits of E-commerce to the SME marketplace. Studies as far back as 1996 (see Abell & Lim 1996, Poon & Swatman 1997) have suggested that in certain circumstances E-commerce can reduce costs for both administration and production. More recent studies (Quayle 2002) support this claim. Gulledge & Sommer (1998) and Vescovi (2000) have noted that E-commerce adoption leads to enhanced opportunities to increase competitiveness, to reach new customers and markets and to develop buyer/seller relationships. Studies by Radstaak & Ketelaar (1998), Reynolds (2000) and Quayle (2002) suggest that, when properly implemented, E-commerce can reduce inventory overheads and supply real-time inventory levels to the SME. Other benefits pointed to in the literature include more effective organisation of supply chains (Achrol & Kotler 1998, Kalakota & Whinston 1997), reduced lead-time (Quayle 2002) and the development of new markets (Ritchie & Brindley 2001, Raymond 2001).

While a number of benefits might be achievable through the use of E-commerce, these need to be critically examined in terms of the motivation of the SME sector. A number of studies over the past decade (Fink & Tjarka 1994, MacGregor et al 1998, Martin & Matlay 2001, Culkin & Smith 2000) have shown that, while many SMEs have adopted E-commerce in

10

order to gain a greater share of the global market, many other SMEs are simply intent on improving internal efficiency. Thus, while many studies have shown that certain benefits are achievable, the applicability of these benefits to the SME sector needs to be critically assessed.

2.2.2 Initiatives for E-commerce adoption by SMEs

The second component was first proposed by the Department of Trade and Industry in the UK and is termed the DTI adoption ladder. According to Sergeant (2000), the DTI ladder

'lies at the heart of governmental understanding of the adoption of Information Communications Technology (ICT) ... and purports to represent ICT adoption processes in smaller businesses' (Sergeant 2000, cited Martin & Matlay 2001, pp 400)

The model, termed sequential or step-wise (Martin & Matlay 2001) proposes the approach to E-business through a series of stages beginning with email, progressing through website development, E-commerce and finally transforming the organization.

A number of authors have focused their attention on the SME sector and have questioned not only the similarity of SMEs to their larger counterparts, but the adoption model itself. Martin & Matlay (2001) describe the government DTI model as 'generalist' suggesting that:

'while there is some room for organisational differences since it is implied that not all businesses will begin the adoption process at the same stage... no further flexibility is built into the model to encompass the impact of key factors such as business size, sector, ethnicity, gender, human and financial resources, customer base or levels of internationalisation.' (Martin & Matlay 2001, pp 400)

Culkin & Smith (2000) describe the DTI model in even more emotive terms suggesting that it has:

'naïve, over-simplistic understanding of the motivations of those in the small business sector, that means that these interventions are inevitably blunt instruments destined to fail given the limited understanding shown of the complexity of the small business market.' (Culkin & Smith 2000, pp 145)

There are a number of inherent disadvantages in attempting to use a sequential or step-wise model for E-commerce adoption. Martin (1999) found that moves towards internationalization by many SMEs could not be described in terms of linear steps. She added that different SMEs very often followed different paths to reach international exposure. Fletcher (2000) found that while some SMEs sought rapid globalisation, others remained locally focused. Studies by Fallon & Moran (2000) found that sequential or step-wise models failed to account for business characteristics such as business size, while Matlay & Fletcher (2000) and Schuknecht & Perez-Esteve (1999) noted that 'the homogeneous approach' failed to account for business characteristics such as business sector or the location of the SME. The findings of Fletcher (2000), Fallon & Moran (2000), Matlay & Fletcher (2000) and Schuknecht & Perez-Esteve (1999), concerning decisions, by many SMEs, to remain locally focused, are of particular importance to this current study, which seeks to examine regional SMEs. Regional SME are one section of the SME population that has begun to be examined in detail over the past 5 years. Regional SMEs are defined as being outside metropolitan areas and are characterized as having a shortage of skilled personnel, limited access to resources and a lack of infrastructure (Larssen et al 2003, Keniry et al 2003). Unlike their 'city cousins', despite government promises of 'telecommunication enhanced communities', there has been a resistance by many regional SMEs to adopt and use E-commerce (Martin &

Matlay 2001). A number of barriers have been noted in the literature. These include poor cabling and frequent line outages compared to major cities (Wilde et al 2000), deterioration of long established client links and business practices (Wilde & Swatman 2001) and geographic separation from vital infrastructure (Martin 2001). These differences between metropolitan and regional SMEs means that they are disadvantaged by any application of a 'homogeneous approach' to E-commerce, which fails to take these inherent limitations into account.

A number of studies (Martin & Matlay 2001, MacGregor et al 1998) have questioned the linear or step-wise approach even further suggesting that much of it is based on pre-E-commerce criteria that are not viable in the post-E-commerce context. As can be seen (see Section 2.4), pre-E-commerce criteria tend to be based on the ability to place boundaries around the organization and to maintain a strict focus towards activities and strategies within those boundaries. E-commerce, by comparison, removes those organizational boundaries and re-focuses activities and strategies between interacting organizations. As such, the applicability of many of the criteria for the adoption of computer technology, prior to the advent of E-commerce, need to be re-examined in the light of E-commerce.

2.2.3 Development of small business strategic alliances

As already stated, the first government initiative proposed for SME adoption and use of E-commerce by SMEs is the development of a small business strategic alliance, such that member SMEs can compete with their large business counterparts. As with the notion of the step-wise or linear adoption models, the development of small business strategic alliances, as portrayed in the government literature, fails to adequately consider many business characteristics affecting the SME community. Indeed, the view that member SMEs are able to compete with large businesses is based on the assumption that SMEs are really "small large businesses", a view criticised in the literature (see Barnet & Mackness 1983, Westhead & Storey 1996). Under such models, business characteristics such as business size, business age, business sector, geographic location, level of internationalisation are simply removed and replaced by the simplistic notion that all SMEs are intent on gaining a proportion of global market share. Furthermore, such an approach fails to take into account substantial research (Hadjiminolis 1999, Lawrence 1997, MacGregor & Bunker 1996, Westhead & Storey 1996, Walczuch et al 2000, Quayle 2002) that suggests that many SMEs have little desire to reach a larger marketplace either alone or in some form of an alliance. Thus, while small business strategic alliances might be a valuable source of technical or marketing information (see Jarrat 1998, Copp & Ivy 2001, Tetteh & Burn 2001, O'Donnell et al 2001), this does not presuppose that small business strategic alliances are part of any attempt to reach global markets or are part of the decision making process for the adoption of E-commerce.

It would seem, then, that government initiatives directed towards adoption and use of E-commerce by SMEs are based on simplistic models of the nature of the SME community, and in some cases, are based on approaches that do not adequately address the special nature of E-commerce. The inappropriateness of the government initiatives is exacerbated by the fact that no rigorous study has been carried out comparing the adoption of E-commerce by SMEs that are part of a small business strategic alliance and those that are not.

2.2.4 Goals of the study

The goals of this study are fourfold. They are:
- To determine if membership in a small business strategic alliances is associated with business characteristics (business size, business age, business sector, market focus or the level of IT skill).
- To determine if the membership of small business strategic alliances alters perceptions of any of the adoption factors (barriers to adoption, criteria for adoption, benefits of adoption or disadvantages of adoption) of E-commerce technologies.
- To determine if the membership in a small business strategic alliances alters perceptions of any of the adoption factors (barriers to adoption, criteria for adoption, benefits of adoption or disadvantages of adoption) of E-commerce technologies for specific sectors of the SME population (certain business ages, business sizes, business sectors, market focuses, particular levels of IT skill).
- To determine if the associations between business characteristics (business size, business age, business sector, market focus or level of IT skills) and adoption factors (barriers to adoption, criteria for adoption, benefits of adoption or disadvantages of adoption) of E-commerce technologies differ, depending on whether the SME is part of a small business strategic alliance or not.

This chapter examines the literature concerning the nature of small to medium enterprises (SMEs), their use of computer technology and their adoption and use of E-commerce technologies. As E-commerce is considered to be a special case, with regard to its effect on organisations, the following section begins by examining the nature of SMEs and their use of computer technology. We then focus on the use of E-commerce in SMEs. Finally we examine the role of strategic alliances in the acquisition and use of E-commerce in SMEs.

2.3 The nature of small to medium enterprises (SMEs)

There are a number of definitions of what constitutes an SME. Some of these definitions are based on quantitative measures such as staffing levels, turnover or assets, while others employ a qualitative approach. Meredith (1994) suggests that any description or definition must include a quantitative component that takes into account staff levels, turnover, assets together with financial and non-financial measurements, but that the description must also include a qualitative component that reflects how the business is organised and how it operates.
Not only is there a myriad of views concerning the nature of SMEs, but from a governmental standpoint there are a variety of definitions of an SME, depending on the country being considered.
For example, in the late 1960's the Australian Federal Government commissioned a report from a committee known as the Wiltshire Committee. This report suggested a flexible definition of any SME (Meredith, 1994):
'Small business is one in which one or two persons are required to make all of the critical decisions (such as finance, accounting, personnel, inventory, production, servicing, marketing and selling decisions) without the aid of internal (employed)

13

specialists and with owners only having specific knowledge in one or two functional areas of management.' (Meredith, 1994, pp 31)

The Wiltshire Committee concluded that normally this definition could be expected to apply to the majority of enterprises in Australia with fewer than 100 employees.

The United States based its definition on the position of the organisation within the overall marketplace. According to the United States Small Business Administration (SBA) which is based on section 3 of the Small Business Act of 1953:

'An SME shall be deemed to be one which is independently owned and operated and which is not dominant in its field of operation.'

By comparison, the United Kingdom took a more quantitative approach, defining an SME as:

'Having fewer than 50 employees and is not a subsidiary of any other company.'

Like the governmental definitions of SMEs, research initiatives have applied a variety of definitions to the nature of SMEs. A study of Canadian SMEs by Montasemi (1988) based its definition on the number of employees, this being in accordance with the Canadian Small Business Guide (1984). Many studies (see Bradbard, Norris & Kahai (1990), Chen (1993)) have based their model on the UK Companies Act – 50 employees or less.

Indeed, while most studies of SMEs state the average size is far less, a business is deemed small in Sweden if it has 50 or less employees (Gustafsson et al 2001). Although the definition of SMEs in Australia (Wiltshire-Meredith 1994) is 100, this definition is inconsistent with most definitions found in the literature.

More recently there has been a tendency for researchers to simply utilise a mailing list of SMEs supplied by a government agency, thus making decisions about the definitions of SMEs is the responsibility of government agencies, rather than the researcher. Examples of this approach can be seen in studies by Pendergraft, Morris & Savage (1987) and Delone (1988). An alternative approach was adopted by Chen (1993) who based his study on 260 companies randomly selected from the Norfolk Industrial Directory (1990 cited Chen 1993), but where companies conformed to the definition of SMEs in the UK (i.e. they had fewer than 50 employees and were not a subsidiary company).

For this study the Swedish definition, viz., less than 50 employees will be used.

Not only do the definitions of SME vary, but there are wide ranging views on the characteristics of SMEs.

There have been many studies in the literature that have attempted to define the characteristics of SMEs. Central to all of these studies is the underlying realization that many of the processes and techniques that have been successfully applied in large businesses, do not necessarily provide similar outcomes when applied to SMEs. This is perhaps best summed up by Barnet & Mackness (1983) and Westhead & Storey (1996) who stated that SMEs are not 'small large businesses' but are a separate and distinct group of organizations compared to large businesses.

It is appropriate that we examine some of the characteristics found in the literature.

Brigham & Smith (1967) found that SMEs tended to be more prone to risk than their larger counterparts. This view is supported in later studies (Walker,1975, Delone,1988). Cochran (1981) found that SMEs tended to be subject to higher failure rates, while Rotch (1987) suggested that SMEs had inadequate records of transactions. Welsh & White (1981), in a comparison of SMEs with their larger counterparts found that SMEs suffered from a lack of trained staff and had a short-range management perspective. They termed these traits 'resource poverty' and suggested that their net effect was to magnify the effect of environmental impact, particularly where information systems were involved.

14

These early suggestions have been supported by more recent studies that have found most SMEs lack technical expertise (Barry & Milner 2002), most lack adequate capital to undertake technical enhancements (Gaskill et al (1993, Raymond 2001), most SMEs suffer from inadequate organisational planning (Tetteh & Burn 2001, Miller & Besser 2000) and many SMEs differ from their larger counterparts in the extent of the product/service range available to customer (Reynolds et al, 1994).

A number of recent studies (see Reynolds et al (1994), Murphy (1996), Bunker & MacGregor 2000)) have examined the differences in management style between large businesses and SMEs. These studies have shown that, among other characteristics, SMEs tend to have a small management team (often one or two individuals), they are strongly influenced by the owner and the owner's personal idiosyncrasies, they have little control over their environment (this is supported by the studies of Westhead & Storey (1996) and Hill & Stewart (2000) and they have a strong desire to remain independent (this is supported by the findings of Dennis 2000 and Drakopolou-Dodd et al 2002).

These findings are summarised in Table 2.1.

Table 2.1
Features of the Small Business Sector

Findings about SMEs	Researcher
Differ from large businesses	Barnett & Mackness (1983) Reynolds et al (1994) Westhead & Storey (1996) Bunker & MacGregor (2000)
Are externally uncertain	Westhead & Storey (1996)
Are product oriented	Reynolds et al (1994)
Decisions are intuitive	Bunker & MacGregor (2000) Reynolds et al (1994)
Decision making does not entail exhaustive study	Reynolds et al (1994)
Strong Owner Influence	Murphy (1996)
IT decisions are usually made by the owner	Bunker & MacGregor (2000)
Little use of consultants in decision making	Reynolds et al (1994)
More risky than big business	Brigham & Smith (1967) Walker (1975)
Fail more easily than large businesses	Brigham & Smith (1967) Walker (1975)

15

Difficulties obtaining finance	Gaskell & Gibbs (1994) Reynolds et al (1994)
Informal and inadequate planning	Reynolds et al (1994) Tetteh & Burn (2001) Miller & Besser (2000)
Decisions are often made with community in mind rather than business	Miller & Besser (2000)
Poor Record keeping	Markland (1974)
Reluctance to take risks	Walczuch et al (2000)
Are more reluctant to spend on technology	Walczuch et al (2000) Dennis (2000)
Are very often family concerns	Reynolds et al (1994)
Family often used in place of consultants	Dennis (2000) Bunker & MacGregor (2000)
Strong desire for independence	Reynolds et al (1994)
Owners often withhold details from colleagues	Dennis (2000)
Tend to avoid joint business ventures if it impinges on independence	Reynolds et al (1994)
Small centralised management	Bunker & MacGregor (2000)
Lack of technical staff	Martin & Matlay 2001 Bunker & MacGregor (2000)
Lack of control over environment	Westhead & Storey (1996) Hill & Stewart (2000)
Limited market share	Hadjimonolis (1999) Lawrence (1997) Quayle (2002)
Often move towards niche markets	Hadjimonolis (1999) Quayle (2002)
Can't compete with their larger counterparts	Lawrence (1997)

Heavy reliance on few customers	Reynolds et al (1994)
Narrow product/service range	Bunker & MacGregor (2000) Reynolds et al (1994)
Education/experience/skill practical but narrow	Bunker & MacGregor (2000) Reynolds et al (1994)
Little training provided for staff	Reynolds et al (1994)
Are product oriented not customer oriented	Bunker & MacGregor (2000) MacGregor et al (1998)
Are not interested in large shares of the market	MacGregor et al (1998) Reynolds et al (1994)
Are intent on improving day-today procedures	MacGregor et al (1998)

The differences between SMEs and their larger counterparts are highlighted even more when their approaches to IT are considered. Khan & Khan (1992) suggest that most SMEs avoid sophisticated software and applications. This view is supported by studies carried out by Chen (1993), Cragg & King (1993), Holzinger & Hotch (1993) and Delvecchio (1994).

It is appropriate that we now examine the acquisition and use of computer technology by SMEs prior to the onset of E-commerce.

2.4 Pre-E-commerce acquisition and use of IT by SMEs

This section is premised on the view that E-commerce is not just another technology that sustains and enhances business practice: it is an innovation that has disrupted traditional ways of doing business. This premise, which is elaborated upon in section 2.5, is well supported in the literature (see Lee 2001, Kuljis et al 1998, Giaglis et al 1988, Fuller 2000, Kendall & Kendall 2001).

The premise is important for several reasons. Firstly, E-commerce has altered the day-to-day practices of many businesses (Fuller 2000). According to Lee (2001), where once a company used raw materials, transformed those raw materials into products, displayed those products, and ultimately sold those products to customers, with E-commerce this has changed. Now, the raw materials are information about the customer, the transformation is the synthesis and packaging of this information, the products are designed, very often, by the customer and are sold with information services to entice future interaction.

Secondly, the focus of technology acquisition has altered from production within the organization to marketing between organizations. Indeed, Treacy & Wiersema (1997) have suggested that E-commerce transforms organizations that were 'geared towards' production excellence into organizations 'geared towards' customer intimacy.

Thirdly, in a pre-E-commerce environment, benefits, or disadvantages, of technology were planned, tangible and controllable by the organization. With E-commerce, many of the benefits and disadvantages have become less tangible and far more difficult to plan for and manage. Added to this is the fact that many of the benefits, as well as the disadvantages, are unique to E-commerce. Some of the benefits include new customers and markets (Ritchie & Brindley 2001, Quayle 2002, Raymond 2001, Vescovi 2000), improved marketing techniques (Sparkes & Thomas 2001) and improved relations with business partners (Poon & Swatman 1997). Some of the disadvantages of E-commerce adoption, reported in the literature included security risks (Ritchie & Brindley 2001), reduced flexibility of work (Lee 2001) and duplication of work effort (MacGregor et al 1998).

Perhaps the most important reason for distinguishing E-commerce from other technologies is the notion that the adoption and use of E-commerce cannot be based on the same criteria as was used for other technology adoption. As already stated (see section 2.1.2), a number of authors suggest that to base E-commerce adoption and use on criteria used in other technology adoption produces a naïve, over-simplistic, linear model, whose focus is organizationally based rather than interorganisationally directed (Culkin & Smith 2000, Martin & Matlay 2001).

This section, then, is a prelude to an examination of E-commerce, and considers the adoption and use of technology prior to the advent of E-commerce. In line with the views of Faia-Correia et al (1999), who suggest that technology shapes and is shaped by the organization, it is appropriate to consider the organizational context prior to the advent of E-commerce, and in turn, the acquisition and use of technology in that context.

Prior to the advent of E-commerce, most organizations were essentially hierarchical in nature. They exhibited a unity of purpose and were primarily concerned with extending control over resources considered essential to the quality of their products. Communications within such a structure was essentially uni-dimensional (i.e. information flowed in a single direction only), and technology introduced into the business was normally focused on production. As such, the acquisition of technology could be evaluated against tangible inputs and outputs. Thus, while technology might have re-shaped the organisation, these changes were predictable and planned, reinforcing rather than disrupting organisational boundaries.

Prior to the advent of E-commerce, organizations relied primarily on a product base that was supported by stand-alone technology (Lee 2001). The products themselves were tangible, requiring physical inputs and processes, which could be clearly evaluated. This meant that the introduction of technology into these processes could be evaluated and directed towards aggregated financial effects, and outcomes were related to the revenue goals of the entire organization (Dignum 2002). Technology was designed to embody existing organisational values and practices, power relationships and conventions. As such, strategies were fixed and controllable (Treacy & Wiersma 1997). While technology supported these strategies and the products offered by the organisation, it was bounded by the nature of those same products. Its role was simply to increase efficiency, within the boundaries of the products at a procedural level (Lee 2001).

Prior to E-commerce, organizations were also able to utilise technology to enforce the use of specific products and product boundaries. This was achievable by limiting the number and types of products and by placing the boundaries within the operational level of the organisation. Factors that might be termed "informal social ties" (customers, competitors, environmental trends) were 'shadows' to the formal organisation. The focus, instead, was on computerising procedures to achieve low-level operational competence, and the decision to invest in computer technology was primarily concerned with improvements in efficiency and effectiveness. Investment decisions were carried out in terms of strict boundaries and were judged on rigid internal perspectives. An organisation considering the adoption of technology

18

examined the Return on Investment (ROI) of such technology where the ROI was defined within a pre-stated set of strategic guidelines. Willcocks et al (1998) consider that, under such organisational models, the metrics used in the acquisition of computer technology remained static and were still able to give a valid picture of organisational requirements.

As with the literature on the nature of SMEs, many of the studies carried out on the adoption of computer technology by SMEs attempted to portray differences between SMEs and their larger counterparts. These studies are summarized in Table 2.2.

Table 2.2
IT Adoption and Use in SMEs

Findings of SMEs	Researcher
Decision making on IT adoption differs from those made by large businesses	Bunker & MacGregor (2000)
IT decisions are not based on detailed planning	Bunker & MacGregor (2000) Tetteh & Burn (2001)
IT decisions are usually made by the owner	Bunker & MacGregor (2000)
Are more reluctant to spend on technology	Walczuch et al (2000) Dennis (2000)
Lack of technical staff	Martin & Matlay 2001 Bunker & MacGregor (2000)
Lack of IT expertise	Martin & Matlay 2001 Bunker & MacGregor (2000) Klatt (1973) Schollhammer & Kuriloff (1979) Neergaard (1992)
Limited use of technology	MacGregor & Bunker (1996) Poon & Swatman (1997) Abell & Lim (1996)
Little IT skill or training	Bunker & MacGregor (2000) MacGregor & Cocks (1994) Wood & Nosek (1994)
IT more often used for better record keeping	Fink & Tjarka (1994) Neergaard (1992) MacGregor & Bunker (1996)

Vendor a surrogate for IT department	Yap et al (1992)
	MacGregor & Bunker (1996)
	Thong (1999)
	Wood & Nosek (1994)
Informal and inadequate IT planning	Reynolds et al (1994)
	Tetteh & Burn (2001)
	Miller & Besser (2000)
Studies of IT success in SMEs is usually based on management, vendor and user issues	MacGregor & Bunker (1996)
	Schultz et al (1984)
	McDoniel et al (1993)
User information satisfaction is a surrogate for IS success in SMEs	Yap et al (1992)
	McDoniel et al (1993)
	Bailey & Pearson (1983)
	Ives et al (1983)
	Doukidis et al (1992)
	Igbaria (1992)
User attitudes impact on their behaviour with new systems	Ginzberg (1982)
	Desanctis (1983)
	Baroudi et al (1986)
	Amoaka-Gyampah & White (1993)
	MacGregor & Bunker (1996)
Management involvement is essential to IT success	Bergeron & Berube (1988)
	Bergeron et al (1990)
	Javenpaa & Ives (1991)
	Yap et al (1992)
	Black & Porter (2000)

Not only are many of the processes of adoption and use of pre-E-commerce IT different for SMEs, but many of the criteria used by SMEs in the decision-making process about IT differ from larger businesses. The next section examines the criteria used in the Pre-E-commerce adoption of IT by SMEs.

2.4.1 Criteria used in the pre-E-commerce adoption of IT by SMEs

A combined study of Danish, Irish and Greek SMEs carried out in the early 1990's by Neergaard (1992) concluded that there were four main reasons for the acquisition of IT by SMEs. These were increased productivity, streamlining work procedures, better client service and better record keeping. Fink and Tjarka (1994) in a study of Australian executives collapsed two of the categories (streamlining work procedures and better client services) but provided similar reasons to Neergaard for IT acquisition. They described their three reasons for acquisition as 'doing the right thing', 'doing things right' and 'improving the bottom line'. Table 2.3 provides a mapping of the two sets of categories.

Table 2.3

Table 2.3
Reasons for IT Acquisition by SMEs

Neergaard	Fink & Tjarka
Increased productivity	Improving the bottom line
Streamlining work procedures	Doing the right thing
Customer service	Doing the right thing
Better record keeping	Doing things right

Fink & Tjarka (1994) concluded that while larger businesses were demonstrating a shift from 'doing things right' to 'doing the right thing', this shift was less visible in SMEs. This conclusion is supported by a number of studies (see Chen 1993, MacGregor & Bunker 1996 a & b, Amer & Bain 1990).

A number of reasons were suggested to explain SMEs' continued focus on the operational use of technology. MacGregor & Bunker (1996a), in line with the findings of Welsh & White (1981), suggested that most SMEs tended to have a short-range management perspective and appeared more concerned with improving the day-to-day internal nature of the business than with seeking new markets or customers. They added that control mechanisms were often informal, were centralised and were coupled with reluctance, by most SMEs, to take risks. This reduced the need for long-term decision-making. Added to this was a management that, more often than not, was product oriented rather than customer oriented (Reynolds et al 1994, MacGregor et al 1998, Bunker & MacGregor 2000).

It is interesting to note that Fink & Tjarka (1994) posit a gradual movement from 'doing things right' to 'doing the right thing' in larger businesses. MacGregor & Bunker (1996a) found that SMEs that had based their IT acquisition criteria on 'doing the right thing' or 'improving the bottom line' reported significantly less success than those that based their acquisition criteria on 'doing things right'.

2.4.2 Factors affecting pre-E-commerce IT acquisition and use in SMEs

Martin & Matlay (2001) suggest that many initiatives aimed at promoting IT acquisition and use in SMEs fall into the trap of viewing the SME sector as a homogeneous group that are able to take a well ordered, sequential approach to technology adoption. They continue by suggesting that:

'the targets and, in particular, the way in which they are defined, point towards a 'generalist' view of small business operation that largely fails to differentiate between businesses of varying business sizes, ethnic origin, stages of adoption etc.' (Martin & Matlay 2001, pp 400)

There are a number of studies in the literature that point to a variety of business characteristics affecting the adoption and use of IT in SMEs. Indeed, several researchers (Poon & Swatman 1997, Hyland & Matlay 1997) stress that the differing effects of some of these business characteristics often makes it impossible to generalise findings across the entire SME community.

It is appropriate, then to consider some of these findings.

A number of studies (Fallon & Moran 2000, Lal 2002, Matlay 2000, Matlay & Fletcher 2000, Culkin & Smith 2000, Riquelme 2002) have found that business size (in terms of the number of employees as well as turnover) is significantly associated with the adoption of IT. Culkin

& Smith (2000) suggest that larger SMEs are by nature inherently more complex and thus decisions concerning IT acquisition require more detailed examinations of the impact of IT. Larger SMEs tend to adopt more sophisticated systems and very often are more likely to 'computerise' far more of their business than smaller SMEs. Matlay & Fletcher (2000) noted that these findings did not appear to be localised or country-specific.

Recent studies (Martin 1999, Martin et al 2001) have examined SMEs in terms of location. These studies suggest that those SMEs in rural or regional locations often report lower levels of success with IT adoption when compared to those in capital cities or large economic centres. A number of explanations have been put forward, including a heavier reliance on vendors in regional areas than in larger centres and the failure of vendor groups to fully understand the nature of the business they are servicing.

Kai-Uwe Brock (2000), in a study of SME adoption of IT suggests that another important business characteristic appears to be business age. Businesses that have a long-established set of work practices will very often avoid any form of IT intervention that threatens to disrupt those long-held practices.

Studies by Dibb (1997), MacGregor & Bunker (1999), Bennett & Robson (1998), Meikle & Willis (2002), MacGregor et al (2002) have found that business sector is significantly associated with the level and type of IT use in SMEs. These studies found that the manufacturing and retail sectors tended to adopt IT far more quickly than professional or service related SMEs. Unlike the studies relating to business size, the business sector studies cannot be considered 'global'. For example, while Australian studies (MacGregor & Bunker 1999, MacGregor et al 2002) found a higher uptake of IT in the manufacturing and retail sectors, Riquelme (2002), in a study of adoption of technology in China found that service related businesses were adopting IT at the same rate as retail groups.

A number of studies (Poon & Swatman 1997, Donckels & Lambrecht 1997, Lauder & Westhall 1997, Blackburn & Athayde 2000) have examined the impact of internationalisation by SMEs in their adoption of IT. While all studies have been prescriptive, enunciating the steps to be taken in order to utilise technology in an international market, each identifies market focus as being a business characteristic associated with the level and depth of IT adoption and use.

Another business characteristic that appears to be significantly associated with IT adoption and use is the level of IT expertise. Studies in Singapore (Yap et al 1992, Thong et al 1996) and Australia (MacGregor & Bunker 1996, MacGregor et al 1998) have shown that the level of IT skill within the SME is a strong determinant of the type of IT acquired as well as the ongoing success with that IT.

Thus, it can be seen that a number of business characteristics, including business size, business age, business sector, market focus and level of IT expertise are associated with adoption and use of IT in SMEs.

Before examining the nature of post-E-commerce technology adoption, it is appropriate that we consider the nature of E-commerce itself.

2.5 E-commerce

There are nearly as many definitions of E-commerce as there are contributions to the literature. Turban et al (2002) define E-commerce as:

> 'an emerging concept that describes the process of buying, selling or exchanging services and information via computer networks.' (Turban et al 2002, pp 4)

Choi et al (1997 cited Turban et al 2002) draw a distinction between what they term pure E-commerce and partial E-commerce. According to Choi et al, 'pure E-commerce' has a digital product, a digital process and a digital agent. All other interactions (including those that might have one or two of the three nominated by Choi et al) are termed 'partial E-commerce'. Raymond (2001) defines E-commerce as:

> 'functions of information exchange and commercial transaction support that operate on telecommunications networks linking business partners (typically customers and suppliers).' (Raymond 2001 pp 411)

Damanpour (2001), by comparison, defines E-commerce as:

> 'any 'net' business activity that transforms internal and external relationships to create value and exploit market opportunities driven by new rules of the connected economy' (Damanpour 2001, pp 18)

For the purposes of this study, which examines changes to the organisation brought about by involvement in E-commerce, the definition provided by Damanpour is used. While it may be argued that other definitions do not preclude organisational transformation, only the definition of Damanpour 'demands' those transformations and it is consistent with the concept in the literature, generally.

It is these organisational changes, rather than the definition, that needs to be addressed.

As already stated, E-commerce is not just another mechanism to sustain or enhance existing business practices. It is a paradigm shift that is radically changing traditional ways of doing business. Dignum (2002) believes that although IT is an important component, the biggest mistake made by many organizations is that they believe that by simply introducing E-commerce technology, they would succeed without having to worry about their organisational structure. If, as suggested by Treacy & Wiersema (1997), E-commerce transforms a company from one geared towards 'production excellence' to one geared towards 'customer intimacy', E-commerce is not about technology but about a new way of treating customers and suppliers. Achrol & Kotler (1999), in a discussion of marketing within a network economy, describe this transformation as a shift from being an 'agent of the seller' to being an 'agent of the buyer'. Thus, according to Lee (2001), the biggest challenge for most organisations is not how to imitate or benchmark the best E-commerce model, but how to fundamentally change the mindset of management away from operating as a traditional business.

Fundamental to any changes to traditional business procedures is the realisation that E-commerce, unlike any previous technological innovation, has a locus of impact not within the organisation but at an interorganisational level. Thus, a traditional management focus, which included total quality management, lean manufacturing and business process re-engineering (collectively termed economics of scarcity by Lee 2001), are replaced by gathering, synthesis and distribution of information (collectively termed economics of abundance by Lee). Output for organisations can no longer simply be finished products, but must include information and information services, bundled for customer use.

Not only has E-commerce changed the rules pertaining to processes within the organisation, it has had a profound effect on the structure of organisations.

The advent of E-commerce has seen a radical change away from the hierarchical-based philosophy. Organisations that were once 'housed' within strict product-based boundaries are now having to operate and compete at a global level and strict hierarchies appear less adept in the turbulent global market. Functions such as marketing, that were once organisational and product-based (i.e. a select set of products was marketed by an individual organization) are now becoming interorganisational and knowledge-based (multiple organizations continually adjusting their operations to meet changing customer needs and passing on information, rather than products, to their customers). Indeed, Achrol & Kotler suggest that

> "Driven by a dynamic and knowledge-rich environment, the hierarchical organisations of the 20th century are disaggregating into a variety of strategic alliance forms." (p 146)

Not only has E-commerce altered perceptions of organisational structure and function (see Kuljis et al 1998, Giaglis et al 1999) it has altered the use of technology within the organisation (Fuller 2000, Kendall & Kendall 2001). Where once technology supported the hierarchical structure, it is technology that is driving the evolution away from it.

For larger businesses there have been a variety of approaches. Some businesses are moving entirely to a web-based presence (Lee 2001), some are establishing subsidiaries that ultimately become stand-alone, online businesses (see Gulati & Garino 2000), others are merging with online businesses. In all cases, there has been a realisation that multi-level hierarchies, with their inability to react to external change, need to be replaced by flatter structures that are adaptable to an ever-changing external environment.

The changes brought about by E-commerce have not only affected large businesses, but have had a profound effect on SMEs. Where large business is being encouraged to outsource many of its activities and evolve from a hierarchical structure to a flatter network structure, SMEs are being encouraged to pool their limited skills into small business strategic alliances (Dean et al 1997, Blair 2000, NOIE 1998, European Commission 2000).

The development of small business strategic alliances, together with the differing natures of large businesses and SMEs (see Sections 2.3 and 2.4) has meant that when decisions regarding acquisition and use of technology are concerned, SMEs cannot simply be considered a 'mirror' of their larger counterparts (Thong et al (1996), MacGregor & Bunker (1996), Reimenschneider & Mykytyn (2000), Bunker & MacGregor (2000)).

It is appropriate to consider the adoption and use of E-commerce in SMEs.

2.5.1 E-commerce and SMEs

Studies carried out at the onset of E-commerce (Nooteboom (1994), Acs et al (1997), Murphy (1996), McRea (1996), Gessin (1996), Auger & Gallaugher (1997)) predicted that, since SMEs had always operated in an externally uncertain environment, they were more likely to benefit from E-commerce.

Other authors, while agreeing in principle with this viewpoint, did so with a degree of caution. Hutt & Speh (1998) felt that most areas of the SME sector, with the exception of those SMEs involved in the industrial market, would benefit from E-commerce. They suggest that the industrial SMEs already concentrated on an established base of customers and product offerings. Swartz & Iacobucci (2000) felt that the service industries would benefit far more than other areas of the SME community.

Other studies (Reuber & Fischer 1999, Donckels & Lambrecht 1997) felt that the business age was a strong predictor of relative benefit of E-commerce adoption, suggesting that older businesses would not adopt as easily as newer ones.

Among the predicted benefits available to SMEs were:

- A global presence presenting customers with a global choice (Barry & Milner 2002)

- Improved competitiveness (Auger & Gallaugher 1997)
- Mass customisation and 'customerisation', presenting customers with personalised products and services (Fuller 2000)
- Shortening of supply chains, providing rapid response to customer needs (Barry & Milner 2002)

Recent studies have found that these predictions have not eventuated and that it has been the larger businesses that have been more active with respect to E-commerce (see Riquelme 2002, Roberts & Wood 2002, Barry & Milner 2002). A number of reasons have been put forward, including poor security, high costs, a lack of requisite skills. However, some researchers have begun to examine how decisions concerning IT adoption and use are made in the SME sector.

As already stated, there have been many governmental as well as privately funded projects attempting to further the cause of adoption of E-commerce by SMEs. Unfortunately many of these projects relied on pre-E-commerce criteria and focussed on internal systems within the SME rather than interorganisational interaction (Poon & Swatman 1997, Fallon & Moran 2000, Martin & Matlay 2001). The resulting models were step-wise or linear, beginning with email, progressing through website, to E-commerce adoption and finally organisational transformation. Not only are these models based on inappropriate or oversimplified criteria (Kai-Uwe Brock 2000), but they recommend the adoption of E-commerce prior to any form of organisational change.

E-commerce brings with it changes in communication (Chellappa et al 1996), business method (Henning 1998), market structure and approach to marketing (Giaglis et al 1999) as well as changes in day-to-day activities (Doukidis et al 1998). These changes are exacerbated in the SME sector as many SMEs have no overall plan and, for the most part, fail to understand the need for competitive strategies (Jeffcoate et al (2002)).

For SMEs, the changes associated with E-commerce have produced both positive and negative effects. Studies by Raymond (2001) and Ritchie & Brindley (2000) found that, while E-commerce adoption has eroded trading barriers for SMEs, this has often come at the price of altering or eliminating commercial relationships and exposing the business to external risks. Lawrence (1997), Tetteh & Burn (2001) and Lee (2001) contend that E-commerce adoption fundamentally alters the internal procedures within SMEs. Indeed, Lee (2001) adds that the biggest challenge to SMEs is not to find the best E-commerce model but to change the mindset of the owner/managers themselves. For those who have developed an organisation-wide strategy (in anticipation of E-commerce), these changes can lead to an increase in efficiency in the business for those who have not, this can reduce the flexibility of the business (Tetteh & Burn 2001) and often lead to a duplication of the work effort (MacGregor et al 1998).

A number of studies have examined both the tangible and intangible benefits achieved by SMEs from the adoption of E-commerce. Studies by Abell & Lim (1996), Poon & Swatman (1997) and Quayle (2002) found that the tangible benefits derived from E-commerce (such as reduced administration costs, reduced production costs, reduced lead-time, increased sales), were marginal in terms of direct earnings. These same studies found that the intangible benefits (such as improvement in the quality of information, improved internal control of the business, improved relations with business partners) were of far greater value to SMEs.

Unlike previous technological innovations, E-commerce brings with it changes to both procedures within the organisation as well as changes to the structure of the organisation itself. These changes include the way businesses interact, their approaches to marketing, products and customers and the way decisions are made and disseminated, particularly decisions concerning technology adoption and use. For SMEs, these changes can have both positive and negative effects. Those SME owner/managers who have developed an organisation-wide strategy for E-commerce adoption, report increases in efficiency. Those who have not, often find that the changes reduce flexibility within their business.

The next section examines the adoption and use of E-commerce by SMEs.

2.6 The acquisition and use of E-commerce by SMEs

There have been many studies carried out over the last decade that have examined the adoption/non-adoption, benefits/disadvantages of E-commerce in SMEs. A comparison of some of these studies has revealed conflicting results. For example, Poon & Swatman (1997) found that E-commerce led to improved relationships with customers, while Stauber (2000) noted a decline in contact with customers. Some of these differences are clearly due to the nature of the research. However, many of the differences are a consequence of the non-homogeneous nature of the SME sector.

It is not in the scope of this present study, to examine the nature and reasons for differences found in previous studies of SMEs.

Much of the recent research carried out in examining E-commerce adoption and use in SMEs falls under one of four headings:

- criteria employed for the adoption and use of E-commerce in SMEs,
- benefits derived from the adoption and use of E-commerce by SMEs,
- disadvantages encountered through the adoption and use of E-commerce by SMEs and
- barriers to the adoption and use of E-commerce in SMEs.

These will now be examined separately.

2.6.1 Criteria employed for the adoption and use of E-commerce in SMEs

A study carried out on 146 SMEs by Poon & Swatman (1997) provided 5 'drivers' or criteria for E-commerce adoption by respondents. These were: new modes of direct or indirect marketing, strengthening of relationships with business partners, the ability to reach new customers, improvement to customer services and the reduction of costs in communication. Similar studies have been carried out in a variety of SME communities. Some of the criteria for adoption and use have been similar to those found by Poon & Swatman, others have provided alternative responses. Abell & Lim (1996) found that reduction in communication costs, improvement in customer services, improvement in lead time and improvement in sales were the major criteria for E-commerce adoption and use, adding that external technical support was considered vital to any adoption and use strategies.

Lawrence (1997), in an examination of Tasmanian SMEs noted that improved marketing and the ability to reach new customers were the most common criteria for adopting and using E-commerce. Lawrence also noted that decisions concerning E-commerce adoption were often forced onto SMEs by their larger trading partners. This is supported by studies carried out MacGregor & Bunker (1996), MacGregor, Bunker & Waugh (1998), Reimenschneider & Mykytyn (2000) and Raymond (2001).

Auger & Gallaugher (1997) noted that improvement in customer services and improvement to internal control of the business were strong criteria for E-commerce, adoption in SMEs. The strong desire for control was also noted in studies carried out by Reimenschneider & Mykytyn (2000), Poon & Joseph (2001) and Domke-Damonte & Levsen (2002).

A number of studies (Reimenschneider & Mykytyn 2000, Price-Waterhouse Cooper 1999, Power & Sohal 2002) have found that some SMEs have adopted E-commerce nominating pressure from customers as one of the motivating criteria.

For convenience, a summary of research on criteria is provided in Table 2.4.

Table 2.4
Summary of Research on Criteria Used by SME's in the Decisions to Adopt and Use E-Commerce

Criteria	Researcher
Demand/Pressure from Customers	Reimenschneider & Mykytyn 2000 (US) Price Waterhouse Coopers 1999 (Aus) Power & Sohal 2002 (Aus)
Pressure of competition	Raisch 2001 (Can) Poon & Strom 1997 (Aus)
Pressure from Suppliers	Reimenschneider & Mykytyn 2000 (US) MacGregor & Bunker 1996b (Aus) Lawrence 1997 (Aus) Raymond 2001 (Can)
Reduction of costs	Abell & Lim 1996 (NZ) Raisch 2001 (Can) Auger & Gallaugher 1997 (US/Aus)
Improvement to customer service	Abell & Lim 1996 (NZ) Senn 1996 (US) Auger & Gallaugher 1997 (US/Aus) Power & Sohal 2002 (Aus)
Improvement in lead time	Power & Sohal 2002 (Aus) Reimenschneider & Mykytyn 2000 (US) Abell & Lim 1996 (NZ)
Increased sales	Abell & Lim 1996 (NZ) Lee 2001 (US) Phan 2001 (US)
Improvement to internal efficiency	Porter 2001 (US)
Strengthen Relations with Business	Raymond 2001(Can)

Partners	Evans & Wurster 1997 (US)
	Poon & Swatman 1997 (Aus)
Reach new customers/markets	Poon & Swatman 1997 (Aus)
	Lawrence 1997 (Aus)
	Power & Sohal 2002 (Aus)
	Reimenschneider & Mykytyn 2000 (US)
Improve competitiveness	Turban et al 2000 (US)
	Raymond 2001 (Can)
	Reimenschneider & Mykytyn 2000 (US)
External Technical Support	Abell & Lim 1996 (NZ)
Improve marketing	Poon & Swatman 1997 (Aus)
	Lawrence 1997 (Aus)
	Power & Sohal 2002 (Aus)
	Reimenschneider & Mykytyn 2000 (US)
Improve control and follow-up	Reimenschneider & Mykytyn 2000 (US)
	Domke-Damonte & Levsen 2002 (US)
	Poon & Joseph 2001 (Aus)
	Auger & Gallaugher 1997 (Aus/US)

As can be seen in Table 2.4, most of the criteria appear to cross cultural/national borders and could be assumed applicable both to the Swedish and Australia condition.

2.6.2 Benefits derived from the adoption and use of E-commerce by SMEs

As already suggested in section 2.4.1, many of the substantial benefits provided by E-commerce fall into the category of intangible benefits and are often not realised by owner managers at the time of E-commerce adoption.

Studies by Poon & Swatman (1997) and Abell & Lim (1996) found that SMEs benefited in their ability to reach new customers and new markets through the use of E-commerce. This finding has been supported in more recent studies (Vescovi 2000, Ritchie & Brindley 2001, Sparkes & Thomas 2001, Raymond 2001, Quayle 2002).

Earlier studies found that other benefits reported by SME operators included reduced production costs (Poon & Swatman 1997, Abell & Lim 1996), lowering of administration costs (Poon & Swatman 1997, Abell & Lim 1996), reduced lead time (Abell & Lim 1996), increased sales (Abell & Lim 1996), improved relations with business partners (Poon & Swatman 1997) and improved quality of information (Poon & Swatman 1997, Abell & Lim 1996).

A recent study by Quayle (2002) found that benefits derived from E-commerce use, as reported by SME owner/managers, included reduced administration costs, reduced production costs, reduced lead time, reduced stock, improved marketing and improved quality of information.

Again, for convenience these results are summarised in Table 2.5.

Table 2.5
Benefits found by SME's in their use of E-commerce

Benefits	Researcher
Lower administration costs	Poon & Swatman 1997 (Aus) Abell & Lim 1996 (NZ) Quayle 2002 (UK)
Lower production costs	Poon & Swatman 1997 (Aus) Abell & Lim 1996 (NZ) Quayle 2002 (UK)
Reduced lead time	Poon & Swatman 1997 (Aus) Abell & Lim 1996 (NZ) Quayle 2002 (UK)
Reduced Stock	Quayle 2002 (UK)
Increased Sales	Abell & Lim 1996
Increased internal efficiency	Tetteh & Burn 2001 (Aus) MacGregor et al 1998 (Aus)
Improved relations with business partners	Poon & Swatman 1997 (Aus)
New customers and markets	Ritchie & Brindley 2001(UK) Quayle 2002 (UK) Raymond 2001 (Can) Vescovi 2000 (US) Sparkes & Thomas 2001 (UK) Poon & Swatman 1997 (Aus) Abell & Lim 1996 (NZ)
Improved competitiveness	Vescovi 2000 (US)
Improved marketing	Vescovi 2000 (US) Quayle 2002 (UK) Sparkes & Thomas 2001 (UK)
Improved quality of information	Poon & Swatman 1997 (Aus) Abell & Lim 1996 (NZ) Quayle 2002 (UK)

AS with the criteria (Table 2.4) studies involving benefits appear to cross cultural/national borders and are assumed applicable to the Swedish and Australian studies. AS has already been pointed out (see Section 2.2.2) regional SMEs are often portrayed as falling behind in terms of resources, customer base and infrastructure. As such, a number of benefits would appear to be more applicable to the regional SME sector.

2.6.3 Disadvantages encountered through the adoption and use of E-Commerce by SMEs

E-commerce has always carried the stigma of poor security. Innumerable studies have pointed to the perceived lack of visible security as a reason for non-acceptance of the technology, both by businesses and customers (see as examples Lawrence 1997, MacGregor et al 1998). Recent studies, however, have identified a number of other disadvantages incurred by SME operators in their day-to-day use of E-commerce technologies.

Raymond (2001), in examining the removal of business intermediaries by E-commerce, noted a deterioration of relationships with business partners and customers. He termed this effect as 'disintermediation'. Similar findings have been presented by Stauber (2000). Stauber also found that many SME operators complained of increasing costs in their business dealings attributable to E-commerce use.

Lawrence (1997) found that E-commerce, particularly, but not exclusively EDI, resulted in reduced flexibility of work practices and heavier reliance on the technology. Her findings are supported in studies by MacGregor et al (1998), Lee (2001) and Sparkes & Thomas (2001).

MacGregor et al (1998), in a study of 131 regional SMEs in Australia found that many respondents complained that they were doubling their work effort, this, in part, being due to the E-commerce systems not being fully integrated into the existing business systems in the organisation. They also found that many respondents complained that the technology had resulted in higher computer maintenance costs.

Again, for convenience, these studies are summarised in Table 2.6.

Table 2.6
Disadvantages found by SME's in their use of E-commerce technology

Deterioration of relations with business partners	Raymond 2001 (Can) Stauber 2000 (Aus)
Higher costs	Stauber 2000 (Aus) MacGregor et al 1998 (Aus)
Increased computer maintenance	MacGregor et al 1998 (Aus)
Doubling of work	MacGregor et al 1998 (Aus)
Reduced flexibility of work	Lee 2001 (US) Lawrence 1997 (Aus) MacGregor et al 1998 (Aus)
Security risks	Ritchie & Brindley 2001 (UK)
Dependence on E-commerce (non-E-commerce procedures having	Sparkes & Thomas 2001 (UK) MacGregor et al 1998 (Aus)

to be done through E-commerce formats)   Lawrence 1997 (Aus)

Given difficulties with lack of expertise, lack of adequate cabling and lack of infrastructure in regional areas (see Section 2.2.2), a number of these disadvantages are particularly pertinent.

2.6.4 Barriers to the Adoption of Electronic Commerce in SMEs

Hadjimanolis (1999), in a study of E-commerce adoption by SMEs in Cyprus, considers that barriers to adoption can be categorised as either <u>external</u> or <u>internal</u> to the organisation. External barriers include difficulties in obtaining finance, difficulties in obtaining technological information and difficulties choosing the appropriate hardware and software. These difficulties he terms <u>supply barriers</u>. He further nominates two other sub-categories of external barriers that he terms <u>demand barriers</u> and <u>environmental barriers</u>. Demand barriers found by Hadjimanolis include E-commerce not fitting with products and services offered or not fitting with the way their customers wished to conduct their business. Environmental barriers found by Hadjimanolis included complicated governmental regulations and security concerns.

Hadjimanolis subdivided his internal barriers into two categories. These he termed <u>resource barriers</u> (which included lack of management enthusiasm and lack of technical expertise) and <u>systems barriers</u> (which included E-commerce not fitting with current business practices).

In a similar study, Lawrence (1997) defined three categories. These she termed <u>company</u>, <u>personal</u> and <u>industry</u> barriers.

Company barriers, found by Lawrence, included low level of technology use within the business, limited financial and technical resources available, organisational resistance to change and lack of perceived return on investment.

Barriers categorised as personal included lack of information on E-commerce, management preferring conventional approaches to business practice and inability to see the advantages of using E-commerce.

Industry barriers included some respondents believing that the industry, as a whole was not ready for E-commerce technology.

A number of other research initiatives, while not providing categories of perceived barriers have produced similar findings to those of Lawrence and Hadjiminolis. Purao & Campbell (1998), who conducted a series of interviews with SME owners, found that major barriers included a failure to see any advantage in using E-commerce. They also found that lack of technical know how, prohibitive set up costs and security concerns were strong disincentives to many SME owner/managers. Abell & Lim (1996) found many SME owner/managers felt that E-commerce did not suit either their day-to-day business procedures or the product mix offered by their business.

In a cross-cultural study of SMEs in Hong Kong and Finland, Farhoomand et al (2000) found that both cultures reported a lack of technical know how and a failure to see how E-commerce fitted the current mode of business practices.

Recent studies have shown that many of the barriers reported in the late 1990's by Lawrence and Hadjimanolis are still current in today's SMEs. Tambini (1999) and Eid et al (2002) found that SME managers are still not convinced that E-commerce fits the products or services that their businesses offer. Studies by Bakos & Brynjolfsson (2000), Sawhney & Zabin (2002), Merhtens et al (2001) have found that there is still a reluctance for SME managers to adjust their businesses to the requirements and demands placed on it by E-

31

commerce participation. Bakos & Brynjolfsson (2000) and Kulmala et al (2002) found that many SMEs felt that E-commerce did not suit the current mix of customers while Chau & Hui (2001) have reported that many respondents did not see any advantage to using E-commerce in their businesses. Other barriers reported in the literature include a reported lack of technical know how (Mirchandani & Motwani 2001), security concerns (Oxley & Yeung 2001, Reimenschneider & McKinney 2001) and cost concerns (Ratnasingham 2000, Reimenschneider & McKinney 2001).

For convenience these barriers are arranged in Table 2.7.

Table 2.7
Barriers to E-commerce adoption by SME's

Factor	Researcher
E-commerce doesn't fit with products/services	Kendall et al 2001 (HK) Tambini 1999 (US) Abell & Lim 1996 (NZ) Eid et al 2002 (UK) Hadjimanolis 1999 (Greece)
E-commerce doesn't fit with the way we do business	Abell & Lim 1996 (NZ) Bakos & Brynjolfsson 2000 (Swed) Hadjimanolis 1999 (Greece) Farhoomand et al 2000 (Fin/HK) Sawhney & Zabin 2002 (US) Iacovou et al 1995 (US) Poon & Swatman 1997 (Aus) Mehrtens et al 2001 (Aus) Lawrence 1997 (Aus)
E-commerce doesn't fit the way our customers work	Abell & Lim 1996 (NZ) Bakos & Brynjolfsson 2000 (Swed) Kulmala et al 2002 (US) Hadjimanolis 1999 (Greece)
We don't see the advantage of using E-commerce	Purao & Campbell 1998 (US) Lee & Runge 2001 (US) Chau & Hui 2001 (US) Lawrence 1997 (Aus) Hadjimanolis 1999 (Greece)
Lack of technical know how	Purao & Campbell 1998 (US) Farhoomand et al 2000 (Fin/HK) Mirchandani & Motwani 2001 (US) Hadjimanolis 1999 (Greece)

Security risks	Purao & Campbell 1998 (US)
	Aldridge et al 1997 (US)
	Oxley & Yeung 2001 (US)
	Reimenschneider &
	McKinney 2001 (US)
	Hadjimanolis 1999 (Greece)
Cost too high	Reimenschneider &
	McKinney 2001 (US)
	Purao & Campbell 1998 (US)
	Hadjimanolis 1999 (Greece)
	Ratnasingam 2000 (Aus)
	Lawrence 1997 (Aus)
Not sure what H/W or S/W to choose	Purao & Campbell 1998 (US)
	Hadjimanolis 1999 (Greece)
	Farhoomand et al 2000 (Fin/HK)

The various studies described in Tables 2.4 – 2.7 present a significant variety of criteria, benefits, disadvantages and barriers to E-commerce adoption in SMEs. What is significant about these studies is that the vast majority have been conducted within a single country. It would be of interest to discover whether these criteria, benefits, disadvantages and barriers derived for use within a single country were applicable to other countries. Studies by Auger & Gallaugher (1997) and Farhoomand et al (2000) have attempted to address this gap in the literature but have only done so for barriers (Farhoomand et al 2000) and criteria (Auger & Gallaugher 1997). Even these studies have used a limited number of criteria and barriers. Clearly, there is a need for a comprehensive study that takes all the criteria, benefits, disadvantages and barriers and tests their appropriateness in different national settings.

2.6.5 Business characteristics affecting the adoption of E-commerce by SMEs

A number of studies have been carried out to determine which business characteristics may affect SME adoption of E-commerce technology. Hawkins et al (1995), Hawkins & Winter (1996) and Hyland & Matlay (1997) have noted that because SMEs are diverse in terms of business size, business sector, market etc, results are not generalisable across the entire SME sector.
Fallon & Moran (2000) found significant links between the business size (defined in terms of the number of employees) of the SME and the level of internet adoption. Matlay (2000) showed that the business sector was significantly associated with E-commerce adoption. Both studies showed that the same results were achievable despite varying geographic spread or market focus. These studies showed that smaller SMEs (fewer than 10 employees) were less likely to adopt E-commerce technology than larger SMEs. They also found that service organisations were more likely to adopt E-commerce than manufacturing or retail based SMEs. Riquelme (2002), in a study of 75 Chinese SMEs found that those involved in service tended to adopt E-commerce far more than their manufacturing counterparts.

Blackburn & Athayde (2000) identified not only business size and business sector but also the level of international marketing as a business characteristic associated with adoption of E-commerce technology.

As with the pre-E-commerce adoption of IT, a number of studies (Tetteh & Burn 2001, O'Donnell et al 2001) have concluded that successful E-commerce adoption is associated with both the level of IT skill within the SME as well as with the development, prior to E-commerce adoption, of business wide systems. These studies support earlier findings with EDI adoption (see MacGregor et al 1998, Iacovou et al 1995, Turban 2000)

In a study of 102 SMEs, Mazzarol et al (1999) found that the gender of the CEO was significantly associated with the level of adoption of E-commerce, while the age and level of education of the CEO did not show any significant association. This study is supported by the findings of Venkatash & Morris (2000).

For convenience, these studies are summarized in Table 2.8

Table 2.8
Business characteristics affecting the adoption of E-commerce by SMEs

Business characteristics	Researcher
Business size	Hawkins et al 1995 Hawkins & Winter 1996 Hyland & Matlay 1997 Fallon & Moran 2000 Blackburn & Athayde 2000 Matlay 2000
Business age	Kai-Uwe Brock (2000) MacGregor et al (2002) Donckels & Lambrecht (1997)
Business sector	Matlay 2000 MacGregor et al (2002) Schindehutte & Morris (2001) BarNir & Smith (2002) Blackburn & Athayde 2000
Market focus	Blackburn & Athayde 2000 Schindehutte & Morris (2001) BarNir & Smith (2002)
Level of IT skills	Tetteh & Burn (2001) O'Donnell et al (2001)

2.6.6 Summary of the acquisition and use of E-commerce by SMEs

This chapter began by noting three initiatives for E-commerce adoption by SMEs. These were:

> An essentially linear model that began with email, progressed through website design, to finally developing E-commerce.
> A description of the many benefits derivable through E-commerce adoption by SMEs.
> The development, prior to E-commerce adoption, of strategic alliances with other SMEs.

In summary, the first component has been questioned, and indeed criticized in the literature, from a number of perspectives. These include:

- The appropriateness of a linear model, particularly one that places planning as the last step, as a guide to E-commerce adoption
- The appropriateness of a linear model to depict internationalization of SMEs, through E-commerce adoption, when internationalization is not linear in nature.
- The inappropriate treatment of SMEs as a homogeneous group.
- The failure of the model to account for business characteristics such as business size, business age, location of the business etc.
- The use of inappropriate pre-E-commerce criteria for SMEs decision-making.

Likewise, the second component, the benefits to SMEs from E-commerce adoption, has been criticized in the literature. These criticisms include:

- The inappropriate treatment of SMEs as a homogeneous group.
- The application of benefits that are more applicable to large businesses
- The application of benefits that are often not seen as important by many SMEs

While these components are important, an examination of much of the government literature (Culkin & Smith 2000, Martin & Matlay 2001, Blair 2000) would suggest that their success hinges on the development of small business strategic alliances. As such, this is the main focus of this present study. While some studies have been carried out to examine the role of small business strategic alliances, few have attempted to compare SMEs within small business strategic alliances to SMEs outside such arrangements.

It is now appropriate that we examine the third component, the development of strategic alliances, to determine their applicability in the adoption and use of E-commerce by SMEs. The following sections consider the nature of strategic alliances, in particular their role within the SME sector.

2.7 Strategic Alliances

The advent of E-commerce has not only altered organisational procedures (Kuljis et al 1998) but has radically altered interorganisational procedures (Overby & Min 2000). Bakos (1998) suggests that boundaries between organisations have become blurred while Hitt et al (1999) take this a step further by suggesting that organisations are becoming borderless. While this 'expansion' of the organisation has provided a wider marketplace for many businesses, Overby & Min (2000) suggest that there is also the risk of a reduction in the overall efficiency of the organisation as it strives to meet increased customer demands.

This reduction in boundaries and increase in market scope has led to changes in the structure of many organisations. Frequently, it has been argued that multi-level hierarchical structures no longer fit the marketplace (Overby & Min 2000, Tikkanen 1998). Not only has this meant a re-examination of organisational structure, but many factors previously considered 'informal procedures', such as sharing expertise and advice, have now become prominent in day-to-day organisational procedures. This reduction in hierarchical structure, together with the increasing importance of informal interorganisational links, has meant that organisations are not only interacting economically but are tied together by factors that Storper (1995) describes as 'untraded interdependencies'. These links, which include sharing of practical experience, sharing of technical expertise, collective learning and market knowledge (see Keeble et al 1999, O'Donnell et al 2001, Overby & Min 2001, Tikkanen 1998) have been termed strategic alliances or networks and are based on relationships of trust and reciprocity.

There are many definitions of strategic alliances in the literature. Dennis (2000) suggests that strategic alliances

".. are dynamic arrangement(sic) that are constantly evolving and adjusting in order to accommodate changes in the business environment. Member companies have interconnected linkages that allow them to move more efficiently towards set objectives than those operating as a separate entity" (Dennis 2000 p287)

She adds that while all companies form relationships with suppliers, customers etc., it is the extent of the closeness, interdependence and consciousness of these relationships that determines whether they are truly part of a strategic alliance. This definition implies that only those interorganisational links that have formal governance can be termed strategic alliances. By comparison, Yeung (1994) defines a strategic alliance as

"an integrated and coordinated set of ongoing economic and non-economic relations embedded within, among and outside businesses." (Yeung 1994 p 476)

Thus, for Yeung, a strategic alliance is not only a structure but embodies processes between organisations. These processes may be formal economic processes or may be informal cooperative relationships, sharing expertise and know-how.

While recent studies (Keeble et al 1999, O'Donnell et al 2001, Overby & Min 2001) stress the importance of informal interorganisational links, the definition of these links in the SME sector varies widely. As this study has as its focus SME strategic alliances with some form of governance (be they organisationally linked SMEs or businesses who have made use of SME associations), the definition provided by Achrol & Kotler (1999) is adopted, viz.

"an independent coalition of task- or skill-specialised economic entities (independent businesses or autonomous organisational units) that operates without hierarchical control but is embedded by dense lateral connections, mutuality, and reciprocity, in a shared value system that defines "membership" roles and responsibilities" (Achrol & Kotler 1999 p 148).

There are a variety of reasons in the literature as to why strategic alliances have developed. Black & Porter (2000) argue that the more complex and dynamic the environment, the more need there is for some structure to coordinate disparate groups. Christopher (1999) suggests that businesses need to achieve greater agility with supply chain partners. Gilliland & Bello (1997) point to market volatility and technological uncertainty as a source of need for some form of controlling structure, while Tikkanen (1998) suggests a need to re-align organisational structure to market structure.

As with the origin of strategic alliances, there are a number of differing taxonomies of strategic alliances in the literature. These taxonomies are normally based on structure, power or process. It is appropriate to consider each of these styles of classification.

Structure

O'Donnell et al (2002) suggest that strategic alliances can be subdivided into four groups: vertical (linking functional aspects of organisations that result in joint manufacturing, marketing or product development), horizontal (developing relationships either nationally or internationally), industrial (building relationships through resource pooling), social (sharing of marketing and technological know-how). This is similar to the subdivisions suggested by Veradarajan & Cunningham (1995) who termed their subdivisions functional, intra-interorganisational, intra-industry and motivational.

Process

Whereas O'Donnell et al (2002) and Veradarajan & Cunningham (1995) subdivided strategic alliances in terms of structure, Johannisson et al (2002) suggest that strategic alliances can be subdivided into four groups based on process. The four groups are: resource-based (each business controls their own unique resources which are combined to strategic advantage), industrial organisation (businesses as autonomous entities establishing their own unique market position), virtual organisation (independent yet interdependent organisations striving for "joint variety" Veradarajan & Cunningham (1995) using advanced technology), industrial district (SMEs characterised by production type, organised for internal cooperation and external competition).

Achrol & Kotler (1999) also suggested that strategic alliances could be subdivided in terms of process. They provide four types: internal (designed to reduce hierarchy and open businesses to the environment), vertical (strategic alliances that maximise the productivity of serially dependent functions by creating partnerships among independent skill-specialised businesses), intermarket (strategic alliances that seek to leverage horizontal synergies across industries), opportunity (strategic alliances that are organised around customer needs and market opportunities and are designed to seek the best solutions to them).

An examination of the two process taxonomies of strategic alliance shows that while there are similarities between the two, the subdivisions are based on very different perspectives. Johannison et al (2002) appears to have as its focus the individual SME. In contrast, Achrol & Kotler's model appears to have the external environment as its focus. If, as suggested, E-commerce has moved the focus outside the individual organization, the subgroups suggested by Achrol & Kotler would appear to more closely match E-commerce.

Power

Dennis (2000) considers power to be the most important factor upon which to classify strategic alliances. She provides two classifications dominated strategic alliances (a group of smaller companies dominated by a single larger company), equal partner strategic alliances (where there is no governing partner and each relationship is based on reciprocal, preferential, mutually supportive actions).

While power is clearly an important factor, there are too few subgroups in the Dennis model to adequately describe the SME environment.

Clearly, an understanding of these taxonomies adds to our understanding of strategic alliances. An examination of O'Donnell et al's (2002) four subdivisions would suggest that only two, <u>industrial</u> and <u>social</u> adequately describe SMEs. An examination of Achrol & Kotler's (1999) four subdivisions, again, would suggest that only two, <u>intermarket</u> and <u>opportunity</u> adequately describe SMEs. It is appropriate that we examine the role of strategic alliances in SMEs.

2.7.1 Strategic Alliances and SMEs

It could be argued that by the very nature of business, all organisations relate to others and are thus part of some form of strategic alliance. On the surface these relationships may appear to be nothing more than exchanges of goods and payments, but relationships with customers, suppliers, competitors can never be simply described in terms of financial transactions. Dennis (2000) suggests that any dealing with other organisations must impinge on the decision making process even if these decisions only involve the strengthening or relaxing of the relationships themselves. Nalebuff & Brandenburg (1996) state that for a relationship to be truly a strategic alliance it must be conscious, interdependent and cooperating towards a predetermined set of goals.

Viewed then as 'self designing' partnerships Eccles & Crane (1998 cited in Dennis 2000) suggest that strategic alliances are dynamic arrangements evolving and adjusting to accommodate changes in the business environment. Achrol & Kotler (1999) take this a step further by stating that strategic alliances

' .. are more adaptable and flexible because of loose coupling and openness to information. Environmental disturbances transfer imperfectly through loose coupled networks and tend to dissipate in intensity as they spread through the system' (Achrol & Kotler 1999 p 147)

Thus member organisations have interconnected linkages that allow more efficient movement towards predetermined objectives than would be the case if they operated as a single separate entity. By developing and organising functional components strategic alliances provide a better mechanism to learn and adapt to changes in their environment.

In addition to providing much needed information, strategic alliances often provide legitimacy to their members. For businesses that provide a service and whose products are intangible, company image and reputation becomes crucial since customers can rarely test or inspect the service before purchase. Cropper (1996) suggests that membership of a strategic alliance very often supplies this image to potential customers.

The advent of E-commerce has given rise to a 'new wave' of research examining the role of strategic alliances, particularly in SME's. Much of this research has been prompted by the realisation that old hierarchical forms of company organisation produced relationships which are too tightly coupled (Marchewka & Towell 2000), and do not fit an often turbulent marketplace (Overby & Min 2000, Tikkanen 1998).

Schindehutte & Morris (2001) state that organisations, particularly SMEs, survive or fail as a function of their adaptability to the marketplace. Those organisations that can interpret patterns in the environment and adapt their structure and strategy to suit those changing patterns will survive. While adaptability may be a function of prior experience or business sector focus, in the SME sector adaptability often relies on strategic alliance partners.

Properly utilised, strategic alliances can provide a number of advantages over stand-alone organisations. These include the sharing of financial risk (Jorde & Teece 1989), technical knowledge (Marchewka & Towell 2000), market penetration (Achrol & Kotler 1999) and internal efficiency (Datta 1988).

Early studies of SME strategic alliances (Gibb 1993, Ozcan 1995) concentrated on formal strategic alliances. Indeed Golden & Dollinger (1993), in a study of small manufacturing businesses concluded that few SMEs were able to function without some form of inter-organisational relationship having been established. They added that these inter-organisational relationships were associated with successful strategic adaptation by SMEs. Dean et al (1997) suggested that formal strategic alliances were used by SME's to

"pool resources and talents together to reap results which would not be possible (due to cost constraints and economies of scale) if the enterprise operated in isolation." (p 78)

In the 1990's many SME strategic alliances took a more 'semi-formal' approach. Local or government agencies, such as SME associations and chambers of commerce, provided a formal umbrella in the form of advisory services that assisted in legal, financial, training or technical advice. Individual members operated formally within the umbrella organisation but could interact informally with fellow members.

While researchers, government agencies and practitioners have continued to examine and refine both formal and semi-formal strategic alliances, recent literature (Rosenfeld 1996, Premaratne 2001) suggests that informal or social linkages often ensure a higher and more stable flow of information and resources in the SME environment.

Thorelli (1986) states that central to the concept of working within a strategic alliance is the distribution of power that he defines as the ability to influence the decision of others. The five factors he cites as the potential sources of power for members are economic base, technology, expertise, trust and legitimacy. Miles et al (1999) suggest that for SMEs the decision to form a strategic alliance comes from a perception of goals by the individual organisation. If the organisation sees itself as strong in its own right, a strategic alliance may be seen as an option to increase that strength. The distribution of power moves in favour of the strong organisation allowing it to capitalise and influence weaker members without losing its own identity.

If, on the other hand, the organisation sees itself as weak, a strategic alliance may be a necessity in order to survive and compete in the larger marketplace. For these organisations the distribution of power leaves them in a weak position in exchange relationships.

This of course varies from strategic alliance to strategic alliance. In a small strategic alliance (few participating organisations) there is more likely to be an asymmetric relationship between partners. As the size of the strategic alliance increases there are a greater number of potential partners, providing a greater chance to benefit for all members.

Foy (1994 cited Dennis 2000) suggests that

".. by taking advantage of the coordination and economies of scale of large vertical organisations whilst embracing the flexibility, creativity and lower overheads of small businesses, members of a network (*strategic alliance*) are able to enjoy the best of both worlds" (p288, my italics)

this raises the question as to why many SMEs have not become members of some type of formal strategic alliance.

A number of reasons are suggested in the literature. Drakopoulou-Dodd et al (2002) found that, in studies of European SMEs, more than 50% reported that they derived their technical support, financial advice and business know how from family and friends. Gimeno et al (1997 cited Dennis 2000 and Gimeno & Woo 1999) found that many SME owners negatively affect potential strategic alliances by withholding necessary information from their alliance partners. McBer & Company (1986 cited Dennis 2000 and Gimeno & Woo 1999) found that SME owners refuse to trust or cooperate with similar business owners in the same industry.

As with E-commerce adoption, a number of business characteristics appear to impinge upon the choice and nature of SME involvement in strategic alliances. In a study of 591 SMEs Smith et al (2002) found that business size and culture appeared to affect both the amount of strategic planning carried out by the organisation and decisions by the organisation to involve in a strategic alliance. Donckels & Lambrecht (1997) found that business characteristics such as business size, business sector and number of years in business were significantly related to both the choice of, and the type of strategic alliance entered into, while studies by Schindehutte & Morris (2001) and BarNir & Smith (2002) concluded that business sector and market focus dictate SME decisions to form strategic alliances.

2.8 Restatement of Research Question

This chapter has shown that there is substantial advocacy both from researchers as well as government bodies (Blair 2000) for SMEs to develop small business strategic alliances. While some research has examined the role of these alliances in the acquisition and use of E-commerce, there is no critical research that has attempted to compare E-commerce adoption by those SMEs that are part of a small business strategic alliance and those that are not. A review of the literature has confirmed the need for such research and has presented a number of business characteristics that may impinge both on the nature of the membership of such alliances and their effectiveness in the processes surrounding the adoption and use of E-commerce.

As can be seen in the preceding sections, not only are the criteria for adoption and the barriers to non-adoption of E-commerce by SMEs different to their larger counterparts, but the perceived benefits and disadvantages are also specific to the sector.

Over the past decade there has been a 'push', both at a research level as well as a government level, for SMEs to enter into some form of strategic alliance to more fully adapt their organisations to a global market perspective. While the literature has both advocates as well as critics of this approach, little real comparison between members and non-members of SME strategic alliances has been carried out. The current study attempts to bridge that gap. A number of business characteristics affecting E-commerce adoption continue to re-appear in the literature. These business characteristics are the business size (in terms of employee numbers), the business age, the business sector upon which the SME is focussed, the market share on which they focus and the level of IT skills of the SME.

This chapter began by questioning the three government initiatives for E-commerce adoption by SMEs. In particular, this chapter has focused on the role of small business strategic alliances in the adoption of E-commerce by SMEs. As indicated, a number of business characteristics (business size, business age, business sector, market focus or the level of IT skill) appear to be associated with E-commerce adoption in SMEs As such, a number of research questions arise:

- Are certain business sizes more likely to enter into some form of strategic alliance?
- Does business age have a bearing on whether an SME is more likely to enter into some form of strategic alliance?
- Does the business sector have a bearing on whether an SME is more likely to enter into some form of strategic alliance?
- Are SMEs that purport to have a high level of IT expertise more likely to enter into some form of strategic alliance?

- Does the market focus have a bearing on whether an SME is more likely to enter into some form of strategic alliance?
- Does membership of a strategic alliance alter the perceived importance of E-commerce adoption criteria in SMEs?
- Does membership of a strategic alliance alter the perceived importance of E-commerce adoption criteria for particular business sizes, particular business ages, particular business sectors, particular market focuses or particular levels of IT skill?
- Does membership of a strategic alliance alter the perception of barriers for non-adoption of E-commerce in SMEs?
- Does membership of a strategic alliance alter the perception of barriers for non-adoption of E-commerce for particular business sizes, particular business ages, particular business sectors, particular market focuses or particular levels of IT skill?
- Does membership of a strategic alliance alter the perception of benefits for SMEs that have adopted E-commerce?
- Does membership of a strategic alliance alter the perception of benefits for particular business sizes, particular business ages, particular business sectors, particular market focuses or particular levels of IT skill?
- Does membership of a strategic alliance alter the perception of disadvantages for SMEs that have adopted E-commerce?
- Does membership of a strategic alliance alter the perception of disadvantages for particular business sizes, particular business ages, particular business sectors, particular market focuses or particular levels of IT skill?

These are summarised into the following four goals of the study:
- To determine if membership in a small business strategic alliances is associated with business characteristics (business size, business age, business sector, market focus or the level of IT skill).
- To determine if the membership of small business strategic alliances alters perceptions of any of the adoption factors (barriers to adoption, criteria for adoption, benefits of adoption or disadvantages of adoption) of E-commerce technologies.
- To determine if the membership in a small business strategic alliances alters perceptions of any of the adoption factors (barriers to adoption, criteria for adoption, benefits of adoption or disadvantages of adoption) of E-commerce technologies for specific sectors of the SME population (certain business ages, business sizes, business sectors, market focuses, particular levels of IT skill).
- To determine if the associations between business characteristics (business size, business age, business sector, market focus or level of IT skills) and adoption factors (barriers to adoption, criteria for adoption, benefits of adoption or disadvantages of adoption) of E-commerce technologies differ, depending on whether the SME is part of a small business strategic alliance or not.

2.9 Conclusion

This chapter has presented an in-depth analysis of the literature concerned with three main factors of E-commerce adoption in SMEs, namely:
- The E-commerce adoption factors
- The business characteristics associated with E-commerce adoption in SMEs

- The nature and role of small business strategic alliances in the adoption of E-commerce in SMEs
- The review of the literature supports several premises of this study, namely:
- When considering E-commerce adoption in SMEs, there is a need to examine the criteria for adoption, the barriers to adoption, the benefits of adoption and the disadvantages of adoption
- A number of business characteristics (business size, business age, business sector, market focus and the level of IT skill) appear to be associated with E-commerce adoption in SMEs. Clearly, these need to be examined against the adoption factors (criteria for adoption, the barriers to adoption, the benefits of adoption and the disadvantages of adoption).
- There is a gap in the literature specifically concerning the role of small business strategic alliances in the adoption of E-commerce in SMEs.

This chapter has provided the necessary theoretical framework, upon which a study of small business strategic alliances, business characteristics and E-commerce adoption factors in regional SMEs may be undertaken.

The following chapter presents a detailed methodology of that study.

Chapter 3
Research Methods and Procedures

3.1 Introduction

The preceding chapters have shown that there is substantial advocacy both from researchers as well as government bodies for SMEs to develop small business strategic alliances. While some research has examined the role of these alliances in the acquisition and use of E-commerce, there is no critical research that has attempted to compare E-commerce adoption by those SMEs that are part of a small business strategic alliance and those that are not. A review of the literature has confirmed the need for such research and has presented a number of business characteristics that may impinge both on the nature of the membership of such alliances and their effectiveness in the processes surrounding the adoption and use of E-commerce.

This chapter describes methods that are appropriate to the goals of this research and provides details of the procedures used in this study.

3.2 Research methods

As stated in the previous chapter (section 2.8), this study poses four research goals. These are:

- To determine if membership in a small business strategic alliances is associated with business characteristics (business size, business age, business sector, market focus or the level of IT skill).
- To determine if the membership of small business strategic alliances alters perceptions of any of the adoption factors (barriers to adoption, criteria for adoption, benefits of adoption or disadvantages of adoption) of E-commerce technologies.
- To determine if the membership in a small business strategic alliances alters perceptions of any of the adoption factors (barriers to adoption, criteria for adoption, benefits of adoption or disadvantages of adoption) of E-commerce technologies for specific sectors of the SME population (certain business ages, business sizes, business sectors, market focuses, particular levels of IT skill).
- To determine if the associations between business characteristics (business size, business age, business sector, market focus or level of IT skills) and adoption factors (barriers to adoption, criteria for adoption, benefits of adoption or disadvantages of adoption) of E-commerce technologies differ, depending on whether the SME is part of a small business strategic alliance or not.

One approach to meet these goals is to conduct a series of case studies for SMEs. While such an approach will produce substantive detail concerning business characteristics affecting decisions to adopt/not adopt E-commerce, there are just too many permutations of business characteristics that need to be considered. Attempting to include all possible permutations of business characteristics would tend to bias decisions as to which SMEs should be included/excluded from the study, resulting in a set of findings that is not generalizable beyond the sample used in the study.

The second approach is to undertake a large data gathering survey. This approach allows SMEs with differing ages, sizes, sectors, market foci and IT skill levels to be included in the study and reduces any bias of data brought about through decisions concerning inclusion/exclusion of candidate SMEs in the study.

The possibility of using a factorial experimental design was considered, however, as the aim of the study was both to consider overall and specific effects of small business strategic alliances to E-commerce adoption, this was rejected.

3.3 Choice of Location for Data Gathering

An examination of the literature concerned with E-commerce adoption by SMEs (see Section 2.6) shows that findings differ from location to location. Where, for example, in Australia Poon & Swatman (1997) found that E-commerce improved relationships with business partners, a similar study in Canada (Raymond 2001) found the opposite. Similarly where in a UK study Quayle (2002) found a benefit of E-commerce adoption was reduced costs, studies in Australia (MacGregor et al 1998, Stauber 2000) showed cost was increased. It appears, then, that the location of the study may have some bearing on the findings, rendering them inapplicable to other groups of SMEs.

As this study's primary aim was the role of small business strategic alliances, it was determined that more than one location was warranted for the data gathering. As one of the locations was Wollongong, a second regional location of similar size was sought.

A number of recent studies (Kjellberg et al 1998, Barry et al 2003, Klofsten 2000) Dobers & Strannegard 2001) have examined the interaction of Swedish businesses with one another, with government agencies and with educational institutions. These studies suggest along and powerful cooperation between Swedish businesses of all sizes and their employees, government agencies and education.

Since 1977 Swedish tertiary education has extensively involved in short course and distance education primarily aimed at regional small business employees (Kjellberg et al 1998). More recently there have been a number of new initiatives aimed at entrepreneurship and new business development (Klofsten 2000).

A number of studies (Dobers & Strannegard 2001, Gibbons-Wood & Lange 2000) have shown that government involvement in E-commerce adoption has been directed both at the proliferation of technology as well as the development of core competencies through joint business cooperation and education.

As this study sought to examine the role of small business strategic alliances, it was determined that a comparably sized regional location in Sweden may not only provide differences in the level of small business strategic alliance membership, but would provide differences across two political/geographic locations.

While it is important to examine differences across two political/geographic locations, it is equally important that these two locations are sufficiently similar such that comparisons can be made. As such, a number of details needed to be met. These were:

- The location must be a large regional centre rather than a capital city
- As the studies were quantitative in nature, both locations must have a sufficient number of SMEs within the region
- As the study will examine business characteristics such as business age, size, sector, market focus, the community must represent a cross section of business ages, sizes, sectors, market foci.

As the study is examining the role of small business strategic alliances
- A viable government initiated chamber of commerce for SMEs must exist and be well patronised by the SME community
- SMEs must be geographically close such that alliances with customers, suppliers or other businesses was possible.
- The SME community included SMEs that had adopted E-commerce as well as SMEs that had not adopted E-commerce.
- In line with the findings of Kjellberg et al (1998) and Klofsten (2000)
- The locations should have a full range of educational facilities including a university
- Questionnaire distribution and gathering must be possible in the location.
- Locations must be 'economically similar'

Two locations were chosen. The first was a community surrounding Karlstad, Sweden, which has a population between 50,000 and 100,000 and satisfies all of the criteria above. The second was Wollongong, Australia, which has a population of over 100,000 and again satisfies all of the criteria above. Both locations are classified as high income by the World Bank Group and are members of the Organisation for Economic Cooperation and Development (OECD), satisfying the last of the location needs.

The Swedish questionnaire was developed from three previous surveys carried out by the author prior to the current candidature (see Appendix 5). These original surveys examined the adoption of IT by SMEs (MacGregor & Cocks 1994, MacGregor & Bunker 1995, MacGregor & Bunker 1996a,b, MacGregor et al 1996, MacGregor et al 1997, MacGregor & Bunker 1999) as well as the adoption of E-commerce and EDI by SMEs in regional Australia (MacGregor et al 1998a,b) The Swedish questionnaire was sent back to Australia and translated by a visiting Swedish student back into English for accuracy and completeness (copies of the Swedish questionnaires can be found in Appendix 1). The Swedish questionnaire was sent out and returned by mail. Businesses surveyed were randomly selected from a government-produced list and all businesses were from one of four areas. These were Saffle, Arvika, Filipstad, Karlstad. As can be seen from the Swedish survey, the current study forms part of a much larger data collection effort coordinated by the author.

The Australian questionnaire was re-developed from the Swedish questionnaire, so that it could be administered by phone. Questions were in no way altered, however, in some case the order of questions was altered. As with the Swedish questionnaire, the data used in this current study was part of a much larger study coordinated by the author.

Both the Swedish and Australian studies were comprehensive studies of businesses and the portions of both studies used to gather data for the current research were embedded within the larger studies. The larger studies were of approximately the same size and the location of the questions for this current study was similar in the two questionnaires. An analysis of the questions preceding the questions relevant to the current research reveals that that the preceding questions in both studies were similar in nature and would have been most unlikely to introduce any contextual bias.

In both the Swedish and Australian surveys a quota-based approach was considered. However, as five separate business characteristics were being examined (each with five categories) it was considered that forcing so many quotas would potentially bias any results obtained.

It should be noted that where previous studies (Thong et al 1996) have placed finance respondents into service categories, the results of the two pilot studies indicated that this category be separated from the service sector and maintained as its own separate category.

The Australian questionnaire was administered by phone. Those administering the questionnaire chose SMEs from the yellow (business) pages of the phone book. 5 – 15 SMEs were phoned during each session – a different letter of the alphabet (different part of the phone book) was chosen for each session.

3.4 Survey instrument

Prior to any discussion regarding the development of a survey instrument, it is important to analyze the objectives of the study and the data that is necessary to support these goals.

3.4.1 Analysis of objectives and data requirements

To achieve the four goals stated above it is necessary to gather a variety of types of data about significantly different entities and to analyze these in a number of different ways. It is appropriate to examine each of the goals individually to determine the data requirements for each.

Goal 1
The objective of goal 1 is:
- To determine if membership in a small business strategic alliances is associated with business characteristics (business size, business age, business sector, market focus or the level of IT skill).

(see figure 3.1)

The data required to support Goal 1 are the categories of:
- Business Age
- Business Size
- Business Sector
- Market Focus
- Level of IT Skill

together with a mechanism for respondents to indicate whether they are members of a small business strategic alliance.

Figure 3.1

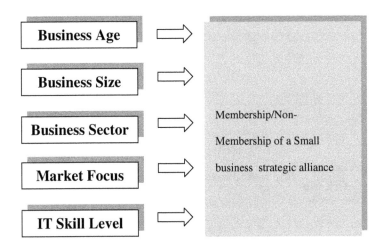

Goal 2

The objective of goal 2 is:

- To determine if the membership of small business strategic alliances alters perceptions of any of the adoption factors (barriers to adoption, criteria for adoption, benefits of adoption or disadvantages of adoption) of E-commerce technologies.

(see figure 3.2)

The data required by Goal 2 is a complete and tested set of adoption factors (criteria for adoption, barriers to adoption, benefits derived from adoption and disadvantages from adoption) of E-commerce, together with a mechanism for respondents to indicate whether they are members of a small business strategic alliance.

Figure 3.2

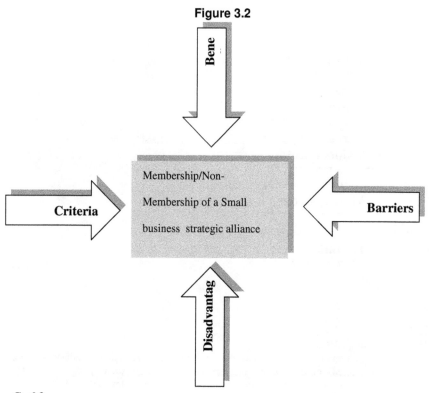

Goal 3
The objective of goal 3 is:
- To determine if the membership in a small business strategic alliances alters perceptions of any of the adoption factors (barriers to adoption, criteria for adoption, benefits of adoption or disadvantages of adoption) of E-commerce technologies for specific sectors of the SME population (certain business ages, business sizes, business sectors, market focuses, particular levels of IT skill).

(see figure 3.3)

The data required by Goal 3 is a complete and tested set of adoption factors (criteria for adoption, barriers to adoption, benefits derived from adoption and disadvantages from adoption) of E-commerce, together with a mechanism for respondents to indicate whether they are members of a small business strategic alliance. Goal 3 also requires the categories of:
- Business Age
- Business Size
- Business Sector
- Market Focus
- Level of IT Skill

Figure 3.3

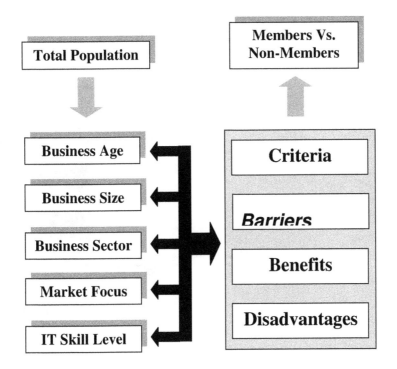

Goal 4

The objective of goal 4 is:
- To determine if the associations between business characteristics (business size, business age, business sector, market focus or level of IT skills) and adoption factors (barriers to adoption, criteria for adoption, benefits of adoption or disadvantages of adoption) of E-commerce technologies differ, depending on whether the SME is part of a small business strategic alliance or not.

(see figure 3.4)

Figure 3.4

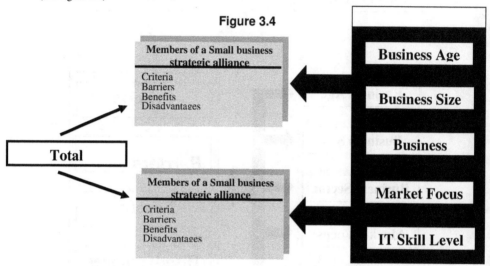

The data required by Goal 4 is a complete and tested set of adoption factors (criteria for adoption, barriers to adoption, benefits derived from adoption and disadvantages from adoption) of E-commerce, together with a mechanism for respondents to indicate whether they are members of a small business strategic alliance. Goal 3 also requires a delineation of the categories of:
- Business Age
- Business Size
- Business Sector
- Market Focus
- Level of IT Skill

3.4.2 Development of the Survey Instrument

Three sets of questions need to be developed to address the goals of the current study. These are:
- Business characteristics– business size, business age, business sector, market focus, level of IT skill

- Membership/non-membership of a small business strategic alliance
- Adoption/non-adoption of E-commerce – adoption factors (barriers to non-adoption, criteria for adoption, benefits of adoption, disadvantages from adoption) of E-commerce.

The development of each of these question types is discussed below.

3.4.2.1 Business characteristics

The development of the business characteristics was based both on previous studies in the literature (see section 2.7), together with two pilot studies and follow-up interviews (see Appendix 8) carried out prior to the present study. (MacGregor & Bunker 1996a, MacGregor et al 1998, Bunker & MacGregor 2000).

The first of these pilot studies examined factors associated with the uptake and use of IT by SMEs (MacGregor & Bunker 1996a). 131 SMEs from Wollongong, NSW took part in the survey. Wollongong was chosen as it represented a regional area, it had an established small business chamber of commerce and a variety of business sectors were represented.

The second pilot study was also carried out in Wollongong and involved factors associated with the decision to adopt and use E-commerce, particularly EDI (MacGregor et al 1998). 87 businesses were involved in the second study with follow up interviews of 6 of the businesses (Bunker & MacGregor 2000).

Business size

A number of authors (Hawkins et al 1995, Hawkins & Winter 1996) have noted that the business size (in terms of the number of employees) appears to be significantly associated with the level and type of adoption of E-commerce technology. While most studies categorise SMEs with less than 5 employees as micro businesses, a number of studies (Fallon & Moran 2000, Matlay 2000) suggest that SMEs with fewer than 10 employees is a far more significant subdivision than comparing 'micro' to 'small'. Similar views were found in the two pilot studies carried out by the author. In both cases significant differences were found when business with 10 or less employees were compared to businesses with more than 10 employees. As both these studies were with regional SMEs and as both gave rise to the questionnaire used in the current study, 10 employees rather than the usual 5 was adopted.

The pilot studies carried out as part of this present study support these findings, but add a separate category for single owner-operated businesses (termed sole trader). The pilot studies also suggested that SMEs with 20-50 employees tended to operate similarly and thus did not need to be split into smaller groupings.

Thus four categories of business size are adopted. These are:
- Sole owner-operated (0 employees)
- 1 – 10 employees
- 11 – 20 employees
- 21-50 employees

51

Business age

A number of studies (Donckels & Lambrecht 1997, Martin & Matlay 2001) have indicated that there appears to be some association between the business age of the SME and decisions regarding E-commerce adoption and use. Many studies have simply categorised business age in 'sets of 5' (0-5years, 6-10 years etc). The pilot study (see Appendix 8) found that within the first of these groups (0 – 5 years), three subsets existed, the first was the very new businesses (less than 1 year in business), the second included a number of businesses that had joined the dot-com revolution and were usually 1 – 2 years old. The second group also included SMEs that were acting as outsourcers to larger businesses. The third group was the residue (3 – 5 years in business). The pilot study showed that all three of these groups acted very differently where IT or E-commerce adoption and use were concerned. The pilot studies also found that for older businesses, subgroups 6 - 10 years, 11 – 20 years and over 20 years were adequate groupings.

Thus, 6 categories of business age are used. These are:
- Very new business (less than 1 year)
- 2 – 3 years
- 3 – 5 years
- 6 – 10 years
- 10 – 20 years
- over 20 years

Business Sector

A study examining internet training in SMEs carried out by Blackburn & Athayde (2000) found an association between business sector and E-commerce adoption and use.

In the pilot studies, four categories of business sector were determined as adequately covering the SME community. These are:
- Industrial – this includes manufacturing, engineering and transport
- Service – this includes professional SMEs such as lawyers, doctors etc.
- Retail – this includes both business to business as well as business to customer
- Finance – insurance, banking, accounting

It should be noted that while previous studies (Thong et al 1996, Blackburn & Athayde 2000) have placed finance respondents into the service category, the results from the two previous pilot studies in Wollongong (MacGregor & Bunker 1996a,b, MacGregor et al 1998, Bunker & MacGregor 2000) suggested that the financial sector was sufficiently different to warrant a separate category.

Market Focus

Market focus refers to the major 'push' of the organization to attract customers/clients and to sell its products/services.

A number of studies (Achrol & Kotler 1997, Blackburn & Athayde 2000) suggest that market focus is associated with the level of adoption of E-commerce in SMEs. Based on the pilot study findings, location of major customer base was found to be an adequate surrogate for market focus. Four distinct location bases were found. These were:

- Local – customer normally in a boundary of 5 – 10 kilometres
- Regional – customers within a 50 kilometre radius
- National – trading extend across the whole nation
- International – products and services are exported.

<u>Level of IT Skill</u>

A number of studies (Thong et al 1996, MacGregor et al 1998, O'Donnell et al 2001) have suggested that the level of IT skill within the organisation is associated with the level of adoption of E-commerce in SMEs. Based on the pilot studies, 5 levels of IT skill are identified. These are:

- No computer knowledge
- Low computer knowledge
- Normal computer knowledge
- High computer knowledge
- Expert computer knowledge

The descriptions for the level of computer skills were tested in the pilot study and appeared to be consistently understood by the majority of the respondents of the pilot study.

3.4.2.2 Strategic Alliance Question

The previous chapter (section 2.8) provides a variety of perspectives on the nature of small business strategic alliances in SMEs. The two pilot studies provided further evidence as to the importance of strategic alliances for gaining technical and organizational knowledge necessary for the adoption and use of E-commerce.

The results of the pilot studies and follow-up interviews revealed that, with the exception of those SMEs that were 'forced' to adopt E-commerce in order to trade with specific larger businesses, owner/managers believed that decisions concerning IT and E-commerce adoption came from within the SME. While many of these SMEs had formed 'loose' strategic alliances with others in order to minimise costs etc., most suggested that these alliances did not involve governance where IT or E-commerce adoption was concerned. Furthermore, those within a small business strategic alliance arrangement indicated that knowledge and technical expertise came from a combination of business partners as well as government-based associations.

Those SMEs that indicated that they had been forced to adopt E-commerce indicated that, in some cases, they used an entirely different set of technology with every other customer. They further indicated that little assistance was forthcoming from the larger businesses, forcing help to be sought from SME partners, customers, suppliers or government-backed agencies.

As no clear distinction appeared to be made between trading partnerships, alliances and government based associations, a single question is proposed asking whether the company make use of any or all of these facilities or whether the company handles decisions concerning E-commerce entirely from within.

3.4.2.3 Questions related to adoption/non-adoption of E-commerce

The final set of questions concerns the adoption factors (criteria for adoption, barriers to adoption, benefits derived from adoption and disadvantages derived from adoption) of E-commerce. The previous chapter contains four sets of tables (Table 2.4 – criteria for adoption, Table 2.5 perceived benefits of adoption, Table 2.6 perceived disadvantages of adoption and Table 2.7 barriers to adoption).

A series of 6 interviews with SMEs was carried out in the Wollongong area. Three of the SMEs had adopted E-commerce, three had not. The purpose of the interviews was to determine whether the four sets of adoption factors (Tables 2.4 – 2.7) were applicable to those SMEs and whether they were complete. The interviews were open-ended. For those that had adopted E-commerce, the criteria for adoption, benefits from having adopted and disadvantages for having adopted were asked. For those that had not adopted E-commerce, the interview sought reasons for non-adoption. The interviews took approximately 45 minutes and were taped for later analysis. The result of the case studies showed that all the criteria, barriers, benefits and disadvantages were identified by at least one SME owner and that no additional criteria, barriers, benefits or disadvantages were nominated. Results of the interviews were that all of the adoption factors were applicable and that no additional adoption factors needed to be added.

Based on the interview data, a 5 point Likert scale was used having anchors 'Is not applicable to my situation at all' and 'Is very applicable to my situation'.

3.5 Data recording

Using the constraints listed above (see Sections 3.4.2.1 – 3.4.2.3), the following data was collected for each respondent:

- The business age. One of
  - Less than 1 year
  - 1-2 years
  - 3-5 years
  - 6-10 years
  - 11-20 years
  - over 20 years
- The business size. One of
  - 0 employees
  - 1-9 employees
  - 10-19 employees
  - 20-50 employees
  - >50 employees
- Business sector. One of
  - Industrial
  - Service
  - Retail Trading
  - Financial
- Market focus. Collected as a percentage of customers from:
  - Local area
  - Regional area

                    National
                    International
- A description of the level of IT skill within the company
                    No computer skill
                    Low computer skill
                    Normal computer skill
                    High computer skill
                    Expert computer skill
- Whether the business had adopted E-commerce
- Whether the business was part of a small business strategic alliance or association for companies

For those businesses that **had adopted** E-commerce, respondents were asked to rate 1 – 5 (not applicable to my situation – very applicable to my situation) the applicability to their business of the following criteria for adoption:

> *Demand/pressure from customers*
> *Pressure of competition*
> *Pressure from suppliers*
> *Reduction of costs*
> *Improvement to customer service*
> *Improvement in lead-time*
> *Increased sales*
> *Improvement to internal efficiency*
> *Strengthen relations with business partners*
> *Reach new customers/markets*
> *Improve competitiveness*
> *External technical support*
> *Improve marketing*
> *Improve control and follow-up*

The benefits of having adopted E-commerce:

> *Lower administration costs*
> *Lower production costs*
> *Reduced lead time*
> *Reduced stock*
> *Increased sales*
> *Increased internal efficiency*
> *Improved relations with business partners*
> *New customers and markets*
> *Improved competitiveness*
> *Improved marketing*
> *Improved quality of information*

And the perceived disadvantages of having adopted E-commerce

> *Deterioration of relations with business partners*
> *Higher costs*
> *Computer maintenance*

Doubling of work
Reduced flexibility of work
Security
Dependence on E-commerce

For those businesses that **had not adopted** E-commerce, respondents were asked to rate (not applicable to my situation – very applicable to my situation) the applicability of the following barriers to their situation:

E-commerce doesn't fit with products/services
E-commerce doesn't fit with the way we do business
E-commerce doesn't fit the way our customers work
We don't see the advantage of using E-commerce
Lack of technical know how
Security risks
Cost too high
Not sure what to choose

The data was entered into an Excel spreadsheet.
As the Swedish questionnaire delineated exports in Europe separately from exports elsewhere, these were added to provide a total export figure.
 For both the Swedish and Australian respondents, the highest percentage across local, regional, national and international was deemed to be the major market focus of the business. This approach has been validated by a number of studies (see Bijmolt & Zwart 1994, Dalli 1994, Harvie et al 2003)
All these values were exported to SPSS for statistical analysis.

3.5.1 Statistical analysis

The design of the questions (and the range of answers) in the questionnaire were deliberate, to allow the use of chi-square tests, two-tailed t-tests, and linear regressions, as these were considered the most suitable statistical analyses for the various goals of the study.
313 SMEs completed the questionnaire in Karlstad, Sweden, 160 in Australia.

A formula for sample size was used

$$\mathbf{E = z_{\alpha/2}\ \sigma/\sqrt{n}}$$

or

$$\mathbf{n = (z_{\alpha/2}\ \sigma/E)^2}$$

σ was determined to be 2.01

A 99.9% degree of confidence was considered. The margin of error was 1.

The minimum sample size was 37 (rounded up)

The minimum sample size for 95% degree of confidence was 21 (rounded up)

The two sample sizes were determined to be adequate.

A series of Levene tests was carried out to determine homogeneity of variance. The Levene's tests provided a significance of <.001 for all questions being examined, indicating that data was sufficiently robust to apply t-tests, linear regressions and chi-square tests.

A number of analyses were performed on the data. These are considered separately.

3.5.2 Determination of the applicability of the adoption factors (barriers to adoption, criteria for adoption, benefits of adoption or disadvantages of adoption) of E-commerce

As already stated, the adoption factors denoted as barriers to adoption, criteria for adoption, benefits of adoption or disadvantages of adoption of E-commerce have been derived both from the literature and in-depth interviews. It was important to determine whether these were applicable to the Swedish and Australian respondents SMEs. If these factors were deemed inapplicable, the ratings would cluster around the lower end of the Likert scale (1 and 2), which denoted 'inapplicability to my situation'.
Consequently, a series of simple frequency tables were produced for each factor to ensure that ratings were not clustered around the lower of the anchors of the Likert scale. If ratings clustered around the lower anchor, clearly, the factor was inapplicable.

3.5.3 Business characteristics determining membership of a small business strategic alliance of SMEs

The first of the goals of this study was
- To determine if membership in a small business strategic alliances is associated with business characteristics (business size, business age, business sector, market focus or the level of IT skill).

Based on the literature and two prior pilot studies five business characteristics (business age, business size, business sector, market focus and level of IT skill) were determined to be possibly associated with membership of a small business strategic alliance.
As already noted (Section 3.5.1) the data from both surveys was determined to be normally distributed and an examination of the frequency tables showed that all possible values were represented.
A series of chi-square tests

$$f(x) = e^{-x/2} x^{v/2-1} \frac{}{2^{v/2} \lceil (v/2)}$$

$$\lceil (a) = \int_0^\infty t^{a-1} e^{-t}\, dt$$

were carried out to determine whether there were any associations between business characteristics and membership/non-membership of a small business strategic alliance.

3.5.4 Determining whether the decision to become a member of a small business strategic alliance altered perceptions of importance of the adoption factors (barriers to adoption, criteria for adoption, benefits of adoption or disadvantages of adoption) of E-commerce

The second goal of the study
- to determine if the membership of small business strategic alliances alters perceptions of any of the adoption factors (barriers to adoption, criteria for adoption, benefits of adoption or disadvantages of adoption) of E-commerce technologies.

A series of two-tailed t-tests

$$t = \frac{\mu - x}{SD/\sqrt{n}}$$

was applied to the data comparing the means of ratings of the adoption factors (barriers to adoption, criteria for adoption, benefits of adoption or disadvantages of adoption) of E-commerce between those SMEs that were part of a small business strategic alliance and those that were not.

3.5.5 Determining whether differences in the perception of importance of the adoption factors (barriers to adoption, criteria for adoption, benefits of adoption or disadvantages of adoption) of E-commerce, between members of a small business strategic alliance and non-members was specific to certain business ages, business sizes, business sectors, market foci or level of IT skill of SMEs

The third goal of the study was
- To determine if the membership in a small business strategic alliances alters perceptions of any of the adoption factors (barriers to adoption, criteria for adoption, benefits of adoption or disadvantages of adoption) of E-commerce technologies for specific sectors of the SME population (certain business ages, business sizes, business sectors, market focuses, particular levels of IT skill).

A series of two-tailed t-tests were applied to each of these separate subdivisions of the data to determine whether the means were significantly different between those businesses that were part of a small business strategic alliance and those that were not.

3.5.6 Determining whether different business characteristics affect the perception of the adoption factors (barriers to adoption, criteria for adoption, benefits of adoption or disadvantages of adoption) of E-commerce depending upon whether the SME is part of a small business strategic alliance or not.

The fourth goal of the study was
- To determine if the associations between business characteristics (business size, business age, business sector, market focus or level of IT skills) and adoption

factors (barriers to adoption, criteria for adoption, benefits of adoption or disadvantages of adoption) of E-commerce technologies differ, depending on whether the SME is part of a small business strategic alliance or not.

The data was subdivided into two groups. These were respondents that were members of a small business strategic alliance and respondents that were not. A series of linear regressions

$$y = mx + b$$

where

$$m = \frac{n\sum(xy) - \sum x \sum y}{n\sum(x^2) - (\sum x)^2}$$

$$b = \frac{\sum y - m\sum x}{n}$$

was carried out to determine which, if any, business characteristics (business size, business age, market focus, business sector, level of IT skill) was associated with the rating of the adoption factors (barriers to adoption, criteria for adoption, benefits of adoption or disadvantages of adoption) of E-commerce for each of the two groups. For those that were found to be significant, a cross tabulation was carried out to demonstrate the ratings.

3.5.7 Treatment of data from the two studies

The data could be analysed as 2 separate samples or it could be compared. This study uses both of these approaches.

3.6 Conclusion

This chapter restates the goals of the study and the methods used to gather and interpret data to meet these goals. The following two chapters provide details of the findings of these methods. Chapter 4 presents the findings of the Swedish study, Chapter 5 presents the findings of the Australian study.

Chapter 4
Quantitative Analysis of the Data Gathered by Means of the Survey in Karlstad, Sweden

It should be noted that for the remainder of this study we are using the typographical convention of a change of font to indicate business characteristics and underlying to indicate adoption factors.

As stated in the previous chapter, the results of this study are expected to contribute to a greater understanding of the nature of small business strategic alliances and their role in the process of adoption and use of E-commerce. As such, the study has four goals. These are:

- To determine if the membership of small business strategic alliances is associated with business characteristics (business size, business age, business sector, market focus or the level of IT skill).
- To determine whether the membership of small business strategic alliances alters perceptions of any of the adoption factors (barriers to adoption, criteria for adoption, benefits of adoption or disadvantages of adoption) of E-commerce technologies.
- To determine whether the membership of small business strategic alliances alters perceptions of any of the adoption factors (barriers to adoption, criteria for adoption, benefits of adoption or disadvantages of adoption) of E-commerce technologies for specific sectors of the SME population (certain business ages, business sizes, business sectors, market focuses, particular levels of IT skill).
- To determine whether the associations between business characteristics (business size, business age, business sector, market focus or level of IT skills) and adoption factors (barriers to adoption, criteria for adoption, benefits of adoption or disadvantages of adoption) of E-commerce technologies differ, depending on whether the SME is part of a small business strategic alliance or not.

The specific focus of this study is for regional SMEs.

This study aims to address each of these goals by presenting the results of a quantitative analysis of data gathered through two surveys, one in the Karlstad region of Sweden, the other in the Wollongong region, Australia.

This chapter presents the data for Karlstad, Sweden. The following chapter, chapter 5, presents the data for Wollongong, Australia.

This chapter is divided into seven sections, as follows:

Section 4.1 of this chapter presents descriptive statistics of the Karlstad sample group. This includes:

- The number of the respondent SMEs that had/had not adopted E-commerce.
- The number of respondent SMEs that were/ were not part of a small business strategic alliance.
- The number of respondent SMEs fitting each of the 6 business age categories.
- The number of respondent SMEs fitting each of the 4 business size categories.
- The number of respondent SMEs fitting each of the 4 business sector categories.
- The number of respondent SMEs fitting each of the 4 market focus categories.
- The number of respondent SMEs fitting each of the 5 levels of IT skill categories.

Section 4.2 presents an examination of the four sets of adoption factors denoted as criteria for adoption, barriers to adoption, benefits of having adopted and disadvantages of having adopted E-commerce to determine their applicability to the Swedish regional SME group.

Section 4.3 addresses **Goal 1**,
- to determine if membership in a small business strategic alliances is associated with business characteristics (business size, business age, business sector, market focus or the level of IT skill).

This is determined by means of a series of chi-square analyses (see section 3.6.2).

Section 4.4 addresses **Goal 2**,
- to determine if the membership of small business strategic alliances alters perceptions of any of the adoption factors (barriers to adoption, criteria for adoption, benefits of adoption or disadvantages of adoption) of E-commerce technologies.

This section utilizes a series of two-tailed t-tests (see section 3.6.3) to determine whether there is a significant difference in the compared means (membership versus non-membership).

Section 4.5 addresses **Goal 3**,
- To determine if the membership in a small business strategic alliances alters perceptions of any of the adoption factors (barriers to adoption, criteria for adoption, benefits of adoption or disadvantages of adoption) of E-commerce technologies for specific sectors of the SME population (certain business ages, business sizes, business sectors, market focuses, particular levels of IT skill).

This section utilizes a series of two-tailed t-tests to determine whether the means of perception of adoption factors (criteria to adopt, barriers to adoption, benefits from adoption or disadvantages having adopted E-commerce) are significantly different between members and non-members of a small business strategic alliance, for specific business ages, business size, business sectors, market foci or levels of IT skill.

Section 4.6 addresses Goal 4,
- To determine if the associations between business characteristics (business size, business age, business sector, market focus or level of IT skills) and adoption factors (barriers to adoption, criteria for adoption, benefits of adoption or disadvantages of adoption) of E-commerce technologies differ, depending on whether the SME is part of a small business strategic alliance or not.

This section utilizes a series of linear regressions to determine whether the business size, business age, business sector, market focus or IT skill level impinge on SMEs' perception of adoption factors (criteria to adopt, barriers to adoption, benefits from adoption or disadvantages having adopted E-commerce). For those found to be significant, a chi-square analysis was carried out to determine how the business characteristic is associated with the perceived importance of either the particular adoption factor.

Section 4.7 presents the conclusions for the Karlstad study.

4.1 Descriptive statistics for the sample group, Karlstad, Sweden

1170 questionnaires were distributed to SMEs in the regional area of Sweden known as Karlstad. 350 returns were gathered giving a return percentage of 29.9%. As the general description of an SME in Sweden is considered to be businesses with 50 or less employees, those businesses reporting staffing levels above 50 were eliminated. This left a final sample size of 313, or 26.75%. The data was imported into SPSS and a series of frequency distributions was applied. These were the number of respondent SMEs that:

- Had/had not adopted E-commerce.
- Were/ were not part of a small business strategic alliance.
- Fitted each of the 6 business age categories.
- Fitted each of the 4 business size categories.
- Fitted each of the 4 business sector categories.
- Fitted each of the 4 market focus categories.
- Fitted each of the 5 levels of IT skill categories.

The data was then split into two groups – those that had adopted E-commerce and those that had not. A series of frequency distributions was applied to each group. These were the number of respondent SMEs:

- That were/ were not part of a small business strategic alliance.
- Fitting each of the 6 business age categories.
- Fitting each of the 4 business size categories.
- Fitting each of the 4 business sector categories.
- Fitting each of the 4 market focus categories.
- Fitting each of the 5 levels of IT skill categories.

The complete data was again split into two groups – those that were part of a small business strategic alliance and those that were not. Again, a series of frequency distributions was applied to each group. These were the number of respondent SMEs:

- That had/had not adopted E-commerce.
- Fitting each of the 6 business age categories.
- Fitting each of the 4 business size categories.
- Fitting each of the 4 business sector categories.
- Fitting each of the 4 market focus categories.
- Fitting each of the 5 levels of IT skill categories.

As already stated, a set of frequency distributions was applied, using SPSS. As would be expected with this sample size, some respondents did not answer all questions. These 'non-answers' which were termed 'missing' were examined and showed no intrinsic pattern. The number of 'missing' responses varied from question to question. The minimum valid sample size was 247 responses.

Cooper (1969) states that for chi-square tests that 'a conservative rule is that no expected frequency of a cell should drop below 5', where

$$E_i = N \left(F \left(Y_u \right) - F \left(Y_l \right) \right)$$

Where

$$F \text{ is the cumulative distribution function } \sum_{i=0}^{x} f(i)$$

Y_u is the upper limit

Y_l is the lower limit

The expected frequency for all cells concerned with the adoption of E-commerce is 24.7 which is above the required 5 for validity.

The expected frequency for membership of a small business strategic alliance is 20.3, again above the required 5 for validity.

As already shown (see Section 3.5.1) the minimum sample size for a t-test (at 99.9% degree of confidence) is 37 or 21 (at 95% degree of confidence). The sample size (N=313) for the Swedish respondents is above 37 justifying the use of a t-test analysis. As individual analyses are being conducted, routine checks will be made to ensure sample size conforms to the above limits.

4.1.1 Adoption of E-commerce

The data was examined to determine the number of respondent SMEs that had/ had not adopted E-commerce technology. Table A3.1 provides the frequency distribution.

The figures in Table A3.1 support the assertion that the Swedish sample size was sufficiently large for both adopters of E-commerce (55.3%, N=152) as well as non-adopters (44.7%, N=123).

4.1.2 Membership of a small business strategic alliance

The data was examined to determine the percentage of respondent SMEs that had become members of a small business strategic alliance and those that has not. Table A3.2 provides details.

As the primary goals of this study centre on the comparison of SMEs that are members of a small business strategic alliance and SMEs that are not, the data in Table A3.2 supports the assertion that the Swedish sample is sufficiently large to include both respondents that are members of a small business strategic alliance (46.2%, N=140) as well as respondents that have decided to remain outside such an arrangement (53.8%, N=163).

4.1.3 Business age range of the Swedish study

Table A3.3 provides details of the number of years the respondent SMEs from the Swedish study had been in business.

An examination of the data in Table A3.3 shows that there is a relatively small number of respondents in the < 1 yr and 1 – 2 yrs categories. For the purposes of further analyses these have been combined into a single category. All other business age groups are sufficiently well represented, with over 80.0% (N=252) of the respondents having been in business for over 5 years. It is interesting to note that 60.9% (N=190) of respondents were conducting business prior to the advent of E-commerce.

4.1.4 Business size of respondent SMEs in terms of number of employees

The data was examined to determine the 'spread' of business size across the respondents. Table A3.4 provides details of the business sizes.

An examination of the data in Table A3.4 shows that over 70% of the respondent group were businesses that had fewer than 10 employees, with the largest single group being those businesses that had between 1 and 9 employees (53.1%, N=164). However, all groups are sufficiently well represented in the sample size.

4.1.5 Business sector

Table A3.5 provides the distribution of respondents across the four business sectors.

As can be seen in Table A3.5, the largest respondent group was the service sector (46.2%, N=114). The data also shows that 21.1% (N=66) of the data is deemed other. With the exception of the financial group, all sectors are well represented in the sample.

4.1.6 Market focus

Four categories of market focus were identified from previous studies. These were local, regional, national and international. Table A3.6 provides the numbers in each of these four categories.

An examination of Table A3.6 shows that two types of market focus predominate in the study sample. These were local businesses, accounting for 54.6% (N=171), of the study sample and businesses trading predominantly at a national level, accounting for 26.2% (N=82). It is interesting to note that despite the views of many authors (Quayle 2002, Vescovi 2000, Sparkes & Thomas 2001) that E-commerce adoption promotes the ability to enter the internet market, the international group only accounted for 9.9% (N=31) of the study sample. Despite this, all groups are well represented in the study.

4.1.7 Level of IT Skill within the respondent SMEs

Respondents were asked to rate their perception of the levels of IT skill within their business. Based on previous studies and case studies carried out in Australia, 5 alternative categories of skill were identified. Table A3.7 provides details of the perceived skills of the respondent sample.

As indicated in Section 3.4.2.1 despite self-evaluation, respondents appeared to understand the question and the ratings of the levels of IT skill sufficiently for this elf evaluation to be used.

An examination of Table A3.7 shows that 82.3% (N=222) of the respondents rated the levels of IT skill within their firm as normal or above, with 25.6% (N=70) rating their skill as high or expert.

4.1.8 Comparison of frequencies of adopters and non-adopters

The data was subdivided into two groups – those responses that indicated they had adopted E-commerce and those that had not. A series of frequency analyses was carried out to show any differences in the two groups.

4.1.8.1 Membership of a small business strategic alliance

The data was examined to determine the number of respondents who were part of a small business strategic alliance. Table A3.8 provides the details of responses.
An examination of the data in Table A3.8 shows that of the 152 adopters of E-commerce, only 37.2% (N=54) were members of a small business strategic alliance. By comparison, the percentage of non-adopters that are members of a small business strategic alliance is 51.7% (N=62). This result is statistically significant (p<.01).
These results are contrary to expectation. Much of the literature concerned with membership of small business strategic alliances and E-commerce adoption in SMEs suggests that SMEs that adopt E-commerce would normally be in some form of small business strategic alliance. Similarly, SMEs that had not adopted E-commerce would normally remain outside such alliances. The data from the regional SMEs in Karlstad does not support these expectations.

4.1.8.2 Business age

Table A3.9 provides details of the frequency distribution of business age, for both adopters as well as non-adopters of E-commerce.
The data in Table A3.9 shows that there is no statistical significant association between business age and the adoption of E-commerce.
An examination of Table A3.9 shows no real differences in the distribution of business age between the adopters and non-adopters.

4.1.8.3 Business size

A frequency distribution of business size was carried out on both the adopting SMEs as well as the non-adopters of E-commerce. Table A3.10 (reproduced below) provides the frequencies.
The data in Table A3.10 (reproduced below) is statistically significant (p<.001)
An examination of the data in Table A3.10 (reproduced below) shows that businesses with 1-19 employees are divided evenly in their decision to adopt E-commerce technology. Of the 41 businesses that were a single operator, only 15, or 35.6% had adopted E-commerce. For larger businesses, 75% of businesses with 20 or more employees were making use of E-commerce.

65

Size of Business

		Frequency	Percent	Valid Percent	Cumulative Percent
Valid	Sole trader	15	9.9	9.9	9.9
	1-19 employees	107	70.4	70.4	80.3
	20-50 employees	30	19.7	19.7	100.0
	Total	152	100.0	100.0	

E-Commerce Adopters

		Frequency	Percent	Valid Percent	Cumulative Percent
Valid	Sole trader	26	21.1	21.5	21.5
	1-19 employees	85	69.1	69.1	90.6
	20-50 employees	10	8.1	8.3	100.0
	Total	121	98.4	100.0	
Missing		2	1.6		
Total		123	100.0		

E-Commerce Non-adopters

This result strongly supports previous studies in the literature that suggest that it is the larger SMEs that are more likely to adopt E-commerce.

4.1.8.4 Business sector

Table A3.11 provides details of the frequency distribution of business sector, for both adopters as well as non-adopters of E-commerce.
The data in Table A3.11 is statistically significant (p<.001)
An examination of the data in Table A3.11 shows that in all sectors, more businesses had adopted E-commerce than had not. The data also shows that all financial sector respondents had adopted E-commerce.

4.1.8.5 Market focus

Businesses in the four areas of market focus, (local, regional, national and international), were examined by way of a set of frequency distributions to determine their uptake of E-commerce technology. Table A3.12 provides details of the distributions.
The data in Table A3.12 is statistically significant (p<.001)
An examination of Table A3.12 shows that with the exception of local businesses, all other market focus groups had more respondents that had adopted E-commerce than had not. Of interest, however, is the comparison of the national and international responses. While 70.5% (N=55) of the businesses that had a national market focus had adopted E-commerce, only 54.8% (N=17) of those businesses that had international market focus had done so.
Many of the benefits put forward in the government initiatives for E-commerce adoption by SMEs centre around the ability to acquire a 'global presence'. Indeed, several studies assert that marketing at an international level requires the development and use of E-commerce, particularly for SMEs. The Karlstad study shows that almost half of the international respondents have not adopted E-commerce, and that it was those with a national focus that more readily seemed to be accepting of the technology.

4.1.8.6 Level of IT skills

Table A3.13 provides frequency distributions of perceived levels of IT skills for those SMEs that had adopted E-commerce as well as those that had not.
The data in Table A3.13 is statistically significant (p<.001)
As can be seen in Table A3.13, those firms with low skills or no skills were less inclined to adopt E-commerce (25% and 28% respectively) compared to those who reported high or expert skills (75% and 95% respectively). This was to be expected.

4.1.8.7 Summary

There have been a number of studies that have examined the possible association between business characteristics and E-commerce adoption. More recently, there has been considerable support for the development of small business strategic alliances as a means to E-commerce adoption. The results in Tables A3.8 – A3.13 present some unexpected findings. Table A3.8 shows that it is the non-members of a small business strategic alliance that appear to be adopting E-commerce rather than the small business strategic alliance members, in the Karlstad study. As such, the appropriateness of the government initiatives to develop small business strategic alliances to assist in E-commerce adoption in SMEs, is questionable, at least where regional SMEs are concerned.
Tables A3.9 – A3.13 present the number of E-commerce adopters and non-adopters across the categories of the five business characteristics (business age, business size, business sector, market focus, and levels of IT skill). The data pertaining to two of the business characteristics, business size and levels of IT skill supports earlier findings in the literature. However, the data pertaining to the other three business characteristics, business age, business sector and market focus does not support the earlier findings in the literature.

4.1.9 Comparison of frequencies for respondents that are members of a small business strategic alliance and respondents that are not

The data was divided into two groups, those that had responded that they were members of a small business strategic alliance and those that indicated that they were not members of such an alliance. Again, a series of frequency distributions was carried out to compare the two groups across the business characteristics, business age, business size, business sector, market focus, and levels of IT skill.

4.1.9.1 Business age

Frequency analyses were carried out for both respondents who were part of a small business strategic alliance as well as for those that were not part of such an arrangement, to determine the distribution of business age categories for each. Table A3.14 provides the details of the frequency distributions.
An examination of the data in Table A3.14 shows no real differences in the distribution of business age between those businesses that are members of a small business strategic alliance and those that are not.
A number of recent studies have suggested that business age appears to be associated with membership of a small business strategic alliance. The Karlstad data does not support this.

4.1.9.2 Business size

Frequency analyses were carried out for both respondents who were part of a small business strategic alliance as well as for those that were not, to determine the distribution of business size for each. Table A3.15 provides the details.

An examination of Table A3.15 shows that for larger SMEs there is a tendency to remain outside any form of small business strategic alliance. The opposite appears to be occurring for smaller businesses. Thus while 74.3% of SMEs with 20 or more employees remained independent, only 34.5% of single person SMEs did the same. The data also shows that 25.7% of members of small business strategic alliances are sole-traders (0 employees), while only 10% are SMEs with 10-19 employees. This figure is almost reversed for the non-member's group (11.7% sole traders, 20.2% 10-19 employees).

The development of business size categories (see Section 3.4.2.1) was based on a prior pilot study. The resulting categories (sole trader, 1-9 employees, 10-19 employees, 20-49 employees, >50 employees) are unstandardised and as such comments comparing one category with another need to be made in terms of the unstandardised form of the data. This having been said, however, an examination of the data shows that a higher proportion of sole traders and 1-9 employee respondents are members of a strategic alliance than 20-49 employees and >50 employees respondents. This supports the earlier findings of Marchewka & Towell (2000) and Overby & Min (2000).

4.1.9.3 Business sector

Frequency analyses were carried out for both respondents who were part of a small business strategic alliance as well as for those that were not, to determine the distribution of responses across the 4 business sectors. Table A3.16 provides the responses.

An examination of the data in Table A3.16 shows that with the exception of the financial sector, respondents from all other sectors were more inclined to remain outside the small business strategic alliances rather than becoming members.

4.1.9.4 Market focus

Frequency analyses were carried out for both respondents who were part of a small business strategic alliance as well as for those that were not, to determine the distribution of responses across the 4 areas of market focus. Table A3.17 shows the frequency distributions for both members and non-members of small business strategic alliances.

An examination of Table A3.17 shows that with the exception of those businesses that primarily trade locally, all other market focus groups had more businesses responding that they were outside any form of small business strategic alliance. Those respondents who are locally focused in their business are evenly split between membership and non-membership of a small business strategic alliance.

An examination of much of the government literature concerned with the development of small business strategic alliances (Blair 2000, NOIE 1998, European Union 2000, Copp & Ivy 2001), suggests that membership of these alliances substantially assists SMEs in their 'quest' for wider market representation. An examination of the data in Table A3.17 does not support this premise, for the Karlstad study sample. Indeed, it is only the locally focused respondents that have appeared to become involved in some form of small business strategic alliance.

4.1.9.5 Level of IT skill

Frequency analyses were carried out for both respondents who were part of a small business strategic alliance as well as for those that were not, to determine the distribution of responses across the 5 levels of IT skill. Table A3.18 provides the frequency distributions.

4.1.9.6 Summary of initial analyses

The initial analyses have confirmed several of the assertions in the literature about adoption/non-adoption and the role of small business strategic alliances. However, many of the analyses have found contradictions to the literature.
The next task is to determine the appropriateness of the adoption factors (barriers to adoption, criteria for adoption, benefits of adoption or disadvantages of adoption)
to the study respondents.

4.2 Appropriateness of adoption factors (barriers to adoption, criteria for adoption, benefits of adoption or disadvantages of adoption) to Swedish respondents

This chapter began by stating the major goals of this study. Goals 1, 3, 4 (see Sections 3.5.3 – 3.5.6) are dependent on the adoption factors (barriers to adoption, criteria for adoption, benefits of adoption or disadvantages of adoption) being applicable to the regional SME respondents of Karlstad, Sweden.
Based on the findings in the literature, a set of 6 in-depth case studies was carried out with regional SMEs in Australia. The aim of these case studies was to validate the appropriateness and completeness of the adoption factors (barriers to adoption, criteria for adoption, benefits of adoption or disadvantages of adoption) presented in chapter 2. Six SMEs, three that had adopted E-commerce and three that had not adopted E-commerce were approached and the owners were interviewed as to reasons why they had or had not adopted E-commerce. The interviews were open-ended. For those that had adopted E-commerce, the criteria for adoption, benefits from having adopted and disadvantages for having adopted were asked. For those that had not adopted E-commerce, the interview sought reasons for non-adoption. The interviews took approximately 45 minutes and were taped for later analysis. The result of the case studies showed that all the criteria, barriers, benefits and disadvantages were identified by at least one SME owner and that no additional criteria, barriers, benefits or disadvantages were nominated.
For each of the measures of criteria, barriers, benefits and disadvantages, respondents were asked to rate how applicable these measures were to their particular SME. The ratings were across a 5 point Likert scale with anchors of 1 – does not fit my situation and 5 – fits my situation very well. A series of frequency analyses was applied to each of the measures of criteria, barriers, benefits and disadvantages. As the ratings were concerned with the applicability of the criteria, barriers, benefits and disadvantages to the respondents, any measures for which over 75% of respondents gave ratings of 1, 2, 3 were considered inapplicable to the respondent group. The following sections examine each of the criteria, barriers, benefits and disadvantages separately.

4.2.1 Applicability of the criteria to the Swedish respondents

Based on a number of studies in the literature and case studies carried out in Australia, 14 measures for criteria to adopt E-commerce were considered. A set of frequency analyses of ratings, by respondents, of each of these criteria was carried out. Table 4.1 provides the results of the frequency analysis. Criteria that had a combined rating (ratings 1, 2, 3) above 75% are highlighted.

Table 4.1
Rating of Criteria for E-commerce Adoption
Number and percentage of respondent's rating of each criteria (1, 2, .. 5)

Crit.	1	2	3	4	5
A	54 (41.5%)	33 (25.4%)	19 (14.6%)	19 (14.6%)	5 (3.8%)
B	39 (30.2%)	21 (16.3%)	36 (27.9%)	24 (18.6%)	9 (7.0%)
C	64 (51.2%)	23 (18.4%)	20 (16.0%)	14 (11.2%)	4 (3.2%)
D	16 (12.4%)	14 (9.2%)	30 (23.3%)	41 (31.8%)	28 (21.7%)
E	6 (4.6%)	1 (1.5%)	19 (14.6%)	44 (33.8%)	59 (45.4%)
F	35 (27.8%)	14 (11.1%)	25 (19.8%)	31 (24.6%)	21 (16.7%)
G	19 (15.0%)	14 (11.0%)	33 (26.0%)	29 (22.8%)	32 (25.2%)
H	8 (6.1%)	3 (2.3%)	21 (15.9%)	59 (44.7%)	41 (31.1%)
I	17 (13.2%)	13 (10.1%)	39 (30.2%)	40 (31.0%)	20 (15.5%)
J	17 (13.3%)	11 (8.6%)	30 (23.4%)	36 (28.1%)	34 (26.6%)
K	15 (11.5%)	4 (3.1%)	19 (14.6%)	50 (38.5%)	42 (32.3%)
L	85 (66.9%)	26 (20.5%)	10 (7.9%)	3 (2.4%)	3 (2.4%)
M	20 (15.6%)	8 (6.3%)	20 (15.6%)	43 (33.6%)	37 (28.9%)
N	24 (18.8%)	20 (15.6%)	38 (29.7%)	29 (22.7%)	17 (13.3%)

Legend

A	*Demand/pressure from customers*
B	*Pressure of competition*
C	*Demand/Pressure from suppliers*
D	*Reduction of costs*
E	*Improvement to customer service*
F	*Improvement in lead-time*
G	*Increased sales*
H	*Improvement to internal efficiency*
I	*Strengthen relations with business partners*
J	*Reach new customers/markets*
K	*Improvement in competitiveness*
L	*External technical support*
M	*Improvement in marketing*
N	*Improvement in control and follow-up*

An examination of the data in Table 4.1 shows that for regional SMEs in Karlstad, Sweden, three criteria are not generally applicable. These are:

70

- *Demand or pressure from customers* that had a total rating of 81.6% (at the 1, 2, 3 level).
- *Demand or Pressure from suppliers* that had a total rating of 85.6% (at the 1, 2, 3 level).
- *The availability of External technical support* that had a total rating of 95.2% (at the 1, 2, 3 level).

The data in Table 4.1 shows that the most important criterion for the respondents was *Improvement to customer services* that had a total rating of 79.2% (at the 4 – 5 level).

4.2.2 Applicability of the barriers to the Swedish respondents

Those respondent SMEs that had adopted E-commerce in their day-to-day business were asked to rate 8 barriers to adoption as they pertained to their business, across a 5 point Likert scale (1 – does not fit my situation, 5 – fits my situation very well). 123 respondents indicted that they had not adopted E-commerce. Table 4.2 provides the frequency of the ratings. Barriers that had a combined rating (rating 1, 2, 3) above 75% are highlighted.

Table 4.2
Rating of Barriers for E-commerce Adoption
Number and percentage of respondent's rating of each barrier

Barr.	1	2	3	4	5
A	14 (14.6%)	8 (8.3%)	21 (21.9%)	20 (20.8%)	33 (34.4%)
B	17 (17.3%)	14 (14.3%)	19 (19.4%)	16 (16.5%)	32 (32.7%)
C	11 (11.7%)	15 (16.0%)	21 (22.3%)	20 (21.3%)	27 (28.7%)
D	18 (18.8%)	16 (16.7%)	25 (26.0%)	14 (14.6%)	23 (24.0%)
E	16 (16.7%)	12 (12.5%)	22 (22.9%)	20 (20.8%)	26 (27.1%)
F	14 (15.4%)	27 (29.7%)	22 (24.2%)	18 (19.8%)	10 (11.0%)
G	17 (18.5%)	17 (18.5%)	24 (26.1%)	19 (20.7%)	15 (16.3%)
H	16 (18.0%)	11 (12.4%)	28 (31.5%)	13 (14.6%)	21 (23.6%)

Legend

A	*E-commerce doesn't fit with products/services*
B	*E-commerce doesn't fit with the way we do business*
C	*E-commerce doesn't fit the way our customers work*
D	*We don't see the advantage of using E-commerce*
E	*Lack of technical know how*
F	*Security risks*
G	*Cost too high*
H	*Not sure what to choose*

An examination of the data in Table 4.2 shows that for regional SMEs in Karlstad, Sweden, none of the barriers have a combined rating of 1, 2, 3 above 75%.

4.2.3 Applicability of the benefits to the Swedish respondents

Those respondent SMEs that had adopted E-commerce in their day-to-day business were asked to rate 11 benefits to adoption as they pertained to their business, across a 5 point Likert scale (1 – does not fit my situation, 5 – fits my situation very well). 152 respondents indicted that they had adopted E-commerce. Table 4.3 provides the frequency of the ratings. Benefits that had a combined rating (rating 1, 2, 3) above 75% are highlighted.

Table 4.3
Rating of Benefits for E-commerce Adoption
Number and percentage of respondent's rating of benefits

Ben.	1	2	3	4	5
A	18 (13.1%)	23 (17.6%)	37 (28.2%)	31 (23.7%)	22 (16.8%)
B	27 (21.1%)	22 (17.2%)	27 (21.1%)	34 (26.6%)	18 (14.1%)
C	25 (19.5%)	12 (9.4%)	29 (22.7%)	40 (31.3%)	22 (17.2%)
D	**52 (43.0%)**	**14 (11.6%)**	**32 (26.4%)**	**14 (11.6%)**	**9 (7.4%)**
E	22 (17.2%)	27 (21.3%)	33 (26.0%)	34 (26.6%)	11 (8.7%)
F	20 (13.2%)	11 (7.2%)	9 (5.9%)	31 (20.4%)	57 (37.5%)
G	16 (12.5%)	16 (12.5%)	43 (33.6%)	40 (31.3%)	13 (10.2%)
H	20 (13.2%)	24 (18.9%)	32 (25.2%)	33 (26.0%)	18 (14.1%)
I	11 (8.4%)	18 (14.1%)	34 (26.6%)	47 (35.9%)	21 (16.0%)
J	**48 (37.2%)**	**29 (22.5%)**	**27 (21.3%)**	**15 (11.6%)**	**10 (7.8%)**
K	17 (13.2%)	13 (10.1%)	27 (21.3%)	37 (28.7%)	35 (27.1%)

Legend

A	*Lower administration costs*
B	*Lower production costs*
C	*Reduced lead-time*
D	*Reduced stock*
E	*Increased sales*
F	*Increased internal efficiency*
G	*Improved relations with business partners*
H	*New customers and markets*
I	*Improved competitiveness*
J	*Improved marketing*
K	*Improved quality of information*

An examination of Table 4.3 shows that for regional SMEs in Karlstad, Sweden, two of the benefits are not generally applicable. These are:

- *Reduced stock* that had a total rating of 81% (at the 1, 2, 3 level).
- *Improved marketing* that had a total rating of 80.6% (at the 1, 2, 3 level).

An examination of the data in Table 4.3 shows that 2 of the benefits are rated far higher than any of the others (at the 4 and 5 level). These are *increased internal efficiency*, 57.9%, and *improved quality of information*, 55.8%.

4.2.4 Applicability of **disadvantages** to the Swedish respondents

Finally, respondents that had adopted E-commerce were asked to rated 7 disadvantages, developed from the literature and case studies, carried out in Australia. Again, the ratings were across a 5 point Likert scale (1 – does not fit my situation, 5 – fits my situation very well). 152 respondents indicated that they had adopted E-commerce. Table 4.4 provides the frequency of responses. Disadvantages that had a combined rating (rating 1, 2, 3) above 75% are highlighted.

Table 4.4
Rating of disadvantages for E-commerce Adoption
Number and percentage of respondent's rating of disadvantages

Dis.	1	2	3	4	5
A	90 (70.9%)	20 (15.7%)	15 (11.8%)	1 (0.8%)	1 (0.8%)
B	53 (41.4%)	28 (21.9%)	30 (23.4%)	12 (9.4%)	5 (3.9%)
C	31 (24.2%)	35 (27.3%)	40 (31.3%)	18 (13.1%)	4 (3.1%)
D	52 (40.9%)	42 (33.1%)	18 (14.2%)	12 (9.4%)	3 (2.4%)
E	92 (72.4%)	22 (17.3%)	11 (8.7%)	2 (1.6%)	0 (0.0%)
F	77 (60.6%)	28 (22.0%)	16 (12.6%)	5 (3.9%)	1 (0.8%)
G	61 (48.8%)	25 (20.0%)	32 (25.6%)	5 (3.9%)	2 (1.6%)

Legend

A	*Deterioration of relations with business partners*
B	*Higher costs*
C	*Computer maintenance*
D	*Doubling of work*
E	*Reduced flexibility of work*
F	*Security*
G	*Dependence on E-commerce*

An examination of the data in Table 4.4 shows that for regional SMEs in Karlstad, Sweden, none of the disadvantages can be considered applicable as they all rate above 75% (at the 1, 2, 3 level). As such all the disadvantages are eliminated from the current study.

There are a number of explanations as to why all disadvantages are not considered important by the Swedish respondents. One possibility is that the nature of the scale 1 – 5 was misunderstood. This explanation is rejected as the scales are consistent with those used for criteria, benefits, and barriers (Tables 4.1 – 4.3). Another potential explanation is that respondents did not understand the disadvantages. Again this is rejected because the respondents were sufficiently knowledgeable concerning other factors such as benefits, criteria and barriers.

The data was examined to ensure that rejection of all disadvantages was a chance happening. As similar findings did not occur in any of the other measures, this was rejected.

A number of studies (Poon & Swatman 1997, Raymond 2001, Stauber 2000) have shown that where in one location certain factors appear as a benefit, in another, they become a disadvantage. For example, where Poon & Swatman (1997) found E-commerce adoption improved business relations in Australia, Raymond (2001), in a similar study in Canada, found business relations were reduced. Similarly where Quayle (2002) found E-commerce reduced costs in UK, Stauber (2000) found these increased in Australia. If, as suggested, benefits and disadvantages are interchangeable depending on the geographic/political location of the study, those disadvantages confirmed by pilot study in Australia, may be substantially reduced or eliminated in the regional Swedish location. Clearly further studies need to be carried out to determine whether this is the case.

4.3 Goal 1 – Business characteristics associated with membership of a small business strategic alliance

The first goal of the study was:
*   To determine if the membership of small business strategic alliances is associated with business characteristics (business size, business age, business sector, market focus or the level of IT skill).

Based on the literature and case studies five business characteristics (business age, business size, business sector and market focus, levels of IT skill) were identified as being associated with membership of a small business strategic alliance. A series of chi-square tests were carried out to examine the association, if any, between each of the five business characteristics and membership/non-membership of a small business strategic alliance. Tables 4.5 – 4.9 provide the data from these chi-square analyses.

Table 4.5
A comparison of business age and membership/non-membership of a small business strategic alliance

	Non-members actual	Non-members expected	Members actual	Members expected
1-2 years	9	7.6	9	5.9
3-5 years	22	24.6	20	19.0
6-10 years	33	34.9	27	27.1
11-20 years	35	45.8	43	35.5
> 20 years	64	74.8	41	57.9

$\chi^2 = 44.807$, p=.000

Table 4.6
A comparison of business size and membership/non-membership of a small business strategic alliance

	Non-members	Non-members expected	Members	Members expected
Sole trader	19	30.6	36	23.7
1-9 employees	81	89.5	78	69.3
10-19 employees	33	26.7	14	20.7
20-50 employees	29	21.8	10	16.9

$\chi^2 = 38.048$ p=.000

Table 4.7
A comparison of business sector and membership/non-membership of a small business strategic alliance

	Non-members	Non-members expected	Members	Members expected
Industrial	34	36.4	27	27.9
Service	63	66.0	48	51.2
Retail	33	36.0	29	27.9
Financial	2	4.9	4	3.8

$\chi^2 = 7.509$ p=.346

Table 4.8
A comparison of market focus and membership/non-membership of a small business strategic alliance

	Non-members	Non-members expected	Members	Members expected
Local	83	76.1	82	98.2
Regional	16	17.5	11	13.5
National	47	48.7	33	41.9
International	17	12.6	14	11.0

$\chi^2 = 7.724$ p=.461

Table 4.9
A comparison of the level of IT skill and membership/non-membership of a small business strategic alliance

	Non-members	Non-members expected	Members	Members expected
No skill	3	2.2	1	1.7
Low skill	21	26.2	25	20.3
Normal skill	83	84.1	61	67.8
High skill	30	32.2	19	22.9
Expert skill	11	11.5	9	8.9

$\chi^2 = 15.352$ p=.120

An examination of Tables 4.5 – 4.9 shows that only one business characteristic (business size) was significantly associated with membership/non-membership of a small business strategic alliance. It is interesting to note that while many of the government initiatives suggest membership of a small business strategic alliance promotes 'internationalisation' of SMEs, this is not apparent in the Karlstad study.

4.4 Goal 2 - The effect of membership of a small business strategic alliance on adoption factors (barriers to adoption, criteria for adoption, benefits of adoption or disadvantages of adoption)

The second goal of the current study was:
- To determine whether the membership of small business strategic alliances alters perceptions of any of the adoption factors (barriers to adoption, criteria for adoption, benefits of adoption or disadvantages of adoption) of E-commerce technologies.

This was determined by carrying out a series of two-tailed t-tests that compared the ratings of respondents who were members of a small business alliance with those that were not. The following sections examine the barriers to adoption, criteria for adoption, benefits of adoption or disadvantages of adoption separately.

4.4.1 The effect of membership of a small business alliance on the applicability of criteria for the adoption of E-commerce

Based on an examination of the literature and case studies carried out in Australia, 14 criteria for adoption of E-commerce by SMEs were identified. A set of frequency analyses was carried out to determine the applicability of these criteria for adoption to the Swedish study (see section 4.2.1). Three criteria:

Demand or Pressure from customers
Demand or Pressure from suppliers
The availability of External technical support

were determined to be not applicable to the Swedish study and were eliminated from the study. A series of two-tailed t-tests was applied to the remaining 11 criteria to determine whether there was a significant difference in the mean of the ratings (between respondents that were members of a small business alliance and respondents that were not).

Table 4.10 provides details of the two-tailed t-tests.

An examination of Table 4.10 shows that there were no significant differences in the perception of criteria for adoption of E-commerce technology between those SMEs that were members of a small business strategic alliance and those that were not.

Table 4.10
Comparison of means of rating of criteria for E-commerce adoption (between respondents that were members of a small business alliance and respondents that were not)

Criteria	Mean Members	N Members	Mean Non-members	N Non-members	t-value	Sig.
B	2.60	45	2.52	81	-.338	.736
D	3.52	46	3.30	80	-.929	.355
E	4.26	46	4.05	81	-1.104	.272
F	2.98	45	2.86	79	-.242	.672
G	3.24	45	3.35	80	.414	.680
H	3.81	47	3.98	82	.860	.391
I	3.26	46	3.26	81	.000	1.000
J	3.48	46	3.45	80	-.114	.910
K	3.63	46	3.83	81	.838	.404
M	3.33	46	3.66	80	1.312	.192
N	2.67	45	3.08	80	1.712	.089

Note: missing data accounts for ranges in N
Legend

A	Demand/pressure from customers
B	Pressure of competition
C	Demand/Pressure from suppliers
D	Reduction of costs
E	Improvement to customer service
F	Improvement in lead-time
G	Increased sales
H	Improvement to internal efficiency
I	Strengthen relations with business partners
J	Reach new customers/markets
K	Improvement in competitiveness
L	External technical support
M	Improvement in marketing
N	Improvement in control and follow-up

4.4.2 The effect of membership of a small business strategic alliance on the applicability of barriers to the adoption of E-commerce

Based on an examination of the literature and case studies carried out in Australia, 8 barriers to the adoption of E-commerce by SMEs were identified. A set of frequency analyses was carried out to determine their applicability to the Swedish study (see section 4.2.2). All barriers were determined to be applicable to the Swedish study. A series of two-tailed t-tests was carried out on the barriers to determine whether there was any significant difference in the ratings of the barriers between those respondents that were members of a small business strategic alliance and those that were not.

Table 4.11 provides the details of the two-tailed t-tests.

Table 4.11
Comparison of means of rating of <u>barriers</u> to the E-commerce adoption (between respondents that were members of a small business alliance and respondents that were not)

<u>Barriers</u>	Mean Members	N Members	Mean Non-members	N Non-members	t-value	Sig.
A	3.68	53	3.30	40	-1.281	.204
B	3.48	52	3.12	43	-1.184	.239
C	3.20	51	3.70	40	1.777	.079
D	3.31	54	2.74	39	-1.916	.058
E	3.37	52	3.12	41	-.814	.418
F	2.82	50	2.79	38	-.113	.910
G	2.86	51	3.13	38	.936	.352
H	3.06	48	3.21	38	.480	.632

Note: missing data accounts for ranges in N
Legend

A	*E-commerce doesn't fit with products/services*
B	*E-commerce doesn't fit with the way we do business*
C	*E-commerce doesn't fit the way our customers work*
D	*We don't see the advantage of using E-commerce*
E	*Lack of technical know how*
F	*Security risks*
G	*Cost too high*
H	*Not sure what to choose*

An examination of Table 4.11 shows that there were no significant differences in the perception of <u>barriers</u> between those respondents that were members of a small business strategic alliance and those that were not.

One of the 'cornerstones' of the government initiatives concerned with membership of a small business strategic alliance, is the reduction of barriers to adoption of E-commerce in SMEs. Studies by Marchewka & Towell (2000) found that technical knowledge is often shared in small business strategic alliances. Datta (1988) and Tikkanen (1998) found that there was a significant improvement in internal efficiency though membership of a small business strategic alliance, while Jorde & Teece (1989) suggested that membership of a small business strategic alliance reduced the financial burdens of its members. While these changes have not been measured by the current study, an examination of Table 4.11 shows that they clearly do no equate to any alteration of perception of barriers to E-commerce adoption.

4.4.3 The effect of membership of a small business alliance on the applicability of <u>benefits</u> derived from the adoption of E-commerce

Based on an examination of the literature and case studies carried out in Australia, 11 <u>benefits</u> derived from the adoption of E-commerce by SMEs were identified. A set of frequency analyses was carried out to determine their applicability to the Swedish study (see section 4.2.3). Two benefits:

>Reduced stock
>Improved marketing

were deemed as not applicable to the study and were eliminated. A series of two-tailed t-tests was carried out on the remaining benefits to determine whether there was any significant difference in the ratings of the benefits between those respondents that were members of a small business strategic alliance and those that were not.
Table 4.12 provides the details of the two-tailed t-tests.

Table 4.12

Comparison of means of rating of benefits to the E-commerce adoption (between respondents that were members of a small business alliance and respondents that were not)

	Mean Members	N Members	Mean Non-members	N Non-Members	t-value	Sig.
A	3.17	48	3.08	80	-.389	.698
B	3.00	47	2.92	79	-.299	.765
C	3.23	47	3.11	79	-.474	.636
E	2.94	47	2.83	78	-.449	.655
F	3.26	46	3.41	82	.713	.477
G	3.06	47	3.19	79	.586	.559
H	3.09	47	3.01	78	-.302	.763
I	3.26	46	3.41	82	.713	.477
K	3.46	48	3.46	79	.000	1.000

Note: missing data accounts for ranges in N
Legend

A	*Lower administration costs*
B	*Lower production costs*
C	*Reduced lead-time*
D	*Reduced stock*
E	*Increased sales*
F	*Increased internal efficiency*
G	*Improved relations with business partners*
H	*New customers and markets*
I	*Improved competitiveness*
J	*Improved marketing*
K	*Improved quality of information*

An examination of Table 4.12 shows that there were no significant differences in the perception of benefits achieved through E-commerce adoption between those respondents that were members of a small business strategic alliance and those that were not.

A number of studies (Marchewka & Towell 2000, Achrol & Kotler 1999, Tikkanen 1998) suggest membership of a small business strategic alliance has been shown to lead to improvement in internal efficiency, technical expertise, marketing knowledge and a reduction in financial burdens. The results in Table 4.12 shows that there are no significant differences in the attribution of these benefits to E-commerce adoption between members of a small business strategic alliance and non-members.

4.4.4 The effect of membership of a small business alliance on the applicability of disadvantages derived from the adoption of E-commerce

Based on an examination of the literature and case studies carried out in Australia, 7 disadvantages derived from the adoption of E-commerce by SMEs were identified. A set of frequency analyses was carried out to determine their applicability to the Swedish study (see section 4.2.4). Based on the frequency distributions, none of the disadvantages was considered applicable to the respondents and thus all disadvantages were eliminated from the study.

As already stated (see section 4.2.4) this result cannot be explained away by misunderstanding of the question, or mere fluke. As such, this is an important and unexpected finding coming from the Karlstad study. While much of the literature, concerned with disadvantages of E-commerce adoption in SMEs has portrayed these disadvantages as 'universal', the Karlstad data suggests that, at least for some regional SME groups, the disadvantages of E-commerce adoption reported in the literature, are of little real concern.

4.5 Goal 3 - To determine whether the membership of small business strategic alliances alters perceptions of adoption factors (barriers to adoption, criteria for adoption, benefits of adoption or disadvantages of adoption) of E-commerce technologies for specific sectors of regional SMEs (certain business ages, business sizes, business sectors, market focuses, particular levels of IT skill).

The third goal of the present study was

- To determine whether the membership of small business strategic alliances alters perceptions of any of the adoption factors (barriers to adoption, criteria for adoption, benefits of adoption or disadvantages of adoption) of E-commerce technologies for specific sectors of the SME population (certain business ages, business sizes, business sectors, market focuses, particular levels of IT skill).

Extensive statistical analyses (as described in Chapter 3) were carried out. In many cases the division of the sample into sub-sets produced sample sizes that were too small to be useful (i.e. they were below the 95% and 99.9% confidence level sample sizes).

Where analyses did meet sample size the results were highly fragmented. Occasionally significant results were found but these results only concerned one adoption factor or one business characteristic. No consistent pattern was observed. Consequently these results will not be reported in detail in the body of the thesis. However, detailed results are provided in Appendix 6 for the sake of completeness.

80

4.6 Goal 4 – To determine if business age, business size, sector, market focus or IT skill level is associated differently with the adoption factors, depending on whether the SME is part of a small business strategic alliance or not

The final goal of the present study was:

- To determine whether the associations between business characteristics (business size, business age, business sector, market focus or level of IT skills) and adoption factors (barriers to adoption, criteria for adoption, benefits of adoption or disadvantages of adoption) of E-commerce technologies differ, depending on whether the SME is part of a small business strategic alliance or not.

One of the fundamental goals of the study (Goal 4) is to determine whether associations between business characteristics and adoption factors differ between respondents that are members of a small business strategic alliance and respondents that are not. As already has been shown (see Section 2.6.5) and the summary table (Table 2.8) there have been numerous studies concluding that business characteristics (business age, size, sector, market focus and level of IT skill) are associated with the adoption of E-commerce by SMEs. The current study has also presented a rigorous examination of the role of small business strategic alliances for each sub-division of these characteristics. It is now important that associations of those characteristics and adoption factors be examined for both respondents that are members of a small business strategic alliance and respondents that are not. If such associations exist, an examination of the scatterplots indicate that there is no reason to expect that these are other than linear. This is further borne out in the literature, which suggests that associations between business characteristics are linear in nature. As such, a series of standard linear regressions has been adopted.

The data was subdivided into two groups, those respondents that were part of a small business strategic alliance and those respondents that were not. A series of linear regressions was applied to both groups of data to determine whether any of the business characteristics (business age, business size, business sector, market focus, levels of IT skill) was associated with perceptions of adoption factors (barriers to adoption, criteria for adoption, benefits of adoption or disadvantages of adoption), for either group of respondents. The following sections examines the criteria, barriers, benefits and disadvantages separately.

4.6.1 An Examination of the business characteristics associated with the perception of criteria for both respondents that were part of a small business strategic alliance and respondents that were not

Based on an examination of the literature and case studies carried out in Australia, 14 criteria for adoption of E-commerce by regional SMEs were identified. A set of frequency analyses was carried out to determine their applicability to the regional Swedish study (see section 4.2.1). Three criteria:

Demand or pressure from customers
Demand or Pressure from suppliers
The availability of External technical support

were determined to be not applicable to the regional Swedish study and were eliminated. A series of linear regressions was applied to the remaining 11 criteria to determine whether there was any association between the business characteristics (business age, business size, business sector, market focus, levels of IT skill) and the perception of importance of any of the criteria, for respondents that were part of a small business strategic alliance and respondents that were not. For those criteria that produced a significant F value, only the significant t values are provided. For those criteria that did not provide a significant F value, no t values are given in the table.

Dependent Variable Pressure from Competition (non-members)		
	Beta	p value
Business size	.263	.006
R Squared	.143	
Adjusted R Squared	.103	
p value for complete regression table	.004	

Table 4.13 Linear Regression for Criterion Pressure from Competition (non-members)

Dependent Variable Reduction in Cost (members)		
	Beta	p value
Level of IT skill	.278	.030
R Squared	.197	
Adjusted R Squared	.124	
p value for complete regression table	.030	

Table 4.14 Linear Regression for Criterion Reduction in Cost (members)

Dependent Variable Reduction in Cost (non-members)		
	Beta	p value
Business size	.288	.004
R Squared	.111	
Adjusted R Squared	.070	
p value for complete regression table	.023	

Table 4.15 Linear Regression for Criterion Reduction in Cost (non-members)

Dependent Variable Improvement in Lead-time (non-members)		
	Beta	p value
Business size	.218	.031
R Squared	.099	
Adjusted R Squared	.058	
p value for complete regression table	.041	

Table 4.16 Linear Regression for Criterion ment in Lead-time (non-members)

Dependent Variable Improvement in Internal Efficiency (non-members)		
	Beta	p value
Business size	.220	.027
Market focus	-.212	.040
R Squared	.131	
Adjusted R Squared	.091	
p value for complete regression table	.009	

Table 4.17 Linear Regression for Criterion Improvement in Internal Efficiency (non-members)

Dependent Variable Improvement in Control and Follow-up		
	Beta	p value
Business age	-.321	.014
Business size	.303	.025
R Squared	.236	
Adjusted R Squared	.166	
p value for complete regression table	.010	

Table 4.18 Linear Regression for Criterion Improvement in Control and Follow-up

The results showed that 5 criteria, Reduction in Cost, Pressure from Competition, Improvement in Lead-time, Improvement in Internal Efficiency and Improvement in Control and Follow-up were associated with some of the business characteristics (business age, business size, business sector, market focus, levels of IT skill). One of the criteria, Improvement in Internal Control and Follow-up showed association for member respondents only. Three criteria Pressure from Competition, Improvement in Lead-time, and Improvement in Internal Efficiency showed association for non-members only. One criterion, Reduction in Cost showed association for both groups of respondents. A detailed discussion of these findings is presented in Section 4.7.

4.6.2 An Examination of the business characteristics associated with the perception of barriers for both respondents that were part of a small business strategic alliance and respondents that were not

Based on an examination of the literature and case studies carried out in Australia, 8 barriers for adoption of E-commerce by SMEs were identified. A set of frequency analyses was carried out to determine their applicability to the Swedish study (see section 4.2.2). All barriers were determined to be applicable. A series of linear regressions was applied to the 8 barriers to determine whether there was any association between the business characteristics (business age, business size, business sector, market focus, levels of IT skill) and the perception of importance of any of the barriers, for respondents that were part of a small business strategic alliance and respondents that were not. For those barriers that produced a significant F value, only the significant t values are provided. For those barriers that did not provide a significant F value, no t values are given in the table.

Dependent Variable E-commerce doesn't fit with our products or services (members)		
	Beta	p value
Business sector	.314	.011
R Squared	.195	
Adjusted R Squared	.124	
p value for complete regression table	.027	

Table 4.19 Linear Regression for Barrier E-commerce doesn't fit with our products or services (members)

Dependent Variable Security Risks (non-members)		
	Beta	p value
Business Sector	-.345	.009
R Squared	.186	
Adjusted R Squared	.113	
p value for complete regression table	.038	

Table 4.20 Linear Regression for Barrier Security Risks (non-members)

The results showed that 2 barriers, Security Risks and E-commerce doesn't fit with our products or services showed and association with Business sector. The barrier E-commerce doesn't fit with our products or services was associated with Business sector for member respondents only. The barrier, Security risks was associated with Business sector for member respondents only. A detailed discussion will be presented in Section 4.7.

4.6.3 An Examination of the business characteristics associated with the perception of benefits for both respondents that were part of a small business strategic alliance and respondents that were not

Based on an examination of the literature and case studies carried out in Australia, 11 benefits derived from the adoption of E-commerce by SMEs were identified. A set of frequency analyses was carried out to determine their applicability to the Swedish study (see section 4.2.3). Two benefits:

> *Reduced stock*
> *Improved marketing*

were deemed as not applicable to the study and were eliminated. A series of linear regressions was applied to the 9 benefits to determine whether there was any association between the business characteristics (business age of business, business size, business sector, market focus, levels of IT skill) and the perception of importance of any of the benefits, for respondents that were part of a small business strategic alliance and respondents that were not. For those benefits that produced a significant F value, only the significant t values are provided. For those benefits that did not provide a significant F value, no t values are given in the table.

An examination of the data in shows that there were no significant associations between any of the business characteristics (business age of business, business size, business sector, market focus, levels of IT skill) and the perception of importance of any of the benefits.

4.6.4 An Examination of the business characteristics associated with the perception of disadvantages for both respondents that were part of a small business strategic alliance and respondents that were not

Based on previous studies in the literature and the two pilot studies in Australia, 7 disadvantages found from the adoption of E-commerce in SMEs were identified. A series of frequency tests was applied to the data (see section 4.2.4) to determine the applicability of the disadvantages to the Swedish study. All disadvantages were found to be inapplicable to the study and were thus eliminated from further consideration.

4.7 Conclusions

This chapter has provided the findings of a detailed study of 313 regional SMEs in Karlstad in Sweden. A comprehensive discussion of these findings will be given in chapter 6. The remainder of this chapter is a summary of the major findings described in the previous sections.

Four goals were posed for this study.

In examining the goals a set of 14 criteria for adoption of E-commerce, 8 barriers to the adoption of E-commerce, 11 benefits derived from E-commerce adoption and 7 disadvantages from E-commerce adoption were posed. Three of the criteria, *demand/pressure from customers*, *demand/pressure from suppliers*, and *existence of technical support* were found to be inapplicable to the regional Swedish study. Two of the benefits, *reduction of stock* and *improvement to marketing* were, likewise found to be inapplicable to the Swedish study. None of the disadvantages were found applicable to the current study.

The fact that all of the disadvantages were rejected in the Swedish study suggests a discrepancy between Swedish and Australian SMEs, since the list of disadvantages was developed in an Australian pilot study. One possible explanation for these differences is the larger proportion of SMEs in small business strategic alliances in Sweden, compared to Australia. Conceivably this may result in a broader acceptance of E-commerce and a dissipation of perceived disadvantages through mutual help. Similarly the greater involvement of the Swedish government may have gone some way to overcome some of the negative impacts of E-commerce adoption. Finally the significant role of universities in the education and development of SMEs in Sweden may have increased the skill base and thereby reduced the negative impact of E-commerce adoption. All of these would have reduced the perception of disadvantages in the Swedish study.

However, this explanation would not be expected to account for the removal of all of the disadvantages, so further study is needed to explain why the disadvantages have been totally rejected.

Turning now to the question of benefits, it is somewhat surprising that two benefits were rejected. Based on the preceding argument one might have expected Swedish SMEs to be more aware of potential benefits and therefore more able to realize them. One possible explanation for this is increased number of strategic alliances and government involvement with SMEs in Sweden. It is possible that Swedish respondents had experienced both the benefits that were eliminated, but that the benefits were associated with factors other than E-commerce adoption such as membership of a small business strategic alliance or government involvement.

The first of these goals was

- To determine if the membership of small business strategic alliances is associated with business characteristics (business size, business age, business sector, market focus or the level of IT skill).

The results, shown in this chapter indicate that only one business characteristic, business size appears to be associated with decisions to become members of a small business strategic alliance in the Swedish study.

The relationship between business size and membership of a small business strategic alliance is in the direction suggested in the literature, i.e. small businesses tend to gravitate towards a small business strategic alliance, more than larger businesses. There are a number of possible explanations for the fact that other business characteristics were not associated with membership of a small business strategic alliance. For example, it is suggested in the literature that an international market focus might cause an SME to seek out membership of a small business strategic alliance and therefore be able to adopt E-commerce. In the Swedish environment there may not be a perception that membership of a small business strategic alliance is a necessary or useful step in E-commerce adoption and consequently even SMEs with an international focus may not feel the need to gravitate to an alliance as a first step in adopting E-commerce. If this were true, we would expect some SME with an international focus to adopt E-commerce regardless of their involvement with a small business strategic alliance. This is in fact the case (see Section 4.1.6).

A similar argument could be made for the lack of relationship between level of IT skill and membership of a small business strategic alliance. Swedish SMEs, because of the availability of government assistance and support from tertiary institutions may not require the support provided by small business strategic alliances.

In contrast to the relationship between business size and membership of a small business strategic alliance, the results of business age and membership of a small business strategic alliance shows that while a relationship exists, it is not in a single direction. While more SMEs in the 11 – 20 year category are members of a small business strategic alliance, all other age group categories show a higher level of non-membership. Thus while the literature would suggest that younger businesses would be expected to gravitate towards a small business strategic alliance and older businesses are more set in their ways, at best the very young SME respondents are equivocal regarding membership. It may be argued that younger SMEs are more pre-occupied with establishing their businesses, however, this does not explain the higher numbers of 11-20 year respondents. The data was examined to determine whether this age group predominated one of the other factors. No such grouping was found. One possibility is that other factors such gender or education level of the CEO may be biasing the current data.

The second goal was

- To determine whether the membership of small business strategic alliances alters perceptions of any of the adoption factors (barriers to adoption, criteria for adoption, benefits of adoption or disadvantages of adoption) of E-commerce technologies.

The results, shown in this chapter indicate that there were no significant differences in the perception of any of the criteria, barriers or benefits between respondents who were members of a small business strategic alliance and respondents who were not.
To put these results in context, let us look at the case of the barriers to adoption. What the results show is that there is no difference in perception to barriers to adoption of E-commerce because of membership of a small business strategic alliance.
To explain this result it should be remembered that the barriers were developed from the literature and pilot studies in Australia. As has already been established there are higher levels of government support and involvement of tertiary institutions in SMEs in Sweden than Australia. This has resulted in a greater awareness of the barriers to E-commerce adoption across SMEs in Sweden generally, regardless as to whether they are members of a small business strategic alliance or not. If this were the case we would not expect to find significant differences between the two groups.
An almost identical argument can be made for the criteria and benefits.
The third goal was

- To determine whether the membership of small business strategic alliances alters perceptions of any of the adoption factors (barriers to adoption, criteria for adoption, benefits of adoption or disadvantages of adoption) of E-commerce technologies for specific sectors of the SME population (certain business ages, business sizes, business sectors, market focuses, particular levels of IT skill).

The results showed that there were significant differences in perception of importance for some of the criteria, barriers and benefits (See Appendix 6)
The final goal of the study was

- To determine whether the associations between business characteristics (business size, business age, business sector, market focus or level of IT skills) and adoption factors (barriers to adoption, criteria for adoption, benefits of adoption or disadvantages of adoption) of E-commerce technologies differ, depending on whether the SME is part of a small business strategic alliance or not.

The results showed that 5 criteria, Reduction in Cost, Pressure from Competition, Improvement in Lead-time, Improvement in Internal Efficiency and Improvement in Control and Follow-up were associated with some of the business characteristics (business age, business size, business sector, market focus, levels of IT skill). One of the criteria, Improvement in Internal Control and Follow-up showed association for member respondents only. Three criteria Pressure from Competition, Improvement in Lead-time, and Improvement in Internal Efficiency showed association for non-members only. One criterion, Reduction in Cost showed association for both groups of respondents.
The criterion, Pressure from competition showed an association with business age for member respondents. Studies in the literature suggest that younger SMEs are more likely to adopt E-commerce than older ones. Reasons for this include the fact that older SMEs are more set in their ways, as are their customers, while younger SMEs are still very much establishing their customers and business procedures. The results would suggest for stand-alone SMEs this is still the case in the Swedish sample. The results would also suggest that

for respondents that were members of a small business strategic alliance this may be 'dampened' through the activities of the small business strategic alliance.

The literature also suggests that smaller SMEs gravitate to small business strategic alliances and that larger SMEs are more able and likely to adopt E-commerce. The lack of any association for either stand-alone or the member respondents might be explained by one factor counteracting the other. That is, while smaller SMEs are gravitating to a small business strategic alliance, larger ones are adopting E-commerce.

The criterion Improved Lead-time showed as being associated with business size for non-members only. Studies in Australia, US and NZ (Power & Sohal 2000, Reimenschneider & Mykytyn 2000, Abell & Lim 1996) suggest that this is a strong motivation amongst SMEs to adopt some form of E-commerce such that products are made once orders are received rather than waiting for customer purchase. Recent studies (Blackburn & Athayde 2000, Matlay 2000) have further suggested that it is the larger SMEs rather than the smaller ones that are tending to adopt E-commerce in the SME sector. One of the benefits of small business strategic alliances is the ability, through formal dealings with members, to conduct trade formally. The results suggest that respondents that are members of a small business strategic alliance appear to already 'enjoy' reduction of lead-time through their mutual interaction, while those respondents outside such an arrangement see this criterion as crucial. In line with the literature, it would appear that larger SMEs see this particularly so, as a means to increase overall profit of the business.

The criterion Improvement to Internal Efficiency showed as being associated with two business characteristics (Business size and market focus) for non-member respondents only. There are many studies in the literature that suggest that for the SME sector, those that are trading outside a local focus benefit from the adoption and use of E-commerce. As with the previous criterion, studies further suggest that it is the larger SMEs that appear to be adopting E-commerce rather than the smaller (often locally focused) ones. In a study in the US, Porter (2001) found that a benefit (and often an underlying criterion) for E-commerce adoption was improvement to internal efficiency.

One of the benefits often cited in the literature concerned with small business strategic alliances is the increase in internal efficiency of member SMEs. The results would suggest that member respondents have achieved a level of increased internal efficiency through the role of the small business strategic alliance, while non-members are attempting to gain this through E-commerce adoption.

One criterion, Improvement to Control and Follow-up was found to be associated with business age and business size for member respondents only. This result is contrary to expectation, as the literature suggests that members of a small business strategic alliance would be benefiting through their membership. Given also the involvement of government and tertiary education in Sweden, the expectation for all SME respondents would be that this would, in part, have been achieved. One possible explanation is that there is a greater realisation of the potential for E-commerce to improve control and follow-up through membership of a small business strategic alliance. Clearly, further study need to be done to determine if this is the case.

One criterion, Reduction in Cost, was shown to be associated with business characteristics for both members of a small business strategic alliance and non-members. For the non-member respondents this criterion was associated with business size, while for the member respondents this was associated with level of IT skill. One possible argument for the 'shift' from business size to level of IT skill is that the combination of small business strategic alliance, government and tertiary involvement has allowed more integrated E-commerce solutions to be considered, while for non-members it is only the larger SMEs that can consider these same solutions.

The results showed that 2 barriers, Security Risks and E-commerce doesn't fit with our products or services showed and association with Business sector. The barrier E-commerce doesn't fit with our products or services was associated with Business sector for member respondents only. The barrier, Security risks was associated with Business sector for member respondents only.

While government studies have attempted to link membership of small business strategic alliances with E-commerce adoption, a number of studies in the literature (see Section 2.7) have reported that membership often has little to do with E-commerce but rather is founded on the need for legitimacy and a sharing of general know-how. It would appear from the data that members, particularly retail and service sector members have deemed E-commerce as being less than suitable for their particular businesses. It would appear that rather than the small business strategic alliance assisting members to adopt E-commerce, it has benefited the members through non-adoption.

One barrier to E-commerce, Security risks has also shown an association with business sector for non-member respondents. One possible explanation is that membership of a small business strategic alliance has dissipated concerns surrounding security, while similar concerns remained heightened in the non-respondents. This would tend to support the views of in the non-respondents. This would tend to support the views of Yeung (1994) and Achrol & Kotler (1999).

No benefits showed any association with any of the business characteristics. This is a somewhat unexpected finding, however it may be argued that many benefits have been achieved through government and tertiary education involvement with SMEs.

The following chapter provides the data for the second of the studies, carried out in Wollongong, Australia.

Chapter 5
Quantitative Analysis of the Data Gathered by Means of the Survey in Wollongong, Australia

As stated in chapter 3, the results of this study are expected to contribute to a greater understanding of the nature of small business strategic alliances and their role in the process of adoption and use of E-commerce. As such, the study has four goals. These are:

- To determine if the membership of small business strategic alliances is associated with business characteristics (business size, business age, business sector, market focus or the level of IT skill).
- To determine whether the membership of small business strategic alliances alters perceptions of any of the adoption factors (barriers to adoption, criteria for adoption, benefits of adoption or disadvantages of adoption) of E-commerce technologies.
- To determine whether the membership of small business strategic alliances alters perceptions of any of the adoption factors (barriers to adoption, criteria for adoption, benefits of adoption or disadvantages of adoption) of E-commerce technologies for specific sectors of the SME population (certain business ages, business sizes, business sectors, market focuses, particular levels of IT skill).
- To determine whether the associations between business characteristics (business size, business age, business sector, market focus or level of IT skills) and adoption factors (barriers to adoption, criteria for adoption, benefits of adoption or disadvantages of adoption) of E-commerce technologies differ, depending on whether the SME is part of a small business strategic alliance or not.

The specific focus of this study is for regional SMEs.
This study aims to address each of these goals by presenting the results of a quantitative analysis of data gathered through two surveys, one in the Karlstad region of Sweden, the other in the Wollongong region, Australia.
This chapter presents that data for Wollongong, Australia.

This chapter is divided into seven sections, as follows:
Section 5.1 of this chapter presents descriptive statistics of the Wollongong sample group. This includes:

- The number of the respondent SMEs that had/had not adopted E-commerce.
- The number of respondent SMEs that were/ were not part of a small business strategic alliance.
- The number of respondent SMEs fitting each of the 6 business age categories.
- The number of respondent SMEs fitting each of the 4 business size categories.
- The number of respondent SMEs fitting each of the 4 business sector categories.
- The number of respondent SMEs fitting each of the 4 market focus categories.
- The number of respondent SMEs fitting each of the 5 levels of IT skill categories.

<u>Section 5.2</u> presents an examination of the adoption factors (barriers to adoption, criteria for adoption, benefits of adoption or disadvantages of adoption) of E-commerce to determine their applicability to the Australian regional SME sector.

<u>Section 5.3</u> addresses **goal 1**
- To determine if membership in a small business strategic alliances is associated with business characteristics (business size, business age, business sector, market focus or the level of IT skill).

This is determined by means of a series of chi-square analyses (see section 3.6.2).

<u>Section 5.4</u> addresses **Goal 2,**
- To determine if the membership of small business strategic alliances alters perceptions of any of the adoption factors (barriers to adoption, criteria for adoption, benefits of adoption or disadvantages of adoption) of E-commerce technologies.

This section utilizes a series of two-tailed t-tests (see section 3.6.3) to determine whether there is a significant difference in the compared means (membership versus non-membership).

<u>Section 5.5</u> addresses **Goal 3**
- To determine if the membership in a small business strategic alliances alters perceptions of any of the adoption factors (barriers to adoption, criteria for adoption, benefits of adoption or disadvantages of adoption) of E-commerce technologies for specific sectors of the SME population (certain business ages, business sizes, business sectors, market focuses, particular levels of IT skill).

This section utilizes a series of two-tailed t-tests (see section 3.6.4) to determine whether the means of perception of adoption factors (barriers to adoption, criteria for adoption, benefits of adoption or disadvantages of adoption) of E-commerce are significantly different for specific business characteristics (business ages, business size, business sectors, market foci or levels of IT skill).

<u>Section 5.6</u> addresses Goal 4
- To determine if the associations between business characteristics (business size, business age, business sector, market focus or level of IT skills) and adoption factors (barriers to adoption, criteria for adoption, benefits of adoption or disadvantages of adoption) of E-commerce technologies differ, depending on whether the SME is part of a small business strategic alliance or not.

This section utilizes a series of linear regressions (see section 3.6.5) to determine whether the business characteristics (business size, business age, business sector, market focus or levels of IT skill) impinge on SMEs' perception of adoption factors (barriers to adoption, criteria for adoption, benefits of adoption or disadvantages of adoption) of E-commerce. For those found to be significant, a chi-square analysis were carried out to determine how the factor is associated with the perceived importance of either the criteria, barriers, benefits or disadvantages in the adoption of E-commerce.

Section 5.7 presents the conclusions for the Wollongong study.

Section 5.8 provides some comparisons between the Swedish respondents and the Australian respondents.

5.1 Descriptive statistics for the Australian study

250 SMEs were contacted by phone in the area, Wollongong, Australia. 164 SMEs agreed to answer questions providing a return percentage of 65.6%. The data was imported into SPSS and a series of frequency distributions was applied. These were the number of respondent SMEs which:
- Had/had not adopted E-commerce.
- Were/ were not part of a small business strategic alliance.
- Fitted each of the 6 business age categories.
- Fitted each of the 4 business size categories.
- Fitted each of the 4 business sector categories.
- Fitted each of the 4 market focus categories.
- Fitted each of the 5 levels of IT skill categories.

The data was then split into two groups - those that had adopted E-commerce and those that had not. A series of frequency distributions was applied to each group. These were the number of respondent SMEs:
- That were/ were not part of a small business strategic alliance.
- Fitting each of the 6 business age categories.
- Fitting each of the 4 business size categories.
- Fitting each of the 4 business sector categories.
- Fitting each of the 4 market focus categories.
- Fitting each of the 5 levels of IT skill categories.

The complete data was again split into two groups - those that were part of a small business strategic alliance and those that were not. Again, a series of frequency distributions was applied to each group. These were the number of respondent SMEs:
- That had/had not adopted E-commerce.
- Fitting each of the 6 business age categories.
- Fitting each of the 4 business size categories.
- Fitting each of the 4 business sector categories.
- Fitting each of the 4 market focus categories.
- Fitting each of the 5 levels of IT skill categories.

As already stated, a set of frequency distributions was applied, using SPSS. As would be expected with this sample size (N=160), some respondents did not answer all questions.

92

These 'non-answers' which were termed 'missing' were examined and showed no intrinsic pattern.

Cooper (1969) states that for chi-square tests that 'a conservative rule is that no expected frequency of a cell should drop below 5', where

$$E_i = N (F (Y_u) - F (Y_l))$$

where

F is the cumulative distribution function $\sum_{i=0}^{x} f(i)$

Y_u is the upper limit
Y_l is the lower limit

The expected frequency for all cells concerned with the adoption of E-commerce is 24.7 which is above the required 5 for validity.

The expected frequency for membership of a small business strategic alliance is 20.3, again above the required 5 for validity.

As already shown (see Section 3.5.1) the minimum sample size for a t-test (at 99.9% degree of confidence) is 37 or 21 (at 95% degree of confidence). The sample size (N=160) for the Australian respondents is above 37 justifying the use of a t-test analysis. As individual analyses are being conducted, routine checks will be made to ensure sample size conforms to the above limits.

5.1.1 Adoption of E-commerce

The data was examined to determine the number of respondents that had/had not adopted E-commerce. Table A4.1 provides the frequency distributions.
The values in Table A4.1 show that, overwhelmingly, the respondent SMEs of Wollongong, Australia had not embraced E-commerce technology. Indeed, only 15.6 % (N=25) of the respondents indicated that they were using E-commerce in their day-to-day activities.

5.1.2 Membership of a small business strategic alliance

The data was examined to determine the percentage of the respondents that had become members of a small business strategic alliance and those that has not. Table A4.2 provides details.
As the primary goals of this study centre on the comparison of regional SMEs that are members of a small business strategic alliance and SMEs that are not, the data in Table A4.2 supports the notion that the Australian sample is sufficiently large to include both respondents that are members of a small business strategic alliance (30%, N=48) as well as respondents that have decided to remain outside such an alliance (70%, N=112).

5.1.3 Business age range of the Australian study

Table A4.3 provides the details of the business age of the respondent SMEs.
An examination of Table A4.3 shows that there is a relatively small number of respondents in the <1 year category. All other business age groups are sufficiently represented, with 67.5% (N=108) of the respondents having been in business for over 5 years.

5.1.4 Business size in terms of the number of employees

The data was examined to determine 'spread' of business size across the respondent SMEs. Table A4.4 provides details of the business sizes.
An examination of the data in Table A4.4 shows that only 11.2% (N=18) of the respondent SMEs had more than 10 employees. This would suggest that no statistical inferences are possible for business sizes 10-19 and 20-50 employees.

5.1.5 Business sector

Table A4.5 provides details of the business sectors.
As can be seen in Table A4.5 the respondent SMEs mainly fell into 2 categories, service (49.8%, N=79) and retail (41.9%, N=67). The data shows that there were only 10 (6.3%) of the respondents that indicated they were in the industrial sector and only 1 financial respondent.

5.1.6 Market focus

Four categories of market focus were identified from previous studies. These were local, regional, national and international. Table A4.6 provides the numbers in each of these four categories.
An examination of Table A4.6 shows that two types of market focus predominate in the Australian study. These were local (27.5%, N=44) and regional (59.4%, N=95). While the national market focus is lower (N=20), there are still sufficient numbers to statistically analyse these. There was only 1 international respondent, so no statistical analysis could be undertaken.

5.1.7 Level of IT skill within the respondent SMEs

Respondents were asked to rate their perception of the levels of IT skill within their business. Based on previous studies and case studies carried out in Australia, 5 alternative categories of IT skill (none, low, normal, high, expert) were provided. Table A4.7 provides details of the perceived skills of the respondent SMEs.
As indicated in Section 3.4.2.1, despite self-evaluation, respondents seemed to understand the question and ratings of levels of IT skills. This was further adequately checked through the use of the phone as the data gathering vehicle.
An examination of Table A4.7 shows that 68.6% (N=110)of the respondent SMEs rated the levels of IT skill within their firm as average or above, with 23.9% (N=38) rating their skill as high or expert.

5.1.8 Comparison of frequencies of adopters and non-adopters

The data was subdivided into two groups - those responses that indicated they had adopted E-commerce and those that had not. A series of frequency analyses was carried out to show any differences in the two groups.

5.1.8.1 Membership of a small business strategic alliance

The data was examined to determine the number of respondent SMEs who were part of a small business strategic alliance. Table A4.8 provides the details of responses.
An examination of the data in Table A4.8 shows that the number of adopters of E-commerce is small in comparison with the non-adopters. The data shows that of the 25 E-commerce adopters, only 40% (N=10) were members of a small business strategic alliance. The data also shows that 71.9% (N=97) of the non-adopters are not members of any form of small business strategic alliance.
The data shows no statistical association between membership of a small business strategic alliance and adoption of E-commerce.
These results are contrary to expectation. Much of the literature concerned with membership of small business strategic alliances and E-commerce adoption in SMEs suggests that SMEs that adopt E-commerce would normally be in some form of small business strategic alliance. Similarly, SMEs that had not adopted E-commerce would normally remain outside such alliances. While the data concerned with non-adopters supports these earlier findings, the data concerned with adopters, in the Wollongong study, does not.

5.1.8.2 Business age

Table A4.9 provides details of the frequency distribution of business age, for both adopters as well as non-adopters of E-commerce.
The data in Table A4.9 shows no statistical association between adoption of E-commerce and business age.
An examination of the data in Table A4.9 shows that the maximum number of respondents in any category was 6, As such, no statistical inferences are possible for the E-commerce adoption group.

5.1.8.3 Business size

A frequency distribution of business size was carried out on both the adopting businesses as well as the non-adopters of E-commerce. Table A4.10 provides the frequencies.
The data in Table A4.10 shows no statistical association between adoption of E-commerce and business size.
An examination of the data in Table A4.10 shows that all E-commerce adopters had employee numbers below 10.
These results are contrary to expectation. Much of the literature concerned with E-commerce adoption in SMEs suggests that it is the larger SMEs that are more likely to adopt E-commerce. The findings from the Wollongong study do not support this premise.

5.1.8.4 Business sector

Table A4.11 provides details of the frequency distribution of business sector, for both adopters as well as non-adopters of E-commerce.

The data in Table A4.11 shows no statistical association between adoption of E-commerce and business sector.

An examination of Table A4.11 shows that 96% (N=24) of the E-commerce adopters were either service or retail SMEs. While, amongst the non-adopters only 10 respondent SMEs were industrial, there is still sufficient data to apply further statistical analyses. There were no financial respondent SMEs.

A number of earlier studies in the literature suggest that retail and service SMEs are more likely to adopt E-commerce. The findings from the regional Wollongong study support these earlier studies.

5.1.8.5 Market focus

Table A4.12 provides details of the frequency distribution of market focus, for both adopters as well as non-adopters of E-commerce.

The data in Table A4.12 shows no statistical association between adoption of E-commerce and market focus.

An examination of Table A4.12 shows that for the market focus groups, local, regional and national, there were more respondents that had not adopted E-commerce than those that had. The data also shows that with the exception of the regional group, the number of respondent SMEs that had adopted E-commerce was insufficient to be able to apply any form of statistical analysis.

5.1.8.6 Level of IT skills

Table A4.13 provides frequency distributions of perceived levels of IT skills for those SMEs that had adopted E-commerce as well as those that had not.

The data in Table A4.13 shows no statistical association between adoption of E-commerce and IT skill level.

As can be seen from the data in Table A4.13, most respondent SMEs rated their IT skills as average or higher. The data shows that of the 92 respondents that rated their IT skills as high or expert, only 9 had adopted E-commerce. This result is unexpected. A number of recent articles in the literature suggest that the greater the level of IT skill, the more likely that the SME will adopt E-commerce. The Wollongong data does not support these conclusions.

Again, the small numbers of no skill or low skill (4%, 16% - .7%, 5.9%) preclude any further statistical analysis.

A number of recent studies have suggested that, while below original expectations, SMEs are moving towards the adoption of some form of E-commerce in their day-to-day activities. The data presented in Tables A4.8 - A4.13 would suggest that this is not the case for the Wollongong study sample.

5.1.9 Comparison of frequencies for respondent SMEs that are members of a small business strategic alliance and respondent SMEs that are not

The data was divided into two groups, those that had responded that they were members of a small business strategic alliance and those that indicated that they were not members of such an alliance. Again, a series of frequency distributions was carried out to compare the two groups across the business characteristics of business age, business size, business sector, market focus, and levels of IT skill.

5.1.9.1 Business age

Frequency analyses were carried out for both respondent SMEs who were part of a small business strategic alliance as well as for those that were not part of such an alliance, to determine the distribution of business age categories for each. Table A4.14 provides the details of the frequency distributions.

An examination of Table A4.14 shows that, with the exception of the respondent SMEs in the < 1 year group, all other groups are well represented.

A number of recent studies have suggested that business age appears to be associated with membership of a small business strategic alliance. The Wollongong data does not support this.

5.1.9.2 Business size

Frequency analyses were carried out for both respondent SMEs who were part of a small business strategic alliance as well as for those that were not, to determine the distribution of business size for each. Table A4.15 provides the details.

An examination of the data in Table A4.15 shows that for all business sizes, there was a tendency to remain outside any form of small business strategic alliance. The development of business size categories (see Section 3.4.2.1) was based on a prior pilot study. The resulting categories (sole-trader, 1 - 9 employees, 10-19 employees, 20-49 employees, >50 employees) are unstandardised and as such any comments comparing one category with another needs to be made in terms of the unstandardised form of the data. This having been said, however, an examination of the data shows that no particular business size appear to be members of a small business strategic alliance. This does not support the earlier findings in the literature.

5.1.9.3 Business sector

Frequency analyses were carried out for both respondent SMEs who were part of a small business strategic alliance as well as for those that were not, to determine the distribution of responses across the 4 business sectors. Table A4.16 provides the responses.

An examination of the data in Table A4.16 shows that, with the exception of the financial sector, respondents from all other sectors were more inclined to remain outside the small business strategic alliance.

5.1.9.4 Market focus

Frequency analyses were carried out for both respondent SMEs who were part of a small business strategic alliance as well as for those that were not, to determine the distribution of responses across the 4 areas of market focus. Table A4.17 shows the frequency distributions for both members and non-members of small business strategic alliances.

An examination of Table A4.17 shows that for all of the market focus categories, there was a tendency to remain outside the small business strategic alliance.

An examination of much of the government literature concerned with the development of small business strategic alliances (Blair 2000, NOIE 1998, European Union 2000, Copp & Ivy 2001), suggests that membership of these alliances substantially assists SMEs in their 'quest' for wider market representation. An examination of the data in Table A4.17 does not support this premise, for the Wollongong study sample.

5.1.9.5 Level of IT skill

Frequency analyses were carried out for both respondent SMEs who were part of a small business strategic alliance as well as for those that were not, to determine the distribution of responses across the five levels of IT skill. Table A4.18 provides the frequency distributions.

An examination of Table A4.18 shows that that there were only 2 respondent SMEs who were members of a small business strategic alliance that indicated that they had no levels of IT skills. All other sectors are well represented.

5.2 Appropriateness of adoption factors (barriers to adoption, criteria for adoption, benefits of adoption or disadvantages of adoption) of E-commerce to Australian respondent SMEs

This chapter began by stating the major goals of this study. Goals 1, 3, 4 (see Sections 3.5.3 - 3.5.6) are dependent on the criteria, barriers, benefits and disadvantages being applicable to the Australian study.

Based on the findings in the literature, a set of 6 in-depth case studies was carried out with regional SMEs in Australia. The details of these can be found in Section 4.2.

For each of the measures of criteria, barriers, benefits and disadvantages, respondents were asked to rate how applicable these measures were to their particular SME. The ratings were across a 5 point Likert scale with anchors of 1 - does not fit my situation and 5 - fits my situation very well. A series of frequency analyses was applied to each of the measures of criteria, barriers, benefits and disadvantages. As the ratings were concerned with the applicability of the criteria, barriers, benefits and disadvantages to the respondents, any measures for which over 75% of respondents gave ratings of 1, 2, 3 were considered inapplicable to the respondent group. The following sections examine each of the criteria, barriers, benefits and disadvantages separately.

5.2.1 Applicability of the criteria to the Australian respondent SMEs

Based on a number of studies in the literature and case studies carried out in Australia, 14 measures for criteria to adopt E-commerce were considered. As stated, a set of frequency analyses of ratings, by respondent SMEs, of each of these criteria was carried out. Table 5.1

provides the results of the frequency analysis. Criteria that had a combined rating (ratings 1, 2, 3) above 75% are highlighted.

Table 5.1
Rating of Criteria for E-commerce Adoption
Number and Percentage of respondents rating each criteria

Crit.	1	2	3	4	5
A	6 (24.0%)	5 (20.0%)	2 (8.0%)	5 (20.0%)	5 (20.0%)
B	6 (24.0%)	3 (12.0%)	4 (16.0%)	7 (28.0%)	3 (12.0%)
C	**17 (68.0%)**	**2 (8.0%)**	**0 (0.0%)**	3 (12.0%)	3 (12.0%)
D	5 (20.0%)	1 (4.0%)	2 (8.0%)	6 (24.0%)	10 (40.0%)
E	2 (8.0%)	2 (8.0%)	3 (12.0%)	8 (32.0%)	9 (36.0%)
F	8 (32.0%)	3 (12.0%)	7 (28.0%)	2 (8.0%)	5 (20.0%)
G	5 (20.0%)	2 (8.0%)	0 (0.0%)	9 (36.0%)	9 (36.0%)
H	3 (12.0%)	0 (0.0%)	4 (16.0%)	9 (36.0%)	9 (36.0%)
I	**19 (76.0%)**	**0 (0.0%)**	2 (8.0%)	4 (16.0%)	**0 (0.0%)**
J	4 (16.0%)	2 (8.0%)	5 (20.0%)	4 (16.0%)	10 (40.0%)
K	5 (20.0%)	0 (0.0%)	3 (12.0%)	8 (32.0%)	9 (36.0%)
L	**19 (76.0%)**	**1 (4.0%)**	**1 (4.0%)**	2 (8.0%)	2 (8.0%)
M	4 (16.0%)	2 (8.0%)	4 (16.0%)	8 (32.0%)	7 (28.0%)
N	4 (16.0%)	2 (8.0%)	5 (20.0%)	8 (32.0%)	6 (24.0%)

Legend

A	*Demand/pressure from customers*
B	*Pressure of competition*
C	*Demand/Pressure from suppliers*
D	*Reduction of costs*
E	*Improvement to customer service*
F	*Improvement in lead time*
G	*Increased sales*
H	*Improvement to internal efficiency*
I	*Strengthen relations with business partners*
J	*Reach new customers/markets*
K	*Improvement in competitiveness*
L	*External technical support*
M	*Improvement in marketing*
N	*Improvement in control and follow-up*

An examination of the data in Table 5.1 shows that for regional SMEs in Wollongong, Australia, three criteria are not generally applicable. These are:

1 *Demand/pressure from suppliers* that had a total rating of 76% (at 1, 2, 3 level)
2 *Strengthen relations with business partners* that had a total rating of 84% (at 1, 2, 3 level)

3   *External technical support* that had a total rating of 84% (at 1, 2, 3 level)

The data in Table 5.1 shows that the most important criterion was *increased sales* that had a total rating of 72% (at the 4, 5 level).

5.2.2 Applicability of the barriers to the Australian respondent SMEs

Those respondent SMEs that had adopted E-commerce in their day-to-day business were asked to rate 8 barriers to adoption as they pertained to their business, across a 5 point Likert scale (1 - does not fit my situation, 5 - fits my situation very well). 135 respondent SMEs indicted that they had not adopted E-commerce. Table 5.2 provides the frequency of the ratings. Barriers that had a combined rating (rating 1, 2, 3) above 75% are highlighted.

Table 5.2
Rating of Barriers for E-commerce Adoption
Number and Percentage of respondents rating each barrier

Barr.	1	2	3	4	5
A	25 (18.5%)	17 (12.6%)	29 (21.5%)	18 (13.3%)	46 (34.1%)
B	17 (12.6%)	20 (14.8%)	25 (18.5%)	28 (20.7%)	44 (32.6%)
C	21 (15.6%)	18 (13.3%)	29 (21.5%)	25 (18.5%)	41 (30.4%)
D	18 (13.3%)	22 (16.3%)	33 (24.4%)	20 (14.8%)	42 (31.1%)
E	28 (20.8%)	31 (23.0%)	12 (8.9%)	18 (13.3%)	46 (34.1%)
F	29 (21.5%)	25 (18.5%)	40 (29.6%)	13 (9.6%)	28 (20.7%)
G	31 (23.0%)	31 (23.0%)	18 (13.3%)	22 (16.3%)	33 (24.4%)
H	36 (26.7%)	29 (21.5%)	27 (20.0)	16 (11.9%)	27 (20.0%)

Legend

A	*E-commerce doesn't fit with products/services*
B	*E-commerce doesn't fit with the way we do business*
C	*E-commerce doesn't fit the way our customers work*
D	*We don't see the advantage of using E-commerce*
E	*Lack of technical know how*
F	*Security risks*
G	*Cost too high*
H	*Not sure what to choose*

An examination of the data in Table 5.2 shows that none of the barriers have a combined rating of 1, 2, 3 above 75%.

5.2.3 Applicability of the benefits to the Australian respondent SMEs

Those respondent SMEs that had adopted E-commerce in their day-to-day business were asked to rate 11 benefits to adoption as they pertained to their business, across a 5 point Likert scale (1 - does not fit my situation, 5 - fits my situation very well). 25 respondent

SMEs indicted that they had adopted E-commerce. Table 5.3 provides the frequency of the ratings. Benefits that had a combined rating (rating 1, 2, 3) above 75% are highlighted.

Table 5.3
Rating of Benefits for E-commerce Adoption
Number and Percentage of respondents rating each benefit

Ben.	1	2	3	4	5
A	4 (16.0%)	4 (16.0%)	3 (12.0%)	9 (36.0%)	5 (20.0%)
B	11 (44.0%)	3 (12.0%)	4 (16.0%)	4 (16.0%)	3 (12.0%)
C	11 (44.0%)	1 (4.0%)	5 (20.0%)	5 (20.0%)	3 (12.0%)
D	**13 (52.0%)**	3 (12.0%)	**3 (12.0%)**	4 (16.0%)	**2 (8.0%)**
E	6 (24.0%)	5 (20.0%)	5 (20.0%)	6 (24.0%)	3 (12.0%)
F	4 (16.0%)	0 (0.0%)	3 (12.0%)	11 (44.0%)	7 (28.0%)
G	**21 (84.0%)**	**0 (0.0%)**	**2 (8.0%)**	**1 (4.0%)**	**1 (4.0%)**
H	8 (32.0%)	1 (4.0%)	5 (20.0%)	5 (20.0%)	6 (24.0%)
I	5 (20.0%)	2 (8.0%)	5 (20.0%)	6 (24.0%)	7 (28.0%)
J	4 (16.0%)	1 (4.0%)	8 (32.0%)	5 (20.0%)	7 (28.0%)
K	6 (24.0%)	1 (4.0%)	7 (28.0%)	4 (16.0%)	7 (28.0%)

Legend

A	*Lower administration costs*
B	*Lower production costs*
C	*Reduced lead time*
D	*Reduced stock*
E	*Increased sales*
F	*Increased internal efficiency*
G	*Improved relations with business partners*
H	*New customers and markets*
I	*Improved competitiveness*
J	*Improved marketing*
K	*Improved quality of information*

An examination of Table 5.3 shows that for regional SMEs in Wollongong, Australia, two of the benefits are not generally applicable. These are:
1   *Reduced stock* that had a total rating of 76% (at the 1, 2, 3 level).
2   *Improved relations with business partners* that had a total rating of 92% (at the 1, 2, 3 level).
An examination of the data in Table 5.3 shows that the highest rated benefit was *Increased internal efficiency*, with 72% of respondents rating this benefit either 4 or 5.

5.2.4 Applicability of disadvantages to the Australian respondent SMEs

Finally, respondent SMEs that had adopted E-commerce were asked to rated 7 disadvantages, identified from the literature and in previous pilot studies, carried out in Australia. Again, the ratings were across a 5 point Likert scale (1 - does not fit my situation, 5 - fits my situation very well). 25 respondent SMEs indicated that they had adopted E-commerce. Table 5.4 provides the frequency of responses. <u>Disadvantages</u> that had a combined rating (rating 1, 2, 3) above 75% are highlighted.

Table 5.4
Rating of <u>disadvantages</u> for E-commerce Adoption
Number and Percentage of respondents rating each disadvantage

Dis.	1	2	3	4	5
A	23 (92.0%)	1 (4.0%)	1 (4.0%)	0 (0.0%)	0 (0.0%)
B	11 (44.0%)	5 (20.0%)	3 (12.0%)	4 (16.0%)	2 (8.0%)
C	6 (24.0%)	1 (4.0%)	2 (8.0%)	7 (28.0%)	9 (36.0%)
D	12 (48.0%)	3 (12.0%)	5 (20.0%)	3 (12.0%)	2 (8.0%)
E	12 (48.0%)	6 (24.0%)	16 (32.0%)	3 (12.0%)	0 (0.0%)
F	6 (24.0%)	6 (24.0%)	6 (24.0%)	6 (24.0%)	1 (4.0%)
G	8 (32.0%)	5 (20.0%)	2 (8.0%)	3 (12.0%)	7 (28.0%)

Legend

A	*Deterioration of relations with business partners*
B	*Higher costs*
C	*Computer maintenance*
D	*Doubling of work*
E	*Reduced flexibility of work*
F	*Security*
G	*Dependence on E-commerce*

An examination of the data in Table 5.4 shows that for regional SMEs in Wollongong, 4 <u>disadvantages</u> are not generally applicable. These are:
  1. *Deterioration of relations with business partners* that had a total rating of 100% (at the 1, 2, 3 level).
  2. *Higher costs* that had a total rating of 76% (at the 1, 2, 3 level).
  3. *Doubling of work* that had a total rating of 80% (at the 1, 2, 3 level).
     4. *Reduced flexibility of work* that had a total rating of 88% (at the 1, 2, 3 level).
An examination of the data in Table 5.4 shows that the most applicable disadvantage was *computer maintenance* that rated 64% (at the 4, 5 level).
A brief comparison with the Swedish data (see section 4.2.4) shows that where, in the Swedish study, all disadvantages were considered inapplicable, only 4 disadvantages are inapplicable for the Wollongong study. This does, however, raise questions concerning the appropriateness of those four disadvantages (*Deterioration of relations with business partners, Higher costs, Doubling of work, Reduced flexibility of work*) that were inapplicable to both studies. These results are considered in detail in concluding statements (see Section 5.7) and in the following chapter (see Section 6.3.2)

5.3 Goal 1 - Factors determining membership of a small business strategic alliance

The first goal of the study was:
  • To determine if the membership of small business strategic alliances is

associated with business characteristics (business size, business age, business sector, market focus or the level of IT skill).

Based on the literature and case studies five business characteristics (business age, business size, business sector and market focus, levels of IT skill) were determined to be the business characteristics associated with membership of small business strategic alliance.
A series of chi-square tests were carried out to examine the association, if any, between each of the five business characteristics and membership/non-membership of a small business strategic alliance. Tables 5.5 - 5.9 provide the data from these chi-square analyses.

Table 5.5
A comparison of business age and membership/non-membership of a small business strategic alliance

	Non-members	Non-members Expected	Members	Members Expected
< 1 year	10	7.7	1	3.3
1-2 years	12	11.2	4	4.8
3-5 years	16	17.5	9	7.5
6-10 years	19	18.9	8	8.1
11-20 years	28	28.3	13	12.1
> 20 years	27	28.4	13	12.2

$\chi^2 = 3.801$ p=.716

Table 5.6
A comparison of business size and membership/non-membership of a small business strategic alliance

	Non-members	Non-members Expected	Members	Members Expected
Sole trader	21	21.0	9	9.0
1-9 employees	80	78.4	32	33.6
10-19 employees	6	6.3	3	2.7
20-50 employees	4	5.6	4	2.4

$\chi^2 = 2.109$ p=.302

Table 5.7
A comparison of business sector and membership/non-membership of a small business strategic alliance

	Non-members	Non-members Expected	Members	Members Expected
Industrial	6	7.7	5	3.3
Service	51	55.3	28	23.7
Retail	55	46.9	12	20.1

$\chi^2 = 14.029$ p=.003

Table 5.8

A comparison of market focus and membership/non-membership of a small business strategic alliance

	Non-members	Non-members Expected	Members	Members Expected
Local	30	30.8	14	13.2
Regional	70	66.5	25	28.5
National	12	14.0	8	6.0

$\chi^2 = 4.604$ p=.330

Table 5.9

A comparison of the level of IT skill and membership/non-membership of a small business strategic alliance

	Non-members	Non-members Expected	Members	Members Expected
No skill	7	6.3	2	2.7
Low skill	34	28.7	7	12.3
Normal skill	49	49.7	22	21.3
High skill	18	18.9	9	8.1
Expert skill	3	7.7	8	3.3

$\chi^2 = 13.689$ p=.018

An examination of Tables 4.5 - 4.9 shows that two business characteristics, business sector and level of IT skill are associated with membership of a small business strategic alliance. It should be noted that 2 cells in Table 5.9 have an expected value less than 5.

5.4 Goal 2 - The effect of membership of a small business strategic alliance on adoption factors (barriers to adoption, criteria for adoption, benefits of adoption or disadvantages of adoption) of E-commerce

The second goal of the current study was

- To determine whether the membership of small business strategic alliances alters perceptions of any of the adoption factors (barriers to adoption, criteria for adoption, benefits of adoption or disadvantages of adoption) of E-commerce technologies.

This was determined by carrying out a series of two-tailed t-tests that compared the ratings of respondent SMEs who were members of a small business alliance with those that were not. The following sections examine the criteria, barriers, benefits and disadvantages separately.

5.4.1 The effect of membership of a small business alliance on the applicability of criteria for the adoption of E-commerce

Based on an examination of the literature and case studies carried out in Australia, 14 criteria for adoption of E-commerce by SMEs were identified. A series of frequency analyses was carried out to determine the applicability of these criteria for adoption, to the Australian regional SMEs (see section 5.2.1). Three criteria:

Demand or pressure from suppliers
Strengthen relations with business partners
The availability of external technical support

were determined to be not applicable to the Australian study and were eliminated. A series of two-tailed t-tests was applied to the remaining 11 criteria to determine whether there was a significant difference in the mean of the ratings (between respondent SMEs that were members of a small business alliance and respondent SMEs that were not). Table 5.10 provides details of the two-tailed t-tests.

Table 5.10
Comparison of means of rating of criteria for E-commerce adoption (between respondent SMEs that were members of a small business alliance and respondent SMEs that were not)

Criteria	Mean Members	N Members	Mean Non-members	N Non-members	t-value	Sig.
A	1.90	10	3.20	15	-1.983	.059
B	1.40	10	3.53	15	-4.290	.000***
D	3.50	10	3.47	15	.047	.963
E	3.20	10	4.00	15	-1.362	.186
F	2.10	10	2.93	15	-1.225	.233
G	2.70	10	4.13	15	-2.339	.028*
H	3.20	10	4.13	15	-1.594	.125
J	2.50	10	4.13	15	-2.349	.038*
K	2.60	10	4.20	15	-2.238	.048*
M	2.90	10	3.73	15	-1.310	.203
N	2.80	10	3.73	15	-1.415	.182

* $p<.05$
** $p<.01$
*** $p<.001$

Legend

A	*Demand/pressure from customers*
B	*Pressure of competition*
C	*Demand/Pressure from suppliers*
D	*Reduction of costs*
E	*Improvement to customer service*
F	*Improvement in lead time*

G	Increased sales
H	Improvement to internal efficiency
I	Strengthen relations with business partners
J	Reach new customers/markets
K	Improvement in competitiveness
L	External technical support
M	Improvement in marketing
N	Improvement in control and follow-up

An examination of Table 5.10 shows that the means of ratings of three criteria, *increased sales, reaching new customers/markets, improvement in competitiveness* showed a significant difference (at the .05 level). The data shows that the means of ratings of one criterion, *pressure from competition* showed a significant difference between members and non-members of a small business strategic alliance (at the .001 level). In all cases, respondent SMEs that were not members of a small business strategic alliance rated these more applicable to their situation than did respondent SMEs that were members of a small business strategic alliance.

5.4.2 The effect of membership of a small business alliance on the applicability of barriers to the adoption of E-commerce

Based on an examination of the literature and case studies carried out in Australia, 8 barriers to the adoption of E-commerce by SMEs were identified. A set of frequency analyses was carried out to determine their applicability to the Australian study (see section 5.2.2). All barriers were determined to be applicable to the Australian study. A series of two-tailed t-tests was carried out on the barriers to determine whether there was any significant difference in the ratings of the barriers between those respondent SMEs that were members of a small business strategic alliance and those that were not.
Table 5.11 provides the details of the two-tailed t-tests.

Table 5.11

Comparison of means of rating of barriers to the E-commerce adoption (between respondent SMEs that were members of a small business alliance and respondent SMEs that were not)

Barriers	Mean Members	N Members	Mean Non-members	N Non-members	t-value	Sig.
A	3.34	38	3.23	97	.372	.711
B	3.41	37	3.42	97	-.059	.953
C	4.08	38	3.21	97	1.962	.052
D	3.31	38	2.74	97	-1.916	.052
E	2.97	38	3.41	97	-1.525	.130
F	2.84	38	2.84	97	0.000	1.000
G	2.21	38	3.16	97	-3.177	.002**
H	2.42	38	2.76	97	-1.185	.238

* $p<.05$
** $p<.01$

*** p<.001
Legend

A	*E-commerce doesn't fit with products/services*
B	*E-commerce doesn't fit with the way we do business*
C	*E-commerce doesn't fit the way our customers work*
D	*We don't see the advantage of using E-commerce*
E	*Lack of technical know how*
F	*Security risks*
G	*Cost too high*
H	*Not sure what to choose*

An examination of table 5.11 shows that means of ratings of one barrier, *cost too high*, showed a significant difference (at the .01 level). The data shows that this barrier was more applicable to respondent SMEs that were not members of a small business strategic alliance. One of the 'cornerstones' of the government initiatives concerned with membership of a small business strategic alliance, is the reduction of barriers to adoption of E-commerce in SMEs. As such, we would expect to find a significant difference in the level of importance of these barriers between members and non-members of a small business strategic alliance. Only one barrier, *cost too high*, showed any significant difference in the means of ratings.

5.4.3 The effect of membership of a small business alliance on the applicability of benefits derived from the adoption of E-commerce

Based on an examination of the literature and case studies carried out in Australia, 11 benefits derived from the adoption of E-commerce by SMEs were identified. A set of frequency analyses was carried out to determine their applicability to the Australian study (see section 5.2.3). Two benefits:
> *Reduce stock*
> *Improved relations with business partners*

were deemed as not applicable to the study sample and were eliminated. A series of two-tailed t-tests was carried out on the benefits to determine whether there was any significance difference in the ratings of the barriers between those respondent SMEs that were members of a small business strategic alliance and those that were not.

Table 5.12 provides the details of the two-tailed t-tests.

Table 5.12
Comparison of means of rating of <u>benefits</u> to the E-commerce adoption (between respondent SMEs that were members of a small business alliance and respondent SMEs that were not)

	Mean Members	N Members	Mean Non-members	N Non-Members	t-value	Sig.
A	3.30	10	3.13	15	.259	.799
B	1.50	10	2.53	15	-1.428	.167
C	2.10	10	2.47	15	-.499	.623
E	1.80	10	3.33	15	-2.815	.010**
F	3.30	10	3.87	15	-.963	.346
H	2.20	10	3.33	15	-1.604	.122
I	2.10	10	3.93	15	-3.051	.006**
J	2.50	10	3.80	15	-2.100	.047*
K	2.70	10	3.40	15	-1.030	.314

* $p<.05$
** $p<.01$
*** $p<.001$
Legend

A	*Lower administration costs*
B	*Lower production costs*
C	*Reduced lead time*
D	*Reduced stock*
E	*Increased sales*
F	*Increased internal efficiency*
G	*Improved relations with business partners*
H	*New customers and markets*
I	*Improved competitiveness*
J	*Improved marketing*
K	*Improved quality of information*

An examination of the data in Table 5.12 shows that the means of ratings of two <u>benefits</u>, *increased sales* and *improvement to competitiveness*, showed a significant difference (at the .01 level). The data also shows that the means of ratings of one <u>benefit</u>, *improved marketing*, showed a significant difference (at the .05 level). In all cases, those respondent SMEs that were not members of a small business strategic alliance rated these <u>benefits</u> more applicable to their situation than those that were members of a small business strategic alliance.

Again, one of the 'cornerstones' of the government initiatives concerned with membership of a small business strategic alliance, is that greater benefits are achievable, for SMEs, through the alliance, when adopting E-commerce. The Wollongong data shows that it is the non-member respondents, not the member respondents that have reported a greater benefit from E-commerce adoption.

5.4.4 The effect of membership of a small business alliance on the applicability of disadvantages derived from the adoption of E-commerce

Based on an examination of the literature and case studies carried out in Australia, 7 disadvantages derived from the adoption of E-commerce by SMEs were identified. A set of frequency analyses was carried out to determine their applicability to the Australian study (see section 5.2.4). Based on the frequency distributions, four of the disadvantages were not considered applicable. These were:

Deterioration of relations with business partners
Higher costs
Doubling of work
Reduction in flexibility of work

A series of two-tailed t-tests was carried out on the disadvantages to determine whether there was any significant difference in the ratings of the disadvantages between those respondent SMEs that were members of a small business strategic alliance and those that were not.

Table 5.13 provides the details of the two-tailed t-tests.

Table 5.13

Comparison of means of rating of disadvantages to the E-commerce adoption (between respondent SMEs that were members of a small business alliance and respondent SMEs that were not)

	Mean Members	N Members	Mean Non-members	N Non-Members	t-value	Sig.
C	2.30	10	4.13	15	-2.935	.007**
F	2.20	10	2.80	15	-1.143	.265
G	2.10	10	3.27	15	-1.715	.100

* p<.05
** p<.01
*** p<.001

Legend

A   *Deterioration of relations with business partners*
B   *Higher costs*
C   *Computer maintenance*
D   *Doubling of work*
E   *Reduced flexibility of work*
F   *Security*
G   *Dependence on E-commerce*

An examination of the data in Table 5.13 shows that the means of ratings of one disadvantage, *computer maintenance*, showed a significant difference (at the .01 level) between respondent SMEs that were members of a small business strategic alliance and respondent SMEs that were not. Respondent SMEs that were not members of a small business strategic alliance rated this disadvantage as more applicable than respondent SMEs that were members of a small business strategic alliance.

This would tend to support previous studies that membership of a small business strategic alliance dissipates disadvantages derived from E-commerce adoption in regional SMEs.

5.5 Goal 3 - To determine whether the membership of small business strategic alliances alters perceptions of adoption factors (barriers to adoption, criteria for adoption, benefits of adoption or disadvantages of adoption) of E-commerce technologies for specific sectors of regional SME (certain business ages, business sizes, business sectors, market focuses, particular levels of IT skill).

The third goal of the present study was

- To determine whether the membership of small business strategic alliances alters perceptions of any of the adoption factors (barriers to adoption, criteria for adoption, benefits of adoption or disadvantages of adoption) of E-commerce technologies for specific sectors of the SME population (certain business ages, business sizes, business sectors, market focuses, particular levels of IT skill).

Extensive statistical analyses (as described in Chapter 3) were carried out. In many cases the division of the sample into sub-sets produced sample sizes that were too small to be useful (i.e. they were below the 95% and 99.9% confidence level sample sizes).

Where analyses did meet sample size the results were highly fragmented. Occasionally significant results were found but these results only concerned one adoption factor or one business characteristic. No consistent pattern was observed. Consequently these results will not be reported in detail in the body of the thesis. However, detailed results are provided in Appendix 7 for the sake of completeness.

5.6 Goal 4 - To determine if business age, business size, sector, market focus or IT skill level is associated differently with the adoption factors, depending on whether the SME is part of a small business strategic alliance or not

The final goal of the present study was:

- To determine whether the associations between business characteristics (business size, business age, business sector, market focus or level of IT skills) and adoption factors (barriers to adoption, criteria for adoption, benefits of adoption or disadvantages of adoption) of E-commerce technologies differ, depending on whether the SME is part of a small business strategic alliance or not.

One of the fundamental goals of the study (Goal 4) is to determine whether associations between business characteristics and adoption factors differ between respondents that are members of a small business strategic alliance and respondents that are not. As already has been shown (see Section 2.6.5) and the summary table (Table 2.8) there have been numerous studies concluding that business characteristics (business age, size, sector, market focus and level of IT skill) are associated with the adoption of E-commerce by SMEs. The current study has also presented a rigorous examination of the role of small business strategic alliances for each sub-division of these characteristics. It is now important that associations of those characteristics and adoption factors be examined for both respondents that are members of a small business strategic alliance and respondents that are not. If such associations exist, an examination of the scatterplots indicate that there is no reason to expect that these are other than linear. This is further borne out in the literature, which suggests that associations between business characteristics are linear in nature. As such, a series of standard linear regressions has been adopted.

The data was subdivided into two groups, those respondent SMEs that were part of a small business strategic alliance and those respondent SMEs that were not. A series of linear regressions was applied to both groups of data to determine whether any of the business characteristics (business age, business size, business sector, market focus, levels of IT skill) was associated with perceptions of adoption factors (barriers to adoption, criteria for adoption, benefits of adoption or disadvantages of adoption) of E-commerce, for either group of respondent SMEs. The following sections examines criteria, barriers, benefits and disadvantages separately.

5.6.1 An examination of the business characteristics associated with the perception of criteria for both respondent SMEs that were part of a small business strategic alliance and respondent SMEs that were not

Based on an examination of the literature and case studies carried out in Australia, 14 criteria for adoption of E-commerce by regional SMEs were identified. A set of frequency analyses was carried out to determine their applicability to the Australian study (see section 5.2.1). Three criteria:

Demand or pressure from suppliers
Strengthen relations with business partners
The availability of external technical support

were determined to be not applicable to the Australian study and were eliminated. A series of linear regressions was applied to the remaining 11 criteria to determine whether there was any association between the business characteristics (business age, business size, business sector, market focus, levels of IT skill) and the perception of importance of any of the criteria, for respondent SMEs that were part of a small business strategic alliance and respondent SMEs that were not. For those criteria that produced a significant F value, only the significant t values are provided. For those criteria that did not provide a significant F value, no t values are given in the table.

Dependent Variable Reach New Customers and Markets (non-members)		
	Beta	p value
Business Sector	.646	.002
Market focus	.753	.012
R Squared	.810	
Adjusted R Squared	.704	
p value for complete regression table	.005	

Table 5.14 Linear Regression for Criterion Reach New Customers and Markets (non-members)

The results showed that one criterion was found to be associated with two business characteristics for non-member respondents only. A detailed discussion will be given in Section 5.7.

5.6.2 An Examination of the business characteristics associated with the perception of barriers for both respondent SMEs that were part of a small business strategic alliance and respondent SMEs that were not

Based on an examination of the literature and case studies carried out in Australia, 8 barriers for adoption of E-commerce by regional SMEs were identified. A set of frequency analyses was carried out to determine their applicability to the regional Australian study (see section 5.2.2). All barriers were determined to be applicable. A series of linear regressions was applied to the 8 barriers to determine whether there was any association between the business characteristics (business age of business, business size, business sector, market focus, levels of IT skill) and the perception of importance of any of the barriers, for respondent SMEs that were part of a small business strategic alliance and respondent SMEs that were not. For those barriers that produced a significant F value, only the significant t values are provided. For those barriers that did not provide a significant F value, no t values are given in the table.

Dependent Variable Lack of Technical Know-how (non-members)		
	Beta	p value
Level of IT skill	-.510	.000
R Squared	.310	
Adjusted R Squared	.270	
p value for complete regression table	.000	

Table 5.15 Linear Regression for Barrier Lack of Technical Know-how (non-members)

Dependent Variable Security Risks (non-members)		
	Beta	p value
Market focus	.326	.003
R Squared	.189	
Adjusted R Squared	.141	
p value for complete regression table	.003	

Table 5.16 Linear Regression for Barrier Security Risks (non-members)

Dependent Variable Not Sure what to Choose (non-members)		
	Beta	p value
Level of IT skill	-.327	.003
R Squared	.162	
Adjusted R Squared	.112	
p value for complete regression table	.009	

Table 5.17 Linear Regression for Barrier Not Sure what to Choose (non-members)

A detailed discussion is provided in Section 5.7.

5.6.3 An Examination of the business characteristics associated with the perception of benefits for both respondent SMEs that were part of a small business strategic alliance and respondent SMEs that were not

Based on an examination of the literature and case studies carried out in Australia, 11 benefits derived from the adoption of E-commerce by SMEs were identified. A set of frequency analyses was carried out to determine their applicability to the Australian study (see section 5.2.3). Two benefits:
> *Reduced stock*
> *Improved relations with business partners*

were deemed as not applicable to the study and were eliminated. A series of linear regressions was applied to the 9 benefits to determine whether there was any association between the business characteristics (business age of business, business size, business sector, market focus, levels of IT skill) and the perception of importance of any of the benefits, for respondent SMEs that were part of a small business strategic alliance and respondent SMEs that were not. For those benefits that produced a significant F value, only the significant t values are provided. For those benefits that did not provide a significant F value, no t values are given in the table.

There was insufficient data to undertake a linear regression.

5.6.4 An Examination of the business characteristics associated with the perception of disadvantages for both respondent SMEs that were part of a small business strategic alliance and respondent SMEs that were not

Based on previous studies in the literature and the two pilot studies in Australia, 7 disadvantages found from the adoption of E-commerce in SMEs were identified. A series of frequency tests was applied to the data (see section 5.2.4) to determine the applicability of the disadvantages to the Australian study. Four disadvantages were deemed not applicable to the study. These were:
> *Deterioration of relations with business partners*
> *Higher costs*
> *Doubling of work*
> *Reduction in flexibility of work*

There was insufficient data to undertake a linear regression.

5.7 Conclusions

This chapter has provided the findings of a detailed study of 160 regional SMEs in Wollongong, Australia. Four goals were posed for the study.

In examining the goals a set of 14 criteria for adoption of E-commerce, 8 barriers to the adoption of E-commerce, 11 benefits derived from E-commerce adoption and 7 disadvantages from E-commerce adoption were posed. Three of the criteria, *demand or pressure from suppliers*, *strengthen relations with business partners*, the availability of *external technical support* were found to be inapplicable to the Australian study. Two benefits, *reduced stock* and *improvement in relations with business partners* were found to be

113

inapplicable to the Australian study. Four <u>disadvantages</u>, *deterioration of relations with business partners, higher costs, doubling of work, reduced flexibility of work* were found to be inapplicable to the Australian study.

Despite the fact that the original pilot study was carried out in Australia (MacGregor et al 1998), three criteria, Demand/Pressure from Suppliers, Strengthen relations with Business Partners and Availability of Technical Support were rejected as inapplicable to the Australian study. At the time of the pilot study many SMEs had undertaken some form of E-commerce with the primary objective of doing business with large organizations. Many of these large organizations actually demanded the use of E-commerce as a basis for business transactions, refusing to undertake business with SMEs in any other format. Clearly, many of these SMEs are doing business in a far wider context than the pilot study. Thus the external pressure for adoption has substantially reduced.

Unlike the Swedish situation, there is a 'culture' in Australian SMEs to remain independent rather than become linked to any other business. This is borne out in the levels of membership of small business strategic alliances (see Section 5.1.2). It would be expected that a lesser motivation for E-commerce adoption amongst Australian SMEs would be to strengthen business relations. Indeed, in many cases this would be a disincentive for E-commerce adoption.

As already indicated, far fewer SMEs tend to gravitate to small business strategic alliances. This coupled with a substantially lower government and educational association in Australia results in little technical support. Where in the pilot study, pressure was exerted by larger firms and some support was inevitably supplied, there appears little expectation of the part of SMEs in Australia to expect or to receive any such support.

Two benefits, reduced stock and improvement in relations with business partners were found to be inapplicable to the Australian study. As already indicated, the pressure from larger companies has waned. Where in the past E-commerce may have enhanced business relationships with larger firms, this has substantially reduced so that while many SMEs trade through E-commerce, they still maintain an 'arms length' attitude to other businesses. The removal of reduced stock as a benefit was somewhat unexpected. One explanation may be that as few SMEs are trading with E-commerce, stock levels are not affected by the adoption of E-commerce.

Four disadvantages were found to inapplicable to the Australian study. The first of these disadvantages, deterioration of relations with business partners has already been explained in terms of the 'arms length culture' that appears to exist in Australian SMEs. The other three disadvantages can be explained in terms of the pilot study. As indicated, when the pilot study was carried out, SMEs often adopted E-commerce as a means to do business with larger firms. This often entailed a reduced level of flexibility in that interaction. Added to this many SMEs, at the time of the pilot study were still maintaining ordinary non-E-commerce business dealings with the large bulk of their customers. This resulted in a duplication of the work effort and an added cost to interact with the larger firms.

The first of these goals was

- To determine if the membership of small business strategic alliances is associated with business characteristics (business size, business age, business sector, market focus or the level of IT skill).

The results are unexpected both in light of the literature concerned with small business strategic alliances and also the data produced by the Swedish study. A number of studies

(Donckels & Lambrecht 1997, Smith et al 2002) found that business size, business age and business sector all appeared to be associated with decisions to become members of a small business strategic alliance. On closer examination, both of these earlier studies showed a far higher percentage of membership in small business strategic alliances than was found in the Australian study, where only 30% (N=48) of the 160 respondents indicated membership. Indeed, there appears to be a 'culture' in Australian SMEs that rejects the notion of cooperation in any form of small business strategic alliance. This coupled with the disproportionately high levels of smaller SMEs (89% N=143 of SMEs had below 10 employees) and the similarly large percentage of respondents in the retail and service sector (93% N=149) may have biased the results such that while the sample size appears sufficient to examine associations between business characteristics and membership of a small business strategic alliance, these results are not observed.

While the nature of the data may explain the lack of association between business sector, business size and membership of a small business strategic alliance, the lack of association between business age and membership cannot be so easily explained. The literature would suggest that younger SMEs would be more likely to form alliances than older businesses set in their way. While the data is not significant, an examination of the data concerned with business age shows that most younger respondents (<5 years) are not members of a small business strategic alliance (only 27%, N=14 of the < 5 year group are members of a small business strategic alliance). One possibility is that younger businesses are pre-occupied with establishing their business to join a small business strategic alliance. However, examining the data overall tend to suggest the nature of small business strategic alliances is not something Australian regional SMEs support or patronize.

The results showed that none of the business characteristics was associated with decisions to become members of a small business strategic alliance.

The second goal was

- To determine whether the membership of small business strategic alliances alters perceptions of any of the adoption factors (barriers to adoption, criteria for adoption, benefits of adoption or disadvantages of adoption) of E-commerce technologies.

The results provided data that showed that 4 criteria showed a significant difference in rating between respondent SMEs that were members of a small business strategic alliance and respondent SMEs that were not. The criteria were:

1 *Pressure of competition*
   2 *Increased sales*
   3 *Reaching new customers/markets*
   4 *Improvement in competitiveness*

In all cases non-members rated these criteria higher than member respondents. The literature concerned with small business strategic alliances suggests that SMEs gain marketing know-how through membership of the alliance and that the alliance structure dissipates external forces such as pressure from competition. The results of the Australian study would tend to support these views. If, as suggested, membership of a small business strategic alliance reduces pressure from competition and enhances competitiveness, marketing know-how and access to increased sales, there is less of a need for these to be achieved through E-commerce adoption. As has been found in the data, it is the non-members that put a greater emphasis on these criteria than the member respondents.

The results showed that 1 <u>barrier</u> showed a significant difference in rating between respondent SMEs that were members of a small business strategic alliance and respondent SMEs that were not. This was:

    1 Cost too high

As has already been suggested, membership of a small business strategic alliance dissipates many of the external barriers presented by the possibility of E-commerce adoption. Perhaps most interesting is the fact that only one barrier was shown to be higher for non-member respondents. The literature suggests that most barriers should be dissipated by membership of a small business strategic alliance. The data does not support this notion for the Australian regional SME study.

The results showed that 3 <u>benefits</u> showed a significant difference in rating between respondent SMEs that were members of a small business strategic alliance and respondent SMEs that were not. These were:

    2 Increased sales
    3 New customers/markets
    4 Improvement to competitiveness

An examination of the data shows that all three benefits were rated higher by non-member respondents than they were for member respondents. Again, one possible explanation is that these benefits were achieved through membership of a small business strategic alliance rather than through E-commerce adoption for member respondents. By comparison, non-members may have only been able to achieve increasing benefit through the adoption of E-commerce. This, again, would support the views of Achrol & Kotler (1999) and Schindehutte & Morris (2000) that marketing expertise is a product of small business strategic alliance membership.

The results showed that 1 disadvantage showed a significant difference in rating between respondent SMEs that were members of a small business strategic alliance and respondent SMEs that were not. This was:

    1 Computer maintenance

A similar argument could be made for disadvantages as has been made for benefits. The data shows that it is the non-member respondents that report a higher level of disadvantage with computer maintenance than the member respondents. The data appears to support the notion in the literature that disadvantages are dissipated far more readily in the context of a small business strategic alliance than by stand-alone SMEs.

The final goal of the study was

- To determine whether the associations between business characteristics (business size, business age, business sector, market focus or level of IT skills) and adoption factors (barriers to adoption, criteria for adoption, benefits of adoption or disadvantages of adoption) of E-commerce technologies differ, depending on whether the SME is part of a small business strategic alliance or not.

The results showed that one criterion, reaching new customers and markets was associated with business sector and market focus for non-members only. This result would tend to support the findings of Matlay (2000), Schindehutte & Morris (2001), Blackburn & Athayde (2000) that these business characteristics are associated with E-commerce adoption. The question arises, however, as to why this is not the case for member respondents. One possible reason is the lower than expected level of membership of small business strategic alliances in the Australian study (30%, N= 48).

The question also arises as to why business size does not appear to be associated with any of the criteria. Studies (Hyland & Matlay 1997, Matlay 2000, Fallon & Moran 2000) found that business size was associated with criteria to adopt E-commerce. Again one possible explanations the larger than expected number of respondents with less than 10 employees (89%, N=143). Previous studies suggest that it is the larger SMEs that are more likely to adopt E-commerce. The lack of larger SMEs in the Australian sample does not allow any valid comparison to be made.

The results show that three barriers, Lack of Technical know-how, Security Risks and Not sure what to choose are associated with business characteristics for non-member respondents only. The barrier security risks needs to be considered very carefully as over 90% of the respondents are either retail or service sector businesses. As such a valid conclusion is impossible.

The barriers, Lack of Technical know-how and Not sure what to choose are associated with levels of IT skill. This result would be expected given that both of these barriers are technical in nature. While it may be argued that similar results were not obtained from the member respondents because of the role of the small business strategic alliance in dissipating these problems, this argument must be made with caution, given the smaller than expected size of the membership.

5.8 Comparison of the Swedish and Australian respondent SMEs

The final task was to compare the rating of adoption factors (barriers to adoption, criteria for adoption, benefits of adoption or disadvantages of adoption) of E-commerce, for both members and non-members of a small business strategic alliance) between the Swedish respondent SMEs and the Australian respondent SMEs. The following sections examine criteria, barriers, benefits and disadvantages separately.

5.8.1 Comparison of the rating of criteria by Swedish and Australian respondent SMEs

A series of two-tailed t-tests were carried out to determine whether there was any difference in the means of ratings of any of the criteria between the Swedish and Australian respondent SMEs (for either those that were members of a small business strategic alliance or those that were not).

Table 5.18 presents the data for the non-members.

Table 5.18

Comparison of means of rating of criteria for E-commerce adoption, between Swedish and Australian respondent SMEs (not members of a small business strategic alliance)

Criteria	Mean Swedish	N Swedish	Mean Aust.	N Aust.	t-value	Sig.
A	1.82	61	3.20	15	-3.326	.001***
B	2.10	61	3.53	15	-3.046	.003**
C	1.61	61	1.73	15	-.325	.746
D	3.03	61	3.47	15	-.862	.391
E	3.64	61	4.00	15	-.732	.466
F	2.44	61	2.93	15	-.988	.327
G	2.70	61	4.13	15	-2.833	.006**
H	3.38	61	4.13	15	-2.594	.012*
I	2.69	61	1.00	15	3.405	.001***
J	2.84	61	4.13	15	-3.881	.000***
K	2.97	61	4.00	15	-2.468	.016*
L	1.16	61	2.07	15	-2.026	.060
M	2.72	61	3.73	15	-2.422	.022*
N	2.25	61	3.73	15	-4.529	.000***

* $p<.05$
** $p<.01$
*** $p<.001$

Legend

A	*Demand/pressure from customers*
B	*Pressure of competition*
C	*Demand/Pressure from suppliers*
D	*Reduction of costs*
E	*Improvement to customer service*
F	*Improvement in lead time*
G	*Increased sales*
H	*Improvement to internal efficiency*
I	*Strengthen relations with business partners*
J	*Reach new customers/markets*
K	*Improvement in competitiveness*
L	*External technical support*
M	*Improvement in marketing*
N	*Improvement in control and follow-up*

An examination of the data in Table 5.18 shows that the means of ratings of four criteria, *demand/pressure from customers, strengthen relations with business partners, reach new customers/markets, improvement in control and follow-up* showed a significant difference (at the .001 level). The data shows that the means of ratings of two criteria, *pressure of competition, increased sales* showed a significant difference (at the .01 level). The data also shows that the means of ratings of three criteria, *improvement to internal efficiency, improvement in competitiveness, and improvement in marketing* showed a significant difference (at the .05 level). With the exception of the criterion *strengthen relations with business partners*, the Australian respondent SMEs rated the criteria more applicable than did the Swedish respondent SMEs.

Table 5.19 presents the data for respondent SMEs that were members of a small business strategic alliance.

Despite the differences in the N values (10 and 115), standard deviations were shown to be sufficiently similar (F =.987 for criterion B, F = .052 for criterion I and F=3.065 for criterion L) to accept the differences in the t values.

An examination of the data in Table 5.19 shows that the means of ratings of one criterion, *strengthen relations with business partners* showed a significant difference (at the .001 level). The data also shows that the means of ratings of two criteria, *pressure of competition, external technical support* showed a significant difference (at the .05 level). In all cases the Swedish respondent SMEs rated the criteria as more applicable to their situation than did the Australian respondent SMEs.

While the F tests support the validity of the comparisons between the Swedish and Australian studies, the relatively low number of Australian respondents (N=10) needs to be considered before any conclusions are made.

Table 5.19

Comparison of means of rating of criteria for E-commerce adoption, between Swedish and Australian respondent SMEs (members of a small business strategic alliance)

Criteria	Mean Swedish	N Swedish	Mean Aust.	N Aust.	t-value	Sig.
A	2.10	115	1.90	10	.417	.677
B	2.34	115	1.40	10	2.056	.042*
C	1.71	115	1.80	10	-.198	.844
D	3.00	115	3.50	10	-.955	.342
E	3.64	115	3.20	10	.850	.397
F	2.59	115	2.10	10	.880	.381
G	2.98	115	2.70	10	.531	.596
H	3.71	115	3.20	10	1.064	.289
I	2.98	115	1.00	10	4.572	.000***
J	2.91	115	2.50	10	.747	.456
K	3.42	115	2.60	10	1.513	.133
L	1.42	115	1.00	10	2.054	.042*
M	3.01	115	2.90	10	.190	.850
N	2.72	115	2.80	10	-.150	.881

* $p<.05$
** $p<.01$
*** $p<.001$

Legend

A	*Demand/pressure from customers*
B	*Pressure of competition*
C	*Demand/Pressure from suppliers*
D	*Reduction of costs*

E	*Improvement to customer service*
F	*Improvement in lead-time*
G	*Increased sales*
H	*Improvement to internal efficiency*
I	*Strengthen relations with business partners*
J	*Reach new customers/markets*
K	*Improvement in competitiveness*
L	*External technical support*
M	*Improvement in marketing*
N	*Improvement in control and follow-up*

5.8.2 Comparison of the rating of <u>barriers</u> by Swedish and Australian respondent SMEs

A series of two-tailed t-tests were carried out to determine whether there was any difference in the means of ratings of any of the <u>barriers</u> between the Swedish and Australian respondent SMEs (for either those that were members of a small business strategic alliance or those that were not).
Table 5.20 presents the data for the non-members.

Table 5.20
Comparison of means of rating of <u>Barriers</u> to the E-commerce adoption between Swedish and Australian respondent SMEs (not members of a small business strategic alliance)

Barriers	Mean Swedish	N Swedish	Mean Aust.	N Aust.	t-value	Sig.
A	2.27	62	3.34	38	-2.874	.005**
B	2.27	62	3.41	38	-3.164	.002**
C	2.47	62	4.08	38	-2.897	.005**
D	1.81	62	2.97	38	-3.487	.001***
E	2.21	62	2.79	38	-1.571	.119
F	1.84	62	2.84	38	-3.142	.002**
G	2.05	62	2.21	38	-.466	.642
H	2.11	62	2.42	38	-.850	.397

* p<.05
** p<.01
*** p<.001

Legend

A	*E-commerce doesn't fit with products/services*
B	*E-commerce doesn't fit with the way we do business*
C	*E-commerce doesn't fit the way our customers work*
D	*We don't see the advantage of using E-commerce*
E	*Lack of technical know how*
F	*Security risks*
G	*Cost too high*
H	*Not sure what to choose*

An examination of the data in Table 5.20 shows that the means of ratings of one barrier, *we don't see the advantage of using E-commerce* showed a significant difference (at the .001 level). The data also shows that the means of ratings of four barriers, *E-commerce doesn't fit with products/services, E-commerce doesn't fit with the way we do business, E-commerce doesn't fit the way our customers work, security risks* showed a significant difference (at the .01 level). In all cases the Australian respondent SMEs rated the barriers as more applicable to their situation than did the Swedish respondent SMEs.

Table 5.21 provides the data for respondent SMEs that were members of a small business strategic alliance.

Table 5.21

Comparison of means of rating of barriers to the E-commerce adoption between Swedish and Australian respondent SMEs (members of a small business strategic alliance)

Barriers	Mean Swedish	N Swedish	Mean Aust.	N Aust.	t-value	Sig.
A	3.14	63	3.23	97	-.304	.762
B	2.92	63	3.42	97	-1.871	.063
C	2.65	63	3.21	97	-2.052	.042*
D	2.86	63	3.41	97	-2.137	.034*
E	2.84	63	3.23	97	-1.371	.172
F	2.29	63	2.84	97	-2.160	.032*
G	2.38	63	3.16	97	-2.971	.003**
H	2.41	63	2.78	97	-1.349	.179

* $p<.05$
** $p<.01$
*** $p<.001$

Legend

A	*E-commerce doesn't fit with products/services*
B	*E-commerce doesn't fit with the way we do business*
C	*E-commerce doesn't fit the way our customers work*
D	*We don't see the advantage of using E-commerce*
E	*Lack of technical know how*
F	*Security risks*
G	*Cost too high*
H	*Not sure what to choose*

An examination of the data in Table 5.21 shows that the means of ratings of one barrier, *cost too high* showed a significant difference (at the .01 level). The data also shows that the means of ratings of three barriers, *E-commerce doesn't fit the way our customers work, we don't see the advantage of using E-commerce, security risks* showed a significant difference (at the .05 level). In all cases the Australian respondent SMEs rated the barriers as more applicable to their situation than did the Swedish respondent SMEs.

5.8.3 Comparison of the rating of <u>benefits</u> by Swedish and Australian respondent SMEs

A series of two-tailed t-tests were carried out to determine whether there was any difference in the means of ratings of any of the <u>benefits</u> between the Swedish and Australian respondent SMEs (for either those that were members of a small business strategic alliance or those that were not).
Table 5.22 presents the data for the non-members.

Table 5.22
Comparison of means of rating of <u>Benefits</u> to the E-commerce adoption between Swedish and Australian respondent SMEs (not members of a small business strategic alliance)

Benefits	Mean Swedish	N Swedish	Mean Aust.	N Aust.	t-value	Sig.
A	2.76	115	3.30	10	-1.082	.281
B	2.80	115	1.50	10	1.018	.311
C	2.75	115	2.10	10	1.157	.249
D	2.06	115	1.00	10	1.999	.048*
E	2.43	115	1.80	10	1.302	.195
F	3.17	115	3.30	10	-.252	.801
G	2.87	115	1.00	10	4.337	.000***
H	2.50	115	2.20	10	.570	.570
I	2.95	115	2.10	10	1.691	.063
J	1.97	115	2.50	10	-1.160	.248
K	2.90	115	2.70	10	.351	.726

* $p<.05$
** $p<.01$
*** $p<.001$

Legend

A	*Lower administration costs*
B	*Lower production costs*
C	*Reduced lead-time*
D	*Reduced stock*
E	*Increased sales*
F	*Increased internal efficiency*
G	*Improved relations with business partners*
H	*New customers and markets*
I	*Improved competitiveness*
J	*Improved marketing*
K	*Improved quality of information*

Despite the differences in the N values (10 and 115), standard deviations were shown to be sufficiently similar (F =.932 for benefit D and F=1.924 for benefit G) to accept the differences in the t values.

An examination of the data in Table 5.22 shows that the means of ratings of one benefit, *improved relations with business partners* showed a significant difference (at the .001 level). The data also shows that the means of ratings of one benefit, *reduced stock* showed a significant difference (at the .05 level). In both cases, the Swedish respondent SMEs rated these benefits as more applicable to their situation than did the Australian respondent SMEs.

While the F tests support the validity of the comparisons between the Swedish and Australian studies, the relatively low number of Australian respondents (N=10) needs to be considered before any conclusions are made.

Table 5.23 provides the data for respondent SMEs that were members of a small business strategic alliance.

Table 5.23
Comparison of means of rating of benefits to the E-commerce adoption between Swedish and Australian respondent SMEs (members of a small business strategic alliance)

Benefits	Mean Swedish	N Swedish	Mean Aust.	N Aust.	t-value	Sig.
A	2.85	61	3.13	15	-.585	.560
B	2.64	61	2.53	15	.214	.831
C	2.82	61	2.47	15	.733	.466
D	1.85	61	2.40	15	-1.279	.205
E	2.51	61	3.33	15	-1.833	.071
F	3.25	61	3.87	15	-1.348	.182
G	2.57	61	1.00	15	4.361	.000***
H	2.56	61	3.33	15	-1.604	.113
I	2.67	61	3.93	15	-2.686	.009**
J	2.00	61	3.80	15	-4.140	.000***
K	2.92	61	3.40	15	-.961	.340

* p<.05
** p<.01
*** p<.001

Legend

A	*Lower administration costs*
B	*Lower production costs*
C	*Reduced lead-time*
D	*Reduced stock*
E	*Increased sales*
F	*Increased internal efficiency*
G	*Improved relations with business partners*
H	*New customers and markets*
I	*Improved competitiveness*
J	*Improved marketing*

An examination of the data in Table 5.23 shows that the means of ratings of two benefits, *improved relations with business partners, improved marketing* showed a significant difference (at the .001 level). The data also showed that the means of ratings of one benefit, *improved competitiveness* marketing showed a significant difference (at the .01 level). The data showed that two of the benefits, *improved competitiveness* and *improved marketing* were more applicable to the Australian respondent SMEs, while *improved relations with business partners* was more applicable to the Swedish respondent SMEs.

5.8.4 Conclusions

As can be seen in the data in Tables 5.18 - 5.23, despite the apparent similarity of the two study groups, there are a lot of differences in the ratings of adoption factors between the Swedish and Australian respondents. This supports the notion that SMEs are not homogeneous across cultures or across business characteristics (as shown earlier in this chapter).

Chapter 6
Interpretive Analysis of Data Gathered from the Two Surveys

6.1 Introduction

The previous two chapters have presented the results of the two surveys carried out in Sweden and Australia on regional SMEs and their adoption and use of E-commerce. Chapter 4 presented the data gathered from 313 SMEs in the Karlstad region of Sweden. Chapter 5 presented the data gathered from 160 SMEs in Wollongong, Australia.

In both the Karlstad study and the Wollongong study, four goals were posed (see Sections 3.5.3 – 3.5.6).

This chapter presents an interpretive analysis of the data gathered by means of the two surveys. Each of the study respondent groups is discussed separately, followed by a comparison of the two respondent groups.

As such, the arrangement of the chapter is as follows:

- Section 6.2 examines the Swedish study

    Section 6.2.1 provides a discussion of the respondents

    Section 6.2.2 provides a discussion on the applicability of the <u>criteria</u> for E-commerce adoption, the <u>barriers</u> to E-commerce adoption, the <u>benefits</u> derived from E-commerce adoption and the <u>disadvantages</u> derived from E-commerce adoption with respect to the Swedish study

    Section 6.2.3, 6.2.4, 6.2.5, 6.2.6 provide a discussion of goals 1 – 4 respectively for the Swedish respondents. Section 6.2.7 is the conclusion to the Swedish findings.

- Section 6.3 examines the Australian study

    Section 6.3.1 provides a discussion of the respondents

    Section 6.3.2 provides a discussion on the applicability of the <u>criteria</u> for E-commerce adoption, the <u>barriers</u> to E-commerce adoption, the <u>benefits</u> derived from E-commerce adoption and the <u>disadvantages</u> derived from E-commerce adoption with respect to the Australian study

Section 6.3.3, 6.3.4, 6.3.5, 6.3.6 provide a discussion of goals 1 – 4 respectively for Australian respondents.

    Section 6.3.7 is the conclusion to the Australian findings.

- Section 6.4 compares the Swedish and Australian studies

    Section 6.4.1 provides a discussion of the respondents

    Section 6.4.2 provides a discussion on the applicability of the <u>criteria</u> for E-commerce adoption, the <u>barriers</u> to E-commerce adoption, the <u>benefits</u> derived from E-commerce adoption and the <u>disadvantages</u> derived from E-commerce adoption with respect to both studies

    Section 6.4.3, 6.4.4, 6.4.5, 6.4.6 provide a comparison of goals 1 – 4 respectively with respect to the Swedish and Australian respondents.

    Section 6.4.7 is the conclusion to the comparative examination.

6.2 Regional SMEs in Sweden

The first of the two surveys was conducted in Karlstad, Sweden.
1170 questionnaires were distributed to SMEs in the regional area of Sweden known as Karlstad. 350 returns were gathered giving a return percentage of 29.9%. As the general description of an SME in Sweden is considered to be businesses with 50 or less employees, those businesses reporting staffing levels above 50 were eliminated. This left a final sample size of 313, or 26.75%.

6.2.1 Swedish sample

A number of studies (Riquelme 2002, Roberts & Wood 2002, Barry & Milner 2002) have suggested that despite the predicted benefits that may be derived from E-commerce adoption, many SMEs are continuing to avoid adopting and using the technology in their day-to-day activities. An examination of the adoption rates for the Swedish respondents (see Table A3.1) shows that over half the respondents (55.3%) indicated that they were using E-commerce.
These figures are substantially higher than studies carried out in comparable locations (Stauber 2000, Lawrence 1997, Riquelme 2002). One possible explanation is the interaction between SMEs, educational institutions and government agencies in Sweden. Recent studies (Klofsten 2000, Barry et al 2003, Dobers & Strannegard 2001) have pointed to the strong links between SMEs (particularly regional SMEs) and government and education institutions. These links, which involve educational course, entrepreneurial initiatives and technology proliferation, it is argued, have resulted in a higher uptake of E-commerce technology in regional SMEs.
Tables A3.3 through A3.7 provide a description of the respondents by business characteristics (business age, business size, business sector, market focus and levels of IT skill). The data shows that with the exception of the financial sector, all categories are well represented in the study, with over 90% of respondents having been in business for more than 2 years, 45.4% of respondents trading outside their local area and 82.8% of respondents indicating that they had an average or higher levels of IT skill. It could be concluded that since the majority of the respondents showed a reasonable level of IT skill, responses to the questionnaire were made by an 'informed' group of respondents.
Tables A3.9 through A3.13 provide data concerning the adoption and use of E-commerce across these five business characteristics (business age, business size, business sector, market focus and levels of IT skill). The data shows that with the exception of sole trader SMEs (0 employees), locally focused SMEs and SMEs with low levels of IT skill, more respondents in each category had adopted E-commerce than had not.
As with the overall E-commerce adoption rates, these figures are 'atypical' when compared to similar studies in Australia (Stauber 2000, Lawrence 1997), UK (Quayle 2002), Canada (Raymond 2001) and the US (Reimenschneider & McKinney 2001). Clearly, with the exception of sole traders, locally focused SMES and those with very low IT skill level, educational and governmental links with SMEs can be seen to be effective for all sectors, with all reporting higher uptake of the technology than rejection.
This shows that the SME sector is not a homogeneous one. Indeed, what we're seeing is that external factors or business characteristics such as government and educational involvement do result in a marked difference in the SMEs involved particularly with E-commerce adoption.

A number of studies (Hutt & Speh 1998, Swartz & Iacobucci 2000, Riquelme 2002) have suggested that, across the SME spectrum, the service sectors benefit more than the industrial sector through the adoption of E-commerce. This is not apparent from the Swedish study.

Indeed, while 54% of the service respondents had adopted E-commerce, 63.6% of the industrial respondents and 58.9% of the retail respondents had, likewise, adopted E-commerce. Again, one possible explanation for the higher than expected adoption rates in the industrial and retail sectors is the long-established links with government and educational institutions.

As part of the study, respondents were asked whether they were part of any form of small business strategic alliance. Table A3.2 shows that 46.2% of the Swedish regional respondents were part of some form of small business strategic alliance. Again, membership/non-membership was investigated across business characteristics (business age, business size, business sector, market focus and levels of IT skill). The resulting data (see Tables 4.5 through 4.9) shows that membership/non-membership is associated with business size and business age. The data shows that the relationship between business size and membership of a small business strategic alliance is in the direction suggested by the literature, i.e. that smaller SMEs are more likely to gravitate towards a small business strategic alliance than larger SMEs. In contrast, the results show that the association between business age and membership of a small business strategic alliance is not as suggested in the literature, i.e. that it is the younger SMEs that will tend to gravitate towards a small business strategic alliance rather than the older, more set in their ways SMEs. Indeed, with the exception of the 11 – 20 year group, all other groups had less members of a small business strategic alliance than non-members. Clearly, further study need to be carried out to determine whether other factors such as gender of CEO, educational level of the CEO may have biased the data.

A number of studies, Smith et al (2002), Donckels & Lambrecht (1997), Schindehutte & Morris (2001) and BarNir & Smith (2002) have suggested that business characteristics such as business sector and market focus often dictate SME decisions to form small business strategic alliances. The data from the regional Swedish SME study does not support these earlier studies.

There are a number of possible explanations for the fact that other business characteristics were not associated with membership of a small business strategic alliance. For example, it is suggested in the literature that an international market focus might cause an SME to seek out membership of a small business strategic alliance and therefore be able to adopt E-commerce. In the Swedish environment there may not be a perception that membership of a small business strategic alliance is a necessary or useful step in E-commerce adoption and consequently even SMEs with an international focus may not feel the need to gravitate to an alliance as a first step in adopting E-commerce. If this were true, we would expect some SME with an international focus to adopt E-commerce regardless of their involvement with a small business strategic alliance. This is in fact the case (see Section 4.1.6).

6.2.2 Applicability of adoption factors (barriers to adoption, criteria for adoption, benefits of adoption or disadvantages of adoption) of E-commerce to the Swedish study

Prior to examining any of the goals of the study, it was necessary to examine the applicability of adoption factors (barriers to adoption, criteria for adoption, benefits of adoption or disadvantages of adoption) of E-commerce, to the Swedish sample.

For each of the adoption factors (barriers to adoption, criteria for adoption, benefits of adoption or disadvantages of adoption), respondents were asked to rate the perceived applicability to their particular SME. The ratings were across a 5 point Likert scale with anchors of 1 (not at all applicable to my situation) and 5 (very applicable to my situation). A series of frequency analyses was applied to each of the adoption factors (barriers to adoption, criteria for adoption, benefits of adoption or disadvantages of adoption). As the ratings were concerned with the applicability of the adoption factors (barriers to adoption, criteria for adoption, benefits of adoption or disadvantages of adoption) to the respondents, any measures for which over 75% of respondents gave ratings of 1, 2, 3 were considered inapplicable to the respondent group.

14 separate criteria were tested. Each of these criteria was gathered from previous studies in the literature and were further tested by in depth interviews with regional SMEs in Wollongong. An examination of Table 4.1 shows that 3 criteria, *demand/pressure from customers*, *demand/pressure from suppliers*, *external technical support* were considered inapplicable to the Swedish study.

Studies concerned with two of the criteria, *demand/pressure from customers*, *demand/pressure from suppliers* (see Reimenschneider & Mykytyn 2000, Power & Sohal 2002, Lawrence 1997, MacGregor & Bunker 1996b) have shown that SMEs are often forced to adopt some form of E-commerce in order to continue in business arrangements with customers or suppliers. The results of the Swedish study would suggest that only 18.4% of the respondents felt that they were in such an enforced situation.

An early study by Abell & Lim (1996) concluded that, for SMEs to successfully adopt E-commerce, there was a need to elicit *external technical support*. The high percentage (82.8%) of average or better IT skill (see Table A3.7) would suggest that for the Swedish SME study, this criterion becomes far less a necessity.

8 barriers to E-commerce adoption by SMEs were gathered from previous studies in the literature and were tested for completeness through in depth interviews with SMEs in Wollongong. An examination of the data in Table 4.2 shows that all of the barriers remain applicable to the Swedish study. Hence the current study confirms that these barriers are in fact relevant to the adoption of E-commerce.

11 benefits derived from the adoption and use of E-commerce by regional SMEs were gathered from previous studies in the literature and were tested for completeness through in depth interviews. Those respondents that had adopted E-commerce were asked to rate each of these benefits in terms of their applicability to their situation.

An examination of Table 4.3 shows that two benefits, *reduced stock* and *improvement to marketing* were eliminated as being inapplicable to the Swedish SME study. Apart from these two benefits, the current study confirms the appropriateness of the other benefits in the literature. In particular it confirms the earlier work of Ritchie & Brindley (2001), Quayle (2002) and Vescovi (2000) who all concluded that E-commerce adoption provides new customers and markets and increases sales. The study also confirms the findings of Poon & Swatman (1997), Abell & Lim (1996) Tetteh & Burn (2001) and Raymond (2001), that E-commerce adoption by SMEs often reduces costs, improves internal efficiency and improves relations with business partners. However, the elimination of the benefit *improvement to marketing* raises and interesting point. There have been many studies (see Ritchie & Brindley 2001, Quayle 2002, Vescovi 2000) that have concluded that E-commerce adoption by SMEs provides new customer and markets, increased sales and actually improves marketing. While clearly the Swedish respondents have perceived that they have benefited in terms of provides new customer and markets and increased sales, a distinction is drawn between these and the marketing process itself, with only 19.4% of the respondents indicating that their marketing improved with the adoption of E-commerce.

7 disadvantages were gathered from previous studies in the literature and were tested for completeness through in depth interviews. Those respondents that had adopted E-commerce were asked to rate each of these disadvantages in terms of their applicability to their situation. An examination of Table 4.4 shows that none of the disadvantages was applicable to the Swedish study. This is a major finding of the current study and raises some important questions concerning the validity of the popularly cited disadvantages derived from E-commerce adoption in SMEs. Much of the literature concerned with disadvantages derived from E-commerce adoption tends to treat them as 'universally applicable' to all SMEs. The data from the regional Karlstad study does not support this view. A number of explanations as to why the disadvantages are rated so low are possible. Recent studies (see MacGregor 2004) suggest that disadvantages may be specific to certain sub-groups of regional SMEs rather than all SMEs. These subgroups may be based on the level of education of the CEO, shown in a Belgian study by Donckels & Lambrecht (1997). These subgroups may be dictated by business sector differentiation or by the focus of the business in terms of major customer source (see BarNir & Smith 2002, MacGregor 2004, Schindehutte & Morris 2001) For example, 'older' SMEs (those that have been in operation for more than 10 years) often report higher levels of disadvantage, particularly in areas such as deterioration of relationships with business partners, *doubling of work* and *reduced flexibility of work*, than do 'younger' SMEs. A chi-square analysis of the disadvantages was undertaken to determine if, in the Karlstad study, there was any association between business age and the ratings of disadvantages. Only one disadvantage, *lower production costs*, showed an association (at the .05 level). One recent study carried out on four sets of SMEs in Canada, Norway, Singapore and the Netherlands (Jutla et al 2002) suggests that one possible sub-group that may be associated with E-commerce adoption factors is the geographic/political one. Thus while certain disadvantages are noted in one geographic/political location, these may be reduced or differ in another. Added to this notion is the previously noted involvement of government and educational institutions with SMEs in Sweden. Greater involvement of these bodies may have gone some way to overcome the negative impacts of E-commerce adoption, through increasing the skill base of the SMEs. However, this explanation would not be expected to account for the removal of all of the disadvantages, so further study is needed to explain why the disadvantages have been totally rejected. Once again, this raises the question of homogeneity as previously discussed in Section 6.2.1.

6.2.3 Goal 1

The first goal of the study was:
- To determine if the membership of small business strategic alliances is associated with business characteristics (business size, business age, business sector, market focus or the level of IT skill).

Based on previous studies in the literature and two pilot studies, five business characteristics (business age, business size, business sector, market focus and levels of IT skill) were determined as possibly being associated with membership of a small business strategic alliance.

129

A series of chi-square analyses were undertaken to determine if there were any associations between any of the business characteristics (business age, business size, business sector, market focus and levels of IT skill) and membership/non-membership of a small business strategic alliance (see Tables 4.5 – 4.9).

An examination of the data in Tables 4.5 – 4.9 shows that only two business characteristics, business size and business age, were associated with and membership/non-membership of a small business strategic alliance. The data shows that 65.5% of the single person SMEs (sole traders) were members of a small business strategic alliance. 49% of the SMEs that had between 1 and 9 employees were members of a small business strategic alliance. By comparison, only 27.9% of respondents with more than 10 employees were members of a small business strategic alliance.

These findings support earlier studies (Smith et al (2002), Donckels & Lambrecht (1997), Schindehutte & Morris (2001) and BarNir & Smith (2002)). The studies carried out by BarNir & Smith (200) on 149 New England small manufacturing firms showed that smaller SMEs were often initially attracted to small business strategic alliances by virtue of their appearance as a professional or voluntary organization. They argue that mutual membership allowed a governance to be developed in an environment of trust. Larger SMEs were less likely to become involved in voluntary organizations where their own dominance may be diminished. As has already been indicated, a number of Swedish studies (Barry et al 2003, Klofsten 2000) suggest that a deliberate development of professional or voluntary organizations with Swedish SMEs. The findings suggest that like the New England study small business strategic alliances are favoured by small SMEs rather than by larger ones.

The results of business age and membership of a small business strategic alliance shows that while a relationship exists, it is not in a single direction. While more SMEs in the 11 – 20 year category are members of a small business strategic alliance, all other age groups show a higher level of non-membership. Thus while the literature would suggest that younger businesses would be expected to gravitate towards a small business strategic alliance, it is the older ones that seem to be seeking out such an arrangement. It may be argued that younger SMEs are more pre-occupied with establishing their businesses, however, this does not explain the higher numbers of 11-20 year respondents. The data was examined to determine whether this age group predominated one of the other factors. No such grouping was found.

6.2.4 Goal 2

The second goal of the current study was

- To determine whether the membership of small business strategic alliances alters perceptions of any of the adoption factors (barriers to adoption, criteria for adoption, benefits of adoption or disadvantages of adoption) of E-commerce technologies.

This was determined by carrying out a series of two-tailed t-tests that compared the ratings of respondents that were members of a small business alliance with those that were not.

11 criteria for E-commerce adoption were tested.

A number of earlier studies (Gibb 1993, Ozcan 1995, Golden & Dollinger 1993) suggested that, without some form of interorganizational relationship, IT and E-commerce adoption by SMEs would be difficult, at best. More recent studies (Premaratne 2001, Miles et al 1999), which have examined the nature of decision making within small business strategic alliances suggest that priorities in decision making may be altered by membership of a small business strategic alliance. An examination of the data in Table 4.10 shows that for the 11 criteria tested, there are no significant differences in the ratings of applicability of any of the criteria between respondents that were members of a small business strategic alliance and respondents that were not.

8 barriers to E-commerce were tested to compare their applicability to respondents that were members of a small business strategic alliance and respondents that were not.

A number of studies have suggested that many SMEs that are contemplating the adoption of E-commerce will seek out membership of a small business strategic alliance as a means of increasing their marketing and technical know-how. Achrol & Kotler (1999) describe the role of a small business strategic alliance as dissipating the intensity of disturbances and providing a greater openness to information. Dennis (2000) adds that small business strategic alliances allow members to move towards a set of objectives more easily than SMEs that are operating as separate entities.

An examination of the resulting data (see Table 4.11) shows that, despite the perception that small business strategic alliances dissipate the intensity of disturbances and allow a more efficient movement towards objectives, there were no significant differences in applicability of barriers to E-commerce between respondents that were members of a small business strategic alliance and respondents that were not.

While at first glance the results appear to refute the findings of Dennis (2000) and Achrol & Kotler (1999), these need to be considered in context. It should be remembered that the barriers have been developed from the literature and tested in pilot studies in Australia. As has already been established there are higher levels of government support and involvement of tertiary institutions in SMEs in Sweden than Australia. This has resulted in a greater awareness of the barriers to E-commerce adoption across SMEs in Sweden generally, regardless as to whether they are members of a small business strategic alliance or not. If this is the case, the differences in ratings of the barriers between member and non-member respondents would be expected to be less significant than findings carried out elsewhere.

9 benefits to E-commerce adoption were tested to determine whether there were any significant differences in applicability between respondents that were members of a small business strategic alliance and respondents that were not.

A number of other studies have suggested that small business strategic alliances provide advantages over stand-alone SMEs. Jorde & Teece (1989) showed that membership of a small business strategic alliance reduced financial risks through the sharing of those risks. More recently, Achrol & Kotler (1999) and Schindehutte & Morris (2001) suggested that market penetration might be enhanced through membership of a small business strategic alliance, while Marchewka & Towell (2000) found that dissemination of technical know how through membership of a small business strategic alliance gave 'an edge' over stand alone SMEs.

The resulting data (see Table 4.12) shows that none of the benefits showed any significant differences in applicability between respondents that were members of a small business strategic alliance and respondents that were not. This would suggest that membership of a small business strategic alliance has not enhanced the applicability of benefits to E-commerce adoption.

A similar argument to that of the barriers could be applied to the benefits of E-commerce. If, as suggested, there is a far greater involvement of government and tertiary education with SMEs, it would be expected that there would be less of an impact of the small business strategic alliance on the perception and realization of benefits.

Hence the current study does not confirm assertions by Keeble et al (1999), Overby & Min (2001), O'Donnell et al (2001) and Dennis (2000) about the benefits of small business strategic alliances in regards to E-commerce adoption.

6.2.6 Goal 4

The final goal of the present study was:
- To determine whether the associations between business characteristics (business size, business age, business sector, market focus or level of IT skills) and adoption factors (barriers to adoption, criteria for adoption, benefits of adoption or disadvantages of adoption) of E-commerce technologies differ, depending on whether the SME is part of a small business strategic alliance or not.

Over the years there have been many studies attempting to examine the business characteristics that affect the adoption of E-commerce by SMEs. Early studies (Hawkins et al 1995, Hawkins & Winter 1996, Hyland & Matlay 1997) noted relationships between business size, business age, business sector, market focus and the adoption of E-commerce technologies. Fallon & Moran (2000) found links between business size and internet adoption, while Matlay (2000) showed an association between business sector and E-commerce adoption.

More recently studies by Riquelme (2002), Tetteh & Burn (2001) and O'Donnell et al (2001) have shown that business sector, market focus and levels of IT skill are associated with E-commerce adoption in SMEs. The aim of goal 4 was to determine whether these associations differed depending on whether the SME was a member of a small business strategic alliance or not.

The data was subdivided into two groups, those respondents that were part of a small business strategic alliance and those respondents that were not. A series of linear regressions was applied to both groups of data to determine whether any of the business characteristics (business age, business size, business sector, market focus, levels of IT skill) was associated with perceptions adoption factors (barriers to adoption, criteria for adoption, benefits of adoption or disadvantages of adoption) for either group of respondents.

Table 4.36 provides a comparison of business characteristics affecting <u>criteria</u> for both respondents that were part of a small business strategic alliance and those respondents that were not. An examination of the data in Table 4.36 shows that 5 criteria, Reduction in cost, Pressure from Competition, Improved lead-time, Improvement in Internal Efficiency and Improvement to Control and Follow-up were associated with some of the business characteristics. The criterion Pressure from Competition showed an association with business age for non-members only. Studies in the literature suggest that younger SMEs are more likely to adopt E-commerce than older ones. Reasons for this include the fact that older SMEs are more set in their ways, as are their customers, while younger SMEs are still very much establishing their customers and business procedures. This appears to be the case for the stand-alone SMEs, however, for respondents that were part of a small business strategic alliance this appears to have been negated by the small business strategic alliances.

The criterion Improvement to Lead-time was associated with business size for non-members only. The literature suggests that this is a strong motivational reason for the adoption of E-commerce, particularly for larger SMEs. While this argument explains the findings for non-members, it does not explain the lack of association for members. The literature suggests that one of the benefits of a small business strategic alliance is the ability to engage in formal trade. The results suggest that respondents that are members of a small business strategic alliance appear to already 'enjoy' reduction of lead-time through their mutual interaction, while those respondents outside such an arrangement see this criterion as crucial. In line with the literature, it would appear that larger SMEs see this particularly so, as a means to increase overall profit of the business.

The criterion Improvement to Internal Efficiency was associated with both business size and market focus. There are many studies in the literature that suggest that for the SME sector, those that are trading outside a local focus benefit from the adoption and use of E-commerce. As with the previous criterion, studies further suggest that it is the larger SMEs that appear to be adopting E-commerce rather than the smaller (often locally focused) ones. Porter (2001) found that an underlying benefit of E-commerce adoption was improvement to internal efficiency. As with the criterion Improvement to Lead-time, one argument is that members of a small business strategic alliance have acquired some improvement to internal efficiency through membership of a small business strategic alliance and thus do not require it from the adoption of E-commerce.

One criterion, Improvement to Control and Follow-up was associated with business age and business size for member respondents only. This result is contrary to expectation, as the literature suggests that members of a small business strategic alliance would be benefiting through their membership. One possible argument is that there is a greater awareness of this through membership of a small business strategic alliance.

One criterion, Reduction in Cost, was shown to be associated with business characteristics for both members of a small business strategic alliance and non-members. For the non-member respondents this criterion was associated with business size, while for the member respondents this was associated with level of IT skill. While the association to business size is expected, the association with level of IT skill is not, particularly given the government and educational input into SMEs in Sweden.

The results show that 2 barriers, E-commerce doesn't fit with our products and services and security risks showed association with some business characteristics.

One barrier, E-commerce doesn't fit with our products and services is associated with business sector for member respondents, while the other barrier, Security risks is associated with business sector for non-members only. While it may be argued that security risks as a barrier is dissipated through membership of a small business strategic alliance, this does not explain the barrier E-commerce doesn't fit with our products and services being more applicable to member respondents. One argument is that there is a heightened awareness, through the small business strategic alliance membership. Clearly, this needs further examination.

The data shows that there were no associations between any of the business characteristics and any of the benefits for either respondents that were part of a small business strategic alliance or not.

6.2.7 Conclusion to the Swedish Study

This section has attempted to interpret the findings of the Swedish study, in particular the four goals of the study.

313 SMEs were surveyed. A number of results were found.

Firstly there was a higher than expected rate of E-commerce adoption by the respondent regional Swedish SMEs (55.3%). The most likely explanation, supported in the literature, was strong government and educational links with SMEs resulted in higher uptakes of E-commerce.

The data further showed that this higher than expected uptake of E-commerce was across the board of the respondent SMEs.

Data pertaining to the first of the goals showed membership of small business strategic alliances was associated with business size and business age. While the association with business size was as expected from the literature, the association with business age differed from the findings of earlier studies that found that younger SMEs are more likely to gravitate to a small business strategic alliance. No clear reason for this difference was found from the data, however it was speculated that factors such as gender or education level may be possible underlying reasons.

No other factors were associated with membership of a small business strategic alliance. Again, the most likely reason, supported by the literature is the strong government and educational links found in Sweden.

The results of the second goal for the Swedish respondents was that there were no differences in criteria, barriers or benefits between SMEs that were members of a small business strategic alliance and respondents that were not. As with the higher than expected uptake of E-commerce, the most likely reason for the lack of significant differences is that government and educational links provide the respondents (both members and non-members) with sufficient information and know-how to 'dampen' the differences that might otherwise be apparent. Where other studies have found a discernible difference between members of a small business strategic alliance and non-members, the education and training appears to have negated those differences.

The results of goal 3 showed no discernible pattern, as in many other studies of SMEs. The results, at best, indicate that even in a single location the SME sector is far from homogeneous.

Goal 4 showed that 5 criteria and 2 barriers are comparatively different from member respondents and non-member respondents. One argument is that despite the attempts of government-based literature to link small business strategic alliances and E-commerce adoption, the data clearly show that these are different. In particular, this appears to be brought out in the need for non-members to achieve specific criteria through E-commerce adoption that is available to members without the need for that adoption.

Not only do the results show that Swedish SMEs are not homogeneous, but there are significant differences between Swedish SMEs and those involved in the Australian pilot study. This would call into question the widespread idea that what is good for or true for SMEs in a particular context is good and true for SMEs in another context.

The following section provides a similar interpretation analysis of the data gathered from the Australian study.

6.3 Regional SME in Australia

The second of the two surveys was conducted in Wollongong, Australia.

250 questionnaires were distributed to SMEs in the regional area of Australia known as Wollongong. 350 returns were gathered giving a return percentage of 65.6%.

6.3.1 Australian Study

A number of studies in the 1990's (Nooteboom 1994, Acs et al 1997, Auger & Gallaugher 1997, Gessin 1996) suggested that since SMEs operated in an externally uncertain environment, they were more likely to adopt and <u>benefit</u> from E-commerce. Recent studies (Riquelme 200, Roberts & Wood 2002 and Barry & Milner 2002) have shown that many of these earlier predictions were far too optimistic and that it was the larger businesses that were more actively engaged in E-commerce. An examination of the adoption rates of the Australian study (see Table 4.1) would support these later findings, with only 15.6% of the 160 respondents indicating that they were engaged in E-commerce in their day-to-day activities.

This having been said, the results of the Australian study are substantially lower than the Swedish study and indeed are lower than comparable studies carried out in Canada, US or UK. While clearly the Swedish respondents may be explained through government and educational programs (see Section 6.2.1) this does not address the comparison with other countries. A number of studies (Harvie et al 2003, Gibb 2000, Gilmore et al 2001) have found that where decision making practices are imported into SMEs in US and UK; i.e. alternative approaches to marketing and technology are sought by SME owner/managers, this is not the case with Australian SMEs.

Tables A4.3 through A4.7 provide a description of the respondents by business age, business size, business sector, market focus, levels of IT skill. The data shows that, with the exception of the financial sector, all categories are well represented.

Tables A4.9 through A4.13 provide data concerning the adoption and use of E-commerce across the five business characteristics, business age, business size, business sector, market focus, levels of IT skill.

As with the overall results, the adoption rate across categories of all 5 business characteristics was lower than had been seen in other similar studies. Clearly this lower than expected E-commerce uptake is not confined to any specific sub-group of the respondent sample but permeates all sub-groups. Thus it seems that all sectors or regional SMEs do not appear to be 'importing' skills and know-how from similar businesses around the world.

Several studies carried out by Reuber & Fischer (1999) and Keeley & Knapp (1999) suggested that business age was a strong predictor of E-commerce adoption. An examination of the data in Table A4.9 shows that in fact the Australian data reverses the findings of the previous studies. Where in previous studies it is the older SMEs that appear to be avoiding E-commerce because they and their customers are set in their ways, it is the younger SMEs that are failing to adopt E-commerce with only 2 of the 27 respondents under 2 years in business adopting E-commerce. One possible explanation is the recent introduction of the GST into Australian business. Many businesses, particularly SMEs have noted that adherence to GST regulations has reduced their time and ability to examine any alternate form of trading (Harvie et al 2003).

This is another example of where external factors are having an effect on E-commerce adoption, contrary to what is suggested in the literature.

A number of studies (Hyland & Matlay 1997, Fallon & Moran 2000) have concluded that business size was a strong predictor of E-commerce adoption. An examination of the data in Table A4.10 shows that for the Australian SME respondents this appears not to be the case.

This having been said, it should be noted that there were 18 respondents (11.2%) that had more than 10 employees. Thus the respondent sample is skewed towards the smaller end of the SME spectrum.

A number of studies (Hutt & Speh 1998, Swartz & Iacobucci 2000, Riquelme 2002) suggested that across the SME spectrum the service sector benefited more from the adoption of E-commerce than the industrial sector. The data in Table A4.11 would support these findings, with only 1 of the 11 industrial respondents having adopted E-commerce. This compares to 17.9% (N=14) for the service sector and 14.9% (N=10) for the retail sector.

Again, however, it should be noted that the respondent sample for the Australian study was predominately service and retail SMEs (combined N= 146, 91.2%). Thus, while on the surface it may be argued that there is support for the findings of Hutt & Speh (1998), Swartz & Iacobucci (2000) and Riquelme (2002), the decision to randomly select respondents has resulted in a lower than expected compliment of industrial and financial respondents.

A number of authors (Hawkins et al 1995, Hawkins & Winter 1996) have suggested that E-commerce is particularly suited to SMEs that are conducting business outside their immediate geographic location. While it may be argued that regionally focused SMEs are operating outside their immediate geographic location, an examination of the data in Table A4.12 shows that for the Australian respondent SMEs, only 4 of the 20 respondents that indicated they had a national market focus had adopted E-commerce.

While none of the four market focus categories showed more E-commerce adopters than non-adopters, the largest percentage of adopters was the regional group (17.9%, N=17).

The low number of SMEs that are trading outside the regional area was an unexpected finding of the study. As already noted, there was a high proportion of small SMEs that were either retail or service based. Clearly the major focus of these are customers and businesses in the local area.

As part of the study, respondents were asked whether they were part of any form of small business strategic alliance. Table A4.2 shows that 30% of the respondents were part of some form of small business strategic alliance. Again, membership/non-membership was investigated across business age, business size, business sector, market focus and levels of IT skill. The resulting data (see Tables 5.4 through 5.8) shows that membership/non-membership is associated with business sector only. This result needs to be considered carefully as over 90% of the respondents (N=146) were either retail or service SMEs.

6.3.2 Applicability of adoption factors (barriers to adoption, criteria for adoption, benefits of adoption or disadvantages of adoption) of E-commerce to the Australian study

Prior to examining any of the goals of the study, it was necessary to examine the applicability of adoption factors (barriers to adoption, criteria for adoption, benefits of adoption or disadvantages of adoption) of E-commerce to the Australian study.

For each of the adoption factors (barriers to adoption, criteria for adoption, benefits of adoption or disadvantages of adoption), respondents were asked to indicate a rating as they were perceived to be applicable to their particular SME. The ratings were across a 5 point Likert scale with anchors of 1 (not at all applicable to my situation) and 5 (very applicable to my situation). A series of frequency analyses was applied to each of the measures of criteria, barriers, benefits and disadvantages. As the ratings were concerned with the applicability of the criteria, barriers, benefits and disadvantages to the respondents, any measures that were rated 1, 2, 3 by more than 75% of respondents, were considered inapplicable to the respondent group.

14 separate criteria were tested. Each of these criteria was gathered from previous studies in the literature and was further tested by in depth interviews with SMEs in Wollongong. An examination of Table 5.1 shows that 3 criteria, *demand/pressure from suppliers*, *strengthen relations with business partners*, *external technical support* were considered inapplicable to the Australian study.

Studies concerned with one of the criteria, *demand/pressure from suppliers* (see Reimenschneider & Mykytyn 2000, Power & Sohal 2002, Lawrence 1997, MacGregor & Bunker 1996b) have shown that SMEs are often forced to adopt some form of E-commerce in order to continue in business arrangements with customers or suppliers. At the time of the pilot study many SMEs had undertaken some form of E-commerce to do business with larger organizations. Many SMEs reported that there was an insistence by larger organizations for SMEs to trade via E-commerce. The results of the Australian study would suggest that only 24% of the respondents felt that they were in such an enforced situation.

An early study by Abell & Lim (1996) concluded that, for SMEs to successfully adopt E-commerce, there was a need to elicit *external technical support*. The high percentage (68.6%) of average or better IT skill (see Table A4.7) would suggest that for the Australian study, this criterion becomes far less a necessity.

Where in the pilot study, pressure was exerted by larger firms and some support was inevitably supplied, there appears little expectation of the part of SMEs in Australia to expect or to receive any such support.

A number of studies (Gimeno et al 1997 (cited Dennis 2000), Drakopolou-Dodd et al 2002) have suggested that many SMEs refuse to cooperate with similar business owners, relying on family and friends for technical and financial advice. The data concerning Table 5.1 shows that 76% of the Australian regional SME respondents rated the need to *strengthen relations with business partners* as very inapplicable, supporting these earlier studies.

Clearly this imposition has reduced and many SMEs are trading in a far wider context than with a single larger partner. Thus where there was external pressure, this has not continued to be an issue for E-commerce adoption.

Unlike the Swedish situation, there is a 'culture' in Australian SMEs to remain independent rather than become linked to any other business. This is borne out in the levels of membership of small business strategic alliances (see Section 5.1.2). It would be expected that a lesser motivation for E-commerce adoption amongst Australian SMEs would be to strengthen business relations. Indeed, in many cases this would be a disincentive for E-commerce adoption.

8 barriers to E-commerce adoption by SMEs were gathered from previous studies in the literature and were tested for completeness through in depth interviews with SMEs in Wollongong.

An examination of the data in Table 5.2 shows that all of the barriers remain applicable to the Australian study. Hence the current study confirms that these barriers are in fact relevant to the adoption of E-commerce. It is interesting to note that despite the 'media hype' concerning *security* of E-commerce as a barrier, the most crucial barrier was that it *does not fit with the way they did business*.

11 benefits derived from the adoption and use of E-commerce by SMEs were gathered from previous studies in the literature and were tested for completeness through in depth

interviews. Those respondents that had adopted E-commerce were asked to rate each of these benefits in terms of their applicability to their situation.

Two benefits, *reduced stock* and *improvement in relations with business partners* were eliminated as being inapplicable to the Australian study.

As previously noted, the pressure from large companies for SMEs to adopt E-commerce has substantially reduced, particularly with wider markets being 'tapped'. This combined with the apparent attitude of Australian regional SMEs to maintain an 'arms length' attitude has meant that little real value is seen in improving relationships with business partners. The removal of reduced stock as a benefit was somewhat unexpected. One explanation may be that as few SMEs are trading with E-commerce, stock levels are not affected by the adoption of E-commerce.

7 disadvantages were gathered from previous studies in the literature and were tested for completeness through in depth interviews. Those respondents that had adopted E-commerce were asked to rate each of these disadvantages in terms of their applicability to their situation. An examination of Table 5.4 shows that 4 of the disadvantages, *deterioration of relations with business partners*, *higher costs*, *doubling of work* and *reduced flexibility of work* were inapplicable to the Australian study.

The first of these disadvantages, the deterioration of relationships with business partners has already been explained in terms of criteria and benefits.

As already mentioned, the pilot study showed that E-commerce adoption was very often associated with trading with large organizations. In many cases while E-commerce was required by the larger organization, all other business was conducted in a non-E-commerce environment. This often reduced the flexibility of the E-commerce experience as the SME was 'locked into' a specific mode of operation, it meant a duplication of the work effort and resulted in higher costs. The extension of the E-commerce marketplace has reduced or eliminated these disadvantages so the SME can now dictate the terms of E-commerce rather than being dictated to.

6.3.3 Goal 1

The first goal of the study was:

- To determine if the membership of small business strategic alliances is associated with business characteristics (business size, business age, business sector, market focus or the level of IT skill).

In a study of 591 SMEs, Smith et al (2002) found that the business size of the SME was associated with decisions to become part of a small business strategic alliance. Other studies (see Donckels & Lambrecht 1997, Schindehutte & Morris 2001, BarNir & Smith 2002) have pointed to business characteristics such as business age, business sector, and market focus as being associated with decisions to become members of a small business strategic alliance.

Based on previous studies in the literature and two pilot studies, five business characteristics (business age of business, business size, business sector, market focus and levels of IT skill) were determined as being possibly associated with membership of a small business strategic alliance.

A series of chi-square analyses were undertaken to determine if there were any associations between any of the business characteristics (business age, business size, business sector, market focus and levels of IT skill) and membership/non-membership of a small business strategic alliance (see Tables 5.5 – 5.9).

An examination of the data in Tables 5.5 – 5.9 shows that two business characteristics, business sector and levels of IT skill were associated with membership/non-membership of a small business strategic alliance. The data shows that 45.5% (N=5) of the industrial respondents were members of a small business strategic alliance. By comparison, only 35.4% (N=28) of the service sector and 17.9% (N=12) of the retail sector were members of a small business strategic alliance.

An examination of Table 5.9 shows that 22.2% (N=2) of the no-skill respondents were members of a small business strategic alliance. By comparison, 72.7% (N=8) of the expert skill respondents were members of a small business strategic alliance.

The relatively small sample sizes means that any conclusions based on the data must be made carefully. While in part the results do appear to support the earlier findings of Donckels & Lambrecht (1997) and BarNir & Smith (2002), further studies with a more control sample size need to be carried out.

Recent studies, Donckels & Lambrecht (1997), Schindehutte & Morris (2001), BarNir & Smith (2002) have suggested that business age, business size, business sector, market focus are all associated with membership/non-membership of a small business strategic alliance. The findings from regional Australia do not support these earlier conclusions.

Again, the small sample size needs to be considered before any conclusions are reached.

6.3.4 Goal 2

The second goal of the current study was

- To determine whether the membership of small business strategic alliances alters perceptions of any of the adoption factors (barriers to adoption, criteria for adoption, benefits of adoption or disadvantages of adoption) of E-commerce technologies.

This was determined by carrying out a series of two-tailed t-tests that compared the ratings of respondents who were members of a small business alliance with those that were not.

11 criteria for E-commerce adoption were tested.

A number of earlier studies (Gibb 1993, Ozcan 1995, Golden & Dollinger 1993) suggested that without some form of interorganizational relationship, IT and E-commerce adoption by SMEs would be difficult, at best. More recent studies (Premaratne 2001, Miles et al 1999) that have examined the nature of decision making within small business strategic alliances suggest that priorities in decision making may be altered by membership of a small business strategic alliance. An examination of the data in Table 5.10 shows that four criteria, *pressure of competition, increased sales, reach new customers/markets, improvement in competitiveness* showed a significant difference in the rating of applicability between respondents that were members of a small business strategic alliance and respondents that were not. In all cases, respondents that were not members of a small business strategic alliance rated these criteria as more applicable than respondents that were members of a small business strategic alliance. The data from the Wollongong study supports the views of Miles et al (1999) and Premaratne (2001) who suggest that priorities in decision making are altered through membership of a small business strategic alliance. It is interesting to note, however, that much of the government literature, concerned with the development of small business strategic alliances, tends to suggest that these changes in priorities would result in members rating criteria as more important than non-members. This is not the case in the Wollongong study. One possible explanation is supplied by a study by Dean et al (1997) who suggested that resources such as *increased sales*, *reach new customers/markets* and *improvement in competitiveness* might be achievable through membership of a small business strategic alliance and become less important in the decision making process where E-commerce adoption is concerned.

8 barriers to E-commerce were tested to compare their applicability to respondents that were members of a small business strategic alliance and respondents that were not.

The role of small business strategic alliances has been described as a mechanism for dissipating the intensity of disturbances as well as a forum for greater openness to information and know-how (Achrol & Kotler 1999). As such, SMEs that are members of a small business strategic alliance can move more easily towards objectives than those that operate outside the small business strategic alliance. For E-commerce adoption, which has been described as an external disturbance (Lee 2001), small business strategic alliances are seen as a means of reducing barriers to adoption and increasing know-how in marketing and technology.

An examination of the resulting data (see Table 5.11) shows that one barrier, *cost too high*, provided a significant difference in applicability between respondents that were members of a small business strategic alliance and respondents that were not. Respondents that were not part of a small business strategic alliance rated this barrier more applicable to their situation than members of a small business strategic alliance.

This result supports early findings by Jorde & Teece (1989) who suggest that membership of a small business strategic alliance reduces financial risks of members.

It is interesting to note that while there was a significant difference in the barrier, *cost too high*, no other barrier showed any significant difference between respondents that were members of a small business strategic alliance and respondents that were not. This raises the question as to the applicability of small business strategic alliances, in terms of barriers to E-commerce adoption, for the Wollongong sample.

A closer examination of the data in Table 5.11 shows that, while not significant, respondents that were in a small business strategic alliance rated technological barriers lower than their counterparts, while they rated organizational barriers higher.

This would suggest that some information exchange regarding marketing and technology may have taken place while problems of an organizational nature may have actually been heightened through membership of a small business strategic alliance.

A number of studies (Achrol & Kotler 1999, Schindehutte & Morris 2001) suggested that market penetration might be enhanced through membership of a small business strategic alliance, while Marchewka & Towell (2000) found that dissemination of technical know how through membership of a small business strategic alliance gave 'an edge' over stand alone SMEs.

9 benefits to E-commerce adoption were tested to determine whether there were any significant differences in applicability between respondents that were members of a small business strategic alliance and respondents that were not.

An examination of Table 5.12 shows that 3 benefits, *increased sales, new customers/ markets* and *improved competitiveness* showed a significant difference in applicability between respondents that were members of a small business strategic alliance and respondents that were not. An examination of the data, however, shows that it is the non-member respondents that consider the benefit more applicable to their situation than the member respondents.

A number of authors, Marchewka & Towell (2000) and Schindehutte & Morris (2001) have suggested that SMEs achieve greater benefits from E-commerce adoption, through membership of a small business strategic alliance. The Wollongong results show the reverse of these earlier studies, with non-membership indicating higher perceived benefits when compared to member respondents.

One possibility is that benefits in terms of marketing and competitiveness may have been achieved through small business strategic alliance membership, rather than E-commerce adoption. Indeed, studies by Achrol & Kotler (1999) suggest that it is the small business strategic alliance that provides benefits in terms of marketing and sales.

Achrol & Kotler (1999) and Dennis (2000) suggest that a small business strategic alliance dissipates disadvantages, allowing members to better accommodate changes to their environment. 3 disadvantages were tested to determine whether there were any significant difference in the ratings of applicability between respondents that were members of a small business strategic alliance and respondents that were not.

An examination of the data in Table 5.13 shows that one disadvantage, *computer maintenance* showed a significant difference in the rating of applicability between respondents that were members of a small business strategic alliance and respondents that were not. Respondents that were not part of a small business strategic alliance found the disadvantage more applicable to their situation than respondents that were members of a small business strategic alliance. The results would tend to support the findings of Achrol & Kotler (1999) and Dennis (2000) regarding the dissipation of disadvantages through membership of a small business strategic alliance.

The question, however, arises as to why only one disadvantage appears to show any difference in rating. An examination of the other two disadvantages, security and dependence on E-commerce might suggest that they are less definable or modifiable through membership of a small business strategic alliance. Computer maintenance is, by and large, a more concrete disadvantage and one that is easily measured. It could be argued that given the 'arms length' culture of Australian regional small business owner/managers, that even those within a small business strategic alliance would be more inclined to share concrete knowledge rather than less definable information.

6.3.6 Goal 4

The final goal of the present study was:

- To determine whether the associations between business characteristics (business size, business age, business sector, market focus or level of IT skills) and adoption factors (barriers to adoption, criteria for adoption, benefits of adoption or disadvantages of adoption) of E-commerce technologies differ, depending on whether the SME is part of a small business strategic alliance or not.

A number of studies (Hawkins et al 1995, Hawkins & Winter 1996, Hyland & Matlay 1997) have noted relationships between business size, business age, business sector, market focus and the adoption of E-commerce technologies. Fallon & Moran (2000) found links between business size and internet adoption, while Matlay (2000) showed an association between business sector and E-commerce adoption.

Table 5.35 provides a comparison of business characteristics affecting criteria for both respondents that were part of a small business strategic alliance and those respondents that were not. An examination of the data in Table 5.35 shows that none of the business characteristics are associated with any of the criteria for respondents that were members of a small business strategic alliance. Only one criterion, *reach new customers/markets* was associated with any of the business characteristics (business sector and market focus).

The results show that it is the regionally focused respondents that rated the criterion higher than other respondents. The data also shows that the retail sector respondents rated the criterion higher than other respondents. In both cases the findings are unexpected. Studies carried out in China (Riquelme 2002) and UK (Hyland & Matlay 1997) suggest that it is the service sector that would normally rate this criterion higher, Likewise, studies carried out by Blackburn & Athayde (2000) suggest that it is the SMEs with a 'wider' customer base (national or international) that would normally rate this criterion higher.

Clearly, the lower than expected adoption levels, combine with the lower than expected exporters means valid comparisons with earlier studies cannot be made.

Three barriers, lack of technical know-how, security risks and not sure what to choose are associated with business characteristics for non-members only. One of the barriers, security risks, is associated with business sector, however, this must be discounted as over 90% of the respondents are either retail or service sector businesses.

The other 2 barriers are associated with the level of IT skill. This result would be expected given that both barriers are technical in nature. However, the smaller than expected number of respondents that indicate membership of a small business strategic alliance means that this argument needs to be made with caution.

9 benefits were examined to determine whether any of the business characteristics (business age, business size, business sector, market focus, levels of IT skill) was associated with the applicability of the benefits for both respondents that were part of a small business strategic alliance and those respondents that were not.

Again an examination of the data in Table 5.41 shows that for respondents that were members of a small business strategic alliance, there was no association between any of the business characteristics and any of the benefits. The data shows that for non-member respondents the benefit, *reduced lead time* was associated with the levels of IT skill and the business sector and the benefits, *increased sales* and *lower production costs* were associated with market focus.

3 Disadvantages were examined to determine whether any of the business characteristics (business age, business size, business sector, market focus, levels of IT skill) was associated with the applicability of the benefits for both respondents that were part of a small business strategic alliance and those respondents that were not.

Table 5.42 shows that there were no associations between any of the business characteristics and any of the disadvantages for either respondents that were part of a small business strategic alliance or not.

6.3.7 Conclusion to the Australian Study

This section has attempted to provide some interpretation of the data gathered from the Australian study. As indicated in Section 6.2.7 the literature suggests that there are no adequate frameworks upon which goals 1 – 4 may be developed.

160 SMEs were surveyed. A number of results were found.

Firstly the adoption rate of E-commerce in the Australian study was substantially lower (15.6%) when compared both to the Swedish study and to other studies in the UK and US. While some suggestion exists in the literature to indicate that there is a practice of importing know-how in the US and UK these views cannot be tested with the current data. As with the overall adoption rates, all sub-groups of the Australian sample showed lower than expected E-commerce adoption levels.

A number of studies (Reuber & Fischer 1999, Keeley & Knapp 1999) found that younger SMEs were more likely to adopt E-commerce than older ones. While the data is small, the Australian study found that it was older SMEs that were adopting E-commerce.

While the results for business sector and market focus were as expected, the low number of adopters meant that the findings in both categories must be considered with caution.

Three criteria, demand/pressure from suppliers, strengthen relations with business partners, availability of external technical support were removed as inapplicable to the study. As already indicated, the pilot study was carried out when many SMEs were undertaking E-commerce primarily to trade with larger organizations. As such, there was both pressure to adopt and some technical support to develop E-commerce. With the widening markets, this pressure to adopt appears to be no longer valid.

Of particular note is the criterion improving relationships with business partners (which also emerges as a benefit and its negative as a disadvantage). In all cases, there appears a 'culture' of remaining at arms length from business partners in the Australian SME sector.

Three other disadvantages were also rejected as inapplicable to the Australian study. As mentioned, the pilot study showed that E-commerce adoption was very often associated with trading with large organizations. This often reduced the flexibility of the E-commerce experience as the SME was 'locked into' a specific mode of operation, it meant a duplication of the work effort and resulted in higher costs. The extension of the E-commerce marketplace has reduced or eliminated these disadvantages so the SME can now dictate the terms of E-commerce rather than being dictated to.

The data gathered from goal 1 showed that two business characteristics, business sector and level of IT skill were associated with membership of a small business strategic alliance. While these results were found to support earlier findings in the literature, the relatively small sample sizes means that any conclusions based on the data must be made carefully.

The results of goal 2 showed that four criteria, pressure of competition, increased sales, reach new customers/markets, improvement in competitiveness showed a significant difference in the rating of applicability between respondents that were members of a small business strategic alliance and respondents that were not. Respondents that were not members of a small business strategic alliance rated these criteria as more applicable than respondents that were members.

The results showed that one barrier, cost too high, provided a significant difference in applicability between respondents that were members of a small business strategic alliance and respondents that were not.

The results showed that 3 benefits, increased sales, new customers/ markets and improved competitiveness showed a significant difference in applicability between respondents that were members of a small business strategic alliance and respondents that were not. An examination of the data, however, shows that it is the non-member respondents that consider the benefit more applicable to their situation than the member respondents. One possible explanation, supported by the literature is that these benefits were achieved through membership of a small business strategic alliance and thus were not perceived as a benefit of E-commerce adoption.

As the sample sizes for many of the goal 3 analyses were too small and the results for those analyses showed no consistent patterns, no sensible conclusions can be drawn about the data.

The results for goal 4 showed that only one criterion, reach new customers and markets was associated with business characteristics (for non-members only). The results show that it is the regionally focused respondents that rated the criterion higher than other respondents. The data also shows that the retail sector respondents rated the criterion higher than other respondents. In both cases the results are contrary to expectation and previous findings. However, the low adoption rates in the Australian study means that these results, at best, must be considered with caution.

Three barriers, lack of technical know-how, security risks and not sure what to choose are associated with business characteristics for non-member respondents only. Two of the barriers, lack of technical and not sure what to choose are associated wit IT skill. This result would be expected as both of the barriers are technical in nature. The result of the third barrier must be discounted as there was a higher than expected level of respondents in two business sectors only.

There was no association with either benefits or disadvantages.

Looking at the Australian study in isolation two significant observations can be made. The first is that the differences that exist between the pilot study in Australia and the detailed study reported appear to be temporal in that they are affected by external factors that change over time.

The second is that the results of the Australian study are in many cases contradictory to those in the literature. The most plausible explanation is a difference in 'business culture'. Similar differences in business culture are observed in Scotland (Drakopolou-Dodd et al 2002) and may be observed elsewhere.

Both these observations highlight the differences that may arise in E-commerce adoption due to external factors rather than due to internal business characteristics, widely cited in the literature.

The following section briefly examines differences in findings between the two studies.

6.4 A comparison of the two studies

This study was conducted in two locations, Karlstad, Sweden and Wollongong, Australia. The Swedish data has been presented in chapter 4 and Appendix 3, with an interpretive analysis of the findings presented in section 6.2. The Australian data has been presented in chapter 5 and Appendix 4, with an interpretive analysis of the findings presented in section 6.3.

The role of this section is not to repeat the findings detailed in other parts of this thesis but to note and discuss similarities and differences in the two sets of findings.

In line with section 6.2 and 6.3, this section is subdivided as follows:

- Section 6.4.1 provides a discussion of the studies
- Section 6.4.2 provides a discussion on the applicability of the criteria for E-commerce adoption, the barriers to E-commerce adoption, the benefits derived from E-commerce adoption and the disadvantages derived from E-commerce adoption with respect to both studies
- Section 6.4.3 provides a comparison of goal 1 with respect to the Australian and Swedish respondents, section 6.4.4 provides a comparison of goal 2 with respect to the Australian and Swedish respondents, section 6.4.5 provides a comparison of goal 3 with respect to the Australian and Swedish respondents

and section 6.4.6 provides a comparison of goal 4 with respect to the Australian and Swedish respondents

- Section 6.4.7 is the conclusion to the comparative examination.

6.4.1 A comparison of the respondents used of the studies

313 regional SMEs took part in the Swedish section of the study, 160 SMEs took part in the Australian section. A comparison of the adoption rates of the two studies shows that 55.3% of the Swedish respondents had adopted E-commerce, while only 15.6% of the Australian respondents had done likewise.

As already indicated, the Swedish uptake of E-commerce is higher than expected, while the Australians lower than expected. Explanations have been provided for the higher Swedish uptake. These include strong government and educational links with SMEs. Lower Australian uptake of E-commerce may be a product of failure to gather marketing and technical know-how from other countries (as suggested by Harvie et al 2003, Gibb 2000, Gilmore et al 2001).

A comparison of the two studies across business age, business size, business sector, market focus, **levels of IT skill** shows a number of interesting findings. In both studies there was an even spread across business age and business size, however, in both studies the predominant business size was 1 – 9 employees. In both studies there were few financial respondents and the largest single group was the service sector.

Perhaps most notable is the market focus of each of the studies. In the Swedish study, the largest single group was the locally focused respondents, accounting for 54.6% of the respondents. 9.9% of the Swedish respondents indicated that their focus was international. By comparison, the largest single group in the Australian study was the regional focus group with only one respondent (0.6%) indicating international focus.

Table A3.9 through A3.13 and A4.9 through A4.13 provided data concerning E-commerce adoption across the five business characteristics (business age, business size, business sector, market focus, **levels of IT skill**). Two comparisons are noteworthy. A comparison of Tables A3.10 and A4.10 provides the data concerning the adoption of E-commerce across the business size categories. An examination of the data in Table A3.10 and A4.10 shows that while a larger percentage of the respondents with employee numbers greater than 9 had adopted E-commerce in the Swedish study, no respondent with employee numbers greater than 9 had adopted E-commerce in the Australian study.

A comparison of Table A3.13 and A4.13 provides similar findings for IT skill level. Where most of the high and expert IT skill level respondents had adopted E-commerce in the Swedish study, the majority of similarly skilled respondents in Australia had not adopted E-commerce.

Respondents in both studies were asked whether they were members of a small business strategic alliance. 46.2% of the Swedish respondents indicated they were members, 30% of the Australian respondents did likewise.

6.4.2 Applicability of adoption factors (barriers to adoption, criteria for adoption, benefits of adoption or disadvantages of adoption) of E-commerce

As indicated in Sections 6.2.2 and 6.3.2, 14 criteria were examined for applicability to the respondents in each. Two criteria, *demand/pressure from suppliers* and *external technical support* were found to be inapplicable to respondents in both studies.

As already indicated, the development of adoption factors (criteria, barriers, benefits and disadvantages) began with the literature and was pilot tested on SMEs in Australia MacGregor et al 1998a,b). Notable, during the pilot study, was the pressure being placed on SMEs to adopt E-commerce in order to trade with larger organizations. In many case a 'carrot' of technical assistance was offered by the larger organizations. Clearly, with the widening of E-commerce markets, the pressure of simply doing business with larger organizations has been reduced or disappeared. Thus it is to be expected that these criteria would be less applicable than in the original pilot study.

Perhaps most notable amongst the criteria was *strengthening of relations with business partners*. While 46.5% of the Swedish respondents considered this criterion applicable to their situation, only 16% of the Australian respondents considered it of any applicability.

As has already been pointed out, there is a strong link in Sweden between government, education and SME owner/managers. This link, not apparent in Australia, appears to have fostered a 'business culture' of cooperation between SMEs in Sweden while a more competitive 'business culture' is the norm in Australia. This is borne out by the Australian respondent's rejection of the benefit strengthening relations with business partners and the rejection of its negative in the list of disadvantages. It is further borne out by the marked difference in the percentage of members of a small business strategic alliance.

8 barriers were tested for applicability to both studies. All barriers were applicable to both studies.

11 benefits derived from E-commerce adoption were tested for applicability to both studies. One benefit, *Reduced stock* was found to be inapplicable to both studies. An examination of Table 4.3 and 5.3 provides two interesting differences between the studies. 48% of the Australian respondents rated *improvement to marketing* as a benefit of E-commerce. By comparison, only 19.4% of the Swedish respondents rated it as applicable. One explanation, again, appears to be the government and education input into SME development.

41.5% of the Swedish respondents felt that the benefit *strengthening relations with business partners* was applicable to their situation. By comparison only 8% of Australians found this an applicable benefit. Again, this suggests a 'culture' amongst Australian respondents of greater independence or competitiveness compared to the Swedish respondents.

7 disadvantages derived from E-commerce adoption were tested for applicability to both respondents. An examination of Tables 4.4 and 5.4 shows that none of the disadvantages was applicable to the Swedish study and only 3 were applicable to the Australian study. As already stated, this raises a number of questions as to the appropriateness of previously cited disadvantages, derived from E-commerce adoption, to the regional SME sector.

The rejection of the disadvantages in the Swedish study suggests a discrepancy between Swedish and Australian SMEs, since the list of disadvantages was developed in an Australian pilot study. One explanation for these differences might be the larger proportion of SMEs in small business strategic alliances in Sweden, compared to Australia. Conceivably this may result in a broader acceptance of E-commerce and a dissipation of perceived disadvantages through mutual help. Similarly the greater involvement of the Swedish government may have gone some way to overcome some of the negative impacts of E-commerce adoption. Finally the significant role of universities in the education and development of SMEs in Sweden may have increased the skill base and thereby reduced the negative impact of E-commerce adoption. All of these would have reduced the perception of disadvantages in the Swedish study.

However, this explanation would not be expected to account for the removal of all of the disadvantages, so further study is needed to explain why the disadvantages have been totally rejected.

In the Australian study, one disadvantage, deterioration of relations with business partners has already been addressed. The inapplicability of the other 3 disadvantages appears to be related to the pilot study. As already indicated, SMEs used in the pilot study primarily adopted E-commerce to do business with larger organizations. Often this resulted in duplication of work, an inflexible form of E-commerce and an increased cost.

6.4.3 Goal 1

The first goal of the study was:
- To determine if the membership of small business strategic alliances is associated with business characteristics (business size, business age, business sector, market focus or the level of IT skill).

A comparison of the findings from the two studies shows that while business size and business age was significantly associated with membership of a small business strategic alliance in the Swedish study, business sector and levels of IT skill were associated with membership of a small business strategic alliance in the Australian study.

In the Swedish study, the relationship between business size and membership/non-membership of a small business strategic alliance is in the direction suggested in previous studies, i.e. it is the smaller SMEs that appear to be attracted to membership rather than the larger ones. A number of reasons have been put forward. These include the need for legitimacy and the need to gain expertise in marketing, technology and competitiveness. Added to this is an apparent strong government and educational input to provide some of this expertise.

By contrast, the business age relationship to small business strategic alliances is not in a single direction. Where the expectation would be for younger businesses to be attracted to a small business strategic alliance (and its inherent knowledge base), it is the older SMEs that appear to be moving towards membership. One possibility is that younger SMEs may be pre-occupied with establishing their businesses, and, with the expertise, in part being supplied by the government and educational bodies, there is less of a need to gravitate towards a small business strategic alliance.

The lack of relationship between other business characteristics and membership of a small business strategic alliance might also be explained by the higher than normal input of government and educational agencies.

In the Australian situation, the expected relationship between business age and business size were not apparent. This may, in part, be a product of the 'data mix' of the respondent sample. An examination of the respondent data in the Australian study showed that there was a far lower membership of small business strategic alliances, the sample had a higher concentration of retail and service respondents and a larger than expected number of smaller SMEs (<10 employees). This having been said, however, the data did show that there was an association between membership of a small business strategic alliance and the level of IT skill. Indeed, it was the high and expert IT skill levels that appeared to have gravitated towards small business strategic alliances, not the lower skill respondents. One possible explanation is that there is a stronger realization in the high/expert group that membership of a small business strategic alliance might bring about real value in terms of knowledge and expertise. Clearly, further study needs to be done to examine this possibility.

The results of the two studies show quite clearly a significant difference between SMEs in Sweden and Australia. These differences in many cases contradict those patterns suggested in the literature, indicating that the SME sector is not a homogeneous group.

6.4.4 Goal 2

The second goal of the study was:

- To determine whether the membership of small business strategic alliances alters perceptions of any of the adoption factors (barriers to adoption, criteria for adoption, benefits of adoption or disadvantages of adoption) of E-commerce technologies.

Table 6.1 provides the differences between the two studies.

Table 6.1

Differences in rating of applicability between respondents that were members of a small business strategic alliance and respondents that were not, for both the Swedish and Australian Study Population

	Sweden	Australia
Criteria		*pressure from competition*
		increased sales
		reach new customers /markets
		Improvement in competitiveness
Barriers		*cost too high*
Benefits		*increased sales*
		new customers/markets
		Improved competitiveness
Disadvantage		*computer maintenance*

An examination of Table 6.1 shows that there appeared to be no association between membership of a small business strategic alliance and any of the criteria, barriers, benefits or disadvantages for the Swedish study. By comparison, there was some association for certain criteria, barriers, benefits and disadvantages for the Australian study.

As already indicated, Swedish SMEs enjoy a far higher level of support by government and educational agencies than other comparable economies. This may have resulted in a greater awareness and realization of many of the criteria normally assigned to E-commerce uptake. If this were the case we would not expect significant differences to be found between members and non-members of a small business strategic alliance.

A similar argument could be made for benefits and barriers.

By contrast, four criteria were shown to be more applicable to members respondents in the Australian study. Again, one possible argument is that membership of a small business strategic alliance has heightened priorities in decision making concerned with E-commerce adoption.

While a similar argument may be made for the barriers to E-commerce adoption, the data showed that only one barrier, cost too high, appeared to be 'reduced' through membership of a small business strategic alliance. This raises the question as the applicability of small business strategic alliances, in terms of many of the other technical and organizational barriers concerned with E-commerce adoption.

Three benefits showed a significant difference in their applicability between respondents that were members of a small business strategic alliance and respondents that were not. A closer examination, however, shows that it was the non-members that reported higher perceptions of these benefits. One possible argument is that member respondents may have achieved these benefits through membership of the small business strategic alliance rather than through E-commerce adoption. This raises the question as to why the other benefits appeared not affected.

6.4.5 Goal 4

The fourth goal of the study was:
- To determine whether the associations between business characteristics (business size, business age, business sector, market focus or level of IT skills) and adoption factors (barriers to adoption, criteria for adoption, benefits of adoption or disadvantages of adoption) of E-commerce technologies differ, depending on whether the SME is part of a small business strategic alliance or not.

Table 6.3 provides the differences between respondents in the two studies.

Table 6.2

Business characteristics associated with <u>criteria</u>, <u>barriers</u>, <u>benefits</u> and <u>disadvantages</u> for both members and non-members of a small business strategic alliance, for the two studies

	Sweden	Australia
<u>Criteria</u>		
	Pressure from Competition (business size – non-members)	*Reach new customers/ markets* (market focus and business sector non-members)
	Improved to lead-time (Business size – non-members)	
	Improvement to Internal Efficiency business size, market focus non-members	
	Improvement to control and follow-up business age, business size members	
	Reduced cost business size non-members Level of IT skill members	
<u>Barriers</u>		
	E-commerce doesn't fit our prods/services (business sector – members)	*Lack of technical know how* (IT skill – non-members)
	Security (business sector – non-members)	*Not sure what to choose* (IT skill – non-members)
		Security (business sector – non-members)
<u>Benefits</u>		
<u>Disadvantages</u>		

An examination of the data in Table 6.2 shows that 5 criteria are associated with one or more business characteristics for the Swedish respondents. The criterion pressure from competition, shows an association with business age for non-member respondents. This is as would be expected from the literature, with younger SMEs more ready to alter their day-to-day activities to adjust to competition compared to older SMEs. The literature further suggests that the ability to change to suit market fluctuations is a product of membership of a small business strategic alliance. It is argued that where members of a small business strategic alliance have achieved this through their membership, non-members appear to be seeking this through adoption of E-commerce.

A similar argument can be made for improvement to lead-time and improvement to internal efficiency.

The criterion improvement to control and follow-up was found to be associated with business age and business size for member respondents only. This is contrary to expectation, the literature suggesting that members of a small business strategic alliance should have achieved this benefit with the alliance. One argument is that there is a heightened awareness of the potential of E-commerce by member respondents.

One criterion reduction in cost is associated with business size for non-members and IT skills for members. One possible argument for the 'shift' from business size to level of IT skill is that the combination of small business strategic alliance, government and tertiary involvement has allowed more integrated E-commerce solutions to be considered, while for non-members it is only the larger SMEs that can consider these same solutions.

Two barriers, security risks and E-commerce doesn't fit our products and services showed an association with business characteristics. The barrier security risks is associated with business sector for non-member respondents. Previous studies (Riquelme 2002) have noted that sectors, specifically the industrial sector were more apprehensive regarding the uptake of E-commerce than other sectors. One of the roles of a small business strategic alliance is to dissipate external turbulence that may be affecting their members. It is argued that concerns about security are dissipated through membership of a small business strategic alliance.

When considering the barrier E-commerce doesn't fit our products and services while government involvement in SMEs is primarily aimed at allowing them to become 'wired to the marketplace', it would appear that for the retail and service sectors government and small business strategic alliance intervention has shown members that E-commerce does not suit their specific needs.

For the Australian respondents, one criterion new customers and markets is associated with business sector and market focus. While the findings appear to support the literature, they need to be considered carefully because there was a higher than expected number of small SMEs and retail and service SMEs.

The results show that three barriers lack of technical support, not sure what to choose and security risks are associate with business characteristics. The finding for security can be discounted as there was a higher than expected number of retail and service sector respondents.

The barriers, Lack of Technical know-how and Not sure what to choose are associated with levels of IT skill. This result would be expected given that both of these barriers are technical in nature.

Again, the data in Table 6.3 shows that regional SMEs are far from a homogeneous group. While membership of a small business strategic alliance in Sweden meant that some adoption factors were associated with particular business characteristics, in Australia it was the non-member respondents that produced responses that showed an association between adoption factors and particular business characteristics.

6.4.7 Conclusion

A number of authors (Martin & Matlay 2001, Culkin & Smith 2000, Matlay & Fletcher 2000, Schuknecht & Perez-Esteve 1999) have criticized many of the government based SME E-commerce adoption models as taking a homogeneous approach to SMEs. They suggest that these government-based approaches fail to consider major differences in culture, ethnicity, location etc. that affect the decision making approaches made by SMEs.

Section 6.4 shows that despite similarities in population, infrastructure and economies, there are quite substantial differences in responses from the Australian and Swedish studies. These differences not only appear across the entire study samples, but also appear across categories of each of the business characteristics (i.e. certain business ages, business sizes, business sectors, market focuses, particular levels of IT skill).

The study has supported the notions of Martin & Matlay (2001), Culkin & Smith (2000), Matlay & Fletcher (2000), Schuknecht & Perez-Esteve (1999) that the SME sector is not a homogeneous one. As such, the literature that proposes the homogeneous application of small business strategic alliances must be questioned.

6.5 Conclusion

This chapter has presented an interpretive analysis of the two studies carried out in regional Sweden and Australia. Sections 6.2 and 6.3 have examined the data from the studies and compared this to previous findings in the literature. Section 6.4 has compared the relevant data between the two studies.

A number of important and sometimes unexpected results have come from the study.

The aim of the study was to examine the role of small business strategic alliances in the adoption of E-commerce in regional SMEs. Two similar regional locations were chosen, Karlstad in Sweden, Wollongong in Australia. The two locations were chosen as they had similar populations, similar infrastructures and similar OECD and World Bank ratings.

The first important result from the study was that despite these similarities, there were substantial differences both in the rate of adoption of E-commerce and the rate of membership of a small business strategic alliance.

Four sets of adoption factors, derived from the literature and tested in pilot interviews were applied to the study respondents to determine their applicability. The results show that a number of criteria and benefits were rejected as inapplicable to one or both study samples. Of particular importance was the inapplicability of all the disadvantages to the Karlstad respondents and the inapplicability of 4 of the 7 disadvantages to the Wollongong respondents. As has been pointed out, this raises serious questions as to the validity of these disadvantages to the SME sector as a whole.

Four goals were posed. The results of the first goal showed that differing business characteristics appeared to be associated with membership of a small business strategic alliance, for the two study samples. Again, this raises doubt as to the 'universality' of the effect of business characteristics on decisions to join a small business strategic alliance.

The second goal compared members and non-members across the four sets of adoption factors to determine whether small business strategic alliances do dissipate barriers and disadvantages, and whether they enhance benefits derived from E-commerce adoption. For the Karlstad respondents, no significant differences were found for any of the adoption factors. For the Wollongong study, some significant differences were found, however, many were contrary to expectation. These findings would suggest that not only are the two samples very different, but, more importantly, government predictions as to the role of small business strategic alliances were not applicable to either of the two regional SME study samples.

The third goal compared members and non-members across sub-groups of the five business characteristics (i.e. certain business ages, business sizes, business sectors, market focuses, particular levels of IT skill). In both study samples, significant differences were found for certain sub-groups of the business characteristics. However, again, many of these differences were contrary to expectation and no discernible pattern appeared in the data.

The final goal of the study was to determine if business characteristics (business age, business size, business sector, market focus and IT skill level) are associated with adoption factors differently, depending on whether the SME is part of a small business strategic alliance or not.

The results of this part of the study showed that Karlstad and Wollongong respondents appeared to be acting very differently.

In describing these results, this chapter has increased our understanding of the role of small business strategic alliances in decisions concerning E-commerce adoption and use by SMEs.

The final chapter presents conclusions of the research, the limitations of those conclusions and future directions for research in this field.

Chapter 7
Discussion and Conclusions

7.1 Introduction

The previous three chapters have presented the results of the current study and have used these to address the major goals of the study. This chapter summarizes those results and the conclusions drawn so far. The chapter also describes the significance of the research and the limitations of the study and suggests future directions for research.

The background to this study centred on criticisms in the literature of the appropriateness of government initiatives aimed at promoting E-commerce to SMEs. In particular, the purpose of this study was to examine whether small business strategic alliances were associated with adoption of E-commerce by regional SMEs, by comparing adoption by SMEs that are members of a small business strategic alliance and SMEs that are not.

In noting the recent research concerned with E-commerce adoption by regional SMEs, five business characteristics appeared throughout a variety of studies as impinging on the decision making process. These were the business age, the business size, the business sector, the market focus and the level of IT skill.

Four goals of the study were proposed:

The study involved the development of a questionnaire to provide data that would satisfy the goals of the study. The aim of the study was to examine the role of small business strategic alliances in the adoption of E-commerce in regional SMEs. Two similar regional locations were chosen, Karlstad in Sweden, Wollongong in Australia. The two locations were chosen as they had similar populations, similar infrastructures and similar OECD and World Bank ratings.

Four sets of adoption factors, derived from the literature and tested in pilot interviews were applied to the study respondents to determine their applicability. The results show that a number of criteria and benefits were rejected as inapplicable to one or both study samples. The removal of criteria and benefits from one or both of the study locations has been explained in several ways. Firstly, the original pilot study sample were, by and large adopting E-commerce to do business with larger organizations. In some cases the SMEs that took part in the original pilot study felt that they were under some pressure to adopt E-commerce, however, they also indicated that some external support was forthcoming. The widening of the E-commerce marketplace has reduced or eliminated the pressure and has removed the availability of external support.

For the Swedish study, the second reason for removal of some of the criteria and benefits has been the intervention of government and educational agencies into the SME sector. Studies have shown that unlike comparable locations I UK, US and Europe, there is a 'push' by the Swedish government to assist and enable SMEs to become 'wired to the marketplace'.

Finally, for the Australian respondents, there appears to be a competitive, rather than cooperative mentality among SMEs resulting in the elimination of criteria, benefits and disadvantages that were concerned with business partners. Similar findings have been reported in studies in Scotland (Drakopolou-Dodd et al 2002).

The methods and constructs described above were deemed appropriate to meet the four goals of the study. The results of the first goal showed that differing business characteristics appeared to be associated with membership of a small business strategic alliance, for the two study samples.

For the Swedish study, there was an association between business size and business age and membership of a small business strategic alliance. The association with business size was as predicted by previous studies in the literature. The lack of association with other business characteristics was explained by the higher than normal government and educational input into SMEs, particularly in areas such as marketing and technology use.

Of interest in the Swedish study was the finding that the association with business age was not in the expected direction. Unlike previous studies, it was older SMEs that appeared to be gravitating towards small business strategic alliances.

For the Australian study, there was a lower than expected level of membership of a small business strategic alliance (30%, N=48). Despite the low figures, one interesting finding was that high and expert IT level respondents were part of a small business strategic alliance, rather than those with lower IT skill.

The result of the second goal showed that not only are the two samples very different, but, more importantly, government predictions as to the role of small business strategic alliances were less than applicable to either of the two regional SME study samples.

For the Swedish study, there were no significant differences between respondents that were members of a small business strategic alliance and respondents that were not. This has been explained in terms of government and educational input to SMEs.

By comparison, the Australian study showed that some criteria, barriers, benefits and disadvantages were significantly different between respondents that were members of a small business strategic alliance and respondents that were not. While the criteria, barriers and disadvantages were as predicted by the literature, i.e. the small business strategic alliance appeared to have dissipated the effects of external problems, the benefits showed that it was the non-members that appeared to be gaining greater benefit from E-commerce than the members. One explanation is that some of the benefits may have been achieved through membership of the small business strategic alliance and were not perceived as a product of E-commerce adoption.

The third goal compared members and non-members across sub-groups of the five business characteristics (i.e. certain business ages, business sizes, business sectors, market focuses, particular levels of IT skill).

Results of the third goal showed that in many cases, members of a small business strategic alliance were 'worse off'. The data also showed that the two study samples differed in terms of adoption factors, in terms of business characteristics and in terms of sub-groups of those business characteristics. Indeed, the these findings support the notions of Martin & Matlay (2001), Culkin & Smith (2000), Matlay & Fletcher (2000), Schuknecht & Perez-Esteve (1999) that the regional SME sector cannot be viewed as a homogeneous.

The results of the final goal shows that in both studies there were different business characteristics that were associated with some of the adoption factors. For the Swedish respondents there appear to be three factors 'at work'. Firstly, as mentioned, there is a strong government and educational link with SMEs. This is supported in the literature. Secondly, it could be argued that this has led to a more cooperative approach between SMEs. Again, this is supported in the ratings of benefits and criteria related to business partnership. Finally, there is a stronger level of support for small business strategic alliances.

By comparison, the Australian study has shown a lower than expected adoption rate and an equally low membership level. There clearly exists an 'arms length' attitude between the SMES, this being supported both by the ratings and the level of membership of a small business strategic alliance.

7.2 Significance of the Study

The results of this study are significant in that it is the first time in the context of E-commerce adoption that members of a small business strategic alliance were compared to non-members of a small business strategic alliance. This significance is enhanced by the use of two similar regional locations.

In particular, the study is significant to three groups. These are:

- Government bodies promoting E-commerce adoption by regional SMEs in regional locations
- SMEs that are considering adopting E-commerce
- Information Systems researchers

7.2.1 Government bodies promoting E-commerce adoption by regional SMEs

There is a growing advocacy, at the government level, for SMEs to adopt and use E-commerce. This 'push' by government agencies is particularly directed towards regional SMEs as there is a perception that regional SMEs have fallen behind their city counterparts. Many of the strategies proposed by these government agencies are premised on regional SMEs developing small business strategic alliances. This study has presented a detailed comparison of E-commerce adoption by regional SMEs that are members of a small business strategic alliance and regional SMEs that are not. The results of this study strongly contradict the underlying assumptions and will provide these government agencies with a far clearer picture of the role of small business strategic alliances in the E-commerce adoption process.

7.2.2 SMEs that are considering adopting E-commerce

The results of the study are of significance to SMEs that are considering adopting E-commerce by making them aware of the limitations of membership of a small business strategic alliance. The data has shown that while certain barriers and disadvantages may be 'dissipated' through membership of a small business strategic alliance, others appear unaffected, or, worse, even heightened, through membership of a small business strategic alliance.

7.2.3 Information Systems Researchers

This study has reported on the structure and role of small business strategic alliances in the adoption of E-commerce by regional SMEs. Furthermore, the study has used two locations in the data gathering and subsequent discussions. In doing so, the study has raised a number of interesting research issues.

Firstly, the study showed that in both studies, membership of a small business strategic alliance appeared only to be associated with changes in ratings of applicability of criteria, barriers, benefits or disadvantages for certain subgroups of the SME study populations, rather than the entire sample. These findings contradict a number of earlier assumptions concerning the role of small business strategic alliances. Additional studies need to be carried out to confirm or reject the results of this study.

Secondly, this study concentrated on five business characteristics, found in the literature. These were business age, business size, business sector, market focus and levels of IT skill. The study has called into question the effect of these business characteristics. A number of findings produced during this study have suggested that other factors such as national/cultural differences might be associated both with the membership of a small business strategic alliance as well as E-commerce adoption. Further studies need to be undertaken to determine the role of these factors. Other factors that might be considered in the future are the gender and level of education of the CEO.

One of the findings of the study was that many of the previously accepted disadvantages were inapplicable to the Karlstad and Wollongong regional samples. Clearly, a re-examination of the disadvantages associated with E-commerce adoption by SMEs needs to be undertaken.

Finally, the study has shown that there are differences in the data from the two study locations. The results seem to suggest that the strong government and educational input into SMEs has resulted in a more cooperative relationship between the SMEs themselves in Sweden. The results also point to a far less cooperative, stand-alone attitude by the Australian respondents. While the surveys did not explicitly seek this information, there is strong evidence, both in the relative importance placed on relationships with business partners and the level of membership of small business strategic alliances to point to these conclusions.

Several statistical results of this study were unexpected and warrant further investigation. For example, several criteria and benefits were found inapplicable to both respondent populations, while others were deemed inapplicable to one study sample only. Similarly, four disadvantages were deemed inapplicable to both samples.

The apparent differences in the two studies raises the question as to the effect of government and educational intervention in the SME sector. It appears that not only has this intervention provided the Swedish respondents with a substantial technical and marketing advantage, but it has engendered a more cooperative approach to the sharing of that knowledge through business partnerships and membership of small business strategic alliances. This is clearly evident in comparisons of the data from the two studies.

In addition to raising a number of research issues, this study make several contributions by establishing test procedures that would be of significance to other researchers. There appear to be few, if any, studies that have attempted to compare respondents that were members of a small business strategic alliance and respondents that were not in an E-commerce setting. The results of this study provide a benchmark for future research.

7.3 Limitations of the study

As was pointed out (Section 1.4) a number of theoretical frameworks, including TAM, Diffusion of Innovation and Grounded Theory were explored. In all cases, these were found to be inadequate frameworks on which to conduct the current study. It is argued that a number of previous studies into the adoption of E-commerce (Teo & Tan 1998, Kinder 2002, Daniel 2003, Shiels et al 2003) have expressed similar views. The arguments for this are detailed in Section 1.4. As this study, it is hoped, will lead to a greater understanding of E-commerce adoption in regional SMEs, the normal hypothesis has been replaced by 4 goals that have been tested both in the literature and through pilot studies prior to the commencement of this study. This having been said, a number of limitations are noted.

- As the study questions were part of a larger study, many possible respondents may have been 'put off' by the size of the overall questionnaire. Higher percentage returns may have been achievable if the study detailed herein had been conducted separately.

- The study is reliant on responses of a single person, usually the owner/manager of the SME. Perceptions such as level of IT skill may be different for other employees.
- The low E-commerce uptake figures in the Australian study prevented data analyses that had been possible in the Swedish study
- Subjects were randomly chosen in both locations resulting in some sub-groups having less than adequate data to conduct reasonable analyses.

7.4 Future research

Given that the current research is an exploratory study, there are a significant number of areas for future research. Several have been implied in the discussion of significance to information systems researchers.

The current research has examined the nature and role of small business strategic alliances in the adoption of E-commerce by regional SMEs. This has been considered across two studies and across five business characteristics within each of those studies. As indicated, a number of alternative taxonomies for small business strategic alliances have been developed since the current research was started. Research using these taxonomies would significantly enhance and refine the current findings.

A number of other factors such as sex and educational level of the CEO have been suggested as possibly being associated with E-commerce adoption as well as membership of a small business strategic alliance (Trauth 2002, MacGregor 2004, McIvor & Humphreys 2004). A study examining the roles of these additional factors could be fruitful.

The use of two study locations has provided different findings. These differences and their impact on E-commerce adoption and use in regional SMEs needs to be examined. The results of such a study would elicit reasons for these differences and would add to our understanding of the role of small business strategic alliances.

Finally, the statistical results concerned with the applicability of criteria, barriers, benefits and disadvantages have given rise to a number of possible areas of research. Several criteria, benefits and disadvantages were found to be inapplicable to one or both study locations. Studies need to be undertaken to determine why these are inapplicable, particularly those criteria, benefits and disadvantages that were inapplicable for only one study population.

7.5 Conclusion

A number of results were forthcoming from the two sets of study respondents. Some of these results were as predicted from previous studies in the literature, some were unexpected.

The objectives of the study were to examine the relationships between small business strategic alliances and E-commerce adoption factors and between small business strategic alliances and business characteristics.

Despite popular wisdom suggesting that small business strategic alliances reduced disadvantages and barriers to E-commerce adoption and increased the perception of benefits derived from E-commerce adoption, the results show that, for the most part this was not found in either of the studies. In the Swedish study there was no association between membership of a small business strategic alliance and any of the adoption factors (criteria, barriers, benefits or disadvantages). In the Australian study, while four criteria and one barrier showed some association with membership of a small business strategic alliance, the association found for the benefits was actually in the opposite direction to that predicted in the literature, i.e. it was the non-members that rated benefits higher.

Earlier studies in the literature predicted membership of a small business strategic alliance to be associated with business characteristics such as business size, business age, business sector, market focus and level of IT skill. Neither market focus nor business sector showed any association with membership for either of the studies. Indeed, while the association with business size was as predicted in the literature, the associations with business age and level of IT skill were in the opposite directions to those predicted.

The studies cast considerable doubt on the applicability of disadvantages found in the literature. In the Swedish study, all disadvantages were rejected as inapplicable to the study sample, while 4 of the 7 disadvantages were likewise rejected by the Australian study sample group. The study also raises some doubt concerning the applicability of certain criteria and benefits found in previous studies. Indeed, the only adoption factors that seemed to match previous findings were the barriers to E-commerce adoption.

There have been a number of studies that have suggested that market focus is strongly associated with the adoption of E-commerce in SMEs. This was not found in either of the studies. Indeed, at best, only a few criteria and barriers appeared to be associated with any of the business characteristics, while none of the benefits showed an association with any of the business characteristics.

This study began by examining the components of many of the government initiatives promoting E-commerce adoption in SMEs. One of the components was the development of small business strategic alliances, which, it was argued, reduced barriers to E-commerce adoption, and increased the benefits derivable from such an adoption. The results of both these studies shows that not only is this perception questionable, but as the SME sector is so varied, any single approach to E-commerce adoption is likewise questionable.

This study has demonstrated that, even in environments that are economically similar, SMEs are an incredibly heterogeneous group. Their behaviours vary depending upon their level of mutual cooperation or mutual competition. They vary because of external factors such as support from tertiary institutions, and government agencies. They vary because of differences in the way they are treated by large business partners, and, as has been shown, they vary with time, as problems and opportunities quickly alter in the SME sector.

The results of the studies show that we cannot define a universally applicable set of characteristics that explains E-commerce adoption among SMEs. Nor do they show that we can define a single set of characteristics that explain why SMEs form alliances. They show that the role of alliances is far from universal or predictable across E-commerce adoption factors, and perhaps most importantly, they show that we cannot produce a single universal plan to get SMEs to adopt E-commerce because they are demonstrably non-homogeneous in nature.

References

Abell W. & Lim L. (1996) Business Use of the Internet in New Zealand: An Exploratory Study http//www.scu.edu.au/sponsored/ausweb96

Achrol R.S. & Kotler P. (1999) Marketing in the Network Economy **Journal of Marketing** vol 63 (special issue), pp 146 - 163

Acs Z.J., Morck R., Shaver J.M. & Yeung B (1997) The Internationalisation of Small and Medium Sized Enterprises: A Policy Perspective **Small Business Economics** vol 9, no. 1, pp 7 - 20

Adams W. (1972) New Role for top management in computer applications **Financial Executive** April, pp 54 - 56

Alavi M. (1984) An Assessment of the Prototyping Approach to Information Systems Development **Communications of the ACM** vol 27, pp 556 - 563

Aldridge A., White M & Forcht K. (1997) Security Considerations of Doing Business Via the Internet: Cautions to be Considered **Internet Research-Electronic Networking Applications and Policy** vol 7 – no. 1, p 9 - 15

Amer T.S. & Bain C.E. (1990) Making Small Business Planning Easier **Journal of Accountancy** pp 53 - 60

Amoaka-Gyampah K. & White K.B. (1993) User Involvement & Satisfaction **Information & Management**

Auger P.& Gallaugher J.M. (1997) Factors Affecting Adoption of an Internet-based Sales Presence for Small Businesses **The Information Society** vol 13, no. 1, pp 55 - 74

Australian Bureau of Statistics (2001) URL: www.abs.gov.au, Accessed December 10, 2003.

Bailey J.E. & Pearson S.W. (1983) The Development of a tool for Measuring and Analysing Computer User Satisfaction **Management Science** vol 29, no. 5, p 530 - 545

Baker W.E. (1990) Market Networks and Corporate Behavior **Applied Journal of Sociology** vol 3, pp 589 – 625

Bakos Y. (1998) The Emerging Role of Electronic Marketplaces on the Internet **Communications of the ACM** vol 41, August, pp 35 - 42

Bakos Y. & Brynjolfsson E. (2000) Bundling and Competition on the internet **Marketing Science** vol 19, no. 1, pp 63 - 82

BarNir A. & Smith K.A. (2002) Interfirm Alliances in the Small Business: The Role of Social Networks **Journal of Small Business Management** vol 40, no. 3, pp 219 - 232

Baroudi J.J., Olson M.H. & Ives B. (1986) An Empirical Study of the impact of user involvement on   system usage and information satisfaction' **Communications of the ACM** vol 29, no 3, pp   232 - 238

Barnett R.R. & Mackness J.R.: (1983), An Action Research Study of Small Firm **Management Journal of Applied Systems** 10: 63 - 83

Barry H. & Milner B. (2002) SME's and Electronic Commerce: A Departure from the Traditional Prioritisation of Training? **Journal of European Industrial Training** vol 25, no. 7, pp 316 - 326

Barry J, Berg E & Chandler J (2003) Managing Intellectual Labour in Sweden and England **Cross Cultural Management** Vol 10, no. 3, pp 3 - 22

Bennett R & Robson P. (1998) External Advice and Business Links in Cosh A. & Hughes A. (eds) **Enterprise Britain, Growth, Innovation and Public Policy in the Small and Medium Sized Enterprise Sector 1994 – 1997** ESRC Centre for Business Research, Cambridge

Bergeron F & Berube C. (1988) The Management of the End-User Environment: An Empirical Investigation **TIMS/ORSA**

Bergeron F., Rivard S. & De Serre L. (1990) Investigating the Support Role of the Information Centre **MIS Quarterly**

Bijmolt T. & Zwart P (1994) The Impact of External Factors on the Export Success of Dutch Small and Medium Sized Firms **Journal of Small Business Management** pp 69-83

Bird S.R., Sapp S.G. & Lee M.Y (2001) Small Business Success in Rural Communities: Explaining the Sex Gap **Rural Sociology** vol 66, no. 4, pp 507 - 531

Black J.S. & Porter L.W. (2000) **Management: Meeting New Challenges** Prentice Hall, NJ

Blackburn R. & Athayde R. (2000) Making the Connection: The Effectiveness of Internet Training in Small Businesses **Education and Training** vol 42, no. 4/5

Blair T. (2000) UK Prime Minister, Press release re the launch of UK Online opengov site 11th September

Blili, S. and Raymond, L. (1993) Threats and Opportunities for Small and Medium-Sized Enterprises, **International Journal of Information Management**, 13, 439-448.

Bradbard D.A., Norris D.R. & Kahai P.H. (1990) Computer Security in Small Business: An Empirical Study **Journal of Small Business Management** Vol, 28, No.1, pp 9 - 19

Brigham E.F.: & Smith K.V. (1967), The cost of capital to the small firm **The Engineering Economist** vol. 13, no. 1: 1 - 26

Bunker D.J. & MacGregor R.C. (2000) Successful Generation of Information Technology (IT) Requirements for Small/Medium Enterprises (SME's) – Cases from Regional Australia **Proceedings of SMEs in a Global Economy** Wollongong, Australia, pp 72 – 84

Burton F., Chen Y. & Grover V. (1993) An Application of Expectancy Theory for Assessing User Motivation to Utilise an Expert System **Journal of Management Information Systems**

Canadian Small Business Guide (1984) C.C.H. Limited, Toronto, Canada

Chau P.Y.K. & Hui K.L (2001) Determinants of Small Business EDI Adoption: AN Empirical Investigation **Journal of Organisational Computing and Electronic Commerce** vol 11, no. 4, pp 229 – 252

Chellappa R., Barua A. & Whinston A (1996) Looking Beyond Internal Corporate Web Servers in Kalakota R. & Whinston A. (eds) **Readings in Electronic Commerce** Addison Wesley, Reading MA, pp 311 - 321

Chen J.C.: (1993) The impact of microcomputers on small businesses: England 10 years later **Journal of Small Business Management** vol. 31, no. 3: 96 - 102

Chen J.P., Diehl V.A. & Norman K.L (1988) Development of an instrument measuring user satisfaction of human-computer interface **Human Factors in Computing Systems,**

Cochran A.B. (1981) Small Business Mortality Rates: A Review of the Literature **Journal of Small Business Management** vol 19, no 4, pp 50 - 59

Christopher M.L. (1999) Creating the Agile Supply Chain in Anderson D.L. (ed) **Achieving Supply Chain Excellence Through Technology** Montgomery Research Inc, San Francisco CA, pp 28 - 32

Clarke R (1994) Electronic Support for the Practice of Research **Information Society** vol 10, no. 1, pp 25 - 42

Cooper B.E. (1969) **Statistics for Experimentalists** Pergamon Press, UK

Copp C.B. & Ivy R.L. Networking Trends of Small Tourism Businesses in Post-socialist Slovakia **Journal of Small Business Management** vol 39, no. 4, pp 345 - 353

Cragg P.B. & King M. 1993, Small Firm Computing: Motivators and Inhibitors **MIS Quarterly** vol. 17, no. 1 pp 47 - 60

Cropper S. (1996) Collaborative Working and the Issue of Sustainability in Huxham C. (ed) **Creating Collaborative Advantage** Sage, London, pp 80 - 100

Culkin N. & Smith D. (2000) An Emotional Business: A Guide to Understanding the Motivations of Small Business Decision Takers **Qualitative Market Research: An International Journal** vol. 3, no. 3, pp 145 - 157

Dahlstrand A.L. (1999) Technology-based SMEs in the Goteborg Region: Their Origin and Interaction with Universities and Large Firms **Regional Studies** vol 33, no. 4, pp 379 - 389

Dalli D. (1994) The Exporting Process: The Evolution of Small and Medium Sized Firms Towards Internationalisation **Advances in International Marketing** vol 6, pp 85 - 110

Damanpour F. (2001) E-Business E-Commerce Evolution: Perspective and Strategy **Managerial Finance** vol 27, no. 7, pp 16 - 33

Daniel E. (2003) An Exploration of the Inside-Out Model: E-commerce Integration in UK SMEs **Journal of Small Business and Enterprise Development** vol 10, no. 3, pp 233 - 249

Datta D, (1988) International Joint Ventures: A Framework for Analysis **Journal of General Management** vol 14, pp 78 - 91

Davis F.D (1989) Perceived Usefulness, Perceived Ease of Use and User Acceptance of Information Technology **MIS Quarterly** Sept. pp 319 - 340

Dean J., Holmes S. & Smith S. (1997) Understanding Business Networks: Evidence from Manufacturing and Service Sectors in Australia **Journal of Small Business Management** vol 35, no. 1, pp 79 - 84

Delone W.H.: (1988), Determinants for Success for Computer Usage in Small Business **MIS Quarterly** : 51 - 61

DelVecchio M.: (1994), Retooling the Staff along with the system **Bests Review** vol. 94, no. 11: 82 - 83

Dennis C. (2000) Networking for Marketing Advantage **Management Decision** vol 38, no. 4, pp 287 - 292

Desanctis G. (1983) Expectancy Theory as an Explanation of Voluntary Use of a Decision Support System **Psychological Reports** vol 52, pp 247 - 260

Desanctis G. & Courtney J.F. (1983) Towards Friendly User MIS Implementation **Communications of the ACM** vol 26, no 10, p 732 - 738

Dibb S. (1997) How Marketing Planning Builds Internal Networks **Long Range Planning** vol 30, no. 1, pp 53 - 64

Dignum F. (2002) E-Commerce in Production: Some Experiences **Integrated Manufacturing Systems** vol 13, no. 5, pp 283 - 294

Ditsa G.E.M. (1994) Measures of User Acceptance of Information Systems, Master of Commerce Dissertation, University of Wollongong

Dobbers P. & Strannegard L. (2001) Loveable Networks – A Story of Affection, Attraction and Treachery **Journal of Organisational Change Management** vol. 14, no. 1, pp 28 - 49

Doll W.J. & Torkzadeh G. (1988) The Measurement of End-user Computing Satisfaction **MIS Quarterly** vol 12, no 2, pp 259 - 274

Domke-Damonte D. & Levsen V.B. (2002) The Effect of Internet Usage on Cooperation and Performance in Small Hotels **SAM Advanced Management Journal** summer, pp 31 - 38

Donckels R. & Lambrecht J. (1997) The Network Position of Small Businesses: An Explanatory Model **Journal of Small Business Management** vol 35, no. 2, pp 13 - 28

Doukidis G.I., Smithson S. & Naoum G. (1992) Information systems management in Greece: Issues and perceptions **Journal of Strategic Information Systems** 1: pp 139 - 148

Doukidis G., Poulymenakou A., Terpsidis I, Themisticleous M. & Miliotis P. (1998) **The Impact of the Development of Electronic Commerce on the Employment Situation in European Commerce** Athens University of Economics and Business

Drakopoulou-Dodd S. Jack S. & Anderson A.R. (2002) Scottish Entrepreneurial Networks in the International Context **International Small Business Journal** vol 20, no. 2, pp 213 - 219

Eid R., Trueman M. & Ahmed A.M. (2002) A Cross-Industry Review of B2B Critical Success Factors **Internet Research: Electronic Networking Applications and Policy** vol 12, no. 2, pp 110 - 123

Europa – The European Commission (2003) **SME Definition**, URL: http://europa.eu.int/comm/ enterprise/enterprise_policy/sme_definition/index_en.htm, Accessed December 15, 2003.

European Commission (1999) Strategies for Jobs in the Information Society www.europa

European Commission (2000) European Survey of the Information Society **European Society Indicators in the Member States of the EU** http.www.europa.eu.in/ISPO/esis

Evans P.B. & Wurster T.S. (1997) Strategy and the New Economics of Information **Harvard Business Review** Sept-Oct, pp 70 – 82

Farhoomand A.F., Tuunainen V.K. & Yee L.W. (2000) Barriers to Global Electronic Commerce: A Cross-Country Study of Hong Kong and Finland **Journal of Organisational Computing and Electronic Commerce** vol 10, no. 1, pp 23 - 48

Faia-Correia L. Patriotta G., Brigham M & Corbett J.M. (1999) Making Sense of Telebanking Information Systems: The Role of Organisational Backup **Journal of Strategic Information Systems** vol 8, pp 143 - 156

Fallon M. & Moran P (2000) Information Communications Technology (ICT) and manufacturing SMEs **2000 Small Business and Enterprise Development Conference** University of Manchester, pp 100 - 109

Filho W.L., Larsen K & Snickars F. (2000) A Survey of Requirements and Needs in the Field of Environmental Technology, with Special Emphasis on Environmental Employment in Sweden **Environmental Management and Health** vol 11, no. 4, pp 369 - 381

Fink D. & Tjarka F. (1994) Information Systems Contribution to Business Performance: A Study of Information Systems Executives' Attitudes **Australian Journal of Information Systems** vol 2, no 1, pp 29 - 38

Fletcher D. (2000) Family and Enterprise in Carter S. & Jones D. **Enterprise and Small Business: Principles, Policy and Practice** Addison Welsy Longman, London

Fletcher D. (2002) A Network Prespective of Cultural Organising an 'Professional Management' in the Small Family Business **Journal of Small Business & Enterprise Development** vol. 9, no. 4, pp 400 - 415

Fuller T. (2000) The Small Business Guide to the Internet: A Practical Approach to Going Online **International Small Business Journal** vol 19, no. 1, pp 105 – 107

Galliers R.D. & Land F.F. (1987) Choosing Appropriate Information Systems Research Methodologies **Communications of the ACM** vol 30, no. 11, pp 900 - 902

Gaskill L.R., Van Auken H.E. & Kim H. (1993) The Impact of Operational Planning on Small Business Retail Performance **Journal of Small Business Strategy** vol 5, no. 1, pp 21 – 35

Gaskill L.R. & Gibbs R.M. (1994) Going Away to College and Wider Urban Job Opportunities Take Highly Educated Youth Away fro Rural Areas **Rural Development Perspectives** vol 10 10, no. 3, pp 35 - 44

Gessin J. (1996) Impact of Electronic Commerce on Small and Medium Sized Enterprises **Management** Jan-Feb pp 11 - 12

Giaglas G., Klein S. & O'Keefe R. (1999) Disintermediation, Reintermediation, or Cybermediation? The Future of Intermediaries in Electronic Marketplaces **12ᵗʰ Bled Electronic Commerce Conference**

Gibb A. (1993) Small Business Development in Central and Eastern Europe – Opportunity for a Rethink **Journal of Business Venturing** vol 8, pp 461 - 486

Gibbons-Wood D. & Lange T. (2000) Developing Core Skills – Lessons from Germany and Sweden **Education & Training** vol 42, no. 1, pp 24 - 32

Gilliland D.I. & Bello D.C. (1997) The Effect of Output Controls, Process Controls, And Flexibility on Export Channel Performance **Journal of Marketing** vol 6, no. 1, pp 22 - 38

Gimeno J & Woo C.Y (1999) Multimarket Contact, Economies of Scope, and Firm Performance **Academy of Management Journal** vol 42, no. 3, pp 239 - 259

Ginzberg M.J. (1978) Steps towards more effective implementation of MS and MIS **INTERFACES** vol 8, no. 3, p57 - 63

Ginzberg M.J. (1981) Key Recurrent Issues in MIS Implementation Program **MIS Quarterly** vol 5 no   2, p 47 - 59

Glaser B. (1992) **The Basics of Grounded Theory Analysis** Sociology Press, CA

Golden P.A. & Dollinger M. (1993) Cooperative Alliances and Competitive Strategies in Small Manufacturing Firms **Entrepreneurship Theory and Practice** Summer, pp 43 - 56

Gulati R. & Garino J. (2000) Get the Right Mix of Bricks and Clicks **Harvard Business Review** May-June, pp 107 - 114

Gulledge T. & Sommer R (1998) Electronic Commerce Resource an Industry and University Partnership, Research paper, ECRC, Fairfax, VA

Gustafsson R, Klefsjo B., Berggren E. & Granfors-Wellemets U. (2001) Experiences from Implementing ISO 9000 in Small Enterprises – A Study of Swedish Experiences **The TQM Magazine** vol 13, no. 4, pp 232 - 246

Hadjimonolis A. (1999) Barriers to Innovation for SMEs in a Small Less Developed Country (Cyprus) **Technovation** vol 19, no. 9, pp 561 - 570

Harvie C., Aylward D., Gregory G., Lee B.C., MacGregor R.C. & Vrazalic L. (2003) Profiling Successful SME Exporters **Project Funded by NSW Department of State and Regional Development** 30pp

Hawkins P., Winter J. & Hunter J. (1995) **Skills for Graduates in the 21ˢᵗ Century** Report Commissioned from the Whiteway Research, University of Cambridge, Association of Graduate Recruiters, Cambridge

Hawkins P. & Winter J. (1996) The Self Reliant Graduate and the SME **Education and Training** vol 38, no. 4, pp 3 – 9

Henning K. (1998) **The Digital Enterprise. How Digitisation is Redefining Business** Random House Business Books, New York

Hill R. & Stewart J. (2000) Human Resource Development in Small Organisations **Journal of European Industrial Training** vol 24, no. 2/3/4, pp 105 - 117

Hitt M.A., Ireland D.R. & Hoskisson R.E. (1999) **Strategic Management** Southwestern Publishing Cincinnati OH

Holzinger A.G. & Hotch R.: (1993), Small Firms Usage Patterns **Nations Business** vol. 81, no. 8: 39 - 42

Hutt M.D. & Speh T.W. (1998) **Business Marketing Management: A Strategic View of Industrial and Organisational Markets** Dryden Press, Fort Worth Texas

Hyland T. & Matlay H. (1997) Small Businesses, Training needs and VET Provisions **Journal of Education and Work** vol 10, no. 2

Iacovou C.L., Benbasat I. & Dexter A.S. (1995) Electronic Data Interchange and Small Organisations: Adoption and Impact of Technology **MIS Quarterly** vol 19, no. 4, pp 465 - 485

Igbaria M. (1993) User acceptance of microcomputer technology: An empirical test **International   Journal of Management Science** 21: pp 73 - 90

Ives B., Olsen M.H. & Baroudi J.J. (1983) The Measurement of User Information Satisfaction **Communications of the ACM** vol 26, no. 10, p 785 - 793

Jarratt D.G. (1998) A Strategic Classifiaction of Business Alliances: A Qualitative Perspective Built from a Study of Small and Medium-sized Enterprises **Qualitative Market Research: An International Journal** vol 1, no. 1, pp 39 - 49

Javenpaa S. & Ives B. (1991) Executive Involvement and Participation in the Management of Information Technology **MIS Quarterly**

Jeffcoate J., Chappell C. & Feindt S. (2002) Best Practice in SME Adoption of E-Commerce **Benchmarking: An International Journal** vol 9, no. 2, pp 122 – 132

Jenkins M. (1985) Research Methodologies and MIS Research in Mumford E. et al **Research Methodologies in Information Systems** Elsevier, North Holland

Johansson, U. (2003) **Regional Development in Sweden: October 2003**, Svenska Kommunförbundet,   URL: http://www.lf.svekom.se/tru/RSO/Regional_development_in_Sweden.pdf,   Accessed December 14, 2003.

Johannisson B., Ramirez-Pasillas M. & Karlsson G. (2002) Theoretical and Methodological Challenges Bridging Firm Strategies and Contextual Networking **Entrepreneurship and Innovation** August pp 165 - 174

Jorde T. & Teece D. (1989) Competition and Cooperation: Striking the Right Balance **Californian Management Review** vol 31 pp 25 - 38

Kai-Uwe Brock J. (2000) Information and Technology in the Small Firm in Carter S. & Jones-Evans (eds) **Enterprise and the Small Business** Prentice Hall, Pearson Education, pp 384 - 408

Kalakota R. & Whinston A. (1997) **Electronic Commerce: A Manager's Guide** Addison Wesley, Reading MA

Keeble D., Lawson C., Moore B & Wilkinson F. (1999) Collective Learning Processes, Networking and 'Institutional Thickness' in the Cambridge Region **Regional Studies** vol 33, no. 4, pp 319 - 332

Keeley R.H. & Knapp R (1995) Success and Failure of Start-up Companies: A Longitudinal Study in Bygrave W.D, Bird B.J, Birley S., Churchill N.C. Hay M.G., Keeley R.H. & Wetzel W.E.jr (eds) **Frontiers of Entrepreneurship Research** Babson College of Entrepreneurial Study, MA

Keen P.G.W (1987) MIS Research: Current Status, Trend and Needs in Buckingham et al (eds) **Information Systems Education: Recommendations and Implementation** Cambridge University Press, pp 1 - 13

Kendall J.E. & Kendall K.E. (2001) A Paradoxically Peaceful Coexistence Between Commerce and Ecommerce **Journal of Information Technology, Theory and Application** vol 3, no. 4, pp 1 – 6

Keniry, J., Blums, A., Notter, E., Radford, E. & Thomson, S. (2003) **Regional Business – A Plan for Action**, Department of Transport and Regional Services, URL: http://www.rbda.gov.au/ action_plan, Accessed December 13, 2003.

Khan E.H. & Khan G.M.: (1992), Microcomputers and Small Businesses in **Bahrain Industrial Management and Data Systems** vol. 92, no. 6: pp 24 – 28

Kinder T (2002) Emerging E-commerce Business Models: An Analysis of Case Studies from West Lothian Scotland **European Journal of Innovation Management** vol 5, no. 3, pp 131 - 150

Kjellberg Y, Soderstrom M & Svensson L. (1998) Training and Development in the Swedish Context: Structural Change and a New Paradigm? **Journal of European Industrial Training** pp 205 - 216

Klatt L.A. (1973) **Small Business Management: Essential in Entrepreneurship** Wadsworth, CA

Klofsten M (2000) Training Entrepreneurship at Universities: A Swedish Case **Journal of European Industrial Training** pp 337 - 344

Kuljis J., Macredie R. & Paul R.J. (1998) Information Gathering Problems in Multinational Banking **Journal of Strategic Information Systems** vol 7, pp 233 - 245

Kulmala H.I., Paranko J. & Uusi-Rauva E. (2002) The Role of Cost Management in Network Relationships **International Journal of Production Economics** vol 79, no. 1, pp 33 - 43

Lauder G. & Westhall A. (1997) Small Firms Online **Commission on Public Policy in British Business** no. 6

Larsson, E., Hedelin, L. & Gärling, T. (2003) Influence of Expert Advice on Expansion Goals of Small Businesses in Rural Sweden, **Journal of Small Business Management**, 41(2), 205-212.

Lawrence K.L. (1997) Factors Inhibiting the Utilisation of Electronic Commerce Facilities in Tasmanian Small-to-Medium Sized Enterprises **8th Australasian Conference on Information Systems** pp 587 - 597

Lawson R, Alcock C., Cooper J. & Burgess L. (2003) Factors Affecting the Adoption of Electronic Commerce Technologies by SMEs: An Australian Study **Journal of Small Business and Enterprise Development** vol. 11, no. 2, pp 265 - 276

Lee C.S. (2001) An analytical Framework for Evaluating E-commerce Business Models and Strategies **Internet Research: Electronic Network Applications and Policy** vol 11, no. 4, pp 349 - 359

Lee J. & Runge J. (2001) Adoption of Information Technology in Small Business: Testing Drivers of Adoption for Entrepreneurs **Journal of Computer Information Systems** vol 42, no. 1, pp 44 - 57

Lucas H.C. jr (1978) Empirical Evidence for a Descriptive Model of Implementation **MIS Quarterly** vol 2, No. 2, p 27 - 41

McDoniel P.L., Palko J. & Cronan T.P. (1993) Information Systems Develoment: Issues Affecting Success **Journal of Computer Information Systems** Fall, p 50 - 62

MacGregor R.C. (2004) Factors Associated with Formal Networking in Regional Small Business: Some Findings from a Study of Swedish SMEs, **Journal of Small Business and Enterprise Development**, vol 11, no. 1, pp 60 - 74

MacGregor R.C. (2004) The Role of Formal Networks in the ongoing use of Electronic Commerce Technology in Regional Small Business, **Journal of Electronic Commerce in Organisations,** vol 2, no. 1, pp 1 - 14

MacGregor R.C. & Cocks R.S. (1994) Veterinary Computer Education Requirements: A Survey **Australian Veterinary Practitioner** vol 24 no 1, pp 41 - 46,

MacGregor R.C. & Bunker D.J. (1996a) Does Experience with IT Vendors/Consultnts Influence Small Business Computer Education Requirements **Association of Information Systems Proceedings of the Americas Conference on Information Systems** Phoenix Arizona pp31 - 33

MacGregor R.C. & Bunker D.J.(1996b) The Effect of Priorities Introduced During Computer Acquisition on Continuing Success with It in Small Business Environments **Information Resource Management Association International Conference** Washington pp 271 - 277

MacGregor R.C. & Bunker D.J. (1995) Computer Education Requirements for Small Business: A Survey **Information Resource Management Association International Conference** Atlanta Georgia, pp 392 - 394

MacGregor R.C. & Bunker D.J. A (1999) Comparison of Real Estate Brokers' Computer Training Needs with other Small Business Sectors: An Australian Perspective, **Journal of Real Estate Practice and Education**, pp 1 - 12

MacGregor, R.C.Vrazalic, L., Carlsson, S Bunker, D.J.Magnusson, M. (2002) The Impact of Business size and Business type on small business investment in electronic commerce: A study of Swedish Small businesses **Australian Journal of Information Systems** vol 9, no. 2, pp 31 – 39

MacGregor R.C., Bunker D.J. & Waugh P. (1998) Electronic Commerce and Small/Medium Enterprises (SME's) in Australia: An Electronic Data Interchange (EDI) Pilot Study, **Proceedings of the 11ᵗʰ International Bled Electronic Commerce Conference**, Slovenia, June

McIvor R. & Humphreys P. (2004) The Implications of Electronic B2B Intermediaries for the Buyer-Seller Interface **International Journal of Operations & Production Management** vol. 24, no. 3, pp 241 - 269

McRea P. (1996) Reshaping Industry with the Internet **Management** Jan-Feb pp 7 - 10

Marchewka J.T. & Towell E.R. (2000) A Comparison of Structure and Strategy in Electronic Commerce **Information Technology and People** vol 13, no. 2, pp 137 - 149

Markland R.E. (1974) The Role of the Computer in Small Business Management **Journal of Small Business Management** vol 12, no 1, pp 21 - 26

Martin L.M. (1999) Looking for the Right Stuff, Human Capital Formation in Small Firms unpublished PhD Thesis University of Warwick

Martin L.M. & Matlay H. (2001) "Blanket" Approaches to Promoting ICT in Small Firms: Some Lessons from the DTI Ladder Adoption Model in the UK **Internet Research: Electronic Networking Applications and Policy** vol 11, no. 5, pp 399 - 410

Martin L.M., Halstead A. & Taylor J. (2001) Learning Issues in Rural Areas **Contemporary Readings in Post-compulsory Education** Triangle

Matlay H. (2000) Training in the Small Business Sector of the British Economy in Carter S. & Jones D. **Enterprise and Small Business: Principles, Policy and Practice** Addison Wesley Longman, London

Matlay H. & Fletcher D. (2000) Globalisation and Strategic Change: Some Lesson from the UK Small Business Sector **Strategic Change** vol 9., no. 7

Mazzarol T., Volery T., Doss N & Thein V. (1999) Factors Influencing Small Business Start-ups **International Journal of Entrepreneurial Behaviour and Research** vol 5, no. 2, pp 48 - 63

Maikle F & Willis D. (2002) A Pilot Study of Regional Differences E-Commerce Development in UK SMEs **IRMA** pp 1142 - 1143

Melone N.P. (1990) A Theoretical Assessment of the User-Satisfaction Construct in Information Systems Research **Management Science** vol 36, no. 1, pp 76 - 89

Meredith G.G.: (1994), **Small Business Management in Australia** McGraw Hill, 4th Edition

Mehrtens J., Cragg P.B. & Mills A.M. (2001) A Model of Internet Adoption by SMEs **Information and Management** vol 39, pp 165 - 176

Miles G., Preece S. & Baetz M.C. (1999) Dangers of Dependence: The Impact of Strategic Alliance Use by Small Technology Based Firms **Journal of Small Business Management** pp 20 - 29

Miller N.L. & Besser T.L. (2000) The Importance of Community Values in Small Business Strategy Formation: Evidence from Rural Iowa **Journal of Small Business Management** vol 38, no. 1, pp 68 - 85

Mirchandani D.A. & Motwani J. (2001) Understanding Small Business Electronic Commerce Adoption: An Empirical Analysis **Journal of Computer Information Systems** vol 41, no. 3, pp 70 - 73

Montazemi A.R. (1988) Factors affecting Information Satisfaction in the Context of the Small Business Environment **MIS Quarterly** Vol. 12, No.2, pp 239 - 256

Moynihan T. (1990) What Chief Executives and Managers want from their IT Departments **MIS Quarterly**

Murphy J. (1996) **Small Business Management** Pitman London

Nalebuff B.J. & Brandenburg A.M. (1996) **Co-operation** Harper Collins Business, Philadelphia, PA

National Office of the Information Economy (1998) A Strategic Framework for the Information Economy: Identifying Priorities for Action **Australian Commonwealth Government**

Neergaard P. (1992) Microcomputers in small and medium-size companies: benefits achieved and problems encountered **Proceedings of the Third Australian Conference on Information Systems**, Wollongong p 579 - 604

Nooteboom B. (1994) Innovation and Diffusion in Small Firms: Theory and Evidence **Small Business Economics** vol 6, no. 5, pp 327 - 347

O'Donnell A., Gilmore A, Cummins D & Carson D (2001) The Network Construct in Entrepreneurship Research: A Review and Critique **Management Decision** vol 39, no. 9, pp 749 - 760

Orlikowski W.J. (1992) The Duality of Technology: Rethinking the Concept of Technology in Organisations **Organisational Science** vol 3, pp 398 - 427

Overby J.W. & Min S. (2001) International Supply Chain Management in an Internet Environment A Network-oriented Approach to Internationalisation **International Marketing Review** vol 18, no. 4, pp 392 - 420

Oxley J.E. & Yeung B. (2001) E-Commerce Readiness: Institutional Environment and International Competitiveness **Journal of International Business Studies** vol 32, no. 4, pp 705 - 723

Ozcan G. (1995) Small Business Networks and Local Ties in Turkey **Entrepreneurship and Regional Development** vol 7, pp 265 - 282

Pendergraft N., Morris L & Savage K. (1987) Small Business Computer Security **Journal of Small Business Management** Vol. 25, No.4

Phan D.D. (2001) E-business Management Strategies: A Business-to-Business Case Study **Information Systems Management** Fall, pp 61 - 69

Poon S. & Joseph M. (2001) A Preliminary Study of Product Nature and Electronic Commerce **Marketing Intelligence & Planning** vol 19, no. 7, pp 493 – 499

Poon S. & Strom J. (1997) Small Business Use of the Internet: Some Realities **Association for Information Systems Americas Conference** Indianapolis

Poon S. & Swatman P. (1997) The Internet for Small Businesses: An Enabling Infrastructure **Fifth Internet Society Conference** pp 221 - 231

Porter M. (2001) Strategy and the Internet **Harvard Business Review** March, pp 63 - 78

Power D.J. & Sohal A.S. (2002) Implementation and Usage of Electronic Commerce in Managing the Supply Chain: A Comparative Study of Ten Australian Companies **Benchmarking: An International Journal** vol 9, no. 2, pp 190 - 208

Premaratne S.P. (2001) Networks, Resources and Small Business Growth: The Experience in Sri Lanka **Journal of Small Business Management** vol 39, no. 4, pp 363 - 371

Price Waterhouse and Coopers (1999) **SME Electronic Commerce Study Final Report** 37pp

Purao S. & Campbell B. (1998) Critical Concerns for Small Business Electronic Commerce: Some Reflections Based on Interviews of Small Business Owners **Proceedings of the Association for Information Systems Americas Conference** Baltimore, MD, 14 – 16 August, pp 325 - 327

Quayle M. (2002) E-commerce: The Challenge for UK SMEs in the Twenty-First Century **International Journal of Operations and Production Management** vol 22, no. 10, pp 1148 - 1161

Radstaak B. & Ketelaar H. (1998) **Worldwide Logistics: The Future of the Supply Chain** Holland International Distribution Council: The Hague

Raisch W.D. (2001) **The E-marketplace: Strategies for Success in B2B** McGraw-Hill New York

Ratnasingam P. (2000) The Influence of Power on Trading Partners in Electronic Commerce **Internet Research** vol 10, no. 1, pp 56 – 62

Raymond L. (2001) Determinants of Web Site Implementation in Small Business **Internet Research: Electronic Network Applications and Policy** vol 11, no. 5, pp 411 - 422

Reimenschneider C.K. & Mykytyn P.P. jr (2000) What Small Business Executives Have Learned about Managing Information Technology **Information & Management** vol 37, pp 257 – 267

Reimenschneider C.K. & McKinney V.R. (2001) Assessing Beliefs in Small Business Adopters and Non-Adopters of Web-Based E-Commerce **Journal of Computer Information Systems** vol 42, no. 2, pp 101 - 107

Reuber A.R. & Fischer E (1999) Understanding the Consequences of Founders' Experience **Journal of Small Business Management** vol 3, no. 2, pp 30 - 45

Reynolds W., Savage W. & Williams A. (1994) **Your own business: A Practical guide to success** ITP

Reynolds J. (2000) E-Commerce: A Critical Review **International Journal of Retail and Distribution Management** vol 28, no. 10, pp 417 - 444

Riquelme H. (2002) Commercial Internet Adoption in China: Comparing the Experience of Small, Medium and Large Business **Internet Research: Electronic Networking Applications and Policy** vol 12 , no. 3, pp 276 - 286

Ritchie R. & Brindley C. (2000) Disintermediation, Disintegration and Risk in the SME Global Supply Chain **Management Decision** vol 38, no. 8, pp 575 - 583

Roberts M & Wood M. (2002) The Strategic Use of Computerised Information Systems by a Micro Enterprise **Logistics Information Management** vol 15, no. 2, pp 115 - 125

Robey D. (1987) Implementation and the Organisational Impact of Information Systems **INTERFACE** vol 17, no 3, p 72 - 84

Rosenfeld S. (1996) Does Cooperation Enhance Competitiveness? Assessing the Impacts of Inter-firm Collaboration **Research Policy** vol 25, no. 2, pp 247 - 263

Rotch W. (1967) **Management of small enterprises: Cases and Readings** University of Virginia   Press

Sawhney M. & Zabib J. (2002) Managing and Measuring Relational Equity in the Network Economy **Journal of the Academy of Marketing Science** vol 30, no. 4, pp 313 - 332

Schindehutte M. & Morris M.H. (2001) Understanding Strategic Adaption in Small Firms **International Journal of Entrepreneurial Behaviour and Research** vol 7, no. 3, pp 84 - 107

Schneider P (1999) Australia Unbound **CIO** vol 12, no. 16, pp 40 - 45

Schollhammer H. & Kuriloff A.H. (1979) **Entrepreneurship and Small Business Management**   John Wiley, New York

Schulnecht L. & Perez-Esteve R (1999) A Quantitative Assessment of Electronic Commerce, Working Paper ERAD-99-01, World Trade Organisation

Schultz R.L., Ginzberg M.J. & Lucas H.C. jr (1984) A Structural Model of Implementation in Schultz R.L. & Ginzberg M.J. (eds) **Applications of Management Science** JAI Press, Greenwich CT, pp 55 - 87

Senn J.A. (1996) Capitalisation on Electronic Commerce **Information Systems Management** Summer

Shiels H, McIvor R & O'Reilly D (2003) Understanding the Implications of ICT Adoption: Insights from SMEs **Logistics Information Management** vol 16, no. 5, pp 312 - 326

Smith A.J., Boocock G., Loan-Clarke J. & Whittaker J. (2002) IIP and SMEs: Awareness, Benefits and Barriers **Personnel Review** vol 31, no. 1, pp 62 - 85

Sparkes A. & Thomas B. (2001) The Use of the Internet as a Critical Success Factor for the Marketing of Welsh Agri-food SMEs in the Twenty First Century **British Food Journal** vol 103, no. 4, pp 331 - 347

Srinivasan A. & Davis J.G. (1987) A Reassessment of Implementation Process Models **INTERFACE**   vol 17, no 3, p 64 - 71

Srinivasan A. (1985) Alternative Measures of System Effectiveness: Associations and Implications **MIS Quarterly**

Stauber A (2000) **A Survey of the Incorporation of Electronic Commerce in Tasmanian Small and Medium Sized Enterprises** Tasmanian Electronic Commerce Centre, 37pp

Steyaert C. (1997) A Qualitative Methodology for Process Studies of Entrepreneurship: Creating Local Knowledge Through Stories **International Studies of Management and Organisations** vol 27, no. 3, pp 13 - 34

Storper M. (1995) The Resurgence of Regional Economies, Ten Years Later: The Region as a Nexus of Untraded Interdependencies **European Urban and Regional Studies** vol 2, no. 3, pp 191 - 221

Swanson E.B. (1988) **Information Systems Implementation** Homewood, Il

Swartz T.A. & Iacobucci D. (eds) **Handbook of Services Marketing and Management** Sage CA

Szajna B. & Scamell R. (1993) The effects of Information Systems User Expectations on their Performance and Perceptions **MIS Quarterly**

Tait P. & Vessey I. (1988) The Effect of User Involvement on System Success: A Contingency Approach **MIS Quarterly** vol 12, no. 1, p 91 - 108

Tambini A.M. (1999) E-Shoppers Demand E-Service **Discount Store News** vol 11, no. 38

Teo T.S.H. & Tan M (1998) An Empirical Study of Adopters and Non-adopters of the Internet in Singapore **Information & Management** vol 34, pp 339 - 345

Tetteh E. & Burn J. (2001) Global Strategies for SME-business: Applying the SMALL Framework **Logistics Information Management** vol 14, no. ½, pp 171 – 180

Thong J.Y.L, Yap C.S. & Raman K.S. (1996) Top Management Support, External Expertise and Information Systems Implementation in Small Business **Information Systems Research** vol 7, no. 2, pp 248 – 267

Thorelli H.B. (1986) Networks: Between Markets and Hierarchies **Strategic Management Journal** vol 7, pp 37 - 51

Tikkanen H. (1998) The Network Approach in Analysing International marketing and Purchasing Operations: A Case Study of a European SME's focal net 1992 – 95 **Journal of Business and Industrial Marketing** vol 13, no. 2, pp 109 - 131

Trauth E.M. (2002) Odd Girl Out: An Individual Differences Perspective on Women in the IT Profession **Information Technology and People** vol. 15, no. 2, pp 98 - 118

Treacy M & Wiersema F (1997) **The Discipline of market Leaders** Perseus Press Cambridge MA

Turban E., Lee J., King D. & Chung H. (2000) **Electronic Commerce: A Managerial Perspective** Prentice Hall, NJ

Turban E., King D, Lee J. Warkentin M & Chung H.M. (2002) **Electronic Commerce** Prentice Hall

United States Small Business Act (1953)

Varadarajan P.R. & Cunningham M. (1995) Strategic Alliances: A Synthesis of Conceptual Foundations **Journal of the Acadamy of Marketing Science** vol 23, no. 4, pp 282 - 296

Venkatesh V. & Davis F.C. (1994) Modeling the Determinants of Perceived Ease of Use **ICIS** Vancouver pp 213 - 227

Venkatash V. & Morris M.G. (2000) Why Don't Men Ever Stop to Ask for Directions? Gender, Social Influence and their Role in Technology Acceptance and Usage Behavior **MIS Quarterly** vol 24, no. 1

Vescovi T. (2000) Internet Communication: The Italian SME Case **Corporate Communications: An International Journal** vol 5, no. 2, pp 107 - 112

Vrazalic L., Bunker D., MacGregor R.C., Carlsson S. & Magnusson M. (2002) Electronic Commerce and Market Focus: Some Findings from a Study of Swedish Small to Medium Enterprises **Australian Journal of Information Systems** vol 10, no. 1, pp110 - 119

Walczuch R., Van Braven G. & Lundgren H. (2000) Internet Adoption Barriers for Small Firms in the Netherlands **European Management Journal** vol 18, no. 5, pp 561 - 572

Walker E.W. (1975) Investment and Capital Structure Decision Making in Small Business in Walker E.W. (ed) **The Dynamic Small Firm: Selected Readings** Austin Press, Texas

Welsh J.A. & White J.F. (1981) A Small Business is not a little Big Business **Harvard Business Review** Jul.

Westhead P. & Storey D.J. (1996) Management Training and Small Firm Performance: Why is the Link so Weak? **International Small Business Journal** vol 14, no. 4, pp 13 - 24

Wilde W.D., Swatman P.A. & Castleman T. (2000) Investigating the Impact of IT&T on Rural, Regional and Remote Australia **Collecter USA** Breckenbridge

Wilde W.D. & Swatman P.A. (2001) Studying R-3 Communities: An Economic Lens Deakin University Working paper No. 3

Willcocks L., Graeser V. & Lester S. (1998) 'Cybernomics' and IT Productivity: Not Business As Usual **European Management Journal** vol 16, no. 3, pp 272 - 283

Wood J.G. & Nosek J.T. (1994) Discrimination of Structure and Technology in a Group Support System: The Role of Process Complexity **ICIS** Vancouver, pp. 187 - 199

Yap C.S., Soh C.P.P. & Raman K.S. (1992) Information System Success Factors in Small Business **International Journal of management Science** 20: pp 597 - 609

Yeung H.W. (1994) Critical Reviews of Geographical Perspectives on Business Organisations and the organisation of production: Towards a Network Approach **Progressive Human Geography** vol 18, no. 4, pp 460 – 490

Appendix 1

1. Hur länge har Ert företag varit verksamt?

Mindre än 1 år   1-2 år   2-5 år   6-10 år   11-20 år   Mer än 20 år

2. Hur många är anställda hos Ert företag?

$\lceil$ **0   1-9   10-19   20-49   50-199   Mer än 200**

3. Vilken är Ert företags huvudsakliga näringsgren?

Industriföretag   Tjänsteföretag   Handelsföretag   Bank/Försäkring   Annan

Inom följande bransch:..

4. Hur många unika kunder har Ert företag totalt:..............st

5. Hur stor andel av Ert företags kunder uppskattar Ni finns i:

Kommunen   Övriga länet   Övriga Sverige   EU   Övriga världen
Summa

%	%	%	%	%
				=100%

6. Hur stor andel av Ert företags kunder uppskattar Ni är:

Återförsäljare   Andra företag   Offentliga org.   Privatpersoner   Andra
Summa

%	%	%	%	%	=100%

7. Hur många leverantörer har Ert företag?
0   1-5   6-10   11-20   21-40   Fler än 40

8. Hur stor andel av Ert företags leverantörer finns i:

Kommunen   Övriga länet   Övriga Sverige   EU   Övriga världen
Summa

%	%	%	%	%
				=100%

9. Ingår Ert företag i något nätverk eller organisation för företag?
Nej   Ja, följande:...

10. Hur stor var Ert företags totala omsättning förra året?.................Mkr.

11. Vilket kön, ålder och högsta utbildning har Ert företags VD?
Man   Kvinna   Ålder:____

*Folk/Grundskola   Gymnasium   Högskola/Universitet   Annan
utbildning:....................*

12. Använder Ert företag datorer i verksamheten?
Ja → gå till fråga **14**   Nej → gå till nästa fråga

13. Planerar Ni att införa datorer i er verksamhet inom 2 år?
Ja → gå till fråga **44**   Vet ej → gå till fråga **44**   Nej → avsluta och skicka in
svaret.

Del II. Frågor om företagets datoranvändning i verksamheten

14. Hur många år har Ert företag använt datorer i verksamheten?
Mindre än 1 år   1-2 år   3-5 år   6-10 år   Mer än 10 år

15. Har Ert företag något affärssystem (OLF - Order Lager Fakturering)?
Ja   Nej
Annat...

16. Har Ert företag något produktionsplaneringssystem?
Ja   Nej
Annat...

17. Har Ert företag några andra datoriserade system?
Ja   Nej   Följande..

18. Har Ert företag någon som ansvarar för företagets IT/Datafrågor?
Ja, på företaget   Ja, som outsourcad tjänst   Nej, ingen

19. Hur skulle Ni beskriva Ert företags totala datakunskaper?
Inga kunskaper   Låga   Normala   Höga   Expertkunskaper

174

20. Har Ert företag tillgång till Internet?
Ja → gå till nästa fråga

Nej → gå till fråga **22**

Om Ja, till vad används Internet (exkl. egen hemsida)?

Skicka/Ta emot e-post

Beställa varor/ tjänster

Sköta bankärenden/elektroniska betalningar

Söka information om kunder

Söka information om leverantörer

Ladda hem digitala produkter

Söka information om konkurrenter

Generell informationssökning

Videokonferenser

Annat:....................................………..

21. Har Ert företag hemsida på Internet?
Ja   Nej

Om Ja, vad finns på hemsidan?

Företagsinformation   Support   Produktinformation/katalog
Försäljning till kund   Annat..

Till vem riktar sig hemsidan?

Leverantörer   Återförsäljare   Företagskunder
Privatpersoner
Andra..

22. Använder Ert företag idag elektronisk affärskommunikation i någon form?

d v s skickar eller tar företaget m.h.a datorer emot elektronisk affärsinformation från affärspartners via någon form av data-/telenätverk (ej fax)?

Ja → gå till fråga **25**

Nej → gå till nästa fråga:

23. *Vad är anledningen till att Ert företag inte använder elektronisk affärskommunikation?* Nedan följer ett antal påståenden. Svara på påståendena med utgångspunkt från Din personliga uppfattning. Kryssa den siffra som Du tycker stämmer bäst överens med Din egen uppfattning!

Vi använder inte elektronisk affärskommunikation därför att:	Stämmer inte alls				Stämmer mycket bra
Det passar inte för våra produkter/tjänster	1	2	3	4	5
Det passar inte vårt sätt att arbeta	1	2	3	4	5
Det passar inte våra kunders sätt att arbeta	1	2	3	4	5
Vi ser inga fördelar	1	2	3	4	5
Vi vet för lite/ har för dåliga kunskaper	1	2	3	4	5
Säkerheten verkar tveksam	1	2	3	4	5
Investeringskostnaden är för hög	1	2	3	4	5
Det är svårt att veta vad man ska satsa på/för många standards	1	2	3	4	5

24. Vilka drivkrafter finns för att införa elektronisk affärskommunikation i Ert företag?

Vad skulle kunna motivera Ert företag att införa elektronisk affärskommunikation?	Stämmer inte alls				Stämmer mycket bra
Om våra kunder krävde det	1	2	3	4	5
Om det innebar att vi förbättrade vår kundservice	1	2	3	4	5
Om det innebar att vi förbättrade vår konkurrenskraft	1	2	3	4	5
Om det innebar att vi kunde öka vår försäljning	1	2	3	4	5
Om det innebar att våra kostnader sänktes	1	2	3	4	5
Om det innebar att vi kunde minska vårt lager	1	2	3	4	5
Om det innebar att ledtiderna kunde kortas	1	2	3	4	5
Om det innebar att vi kunde höja vår interna effektivitet	1	2	3	4	5
Om våra konkurrenter införde elektronisk affärskommunikation	1	2	3	4	5
Om våra leverantörer erbjöd bättre affärsvillkor	1	2	3	4	5
Om det innebar att vi fick tillgång till nya kunder/marknader	1	2	3	4	5
Om det förbättrade vår kommunikation med kunder/leverantörer	1	2	3	4	5
Om vi fick finansiellt stöd	1	2	3	4	5

Vad skulle kunna motivera Ert företag att införa elektronisk affärskommunikation?	Stämmer inte alls				Stämmer mycket bra
Om vi fick stöd/utbildning vid utvecklingen	1	2	3	4	5
Om det innebar förbättrad marknadsföring	1	2	3	4	5
Om det passade vårt sätt att arbeta	1	2	3	4	5
Om det innebar bättre möjligheter till kontroll och uppföljning	1	2	3	4	5

Del III. Frågor om företagets elektroniska affärer

25. Hur länge har Ert företag använt elektronisk a[Fortsätt till fråga → **44**]

Mindre än 1 år   1 - 2 år   3 - 5 år
6 - 10 år   Mer än 10 år

26. Med vem eller vilka har Ert företag elektronisk affärskommunikation?

Företagskunder   Leverantörer   Offentliga org.
Privatpersoner   Återförsäljare   Andra:.................................

27. Har Ert företag någon form av försäljning via hemsida på Internet?

Ja mot postförskott/faktura   Ja med elektronisk betalningslösning   Nej

Om Ja, vem utnyttjar den?

Återförsäljare   Företagskunder
Privatpersoner   Andra...

28. Delar Ert företag information/nätverk över Internet, Extranät eller gemensam server?

Ja   Nej

Om ja, med vilka?

Internt i företaget   Leverantörer   Återförsäljare
Kunder   Offentliga org.
Andra:................................

29. Är Ert företag anslutet till något av följande?
Kommunens inköpssystem
Nationell marknadsplats,
följande:..

Internationell marknadsplats,
följande:...

Gemensam produktdatabas på Internet,
följande:...

Gemensam leverantörsdatabas på Internet,
följande:..
Nej, ej ansluten.

30. Vilken information skickas via elektronisk affärskommunikation till Ert företag?

Order	Faktura	Debiteringsbesked
Orderbekräftelse	Fakturalös betalning	Tulldeklaration
Leveransplan	Transportbokning	Reklam
Leveransavisering	Fraktsedel	Prislista/Artikellista
Annat:................................		

31. Vilken information skickas via elektronisk affärskommunikation från Ert företag?

Order	Faktura	Debiteringsbesked
Orderbekräftelse	Fakturalös betalning	Tulldeklaration
Leveransplan	Transportbokning	Reklam
Leveransavisering	Fraktsedel	Prislista/Artikellista

Annat:...

32. Vilka kommunikationslösningar använder sig Ert företag av vid elektronisk affärskommunikation?

Modem	Bredband, ADSL, Fast lina	Privata nätverk
ISDN	VAN-företag	Annan:............................

33. Uppskatta hur stor andel av Företagets kommunikation med kunder/återförsäljare idag sker via:

E-post   Filöverföring Hemsida   OBI   EDI/Edifact EDA   Telefon   Fax
Säljbesök Brev

%	%	%	%	%	%	%	%	%	%

Annat:......%...**summa=10**
0%

34. Uppskatta hur stor andel av Företagets kommunikation med leverantörer idag sker via:

E-post   Filöverföring Hemsida   OBI   EDI/Edifact EDA   Telefon   Fax
Säljbesök Brev

%	%	%	%	%	%	%	%	%	%

Annat:......%...**summa=10 0%**

35. Uppskatta hur stor andel av Företags kommunikation med offentliga org. sker idag via:

E-post   Filöverföring Hemsida   OBI   EDI/Edifact EDA   Telefon   Fax
Säljbesök Brev

%	%	%	%	%	%	%	%	%	%

Annat:......%...
summa=100%

36. Uppskatta hur stor andel av Företags försäljning sker idag via?

E-post   Filöverföring Hemsida   OBI   EDI/Edifact EDA   Telefon   Fax
Säljbesök Brev

%	%	%	%	%	%	%	%	%	%

Annat:......%...
summa=100%

37. Uppskatta hur stor andel av Företags inköp sker idag via?

E-post   Filöverföring Hemsida   OBI   EDI/Edifact EDA   Telefon   Fax
Säljbesök Brev

%	%	%	%	%	%	%	%	%	%

Annat:......%...
summa=100%

38. Är företagets system för elektronisk affärskommunikation integrerat med övriga datasystem?

Ja   Nej
Om ja, med vilka?

179

Affärssystemet   System för produktionsplanering   Andra:
....

39. *Från vem kom initiativet till att börja använda elektronisk affärskommunikation?*

Er själva   Leverantörer   Vet ej
Kunder   Branschen   Annan:.....................................

40. *Vad var drivkraften/erna till införandet av elektronisk affärskommunikation?*

Nedan följer ett antal påståenden. Svara på påståendena med utgångspunkt från Din

personliga uppfattning. Kryssa den siffra som Du tycker stämmer bäst överens med Din egen

uppfattning!

En stark drivkraft till att Vårt företag införde Elektronisk affärskommunikation var:	Stämmer inte alls				Stämmer mycket bra
Krav/Press från kunder	1	2	3	4	5
Konkurrenstrycket i branschen	1	2	3	4	5
Att leverantörer erbjöd bättre affärsvillkor	1	2	3	4	5
Att få lägre kostnader	1	2	3	4	5
Att höja kundservicen	1	2	3	4	5
Att kunna korta ledtider och minska lager	1	2	3	4	5
Att öka försäljningen	1	2	3	4	5
Att öka den interna effektiviteten	1	2	3	4	5
Att stärka relationen till våra handelspartners	1	2	3	4	5
Möjligheten att nå ut till nya kunder/marknader	1	2	3	4	5
Att öka vår konkurrenskraft	1	2	3	4	5
Att vi erbjöds externt stöd vid införandet	1	2	3	4	5
Att förbättra vår marknadsföring	1	2	3	4	5
Att få bättre möjligheter till kontroll och uppföljning	1	2	3	4	5

41. Vilka initiala svårigheter fanns vid Ert företags införande av elektronisk affärskommunikation?

När Vårt företag införde Elektronisk affärskommunikation var det svårt:	Stämmer inte alls				Stämmer mycket bra
Att förändra rutinerna i verksamheten	1	2	3	4	5
Att skaffa egen kunskap/lära sig den nya tekniken	1	2	3	4	5
Att installera, anpassa och driftsätta tekniken	1	2	3	4	5
Att lösa alla tekniska/organisatoriska detaljer med motparten	1	2	3	4	5
Att upphandla hård-/mjukvara	1	2	3	4	5
Att upphandla konsulttjänster	1	2	3	4	5
Att räkna hem investeringen	1	2	3	4	5
Att ansluta nya handelspartners	1	2	3	4	5
Att integrera med övriga interna datasystem	1	2	3	4	5
Att få personalens acceptans	1	2	3	4	5
Att bära kostnaden	1	2	3	4	5
Annat:...	1	2	3	4	5

42. Vilka nyttofördelar anser Ni att införandet av elektronisk affärskommunikation har medfört för Ert företag?

Genom att införa elektronisk affärskommunikation har vi fått:	Stämmer inte alls				Stämmer mycket bra
Lägre kostnader för administration	1	2	3	4	5
Lägre kostnader för produktion/distribution	1	2	3	4	5
Kortare ledtider	1	2	3	4	5
Minskat lager	1	2	3	4	5
Ökad försäljning	1	2	3	4	5
Ökad intern effektivitet	1	2	3	4	5
Starkare relationer till våra handelspartners	1	2	3	4	5
Nya kunder/marknader	1	2	3	4	5
Ökad konkurrenskraft	1	2	3	4	5

Genom att införa elektronisk affärskommunikation har vi fått:	Stämmer inte alls				Stämmer mycket bra
Bättre möjligheter till marknadsföring	1	2	3	4	5
Bättre informationskvalitet/Färre fel	1	2	3	4	5

43. Vilka nackdelar anser Ni uppkom vid införandet av elektronisk affärskommunikation för Ert företag?

Genom att införa elektronisk affärskommunikation har vi fått:	Stämmer inte alls				Stämmer mycket bra
Försämrade relationer till våra handelspartners	1	2	3	4	5
Höjda kostnader	1	2	3	4	5
Tidskrävande underhåll av datasystemet	1	2	3	4	5
Tvingas jobba med dubbla rutiner	1	2	3	4	5
Sämre kundservice	1	2	3	4	5
Minskad flexibilitet i arbetet	1	2	3	4	5
Försämrad säkerhet	1	2	3	4	5
Ökat teknikberoende	1	2	3	4	5

Del IV. Frågor om företagets elektroniska affärer i framtiden.

44. Vad anser Ni om Internets betydelse för Ert företag i framtiden?

Ingen   Liten   Måttlig   Stor   Mycket stor

45. Vad anser Ni i stort om Internets betydelse för hela samhället?
Ingen   Liten   Måttlig   Stor   Mycket stor

46. Vad tror ni om Ert företags användande av elektronisk handel/affärer i framtiden?
Ska börja   Samma omfattning   Utökning   Avveckling   Vet ej

47. Vad anser Ni om framtiden i stort för elektronisk handel/affärer i samhället?
Samma omfattning   Utökning   Avveckling   Vet ej

48. Vad skulle Ni och Ert företag vilja veta mer om angående elektronisk handel/affärer
Allmänna IT/Datakunskaper   Teknik   Säkerhet och betalningar

Juridik	Revision	Olika affärsmodeller
Import/Export	Logistik	Marknadsföring på Internet
Inget		

Annat..

49. Skriv här om Ni har några personliga åsikter eller kommentarer, gällande elektroniska affärer/handel eller själva enkäten:

....

....

....

....

....

....

....

....

Var vänlig och skicka in den besvarade enkäten snarast i det bifogade kuvertet!

Ett stort tack för
Er medverkan!

A Survey Sent to Companies in Värmland Concerning E-commerce

Part I. General questions

1. How long have your company been in business?
Less than a year   1-2 years   6-10 years   11-20 years   More than 20 years

2. How many employees does your company have?
0   1-9   10-19   20-49   50-199 More than 200

3. Which is your branch of business?
Industry   ServiceTrading   Bank/Insurance   Other
Within following business:

4. How many (unique) customers does your company have totally?

5. Of all your customers, how many percent of them is situated in the…
Council   Region Other parts of SwedenEC   Outside EC
Totally 100%

6. How many percent of your customers are…
Retailers   Other private businesses   Public organizations   Private persons
Other   Totally 100%

7. How many suppliers does your company have?
0   1-5   6-10   11-20   21-40   More than 40

8. Of all your suppliers, how many percent of them is situated in the…
Council   Region Other parts of SwedenEC   Outside EC
Totally 100%

9. Is your company part of any network or organizations for companies?
No   Yes, we are part of:

10. How big was your total sale last year?……………….Million kronor.

11. What gender, age and highest degree does your company's vice president have?
Man   FemaleAge:
Junior High School   Senior High School   College/University
Other education:

12. Do the employees in your company use computers in their daily work?
Yes, move to forward to question 15
No, move forward to the question

13. Are you planning on using computers in your business within two years?
Yes, move forward to question 45

I don't know, move forward to question 45
No, thank you for your participation. Please send in the results

Part II. Questions concerning the use of computers in the business

14. For how long have you been using computers within the company?
Less than a year   1-2 years   3-5 years   6-10 years   More than 10 years

15. Does your company have any enterprise business system?
Yes   No   Other

16. Does your company have any system for product planning?
Yes   No   Other

17. Does your company have any other computerized systems?
Yes   No   The following systems:

18. Does your company have any person with special responsibilities for the company's
computer issues?
Yes, situated at the company
Yes, an outsourcer
No

19. How would you describe/estimate the average computer knowledge in your company?
No computer knowledge   Low   Normal   High   Experts

20. Does your company have access to the Internet?
Yes, move forward to the next question
No, go to question number 22

If yes, how do you use the Internet (besides having a homepage)
Send/Retrieve e-mail   Order products/services
Banking transactions/Pay bills electronically Search information about customers
Search information about supplier   Download digital products
Search information about competitors   General information research
Videoconferencing   Other:

21. Does your company have a homepage on the Internet?
Yes   No

If yes, what does it contain?
Information about the company   Support
Information about the products/catalogue   Sales   Other:

For whom is the homepage made?
Suppliers   Retailers   Companies   Private persons   Other:

185

22. Does your company use any kind of e-commerce today?
In other words, if your company retrieve business information from other companies via any computer/phone network (fax is not included).
Yes, go to question number 26
No, move forward to the next question

23. What are the reasons why your company doesn't use e-commerce?
Here follows a few statements. Answer them based on your own opinion. Make a cross on the number that suits your opinion the best.
We don't use e-commerce because:

It doesn't get together with our products/services
It doesn't fit well with our way of working
It doesn't fit well with our customers' way of working
We don't find any advantages
We don't know much about it/our knowledge is scarce
The security seems doubtful
The amount for the investment is too high
It is hard to know what to choose/too many standards

24. Which driving forces would make your company start using e-commerce?
What would motivate your company to start using e-commerce?

If our customers demand it
If it will lead to improved customer service
If it will improve our competitiveness
If our sales will improve
If our costs will get reduced
If our stock will get smaller
If our ledtider could be shortened (If it reduces time between order and delivery/ If it reduces the time between outlay of capital and receipt of products/service)
If we could make our internal efficiency higher
If our competitors started using e-commerce
If our suppliers offered us a better business deal
If it will give us access to new customers/suppliers
If it will improve our communication with customers/suppliers
If we would get financial support
If we will get support/education during the development
If it will improve our marketing
If it will fit our way of working
If it will give us better opportunities to do controls and follow-ups

Part III. Questions about the company's e-commerce

25. For how long has your company been using e-commerce? Less than a year..osv

26. With whom does your company do business with, using e-commerce? Company customers, Suppliers, Public organizations, Private persons, Retailers, Others

27. Does your company have any type of sale via homepage on the Internet? Yes, using payment via C.O.D./invoice Yes, using some sort of electronic payment No
If yes, who's using it?
Retailers, Private persons, Company customers, Others
28. Does your company share information/network over the Internet, extra net, or shared server? Yes No
If yes, with whom?
Inside the company, Suppliers, Retailers, Customers, Public organizations, Others

29. Is your company associated with/connected to any of the following?
The system for purchase at the local authorities
National marketplace, following???....
International marketplace, ...
Shared/joint product database on the Internet, ...
Shared/joint supplier database on the Internet,....
No, not connected/associated.

30. Which information is sent **to** your company via electronic business communication (e-commerce)?
Order, Order confirmation, Plan of delivery, Notification of delivery, Invoice, Payment without invoice, Booking of transport, Consignment note, Information about debiting debiteringsbesked, Customs/toll declaration, Advertisement, Price-list/Article-list, Other

31. Which information is sent **from** your company using electronic business communication (e-commerce)?
Order, Order confirmation, Plan of delivery, Notification of delivery, Invoice, Payment without invoice, Booking of transport, Consignment note, Information about debiting debiteringsbesked, Customs/toll declaration, Advertisement, Price-list/Article-list, Other

32. Which communication techniques do your company use doing electronic business communication (e-commerce)?
Modem   Bredband, ADSL, Fast lina   **Private network/s**
ISDN   VAN-företag   **Other**

33. How many percent of your company's communication with customers/ retailers are by (via).....e-mail, file-transfer, homepage, OBI, EDI/edifact, EDA, telephone, Fax, visit by salesman/ vendor, letter

34. How many percent of your company's communication with suppliers are by (via).....e-mail, file-transfer, homepage, OBI, EDI/edifact, EDA, telephone, Fax, visit by salesman/ vendor, letter

35. How many percent of your company's communication with public organizations are by (via).....e-mail, file-transfer, homepage, OBI, EDI/edifact, EDA, telephone, Fax, visit by salesman/ vendor, letter

36. How many percent of your company's sale are by (via).....e-mail, file-transfer, homepage, OBI, EDI/edifact, EDA, telephone, Fax, visit by salesman/ vendor, letter

37. How many percent of your purchase are by (via).....e-mail, file-transfer, homepage, OBI, EDI/edifact, EDA, telephone, Fax, visit by salesman/ vendor, letter

38. Is the company's system for electronic business-communication (e-commerce) integrated with the other computer(ized) systems? If yes, with which? The enterprise business system. The system for product planning. Other...

39. Who initiated the use of electronic business-communication?
    You, yourself - customers -suppliers- the line of business branschen- don't know - Else

40. What or which were the driving forces that made your company use electronic business-communication (e-commerce)?
    Here follows a few statements. Answer them based on your own opinion. Make a cross on the number that you think suits best with your own opinion!

    Demand/ Pressure from customers
    The pressure of competition in the line of business
    Demand/pressure from suppliers
    To reduce costs
    To improve customer-service
    To shorten time from order to sale and to reduce stock
    To increase sale
    To improve the internal efficiency
    To strengthen the relations with business-partners
    The possibility to reach new customers/markets
    To improve our competitiveness
    We where offered external support at the introduction
    To improve our marketing
    To improve possibilities of control and follow-up
    Else:

41. What difficulties did you experience introducing electronic business-communication (e-commerce) in your company?
    When our company introduced e-commerce it was hard to:

    To change the routines
    To get knowledge/learn about the new technique
    To install, adapt and implement the technique
    To solve the technical/organizational details with the counterpart
    To (upphandla) purchase hard- and software

188

To (upphandla) services by consultant
(To count home) Räkna hem the investment
To connect new associated/ business partners
To integrate with other internal computer systems
To get the acceptance from the personnel
Att bära kostnaden
Else:

42. What benefits have your company experienced introducing/initiating e-commerce?
Introducing/initiating e-commerce led to:
Lower administration costs
Lower costs for production/ distribution
reduced leadtime
Reduced stock
Increased sale
Increased internal efficiency
Stronger/improved relations with business-partners
New customers/ markets
Increased/improved competitiveness
Improved marketing-possibilities
Improved quality on information/ reduced number of errors

43. What disadvantages or drawbacks have your company experienced introducing/initiating e-commerce?
Introducing/ initiating e-commerce led to:
Deteriorated relations with business-partners
Higher costs
Time demanding maintenance of the computer(ized) system
Being/getting forced to "work doubleReduced flexibility in work
Reduced security/ safety
Increased/ higher dependence on technique

Part IV. Questions about the company's electronic businesses in the future

44. What do you think of the meaning of Internet in the future within your company?
None   Small   Good   High importance   Very high importance

45. What do you think of the meaning of Internet, widely speaking, for the whole society?
None   Small   Good   High importance   Very high importance

46. What do you think about the use of e-commerce within your company in the future?
The same extent as before   It will increase   It will decrease   I don't know

47. What would you and your company want to know more about concerning e-commerce?
General computer knowledge Technique   Security and payments
Jurisdiction   Revision   Different business models
Import/Export   Logistic   Marketing via Internet

Nothing
Other…

48. If you have any personal opinions or comments concerning e-commerce or the survey, please write them here:

E-commerce in Australian SMEs

A Survey of SMEs in the Illawarra Region
To be conducted over the **telephone** and **face-to-face interviews** with **SME owners**

Instructions: Please circle the NUMBER corresponding to the Participant's response in PENCIL

Questions about the Owner

1. Gender

1	2
Female	Male

2. How old are you?

1	2	3	4	5	6
Under 21	21 to 30	31 to 40	41 to 50	51 to 60	Over 60

3. What is the highest qualification you hold?

1	2	3	4	5	6	7	8
Primary school	High school	High school certificate	Apprenticeship or trade (TAFE) qualification	Undergraduate degree	Postgraduate degree	PhD	No formal qualification

Part 1 General Questions about the Organisation

4. How many employees, other than yourself, does your organisation have? Please indicate a full-time equivalent.

1	2	3	4	5	6
None	1 to 9	10 to 19	20 to 49	50	51 or more

5. How long has your organisation been in business?

1	2	3	4	5
Less than a year	1 to 2 years	3 to 5 years	6 to 10 years	More than 10 years

6. Which of the following best describes your organisation?

1	2	3
Sole proprietorship	Partnership	Incorporated (limited liability) company

7. How would you describe your <u>main</u> business activities?

_____

8. Where are the <u>majority</u> of your customers located?

1	2	3	4	5
In the local council area	In the Illawarra region	Outside the Illawarra region, but in NSW	Australia wide	Outside Australia

9. What was your (approximate) sales turnover in 2002?

1	2	3	4	5
Less than $100,000	$100,000 to $499,999	$500,000 to $999,999	$1 million to $ 2 million	More than $2 million

10. Is your organisation in any form of partnership arrangement with other businesses?

1	2
Yes	No

11. Is your organisation a member of any formal government organisation, such as a Chamber of Commerce?

1	2
Yes	No

Part 2 Questions About the Use of Computers in the Organisation

12. Does your organisation use computers in daily business activities?

1	2
Yes	No

Skip to Question 16

13. How long have you been using computers in your organisation?

1	2	3	4	5
Less than a year	1 to 2 years	3 to 5 years	6 to 10 years	More than 10 years

14. Does anyone provide IT or computer support (including web site design) in or for your organisation?

1	2
Yes	No

Skip to Question 16

15. Who is responsible for providing IT support in your organisation?

1	2	3
A full-time employee	A part-time employee	A contractor or external party

16. Which of the following best describes the <u>average</u> level of computer knowledge/skill in your organisation?

1	2	3	4	5
No computer knowledge	Low knowledge	Average knowledge	Relatively high knowledge	Expert knowledge

17. *[For the first category (Customers) say:* **Do you use the telephone to communicate with your Customers?** *[Wait for response, tick appropriate box]* **The Fax?** *[Wait for response, tick appropriate box]* **E-mail with or without attachments?** *[Wait for response, tick appropriate box. ETC. Then move on to the next category (Suppliers) and repeat the same process. After participants have responded to all the categories repeat back to him/her the communication types for each stakeholder category and then ask them to rank the top three in <u>order of frequency of use</u>. If a Participant has indicated that they do NOT have Business Partners, do not ask them to respond to that category.]*

Communication Types	Customers		Suppliers		Government Organisations		Business Partners	
	Yes/No	Rank	Yes/No	Rank	Yes/No	Rank	Yes/No	Rank
Telephone								
Fax								
E-mail with or without attachments								
File transfers over computers								
Organisational website								
Personal contact (e.g. a counter, door to door sales, conferences, exhibitions)								
Letters sent via the Post								
Other:								

18. Does your organisation share information over the Internet or any other type of network (for example, intranet, extranet or shared server, but excluding e-mail or a web site) with customers?

1   2
Yes   No

19. With suppliers?

1   2 | If participant has responded YES to this question, he/she must respond to questions in PART 5 of the survey.
Yes   No

20. With government organisations?

1   2 | If participant has responded YES to this question, he/she must respond to questions in PART 5 of the survey.
Yes   No

21. With business partners?

1   2 | If participant has responded YES to this question, he/she must respond to questions in PART 5 of the survey.
Yes   No

22. Do you have Internet access in your organisation?

1   2
Yes   No

Skip to Question 24

23. What type(s) of Internet access does your organisation have?

1	2	3	4	5
Dial up modem connection	ISDN (Integrated Services Digital Network)	ADSL (Asymmetric Digital Subscriber Line)	Cable	Not sure/Don't know

24. Does your organisation have a dedicated web page or web site on the Internet?

1   2
Yes   No

*Skip to
Question 26*

25. I'd like to know more about your web site so I am going to read a list of statements about your web site. Can you please indicate whether each statement is True or False.

Statements	True/False	
Our web site contains information about the organisation, including contact details.		
It contains information about our products or services.		
It contains prices for our products or services.		
It contains an e-mail link for customers to contact us.		
It contains an online form for customers to contact us.		
It contains an online form for ordering products which the customer has to print out and fax to us.		Secure Non-secure
It contains an online form for ordering products which can be submitted online.		Secure Non-secure
It enables customers to complete a full e-commerce transaction, including browsing products, putting them in an electronic shopping basket and paying online using a secure credit card system.		
Customers are able to track the status of their order using our web site.		

26. Have you implemented e-commerce in your organisation?

1	2
Yes	No

GO TO PART 3   GO TO PART 4

Part 3 Questions for Organisations that have implemented e-commerce

27. Who was the <u>main</u> initiator of e-commerce in your organisation?

1	2	3	4	5
You (the Owner)	Customers	Suppliers	Business Partner	Not sure

28. How long has e-commerce been used in your organisation?

1	2	3	4
Less than a year	1 to 2 years	3 to 5 years	6 to 10 years

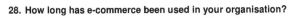

29. The next question relates to <u>the reasons which may have affected your decision to implement e-commerce in your organisation</u>. I am going to read out a list of statements to you and ask you to rank each statement on a scale of 1 to 5 to indicate how important it was to your decision to implement e-commerce. A 1 means that the reason was very unimportant to your decision, 2 means it was unimportant, 3 means it was neutral, 4 means it was important and 5 means the reason was very important to your decision. If a statement is not applicable to your organisation please say "Not Applicable". You can use words instead of numbers if you prefer.

	VU	U	N	I	VI	
You implemented e-commerce because of demands and/or pressure from clients (such as customers and suppliers).	1	2	3	4	5	NA
Your competitors who had implemented e-commerce.	1	2	3	4	5	NA
Your suppliers offered you incentives to implement it.	1	2	3	4	5	NA
You believed that implementing e-commerce would reduce your costs.	1	2	3	4	5	NA
You believed that implementing e-commerce would improve your customer service.	1	2	3	4	5	NA
You believed that implementing e-commerce would lead to increased sales.	1	2	3	4	5	NA
You believed that implementing e-commerce would lead to operational efficiencies inside the organisation.	1	2	3	4	5	NA
You believed that implementing e-commerce would strengthen your relationship with our business partners.	1	2	3	4	5	NA
You believed that implementing e-commerce would allow you to reach new customers and markets.	1	2	3	4	5	NA
You believed that implementing e-commerce would improve your competitiveness.	1	2	3	4	5	NA
You were offered external support (from government or other public and private organisations) to implement e-commerce.	1	2	3	4	5	NA
You believed that implementing e-commerce would improve your marketing strategy.	1	2	3	4	5	NA
You believed that implementing e-commerce would offer you a higher degree of control over managing the business processes (such as orders, accounts, etc.).	1	2	3	4	5	NA

30. The next question relates to <u>the difficulties which you may have experienced while implementing e-commerce in your organisation</u>. I am going to read out a list of statements to you and ask you to rank each statement on a scale of 1 to 5 to indicate how significant it was to your situation. A 1 means it was a very insignificant difficulty that you experienced, 2 means it was insignificant, 3 means it was neutral, 4 means it was significant and 5 means it was a very significant difficulty. If a statement is not applicable to your organisation please say "Not Applicable". You can use words instead of numbers if you prefer.

VU U N I VI

196

It was difficult to change your business processes.	1	2	3	4	5	NA
It was difficult to obtain expertise to assist with the implementation.	1	2	3	4	5	NA
You had difficulties physically installing and adapting e-commerce in your organisation.	1	2	3	4	5	NA
It was difficult to resolve technical and organisational issues with your counterparts (customers, suppliers, government organisations, partners).	1	2	3	4	5	NA
It was difficult to purchase hardware and software.	1	2	3	4	5	NA
It was difficult to obtain the services of a consultant.	1	2	3	4	5	NA
It was difficult to put a "price tag" (or final cost) on the implementation.	1	2	3	4	5	NA
It was difficult to connect to your business partners due to incompatibility between your technical infrastructure.	1	2	3	4	5	NA
It was difficult to integrate e-commerce with your other internal computer systems.	1	2	3	4	5	NA
It was difficult to get employees to accept e-commerce.	1	2	3	4	5	NA
It was difficult to allocate the cost of e-commerce implementation to a particular business unit or activity.	1	2	3	4	5	NA
It was difficult because employees had low computer expertise.	1	2	3	4	5	NA

31. **The next question relates to <u>the benefits which you may have experienced AFTER implementing e-commerce in your organisation.</u> I am going to read out a list of statements to you and ask you to rank each statement on a scale of 1 to 5 to indicate how important each benefit is to your organisation. Would you like me to read the scale to you again?** *[If Participant says "No", go to statements below. If Participant says "Yes" read the following:]* **A 1 means that the benefit was very unimportant to your organisation, 2 means it was unimportant, 3 means it was neutral, 4 means it was important and 5 means the benefit was very important to your organisation. If a statement is not applicable to your organisation please say "Not Applicable". You can use words instead of numbers if you prefer.**

E-commerce lowered your administration costs.	1	2	3	4	5	NA
E-commerce lowered your production and distribution costs.	1	2	3	4	5	NA
E-commerce reduced your lead time from order to delivery.	1	2	3	4	5	NA
E-commerce increased your sales revenues.	1	2	3	4	5	NA
E-commerce led to operational efficiencies inside the organisation.	1	2	3	4	5	NA
E-commerce improved your relationship with business partners.	1	2	3	4	5	NA

E-commerce allowed you to enter new markets and increase your customer base.	1	2	3	4	5	NA
E-commerce improved your ability to compete.	1	2	3	4	5	NA
E-commerce improved your marketing strategy.	1	2	3	4	5	NA
E-commerce reduced the number of errors in your data processing.	1	2	3	4	5	NA

32. The next question relates to <u>the problems which you may have experienced AFTER implementing e-commerce in your organisation</u>. I am going to read out a list of statements to you and ask you to rank each statement on a scale of 1 to 5 to indicate how important each problem was to your organisation. Would you like me to read the scale to you again? *[If Participant says "No", go to statements below. If Participant says "Yes" read the following:]* **A 1 means that the problem was very unimportant to your organisation, 2 means it was unimportant, 3 means it was neutral, 4 means it was important and 5 means the problem was very important to your organisation. If a statement is not applicable to your organisation please say "Not Applicable". You can use words instead of numbers if you prefer.**

E-commerce deteriorated your relationships with business partners.	1	2	3	4	5	NA
E-commerce increased your costs.	1	2	3	4	5	NA
E-commerce has increased the time and resources spent on computer systems maintenance.	1	2	3	4	5	NA
You have experienced major technical problems as a result of implementing e-commerce.	1	2	3	4	5	NA
You have "doubled up" on your business processes since implementing e-commerce (i.e. you do the same thing twice).	1	2	3	4	5	NA
E-commerce has reduced your flexibility.	1	2	3	4	5	NA
E-commerce has reduced the security of your computer systems.	1	2	3	4	5	NA
You have become highly dependent on e-commerce to run the organisation.	1	2	3	4	5	NA

Part 4 Questions for Organisations that have not implemented e-commerce

33. The next question relates to <u>the reasons why your organisation may not be using e-commerce</u>. I am going to read out a list of statements to you and ask you to rank each statement on a scale of 1 to 5 to indicate how important it was to your decision NOT to implement e-commerce. A 1 means that the reason was very unimportant to your decision, 2 means it was unimportant, 3 means it was neutral, 4 means it was important and 5 means the reason was very important to your decision. If a statement is not applicable to your organisation please say "Not Applicable". You can use words instead of numbers if you prefer.

198

E-commerce is not suited to your products/ services	1	2	3	4	5	NA
E-commerce is not suited to your way of doing business.	1	2	3	4	5	NA
E-commerce is not suited to the ways your clients (customers and/or suppliers) do business.	1	2	3	4	5	NA
E-commerce does not offer any advantages to your organisation.	1	2	3	4	5	NA
You do not have the computer knowledge in the organisation to implement e-commerce.	1	2	3	4	5	NA
E-commerce is too complicated to implement.	1	2	3	4	5	NA
E-commerce is not secure.	1	2	3	4	5	NA
You do not have the financial resources to implement e-commerce.	1	2	3	4	5	NA
It is difficult to choose the most suitable e-commerce standard with so many different options available.	1	2	3	4	5	NA

34. The next question relates to the <u>reasons why your organisation may decide to implement e-commerce in the future</u>. I am going to read out a list of statements to you and ask you to rank each statement on a scale of 1 to 5 to indicate how significant it would be to your decision to implement e-commerce. A 1 means it would be very insignificant to your decision, 2 means it would be insignificant, 3 means it would be neutral, 4 means it would be significant and 5 means it would be very significant. If a statement is not applicable to your organisation please say "Not Applicable". You can use words instead of numbers if you prefer.

If your clients (customers and/or suppliers) demand it.	1	2	3	4	5	NA
If it leads to improved customer service.	1	2	3	4	5	NA
If it improves your ability to compete.	1	2	3	4	5	NA
It if leads to increases in your sales.	1	2	3	4	5	NA
If it reduces your operating costs.	1	2	3	4	5	NA
If it offers you more efficient inventory planning and management.	1	2	3	4	5	NA
If it reduces your lead time from order to delivery.	1	2	3	4	5	NA
If it results in operational efficiencies inside the organisation.	1	2	3	4	5	NA
If your competitors implement e-commerce.	1	2	3	4	5	NA
If your suppliers offered you incentives to implement it.	1	2	3	4	5	NA
If it gave you access to new customers.	1	2	3	4	5	NA
If it leads to improvements in your communications with customers and/or suppliers.	1	2	3	4	5	NA
If you received financial support to implement it.	1	2	3	4	5	NA

If you received support in the form of expertise and knowledge to implement it.	1	2	3	4	5	NA
If it leads to improvements in your marketing strategy.	1	2	3	4	5	NA
If it suited your way of doing business.	1	2	3	4	5	NA
If it offered you a higher degree of control over managing the business.	1	2	3	4	5	NA

Part 5 Questions about B2B commerce

35. How often do you share data with your business partners over the Internet or other types of networks?

1	2	3	4
Daily	Weekly	Monthly	Hardly ever

36. Which of the following best describes your relationship with your e-commerce business partners?

1	2	3	4
Equal partners	You are the dominant partner.	Your partners are dominant in the relationship.	The level of dominance varies – in some partnerships you're the dominant partner, in others you're not.

37. Do you make your strategic business decisions in consultation with your business partners?

1	2
Yes	No

Skip to
Question 39

38. What percentage of these strategic business decisions do YOU make?

1	2	3	4	5
100%	More than 50%	50%	Less than 50%	None

39. Do you and your business partner share the costs associated with supporting your partnership (for example, technical costs, staffing costs, administrative costs, etc.)?

1	2
Yes	No

Skip to
Question 41

40. What percentage of these costs do YOU pay for?

1	2	3	4	5
100%	More than 50%	50%	Less than 50%	None

41. Do you have a pre-determined set of criteria which you apply to a potential business partner before entering into a partnership/collaborative arrangement with them?

1	2
Yes	No

Skip to
Question 43

42. To which partners do you apply the criteria?

1	2	3	4	5
All your partners	More than half your partners	Half your partners	Less than half your partners	None

43. What type of systems architecture is employed in your organisation?

1	2	3	4
Microsoft.Net	Websphere (IBM)	Java J2EE	Other

44. Does your organisation use the same systems architecture as your business partners?

1	2
Yes	No

Skip to
Question 46

45. With how many of your partners do you share the same systems architecture?

1	2	3	4	5
All your partners	More than half your partners	Half your partners	Less than half your partners	None

46. Are you experiencing integration difficulties with your business partners as a result of different types of systems architecture?

1	2
Yes	No

Skip to
Question 48

47. With how many of your partners are you experiencing these integration difficulties?

1	2	3	4	5
All your partners	More than half your partners	Half your partners	Less than half your partners	None

48. Are you experiencing communication difficulties with your business partners as a result of different types of systems architecture?

   1   2
  Yes   No

Skip to
Question 50

49. With how many of your partners are you experiencing these communication difficulties?

1	2	3	4	5
All your partners	More than half your partners	Half your partners	Less than half your partners	None

50. Do you have technical compatibility problems with your business partners?

   1   2
  Yes   No

Skip to
Question 52

51. How often do you have compatibility problems with your business partners?

1	2	3	4
Daily	Weekly	Monthly	Hardly ever

52. Is the data shared between you and your business partner encrypted (formatted for security) prior to transmission?

   1   2
  Yes   No

Skip to
Question 54

53. With how many of your partners do you share encrypted data?

1	2	3	4	5
All your partners	More than half your partners	Half your partners	Less than half your partners	None

54. Do you track and maintain statistics on the volume and type of data being shared between you and your business partner through logs?

<pre>
1   2
Yes   No
</pre>

Skip to
Question 56

55. With how many of your partners do you maintain these logs?

1	2	3	4	5
All your partners	More than half your partners	Half your partners	Less than half your partners	None

56. Do you have a secure access arrangement with your business partners?

<pre>
1   2
Yes   No
</pre>

Skip to
Question 58

57. With how many of your partners do you have this secure arrangement?

1	2	3	4	5
All your partners	More than half your partners	Half your partners	Less than half your partners	None

58. Do you allow your business partners direct access to your data?

<pre>
1   2
Yes   No
</pre>

Skip to END

59. How many of your partners do you allow direct access to your data?

1	2	3	4	5
All your partners	More than half your partners	Half your partners	Less than half your partners	None

Appendix 3
Non significant Data from the Swedish study

Table A3.1

Adoption/Non-Adoption of Electronic Commerce

		Frequency	Percent	Valid Percent	Cumulative Percent
Valid	Adopted EC	152	48.6	55.3	55.3
	Not adopted	123	39.3	44.7	100.0
	Total	275	87.9	100.0	
Missing		38	12.1		
Total		313	100.0		

Table A3.2

Membership/Non-Membership of a Small Business Strategic alliance

		Frequency	Percent	Valid Percent	Cumulative Percent
Valid	Non-members	163	52.1	53.8	53.8
	members	140	44.7	46.2	100.0
	Total	303	96.8	100.0	
Missing		10	3.2		
Total		313	100.0		

Table A3.3

Age of the Business

		Frequency	Percent	Valid Percent	Cumulative Percent
Valid	< 1 year	4	1.3	1.3	1.3
	1-2 years	14	4.5	4.5	5.8
	3-5 years	42	13.4	13.5	19.2
	6-10 years	62	19.8	19.9	39.1
	11-20 years	79	25.2	25.3	64.4
	> 20 years	111	35.5	35.6	100.0
	Total	312	99.7	100.0	
Missing		1	.3		
Total		313	100.0		

Table A3.4

Size of Business

		Frequency	Percent	Valid Percent	Cumulative Percent
Valid	Sole trader	56	17.9	18.1	18.1
	1-9 employees	164	52.4	53.1	71.2
	10-19 employees	49	15.7	15.9	87.1
	20-50 employees	40	12.8	12.9	100.0
	Total	309	98.7	100.0	
Missing		4	1.3		
Total		313	100.0		

Table A3.5

Business Sector

		Frequency	Percent	Valid Percent	Cumulative Percent
Valid	Industrial	62	19.8	25.1	25.1
	Service	114	36.4	46.2	71.3
	Retail/Trading	65	20.8	26.3	97.6
	Financial	6	1.9	2.4	100.0
	Total	247	78.9	100.0	
Missing	Total	66	21.1		
Total		313	100.0		

TableA3.6

Market focus

		Frequency	Percent	Valid Percent	Cumulative Percent
Valid	Local business	171	54.6	54.6	54.6
	Regional business	29	9.3	9.3	63.9
	National	82	26.2	26.2	90.1
	International	31	9.9	9.9	100.0
	Total	313	100.0	100.0	

TableA3.7

Computer Skill within the Business

		Frequency	Percent	Valid Percent	Cumulative Percent
Valid	No skill	4	1.3	1.5	1.5
	Low skill	47	15.0	17.2	18.7
	Normal skill	152	48.6	55.7	74.4
	High skill	50	16.0	18.3	92.7
	Expert skill	20	6.4	7.3	100.0
	Total	273	87.2	100.0	
Missing		40	12.8		
Total		313	100.0		

TableA3.8
Membership/Non-Membership of a Small Business Strategic alliance

		Frequency	Percent	Valid Percent	Cumulative Percent
Valid	Non-members	91	59.9	62.8	62.8
	Members	54	35.5	37.2	100.0
	Total	145	95.4	100.0	
Missing		0	7	4.6	
Total		152	100.0		

E-Commerce Adopters

		Frequency	Percent	Valid Percent	Cumulative Percent
Valid	Non-members	58	47.2	48.3	48.3
	Members	62	50.4	51.7	100.0
	Total	120	97.6	100.0	
Missing		0	3	2.4	
Total		123	100.0		

E-Commerce Non-adopters

TableA3.9
Age of Business

		Frequency	Percent	Valid Percent	Cumulative Percent
Valid	1-2 years	7	4.6	4.6	4.6
	3-5 years	22	14.5	14.5	19.1
	6-10 years	34	22.4	22.4	41.4
	11-20 years	37	24.3	24.3	65.8
	> 20 years	52	34.2	34.2	100.0
	Total	152	100.0	100.0	

E-Commerce Adopters

		Frequency	Percent	Valid Percent	Cumulative Percent
Valid	< 1 year	3	2.4	2.5	2.5
	1-2 years	6	4.9	4.9	7.4
	3-5 years	15	12.2	12.3	19.7
	6-10 years	24	19.5	19.7	39.3
	11-20 years	31	25.2	25.4	64.8
	> 20 years	43	35.0	35.2	100.0
	Total	122	99.2	100.0	
Missing		1	.8		
Total		123	100.0		

E-Commerce Non-adopters

TableA3.10
Size of Business

		Frequency	Percent	Valid Percent	Cumulative Percent
Valid	Sole trader	15	9.9	9.9	9.9
	1-9 employees	77	50.7	50.7	60.5
	10-19 employees	30	19.7	19.7	80.3
	20-50 employees	30	19.7	19.7	100.0
	Total	152	100.0	100.0	

E-Commerce Adopters

		Frequency	Percent	Valid Percent	Cumulative Percent
Valid	Sole trader	26	21.1	21.5	21.5
	1-9 employees	67	54.5	55.4	76.9
	10-19 employees	18	14.6	14.9	91.7
	20-50 employees	10	8.1	8.3	100.0
	Total	121	98.4	100.0	
Missing		2	1.6		
Total		123	100.0		

E-Commerce Non-adopters

TableA3.11
Business Sector

		Frequency	Percent	Valid Percent	Cumulative Percent
Valid	Industrial	35	23.0	26.5	26.5
	Service	58	38.2	43.9	70.5
	Retail/Trading	33	21.7	25.0	95.5
	Financial	6	3.9	4.5	100.0
	Total	132	86.8	100.0	
Missing	Total	20	13.2		
Total		152	100.0		

E-Commerce Adopters

		Frequency	Percent	Valid Percent	Cumulative Percent
Valid	Industrial	20	16.3	21.7	21.7
	Service	49	39.8	53.3	75.0
	Retail/Trading	23	18.7	25.0	100.0
	Total	92	74.8	100.0	
Missing	Total	31	25.2		
Total		123	100.0		

E-Commerce Non-adopters

TableA3.12
Market Focus

		Frequency	Percent	Valid Percent	Cumulative Percent
Valid	Local business	66	43.4	43.4	43.4
	Regional business	14	9.2	9.2	52.6
	National	55	36.2	36.2	88.8
	International	17	11.2	11.2	100.0
	Total	152	100.0	100.0	

E-Commerce Adopters

		Frequency	Percent	Valid Percent	Cumulative Percent
Valid	Local business	74	60.2	60.2	60.2
	Regional business	11	8.9	8.9	69.1
	National	24	19.5	19.5	88.6
	International	14	11.4	11.4	100.0
	Total	123	100.0	100.0	

E-Commerce Non-adopters

TableA3.13
Computer Skills

		Frequency	Percent	Valid Percent	Cumulative Percent
Valid	No skill	1	.7	.7	.7
	Low skill	13	8.6	8.6	9.3
	Normal skill	81	53.3	53.6	62.9
	High skill	37	24.3	24.5	87.4
	Expert skill	19	12.5	12.6	100.0
	Total	151	99.3	100.0	
Missing		1	.7		
Total		152	100.0		

E-Commerce Adopters

		Frequency	Percent	Valid Percent	Cumulative Percent
Valid	No skill	3	2.4	2.5	2.5
	Low skill	34	27.6	28.1	30.6
	Normal skill	70	56.9	57.9	88.4
	High skill	13	10.6	10.7	99.2
	Expert skill	1	.8	.8	100.0
	Total	121	98.4	100.0	
Missing		2	1.6		
Total		123	100.0		

E-Commerce Non-adopters

TableA3.14
Age of Business

		Frequency	Percent	Valid Percent	Cumulative Percent
Valid	< 1 year	2	1.2	1.2	1.2
	1-2 years	7	4.3	4.3	5.5
	3-5 years	22	13.5	13.5	19.0
	6-10 years	33	20.2	20.2	39.3
	11-20 years	35	21.5	21.5	60.7
	> 20 years	64	39.3	39.3	100.0
	Total	163	100.0	100.0	

Non-Member of a small business strategic alliance

		Frequency	Percent	Valid Percent	Cumulative Percent
Valid	< 1 year	2	1.4	1.4	1.4
	1-2 years	7	5.0	5.0	6.4
	3-5 years	20	14.3	14.3	20.7
	6-10 years	27	19.3	19.3	40.0
	11-20 years	43	30.7	30.7	70.7
	> 20 years	41	29.3	29.3	100.0
	Total	140	100.0	100.0	

Member of a small business strategic alliance

TableA3.15
Size of Business

		Frequency	Percent	Valid Percent	Cumulative Percent
Valid	Sole trader	19	11.7	11.7	11.7
	1-9 employees	81	49.7	50.0	61.7
	10-19 employees	33	20.2	20.4	82.1
	20-50 employees	29	17.8	17.9	100.0
	Total	162	99.4	100.0	
Missing	0	1	.6		
Total		163	100.0		

Non-Member of a small business strategic alliance

		Frequency	Percent	Valid Percent	Cumulative Percent
Valid	Sole trader	36	25.7	26.1	26.1
	1-9 employees	78	55.7	56.5	82.6
	10-19 employees	14	10.0	10.1	92.8
	20-50 employees	10	7.1	7.2	100.0
	Total	138	98.6	100.0	
Missing	0	2	1.4		
Total		140	100.0		

Member of a small business strategic alliance

TableA3.16
Business Sector

		Frequency	Percent	Valid Percent	Cumulative Percent
Valid	Industrial	34	20.9	25.8	25.8
	Service	63	38.7	47.7	73.5
	Retail/trading	33	20.2	25.0	98.5
	Financial	2	1.2	1.5	100.0
	Total	132	81.0	100.0	
Missing	Total	31	19.0		
Total		163	100.0		

Non-Member of a small business strategic alliance

		Frequency	Percent	Valid Percent	Cumulative Percent
Valid	Industrial	27	19.3	25.0	25.0
	Service	48	34.3	44.4	69.4
	Retail/trading	29	20.7	26.9	96.3
	Financial	4	2.9	3.7	100.0
	Total	108	77.1	100.0	
Missing	Total	32	22.9		
Total		140	100.0		

Member of a small business strategic alliance

TableA3.17
Market Focus

		Frequency	Percent	Valid Percent	Cumulative Percent
Valid	Local business	83	50.9	50.9	50.9
	Regional business	16	9.8	9.8	60.7
	National	47	28.8	28.8	89.6
	International	17	10.4	10.4	100.0
	Total	163	100.0	100.0	

Non-Member of a small business strategic alliance

		Frequency	Percent	Valid Percent	Cumulative Percent
Valid	Local business	82	58.6	58.6	58.6
	Regional business	11	7.9	7.9	66.4
	National	33	23.6	23.6	90.0
	International	14	10.0	10.0	100.0
	Total	140	100.0	100.0	

Member of a small business strategic alliance

TableA3.18
Skill Level

		Frequency	Percent	Valid Percent	Cumulative Percent
Valid	No skill	3	1.8	2.0	2.0
	Low skill	21	12.9	14.2	16.2
	Normal skill	83	50.9	56.1	72.3
	High skill	30	18.4	20.3	92.6
	Expert skill	11	6.7	7.4	100.0
	Total	148	90.8	100.0	
Missing	0	15	9.2		
Total		163	100.0		

Non-Member of a small business strategic alliance

		Frequency	Percent	Valid Percent	Cumulative Percent
Valid	No skill	1	.7	.9	.9
	Low skill	25	17.9	21.7	22.6
	Normal skill	61	43.6	53.0	75.7
	High skill	19	13.6	16.5	92.2
	Expert skill	9	6.4	7.8	100.0
	Total	115	82.1	100.0	
Missing	0	25	17.9		
Total		140	100.0		

Member of a small business strategic alliance

TableA3.19
A comparison of the means of rating of criteria for adoption of E-commerce between those respondents that were members of a strategic alliance and those that were not, that had been in business for between 3 and 5 years

Criteria	Mean Members	N Members	Mean Non-members	N Non-members	t-value	Sig.
B	2.00	12	1.43	7	-.977	.342
D	3.08	12	3.43	7	.429	.673
E	3.92	13	4.14	7	.315	.756
F	2.83	12	2.86	7	.027	.979
G	3.08	13	3.43	7	.446	.660
H	3.50	12	3.50	8	.000	1.000
I	3.00	12	2.86	7	-.194	.849
J	3.77	13	2.86	7	-1.287	.215
K	3.42	12	3.29	7	-.174	.864
M	3.08	13	3.71	7	.782	.444
N	3.00	12	2.86	7	-.185	.855

Legend

A	*Demand/pressure from customers*
B	*Pressure of competition*
C	*Demand/pressure from suppliers*
D	*Reduction of costs*
E	*Improvement to customer service*

F	*Improvement in lead time*
G	*Increased sales*
H	*Improvement to internal efficiency*
I	*Strengthen relations with business partners*
J	*Reach new customers/markets*
K	*Improvement in competitiveness*
L	*External technical support*
M	*Improvement in marketing*
N	*Improvement in control and follow-up*

TableA3.20
A comparison of the means of rating of criteria for adoption of E-commerce between those respondents that were members of a strategic alliance and those that were not, that had been in business for between 6 and 10 years

Criteria	Mean Members	N Members	Mean Non-members	N Non-members	t-value	Sig.
B	2.78	9	2.30	20	-.877	.388
D	3.78	9	3.05	20	-1.559	.131
E	4.22	9	4.15	20	-.209	.836
F	3.44	9	4.15	20	-1.616	.118
G	3.25	8	3.35	20	.169	.867
H	3.80	10	4.00	20	.617	.542
I	3.00	9	3.40	20	.878	.388
J	3.22	9	3.40	20	.296	.769
K	3.00	9	3.85	20	1.438	.162
M	3.22	9	3.60	20	.610	.547
N	2.78	9	2.95	20	.314	.756

Legend

A	*Demand/pressure from customers*
B	*Pressure of competition*
C	*Demand/pressure from suppliers*
D	*Reduction of costs*
E	*Improvement to customer service*
F	*Improvement in lead time*
G	*Increased sales*
H	*Improvement to internal efficiency*
I	*Strengthen relations with business partners*
J	*Reach new customers/markets*
K	*Improvement in competitiveness*
L	*External technical support*
M	*Improvement in marketing*
N	*Improvement in control and follow-up*

TableA3.21
A comparison of the means of rating of criteria for adoption of E-commerce between those respondents that were members of a strategic alliance and those that were not, that had been in business for between 11 and 20 years

Criteria	Mean Members	N Members	Mean Non-members	N Non-members	t-value	Sig.
B	2.92	12	2.33	18	-1.295	.206
D	3.46	13	3.22	18	-.572	.572
E	4.33	12	3.72	18	-1.527	.138
F	2.38	13	2.41	17	.062	.951
G	3.00	12	3.17	18	.321	.751
H	3.62	13	3.83	18	.556	.582
I	3.69	13	2.94	18	-1.602	.120
J	2.83	12	3.44	18	1.226	.231
K	3.85	13	3.56	18	.620	.540
M	3.33	12	3.67	18	.742	.464
N	2.33	12	2.94	17	1.331	.194

Legend

A	*Demand/pressure from customers*
B	*Pressure of competition*
C	*Demand/pressure from suppliers*
D	*Reduction of costs*
E	*Improvement to customer service*
F	*Improvement in lead time*
G	*Increased sales*
H	*Improvement to internal efficiency*
I	*Strengthen relations with business partners*
J	*Reach new customers/markets*
K	*Improvement in competitiveness*
L	*External technical support*
M	*Improvement in marketing*
N	*Improvement in control and follow-up*

A comparison of the means of rating of criteria for adoption of E-commerce between those respondents that were members of a strategic alliance and those that were not, that had been in business for more than 20 years

Criteria	Mean Members	N Members	Mean Non-members	N Non-members	t-value	Sig.
B	2.80	10	2.97	33	.375	.710
D	3.80	10	3.47	32	-.684	.498
E	4.70	10	4.18	33	-1.600	.117
F	3.22	9	3.25	32	.051	.960
G	3.40	10	3.41	32	.014	.989
H	4.30	10	4.18	33	-.389	.699
I	3.20	10	3.42	33	.533	.583
J	3.90	10	3.59	32	-.711	.482
K	4.00	10	4.06	33	.175	.862
M	3.50	10	3.69	32	.382	.704
N	2.50	10	3.19	32	1.613	.115

Legend

A	Demand/pressure from customers
B	Pressure of competition
C	Demand/pressure from suppliers
D	Reduction of costs
E	Improvement to customer service
F	Improvement in lead time
G	Increased sales
H	Improvement to internal efficiency
I	Strengthen relations with business partners
J	Reach new customers/markets
K	Improvement in competitiveness
L	External technical support
M	Improvement in marketing
N	Improvement in control and follow-up

TableA3.23

A comparison of the means of rating of benefits to adoption of E-commerce between those respondents that were members of a strategic alliance and those that were not, that had been in business 6 - 10 years

Benefit	Mean Members	N Members	Mean Non-members	N Non-Members	t-value	Sig.
A	2.56	9	3.16	19	1.219	.234
B	2.89	9	2.32	19	-1.390	.176
C	3.33	9	2.72	19	-1.133	.268
E	3.11	9	2.82	17	-.575	.571
F	3.10	10	3.28	18	.330	.744
G	3.22	9	3.18	17	-.096	.924
H	3.22	9	3.63	19	.120	.906
I	3.22	9	3.63	19	.924	.355
K	3.78	9	3.56	18	-.410	.685

* p<.05
** p<.01
*** p<.001

Legend

A	*Lower administration costs*
B	*Lower production costs*
C	*Reduced lead time*
D	*Reduced stock*
E	*Increased sales*
F	*Increased internal efficiency*
G	*Improved relations with business partners*
H	*New customers and markets*
I	*Improved competitiveness*
J	*Improved marketing*
K	*Improved quality of information*

TableA3.24

A comparison of the means of rating of benefits to adoption of E-commerce between those respondents that were members of a strategic alliance and those that were not, that had been in business 11 - 20 years

Benefit	Mean Members	N Members	Mean Non-members	N Non-Members	t-value	Sig.
A	3.46	13	2.89	18	-1.186	.245
B	2.75	12	2.88	17	.248	.806
C	3.17	12	3.06	17	-.226	.823
E	2.83	12	3.00	18	.367	.717
F	2.83	12	3.22	18	.844	.406
G	3.25	12	3.06	17	-.444	.660
H	2.82	12	3.35	17	1.094	.284
I	3.36	11	3.50	18	.386	.703
K	3.17	12	3.33	18	.317	.753

* p<.05
** p<.01
*** p<.001

Legend

A	*Lower administration costs*
B	*Lower production costs*
C	*Reduced lead time*
D	*Reduced stock*
E	*Increased sales*
F	*Increased internal efficiency*
G	*Improved relations with business partners*
H	*New customers and markets*
I	*Improved competitiveness*
J	*Improved marketing*
K	*Improved quality of information*

TableA3.25

A comparison of the means of rating of benefits to adoption of E-commerce between those respondents that were members of a strategic alliance and those that were not, that had been in business > 20 years

Benefit	Mean Members	N Members	Mean Non-members	N Non-Members	t-value	Sig.
A	2.92	12	3.13	32	.489	.627
B	3.08	12	3.34	32	.579	.566
C	2.92	12	3.38	32	1.046	.302
E	3.08	12	2.78	32	-.710	.482
F	3.00	12	3.38	32	.849	.401
G	2.75	12	3.39	32	1.703	.096
H	3.08	12	2.72	32	-.877	.386
I	3.33	12	3.30	32	-.069	.946
K	3.50	12	3.47	32	-.066	.947

* p<.05
** p<.01
*** p<.001

Legend

A	*Lower administration costs*
B	*Lower production costs*
C	*Reduced lead time*
D	*Reduced stock*
E	*Increased sales*
F	*Increased internal efficiency*
G	*Improved relations with business partners*
H	*New customers and markets*
I	*Improved competitiveness*
J	*Improved marketing*
K	*Improved quality of information*

TableA3.26
A comparison of the means of rating of criteria for adoption of E-commerce between those respondents that were members of a strategic alliance and those that were not, that had 1 - 9 employees

Criteria	Mean Members	N Members	Mean Non-members	N Non-members	t-value	Sig.
B	2.76	25	2.19	32	-1.595	.116
D	3.76	25	3.09	32	-1.937	.058
E	4.42	26	4.06	32	-1.388	.171
F	3.08	24	2.91	32	-.432	.668
G	3.28	25	3.28	32	.000	1.000
H	3.92	26	3.82	34	-.351	.727
I	3.60	25	3.41	32	-.581	.563
J	3.68	25	3.72	32	.099	.921
K	3.72	25	3.97	32	.698	.488
M	3.28	25	3.72	32	1.071	.289
N	2.88	24	3.13	32	.694	.491

* p<.05
** p<.01
*** p<.001

Legend

A	*Demand/pressure from customers*
B	*Pressure of competition*
C	*Demand/pressure from suppliers*
D	*Reduction of costs*
E	*Improvement to customer service*
F	*Improvement in lead time*
G	*Increased sales*
H	*Improvement to internal efficiency*
I	*Strengthen relations with business partners*
J	*Reach new customers/markets*
K	*Improvement in competitiveness*
L	*External technical support*
M	*Improvement in marketing*
N	*Improvement in control and follow-up*

TableA3.27

A comparison of the means of rating of criteria for adoption of E-commerce between those respondents that were members of a strategic alliance and those that were not, that had 20 - 49 employees

Criteria	Mean Members	N Members	Mean Non-members	N Non-members	t-value	Sig.
B	3.25	8	2.62	21	-1.273	.214
D	3.78	9	3.20	20	-1.349	.189
E	4.50	8	3.95	21	-1.371	.182
F	3.33	9	3.00	20	-.577	.569
G	3.63	8	3.15	20	-.959	.3346
H	4.00	9	4.00	20	.000	1.000
I	3.33	9	3.33	20	.000	1.000
J	3.44	9	3.15	20	-.687	.498
K	4.00	9	3.57	21	-1.020	.316
M	3.44	9	3.35	20	-.179	.859
N	3.22	9	3.15	20	-.141	.889

* p<.05
** p<.01
*** p<.001

Legend

A	*Demand/pressure from customers*
B	*Pressure of competition*
C	*Demand/pressure from suppliers*
D	*Reduction of costs*
E	*Improvement to customer service*
F	*Improvement in lead time*
G	*Increased sales*
H	*Improvement to internal efficiency*
I	*Strengthen relations with business partners*
J	*Reach new customers/markets*
K	*Improvement in competitiveness*
L	*External technical support*
M	*Improvement in marketing*
N	*Improvement in control and follow-up*

A comparison of the means of rating of barriers to adoption of E-commerce between those respondents that were members of a strategic alliance and those that were not, that had 1 - 9 employees

Barriers	Mean Members	N Members	Mean Non-members	N Non-members	t-value	Sig.
A	3.83	29	3.74	23	-.250	.804
B	3.50	28	3.46	26	-.096	.924
C	3.26	28	3.88	24	1.553	.127
D	3.17	29	2.91	23	-.610	.545
E	3.07	27	2.96	24	-.288	.775
F	2.62	26	2.83	23	.581	.564
G	2.73	26	2.83	23	.251	.803
H	2.79	24	2.82	22	.063	.950

* p<.05
** p<.01
*** p<.001

Legend

A	*E-commerce doesn't fit with products/services*
B	*E-commerce doesn't fit with the way we do business*
C	*E-commerce doesn't fit the way our customers work*
D	*We don't see the advantage of using E-commerce*
E	*Lack of technical know how*
F	*Security risks*
G	*Cost too high*
H	*Not sure what to choose*

TableA3.29
A comparison of the means of rating of benefits from adoption of E-commerce between those respondents that were members of a strategic alliance and those that were not, that had 1 - 9 employees

Benefit	Mean Members	N Members	Mean Non-members	N Non-Members	t-value	Sig.
A	3.56	27	2.88	32	-1.984	.052
B	3.46	26	2.78	32	-1.806	.076
C	3.65	26	3.19	31	-1.279	.206
E	3.04	26	3.07	30	.077	.939
F	3.19	27	3.16	31	-.064	.949
G	3.31	26	3.31	32	.000	1.000
H	3.27	26	3.25	32	-.053	.958
I	3.56	27	3.56	31	.338	.737
K	3.56	27	3.42	31	-.347	.730

* p<.05
** p<.01
*** p<.001

Legend

A	*Lower administration costs*

B	*Lower production costs*
C	*Reduced lead time*
D	*Reduced stock*
E	*Increased sales*
F	*Increased internal efficiency*
G	*Improved relations with business partners*
H	*New customers and markets*
I	*Improved competitiveness*
J	*Improved marketing*
K	*Improved quality of information*

TableA3.30
A comparison of the means of rating of criteria for adoption of E-commerce between those respondents that were members of a strategic alliance and those that were not, and were from the industrial sector

Criteria	Mean Members	N Members	Mean Non-members	N Non-members	t-value	Sig.
B	1.91	11	2.59	17	1.661	.109
D	3.08	12	2.94	16	-.399	.693
E	4.42	12	4.12	17	-.829	.414
F	3.17	12	2.69	16	-.953	.350
G	3.46	13	3.88	16	1.151	.260
H	3.92	12	4.00	17	.320	.752
I	3.58	12	3.41	17	-.455	.653
J	3.92	12	3.94	16	.041	.968
K	3.67	12	3.88	17	.522	.606
M	3.77	13	4.19	16	1.170	.252
N	3.00	12	3.06	16	.174	.863

* $p<.05$
** $p<.01$
*** $p<.001$

Legend

A	*Demand/pressure from customers*
B	*Pressure of competition*
C	*Demand/pressure from suppliers*
D	*Reduction of costs*
E	*Improvement to customer service*
F	*Improvement in lead time*
G	*Increased sales*
H	*Improvement to internal efficiency*
I	*Strengthen relations with business partners*
J	*Reach new customers/markets*
K	*Improvement in competitiveness*
L	*External technical support*
M	*Improvement in marketing*
N	*Improvement in control and follow-up*

TableA3.31
A comparison of the means of rating of criteria for adoption of E-commerce between those respondents that were members of a strategic alliance and those that were not, and were from the retail sector

Criteria	Mean Members	N Members	Mean Non-members	N Non-members	t-value	Sig.
B	1.75	8	2.41	17	1.316	.201
D	3.13	8	3.47	17	.576	.571
E	4.25	8	4.06	17	-.498	.623
F	2.25	8	3.47	17	1.976	.060
G	3.50	8	3.76	17	.486	.631
H	3.44	8	3.76	17	.592	.559
I	3.00	8	3.76	17	1.488	.150
J	3.75	8	3.12	17	-1.101	.282
K	3.50	8	4.00	17	.989	.323
M	3.71	7	3.41	17	-.424	.676
N	2.63	8	3.18	17	.972	.342

* p<.05
** p<.01
*** p<.001

Legend

A	*Demand/pressure from customers*
B	*Pressure of competition*
C	*Demand/pressure from suppliers*
D	*Reduction of costs*
E	*Improvement to customer service*
F	*Improvement in lead time*
G	*Increased sales*
H	*Improvement to internal efficiency*
I	*Strengthen relations with business partners*
J	*Reach new customers/markets*
K	*Improvement in competitiveness*
L	*External technical support*
M	*Improvement in marketing*
N	*Improvement in control and follow-up*

TableA3.32
A comparison of the means of rating of barriers to adoption of E-commerce between those respondents that were members of a strategic alliance and those that were not, that indicated that they were from the service sector

Barriers	Mean Members	N Members	Mean Non-members	N Non-members	t-value	Sig.
A	3.46	26	3.46	13	.000	1.000
B	3.46	26	3.15	13	-.587	.561
C	3.00	26	3.75	12	1.496	.143
D	3.11	27	2.67	12	-.824	.415
E	2.89	27	3.08	12	.380	.706
F	2.73	26	3.00	12	.592	.557
G	2.59	27	2.92	12	.663	.511
H	2.80	25	3.50	10	1.229	.228

* p<.05
** p<.01
*** p<.001

Legend

A	*E-commerce doesn't fit with products/services*
B	*E-commerce doesn't fit with the way we do business*
C	*E-commerce doesn't fit the way our customers work*
D	*We don't see the advantage of using E-commerce*
E	*Lack of technical know how*
F	*Security risks*
G	*Cost too high*
H	*Not sure what to choose*

TableA3.33
A comparison of the means of rating of criteria for adoption of E-commerce between those respondents that were members of a strategic alliance and those that were not, and were national market respondents

Criteria	Mean Members	N Members	Mean Non-members	N Non-members	t-value	Sig.
B	2.81	16	2.38	32	-1.112	.272
D	3.31	16	3.31	32	.000	1.000
E	4.41	17	4.28	32	-.493	.624
F	2.50	16	2.90	32	.894	.376
G	3.53	17	3.66	32	.325	.747
H	3.88	17	3.81	32	-.195	.846
I	3.88	16	3.31	32	-1.600	.116
J	3.76	17	3.63	32	-.360	.720
K	4.06	16	3.75	32	-.846	.402
M	3.82	17	4.09	32	.802	.426
N	3.00	16	3.03	31	.081	.936

* p<.05
** p<.01
*** p<.001

Legend

A	Demand/pressure from customers
B	Pressure of competition
C	Demand/pressure from suppliers
D	Reduction of costs
E	Improvement to customer service
F	Improvement in lead time
G	Increased sales
H	Improvement to internal efficiency
I	Strengthen relations with business partners
J	Reach new customers/markets
K	Improvement in competitiveness
L	External technical support
M	Improvement in marketing
N	Improvement in control and follow-up

TableA3.34
A comparison of the means of rating of benefits from adoption of E-commerce between those respondents that were members of a strategic alliance and those that were not, for businesses that are nationally focused

Benefit	Mean Members	N Members	Mean Non-members	N Non-Members	t-value	Sig.
A	3.29	17	3.00	31	-.793	.432
B	3.24	17	2.77	30	-1.127	.266
C	3.35	17	3.07	30	-.675	.503
E	3.47	17	3.03	30	-1.197	.238
F	3.17	18	3.13	30	-.081	.936
G	3.53	17	3.24	29	-1.121	.313
H	3.65	17	3.29	31	-1.013	.317
I	3.65	17	3.29	29	-1.069	.291
K	3.94	18	3.80	30	-.405	.687

* p<.05
** p<.01
*** p<.001

Legend

A	Lower administration costs
B	Lower production costs
C	Reduced lead time
D	Reduced stock
E	Increased sales
F	Increased internal efficiency
G	Improved relations with business partners
H	New customers and markets
I	Improved competitiveness
J	Improved marketing
K	Improved quality of information

TableA3.35
A comparison of the means of rating of benefits from adoption of E-commerce between those respondents that were members of a strategic alliance and those that were not, for businesses that indicated their computer skill level was normal

Benefit	Mean Members	N Members	Mean Non-members	N Non-Members	t-value	Sig.
A	3.25	43	2.98	24	-.842	.403
B	2.70	42	2.86	23	.437	.664
C	3.04	42	2.95	23	-.256	.799
E	2.65	42	3.05	23	1.215	.229
F	2.79	42	3.05	24	.778	.440
G	3.09	41	3.15	23	.192	.848
H	2.86	41	3.22	22	1.005	.319
I	3.18	42	3.48	22	.999	.322
K	3.22	42	3.12	23	-.324	.747

* p<.05
** p<.01
*** p<.001

Legend

A	*Lower administration costs*
B	*Lower production costs*
C	*Reduced lead time*
D	*Reduced stock*
E	*Increased sales*
F	*Increased internal efficiency*
G	*Improved relations with business partners*
H	*New customers and markets*
I	*Improved competitiveness*
J	*Improved marketing*
K	*Improved quality of information*

TableA3.36
A comparison of the means of rating of benefits from adoption of E-commerce between those respondents that were members of a strategic alliance and those that were not, for businesses that indicated their computer skill level was high

Benefit	Mean Members	N Members	Mean Non-members	N Non-Members	t-value	Sig.
A	3.09	21	2.95	11	-.295	.770
B	3.00	21	3.19	11	.377	.709
C	2.91	21	3.29	11	.779	.445
E	3.18	20	2.65	11	-1.123	.271
F	3.27	21	3.14	11	-.254	.801
G	3.14	21	3.18	11	-.084	.933
H	3.42	21	2.86	11	-1.177	.248
I	3.45	21	3.43	11	-.055	.956
K	3.45	21	3.24	11	-.457	.651

* p<.05
** p<.01
*** p<.001

Legend

A	*Lower administration costs*
B	*Lower production costs*
C	*Reduced lead time*
D	*Reduced stock*
E	*Increased sales*
F	*Increased internal efficiency*
G	*Improved relations with business partners*
H	*New customers and markets*
I	*Improved competitiveness*
J	*Improved marketing*
K	*Improved quality of information*

Appendix 4
Non Significant data from the Australian Study

Table A4.1
Adoption/Non-Adoption of Electronic Commerce

		Frequency	Percent	Valid Percent	Cumulative Percent
Valid	Adopted EC	25	15.6	15.6	15.6
	Not adopted	135	84.4	84.4	100.0
	Total	160	100.0	100.0	

Table A4.2
Membership/Non-Membership of a Small Business Strategic alliance

		Frequency	Percent	Valid Percent	Cumulative Percent
Valid	Non-members	112	70.0	70.0	70.0
	members	48	30.0	30.0	100.0
	Total	160	100.0	100.0	

Table A4.3
Age of the Business

		Frequency	Percent	Valid Percent	Cumulative Percent
Valid	< 1 year	11	6.9	6.9	6.9
	1-2 years	16	10.0	10.0	16.9
	3-5 years	25	15.6	15.6	32.5
	6-10 years	27	16.9	16.9	49.4
	11-20 years	40	25.0	25.0	74.4
	> 20 years	41	25.6	25.6	100.0
	Total	160	100.0	100.0	

Table A4.4
Size of Business

		Frequency	Percent	Valid Percent	Cumulative Percent
Valid	Sole trader	30	18.8	18.8	18.8
	1-9 employees	112	70.0	70.0	88.8
	10-19 employees	9	5.6	5.6	94.4
	20-50 employees	9	5.6	5.6	100.0
	Total	160	100.0	100.0	

Table A4.5
Business Sector

		Frequency	Percent	Valid Percent	Cumulative Percent
Valid	Industrial	10	6.3	6.3	6.3
	Service	79	49.8	49.8	56.1
	Retail/Trading	67	41.9	41.9	98.0
	Financial	1	0.1	0.1	98.1
	Other	3	1.9	1.9	100.0
	Total	160	100.0	100.0	

Table A4.6
Market focus

		Frequency	Percent	Valid Percent	Cumulative Percent
Valid	Local business	44	27.5	27.5	27.5
	Regional business	95	59.4	59.4	86.9
	National	20	12.5	12.5	99.4
	International	1	0.6	0.6	100.0
	Total	313	100.0	100.0	

Table A4.7
Computer Skill within the Business

		Frequency	Percent	Valid Percent	Cumulative Percent
Valid	No skill	9	5.6	5.6	5.6
	Low skill	41	25.8	25.8	31.4
	Normal skill	71	44.7	44.7	76.1
	High skill	27	18.1	18.1	94.2
	Expert skill	11	5.8	5.8	100.0
	Total	160	100.0	100.0	

Table A4.8
Membership/Non-Membership of a Small Business Strategic alliance

		Frequency	Percent	Valid Percent	Cumulative Percent
Valid	Members	15	60.0	40	40
	Non-members	10	40.0	60.0	100.0
	Total	25	100.0	100.0	

E-Commerce Adopters

		Frequency	Percent	Valid Percent	Cumulative Percent
Valid	Members	97	71.9	28.1	28.1
	Non-members	38	28.1	71.9	100.0
	Total	135	100.0	100.0	

E-Commerce Non-adopters

Table A4.9
Age of Business

		Frequency	Percent	Valid Percent	Cumulative Percent
Valid	< 1yr	1	4.0	4.0	4.0
	1-2 years	1	4.0	4.0	8.0
	3-5 years	6	24.0	24.0	32.0
	6-10 years	5	20.0	20.0	52.0
	11-20 years	6	24.0	24.0	76.0
	> 20 years	6	24.0	24.0	100.0
	Total	25	100.0	100.0	

E-Commerce Adopters

		Frequency	Percent	Valid Percent	Cumulative Percent
Valid	< 1 year	10	7.4	7.4	7.4
	1-2 years	15	11.1	11.1	18.5
	3-5 years	19	14.1	14.1	32.6
	6-10 years	22	16.3	16.3	48.9
	11-20 years	34	25.2	25.2	74.1
	> 20 years	35	25.9	25.9	100.0
	Total	135	100.0	100.0	

E-Commerce Non-adopters

Table A4.10
Size of Business

		Frequency	Percent	Valid Percent	Cumulative Percent
Valid	Sole trader	3	12.0	12.0	12.0
	1-9 employees	22	88.0	88.0	100.0
	10-19 employees				
	20-50 employees				
	Total	25	100.0	100.0	

E-Commerce Adopters

		Frequency	Percent	Valid Percent	Cumulative Percent
Valid	Sole trader	27	20.0	20.0	20.0
	1-9 employees	90	66.7	66.7	86.7
	10-19 employees	9	6.7	6.7	93.4
	20-50 employees	8	5.9	5.9	100.0
	Total	135	100.0	100.0	

E-Commerce Non-adopters

Table A4.11
Business Sector

		Frequency	Percent	Valid Percent	Cumulative Percent
Valid	Industrial	1	4.0	4.0	4.0
	Service	14	56.0	56.0	60.0
	Retail/Trading	10	40.0	40.0	1000.0
	Financial				
	Total	25	100.0	100.0	

E-Commerce Adopters

		Frequency	Percent	Valid Percent	Cumulative Percent
Valid	Industrial	10	7.4	7.4	7.4
	Service	65	48.1	48.1	55.5
	Retail/Trading	57	42.2	42.2	100.0
	Total	132	100.0	100.0	

E-Commerce Non-adopters

Table A4.12
Market Focus

		Frequency	Percent	Valid Percent	Cumulative Percent
Valid	Local business	3	12.0	12.0	12.0
	Regional business	17	68.0	68.0	80.0
	National	4	16.0	16.0	96.0
	International	1	4.0	4.0	100.0
	Total	152	100.0	100.0	

E-Commerce Adopters

		Frequency	Percent	Valid Percent	Cumulative Percent
Valid	Local business	41	30.4	30.4	30.4
	Regional business	78	57.8	57.8	88.2
	National	16	11.8	11.8	100.0
	International				
	Total	123	100.0	100.0	

E-Commerce Non-adopters

Table A4.13
Computer Skills

		Frequency	Percent	Valid Percent	Cumulative Percent
Valid	No skill	1	4.0	4.0	4.0
	Low skill	4	16.	16.0	20.0
	Normal skill	11	44.0	44.0	64.0
	High skill	4	16.0	16.0	80.0
	Expert skill	5	20.0	20.0	100.0
	Total	25	100.0	100.0	

E-Commerce Adopters

		Frequency	Percent	Valid Percent	Cumulative Percent
Valid	No skill	1	.7	.7	.7
	Low skill	8	5.9	5.9	6.6
	Normal skill	37	27.4	27.4	34.0
	High skill	60	44.4	44.4	78.4
	Expert skill	23	21.6	21.6	100.0
	Total	135	100.0	100.0	

E-Commerce Non-adopters

Table A4.14
Age of Business

		Frequency	Percent	Valid Percent	Cumulative Percent
Valid	< 1 year	1	2.1	2.1	2.1
	1-2 years	4	8.3	8.3	10.5
	3-5 years	9	18.8	18.8	29.3
	6-10 years	8	16.7	16.7	46.0
	11-20 years	13	27.0	27.0	73.0
	> 20 years	13	27.0	27.0	100.0
	Total	48	100.0	100.0	

Member of a small business strategic alliance

		Frequency	Percent	Valid Percent	Cumulative Percent
Valid	< 1 year	10	8.9	8.9	8.9
	1-2 years	12	10.7	10.7	19.6
	3-5 years	16	14.3	14.3	33.9
	6-10 years	19	17.0	17.0	50.9
	11-20 years	28	25.1	25.1	76.0
	> 20 years	27	24.0	24.0	100.0
	Total	112	100.0	100.0	

Non-Member of a small business strategic alliance

Table A4.15
Size of Business

		Frequency	Percent	Valid Percent	Cumulative Percent
Valid	Sole trader	9	18.8	18.8	18.8
	1-9 employees	32	66.7	66.7	85.5
	10-19 employees	3	6.7	6.7	92.2
	20-50 employees	4	7.8	7.8	100.0
	Total	48	100.0	100.0	

Member of a small business strategic alliance

		Frequency	Percent	Valid Percent	Cumulative Percent
Valid	Sole trader	21	18.8	18.8	18.8
	1-9 employees	80	71.4	71.4	90.2
	10-19 employees	6	5.4	5.4	95.6
	20-50 employees	4	4.4	4.4	100.0
	Total	112	100.0	100.0	

Non-Member of a small business strategic alliance

Table A4.16
Business Sector

		Frequency	Percent	Valid Percent	Cumulative Percent
Valid	Industrial	5	10.4	10.4	10.4
	Service	28	58.3	58.3	68.7
	Retail/trading	12	25.0	25.0	93.7
	Financial				
	Other	3	6.3	6.3	100.0
	Total	48	100.0	100.0	

Member of a small business strategic alliance

		Frequency	Percent	Valid Percent	Cumulative Percent
Valid	Industrial	6	5.4	5.4	5.4
	Service	51	45.5	45.5	50.9
	Retail/trading	55	49.1	49.1	100.0
	Financial				
	Total	112	100.0	100.0	

Non-Member of a small business strategic alliance

Table A4.17
Market Focus

		Frequency	Percent	Valid Percent	Cumulative Percent
Valid	Local business	14	29.2	29.2	29.2
	Regional business	25	52.1	52.1	81.3
	National	8	16.6	16.6	97.9
	International	1	2.1	2.1	100.0
	Total	48	100.0	100.0	

Member of a small business strategic alliance

		Frequency	Percent	Valid Percent	Cumulative Percent
Valid	Local business	30	26.8	26.8	26.8
	Regional business	70	62.5	62.5	89.3
	National	12	10.7	10.7	100.0
	International				
	Total	112	100.0	100.0	

Non-Member of a small business strategic alliance

Table A4.18
Skill Level

		Frequency	Percent	Valid Percent	Cumulative Percent
Valid	No skill	2	4.2	4.2	4.2
	Low skill	7	14.6	14.6	18.8
	Normal skill	22	45.8	45.8	64.6
	High skill	9	18.8	18.8	83.4
	Expert skill	8	16.6	16.6	100.0
	Total	48	100.0	100.0	

Member of a small business strategic alliance

		Frequency	Percent	Valid Percent	Cumulative Percent
Valid	No skill	7	6.3	6.3	6.3
	Low skill	34	30.4	30.4	36.7
	Normal skill	49	43.8	43.8	80.5
	High skill	18	16.1	16.1	96.6
	Expert skill	3	3.4	3.4	100.0
	Total	112	100.0	100.0	

Non-Member of a small business strategic alliance

Table A4.19
A comparison of the means of rating of barriers to adoption of E-commerce between those respondents that were members of a strategic alliance and those that were not- (retail)

Barriers	Mean Members	N Members	Mean Non-members	N Non-members	t-value	Sig.
A	3.33	9	3.29	48	.068	.946
B	3.56	9	3.54	48	.026	.979
C	3.56	9	3.42	48	.257	.798
D	2.67	9	3.48	48	-1.478	.145
E	3.44	9	3.63	48	-.314	.754
F	2.78	9	3.15	48	-.645	.521
G	2.78	9	3.44	48	-1.117	.269
H	2.89	9	3.10	48	-.365	.717

Table A4.20
A comparison of the means of rating of barriers to adoption of E-commerce between those respondents that were members of a strategic alliance and those that were not (low skill)

Barriers	Mean Members	N Members	Mean Non-members	N Non-members	t-value	Sig.
A	3.29	7	3.50	30	-.304	.763
B	3.71	7	3.60	30	.177	.860
C	3.71	7	3.70	30	.023	.982
D	3.57	7	3.70	30	-.191	.850
E	4.00	7	4.33	30	-.647	.522
F	3.00	7	3.27	30	-.401	.691
G	3.00	7	3.60	30	-.858	.397
H	3.57	7	3.40	30	.265	.792

Legend

A	*E-commerce doesn't fit with products/services*
B	*E-commerce doesn't fit with the way we do business*
C	*E-commerce doesn't fit the way our customers work*
D	*We don't see the advantage of using E-commerce*
E	*Lack of technical know how*
F	*Security risks*
G	*Cost too high*
H	*Not sure what to choose*

Table A4.21
A comparison of the means of rating of barriers to adoption of E-commerce between those respondents that were members of a strategic alliance and those that were not (high skill)

Barriers	Mean Members	N Members	Mean Non-members	N Non-members	t-value	Sig.
A	2.88	8	2.87	15	.011	.991
B	2.25	8	3.47	15	-1.779	.090
C	2.63	8	2.80	15	-.240	.813
D	2.50	8	3.33	15	-1.217	.237
E	1.38	8	1.40	15	-.071	.944
F	2.00	8	2.80	15	-1.733	.098
G	1.50	8	2.33	15	-1.388	.180
H	1.75	8	2.53	15	-1.422	.170

Legend

A	*E-commerce doesn't fit with products/services*
B	*E-commerce doesn't fit with the way we do business*
C	*E-commerce doesn't fit the way our customers work*
D	*We don't see the advantage of using E-commerce*
E	*Lack of technical know how*
F	*Security risks*
G	*Cost too high*
H	*Not sure what to choose*

Pilot Study Questionnaires

SMALL BUSINESS COMPUTER USAGE SURVEY

The University of Wollongong seeks your co-operation in determining which factors are considered important for Small Business satisfaction with computing technology and the educational requirements necessary to better equip Small Business for computerisation.

The survey will provide vital information to assist in the design of courses to meet the need of Small Business.
Thank you for your participation and support.
Please send replies to:
R.MacGregor
Department of Business Systems
University of Wollongong
Northfields Avenue
Wollongong 2500
FAX (042) 21 4474

The survey will take you approximately 10 minutes to complete. Please feel free to attach any comments that you wish to add.

Results of this survey will be supplied <u>free of charge</u> to all survey participants. **All information supplied will be treated confidentially**

Name of Organisation _____

Type of Business_____

How many people does your business employ _____

Does your business use computers   Y [ ]   N [ ]

How many years has your business been using computers _____

Do you use a computer   Y [ ]   N [ ]

How many years have you been using a computer _____

What are the major uses of computers in you company
  Accounting/Finance   [ ]
  Manufacturing/Scheduling   [ ]
  Customer support   [ ]
  Word processing   [ ]
  Research   [ ]

Other (please specify) _____
_____

How many hours (per week) are spent on the following
        Maintenance and repair of computing equipment   _____
        Developing new projects for the computer   _____
        Helping people use the computer systems   _____
        Keeping track of how the computer is being used   _____
        Checking the data from the computer   _____
        Checking the security of your computer systems   _____

Do you have a person devoted to looking after the computers   Y [ ]   N [ ]
If more than one please state how many _____

How many hours per week are spent on this task   _____

How many hours per year are devoted to training people to look after the computer

_____

How many hours per year are devoted to training people to use the computer

_____

How would you rate your company's ability in the following areas (1 = very poor - 5 = excellent)

	1	2	3	4	5	
Using technology to meet business requirements	[ ]	[ ]	[ ]	[ ]	[ ]
Implementation of new hardware and software	[ ]	[ ]	[ ]	[ ]	[ ]
Management of staff who look after the computers	[ ]	[ ]	[ ]	[ ]	[ ]
Knowing what information you need to run your business	[ ]	[ ]	[ ]	[ ]	[ ]
Designing new systems to do your work	[ ]	[ ]	[ ]	[ ]	[ ]
Evaluating hardware and software when purchasing	[ ]	[ ]	[ ]	[ ]	[ ]
Evaluating the benefits of using technology	[ ]	[ ]	[ ]	[ ]	[ ]
Implementing systems for specific staff members	[ ]	[ ]	[ ]	[ ]	[ ]

Rank the following skills, in order of importance for your company, when considering future computer use

	1	2	3	4	5	
Using technology to meet business requirements	[ ]	[ ]	[ ]	[ ]	[ ]
Implementation of new hardware and software	[ ]	[ ]	[ ]	[ ]	[ ]
Management of staff who look after the computers	[ ]	[ ]	[ ]	[ ]	[ ]
Knowing what information you need to run your business	[ ]	[ ]	[ ]	[ ]	[ ]
Designing new systems to do your work	[ ]	[ ]	[ ]	[ ]	[ ]
Evaluating hardware and software when purchasing	[ ]	[ ]	[ ]	[ ]	[ ]
Evaluating the benefits of using technology	[ ]	[ ]	[ ]	[ ]	[ ]
Implementing systems for specific staff members	[ ]	[ ]	[ ]	[ ]	[ ]

Who negotiates the purchase of computer hardware and software

You	[ ]
Someone else	[ ]

(please specify) _____

How much input did staff have on the purchase and use of computing equipment

None	[ ]
very little	[ ]
some	[ ]
a lot	[ ]

Were your requirements for the use of computers and associated software ever documented
Y [ ]

N [ ]

By whom   Rank the following as they related to you
                                          determining your requirements (most important
                                                              to least important)

By whom		Rank	
You	[ ]	increased productivity	[ ]
Your staff	[ ]	streamlining work procedures	[ ]
the supplier	[ ]	better client service	[ ]
		better record keeping	[ ]
		other	[ ]

please specify _____

_____

Were detailed performance measures for equipment and software developed Y [ ]   N [ ]

By whom   Rank the following as they related to you
                                          determining your performance measures
                                          (most important to least important)

By whom		Rank	
You	[ ]	increased productivity	[ ]
Your staff	[ ]	streamlining work procedures	[ ]
the supplier	[ ]	better client service	[ ]
		better record keeping	[ ]
		other	[ ]
		(please specify) _____	

_____

Were either the requirements or the performance measures changed during the course of the
negotiations with vendors   Y [ ] N [ ]

By whom   Rank which areas changes most affected

By whom		Rank	
You	[ ]	increased productivity	[ ]
Your staff	[ ]	streamlining work procedures	[ ]

the supplier   [   ]   better client service   [   ]
                                        better record keeping   [   ]
                                        other   [   ]
                                             (please specify) _____

How many computer vendors did you approach when purchasing your computers _____

Rank in order of importance the major reasons you purchased your computers
    actual performance of the system against your specified performance measures   [   ]
    cost   [   ]
    expected benefits   [   ]
    ease of use   [   ]
    possibility for future enhancements   [   ]

If you were to re-negotiate the purchase of your computing equipment how would you rank
major criteria for your selection (most important to least important)
    actual performance of the system against your specified performance measures   [   ]
    cost   [   ]
    expected benefits   [   ]
    ease of use   [   ]
    possibility for future enhancements   [   ]

How would you rate the vendor support in the following areas (1 = very poor - 5 excellent)
                                                    1   2   3   4   5
delivery and installation of computer systems of equipment [   ]   [   ]   [   ]   [   ]   [   ]
availability of information about the computer   [   ]   [   ]   [   ]   [   ]   [   ]
satisfaction with the equipment and software   [   ]   [   ]   [   ]   [   ]   [   ]
computer system changes   [   ]   [   ]   [   ]   [   ]   [   ]
computer systems training   [   ]   [   ]   [   ]   [   ]   [   ]
computer systems documentation   [   ]   [   ]   [   ]   [   ]   [   ]
computer problem rectification   [   ]   [   ]   [   ]   [   ]   [   ]

Rank, in order of importance, those factors which make up computer systems vendor support
    delivery and installation of computer systems of equipment   [   ]
    availability of information about the computer   [   ]
    satisfaction with the equipment and software   [   ]
    computer system changes   [   ]
    computer systems training   [   ]
    computer systems documentation   [   ]
    computer problem rectification   [   ]

Do you think you got the best possible system, if not
why_____

_____

Did the benefits of the computer system justify the costs   Y [   ] N [   ]

238

Did the benefits of the computer system justify the risks   Y [ ] N [ ]

How accurate in terms of cost were the estimates given for the purchase, installation and maintenance of your computer system (1 = very poor - 5 = very accurate)   [ ]

How accurate in terms of time were the estimates given for the implementation of your
computer system (1 = very poor - 5 = very accurate)   1   2   3   4   5
                                                  [ ]   [ ]   [ ]   [ ]   [ ]

How accurate in terms of time were the estimates given for the support and maintenance of
your computer system (1 = very poor - 5 = very accurate)   1   2   3   4   5
                                                  [ ]   [ ]   [ ]   [ ]   [ ]

How accurate, in terms of skills required by you and your staff to operate the computer system, were the estimates given for your computer system (1 = very poor - 5 = very accurate)
                                        1   2   3   4   5
                                       [ ]   [ ]   [ ]   [ ]   [ ]

If you undertook a computing course how would you rate as important to you the following
(1 = not important; 5 = very important)

	1	2	3	4	5
Structure and function of computer hardware		[ ]	[ ]	[ ]	[ ]	[ ]
Programming	[ ]	[ ]	[ ]	[ ]	[ ]	
The use of Databases and Spreadsheets		[ ]	[ ]	[ ]	[ ]	[ ]
Business Analysis	[ ]	[ ]	[ ]	[ ]	[ ]	
Information Analysis	[ ]	[ ]	[ ]	[ ]	[ ]	
Office Automation	[ ]	[ ]	[ ]	[ ]	[ ]	
Business and Accounting Systems		[ ]	[ ]	[ ]	[ ]	[ ]
Computer Evaluation Techniques		[ ]	[ ]	[ ]	[ ]	[ ]
Accountancy	[ ]	[ ]	[ ]	[ ]	[ ]	
Finance		[ ]	[ ]	[ ]	[ ]	[ ]
Marketing	[ ]	[ ]	[ ]	[ ]	[ ]	
Business Law	[ ]	[ ]	[ ]	[ ]	[ ]	
Statistics	[ ]	[ ]	[ ]	[ ]	[ ]	
Management Principles		[ ]	[ ]	[ ]	[ ]	[ ]
Interpersonal Skills	[ ]	[ ]	[ ]	[ ]	[ ]	

If a Small Business Computing course was introduced at the University what skills should a graduate have:

	1	2	3	4	5
Structure and function of computer hardware		[ ]	[ ]	[ ]	[ ]	[ ]
Programming	[ ]	[ ]	[ ]	[ ]	[ ]	
The use of Databases and Spreadsheets		[ ]	[ ]	[ ]	[ ]	[ ]
Business Analysis	[ ]	[ ]	[ ]	[ ]	[ ]	
Information Analysis	[ ]	[ ]	[ ]	[ ]	[ ]	
Office Automation	[ ]	[ ]	[ ]	[ ]	[ ]	
Business and Accounting Systems		[ ]	[ ]	[ ]	[ ]	[ ]
Computer Evaluation Techniques		[ ]	[ ]	[ ]	[ ]	[ ]
Accountancy	[ ]	[ ]	[ ]	[ ]	[ ]	
Finance		[ ]	[ ]	[ ]	[ ]	[ ]
Marketing	[ ]	[ ]	[ ]	[ ]	[ ]	

Business Law	[ ]	[ ]	[ ]	[ ]	[ ]	
Statistics	[ ]	[ ]	[ ]	[ ]	[ ]	
Management Principles		[ ]	[ ]	[ ]	[ ]	[ ]
Interpersonal Skills	[ ]	[ ]	[ ]	[ ]	[ ]	

Number of Employees_____   Type of business_____

Number of years using computer technology_____

Indicate the number of years, the number of companies you deal with, the percentage of business transactions and the percentage of business (in terms of revenue) using the following Electronic Commerce technologies:

	Number of Years	Number of Companies	Percentage of transactions	Revenue Percentage
Barcoding	[ ]	[ ]	[ ]	[ ]
Computer aided design /manufacturing (CAD/CAM)	[ ]	[ ]	[ ]	[ ]
Computer telephone integration (CTI)	[ ]	[ ]	[ ]	[ ]
Document Imaging Processing (DIP)	[ ]	[ ]	[ ]	[ ]
Electronic Catalogues	[ ]	[ ]	[ ]	[ ]
Electronic Data Interchange (EDI)	[ ]	[ ]	[ ]	[ ]
Facsimile	[ ]	[ ]	[ ]	[ ]
Electronic Mail	[ ]	[ ]	[ ]	[ ]
Internet	[ ]	[ ]	[ ]	[ ]
Telex	[ ]	[ ]	[ ]	[ ]
Mobile Phone	[ ]	[ ]	[ ]	[ ]
Voice Mail	[ ]	[ ]	[ ]	[ ]
Video conferencing	[ ]	[ ]	[ ]	[ ]
Electronic Information Services eg news/tenders	[ ]	[ ]	[ ]	[ ]

How many companies do you deal with altogether _____

Did you set up and document specific standards
when using electronic commerce methods   Y[ ]   N[ ]

Who was involved in the development of these standards
Staff   [ ]
Management   [ ]
Vendors   [ ]
Trading Partners   [ ]
Consultants   [ ]

Did you choose EDI or was it forced on you by businesses you deal with
Chose [ ]   Forced [ ]

Would you choose EDI now if you could re-appraise the situation

Yes [ ]   No [ ]

How important (1 - not very important 5 - very important) are the following to your company in the exchange of business documents

	not very important			very important	
	1	2	3	4	5
Australia Post	[ ]	[ ]	[ ]	[ ]	[ ]
FAX	[ ]	[ ]	[ ]	[ ]	[ ]
Electronic Data Interchange (EDI)	[ ]	[ ]	[ ]	[ ]	[ ]
Electronic Mail (Email)	[ ]	[ ]	[ ]	[ ]	[ ]
Internet	[ ]	[ ]	[ ]	[ ]	[ ]
Telex	[ ]	[ ]	[ ]	[ ]	[ ]

Telephone	[ ]	[ ]	[ ]	[ ]	[ ]

Has there been an improvement/no change/ deterioration in terms of the following in your business because of the introduction of electronic commerce technologies:

	improvement	no change	deterioration
financial	[ ]	[ ]	[ ]
profits	[ ]	[ ]	[ ]
inventory level	[ ]	[ ]	[ ]
employee related expenses	[ ]	[ ]	[ ]
revenue	[ ]	[ ]	[ ]
quality of transactions exchanged	[ ]	[ ]	[ ]
efficiency of the business	[ ]	[ ]	[ ]
information systems development	[ ]	[ ]	[ ]
document cycle time	[ ]	[ ]	[ ]
time spent on manual functions in the business	[ ]	[ ]	[ ]
employee satisfaction	[ ]	[ ]	[ ]
company specialisation	[ ]	[ ]	[ ]
company market share	[ ]	[ ]	[ ]
company's strategic position in marketplace	[ ]	[ ]	[ ]
delivery times	[ ]	[ ]	[ ]
benefits to customers	[ ]	[ ]	[ ]
quality of information exchanged with other companies	[ ]	[ ]	[ ]
shipping costs	[ ]	[ ]	[ ]
strategic alliance with other companies	[ ]	[ ]	[ ]
implementation of strategic programs within the business	[ ]	[ ]	[ ]

How would you rate the following electronic commerce technologies in terms of its value to your business (1 - not very useful - 5 extremely useful)

	not very useful				extremely useful
	1	2	3	4	5
Barcoding	[ ]	[ ]	[ ]	[ ]	[ ]
Computer aided design /manufacturing (CAD/CAM)	[ ]	[ ]	[ ]	[ ]	[ ]
Computer telephone integration (CTI)	[ ]	[ ]	[ ]	[ ]	[ ]
Document Imaging Processing (DIP)	[ ]	[ ]	[ ]	[ ]	[ ]
Electronic Catalogues	[ ]	[ ]	[ ]	[ ]	[ ]
Electronic Data Interchange (EDI)	[ ]	[ ]	[ ]	[ ]	[ ]
Facsimile	[ ]	[ ]	[ ]	[ ]	[ ]
Electronic Mail	[ ]	[ ]	[ ]	[ ]	[ ]
Internet	[ ]	[ ]	[ ]	[ ]	[ ]
Telex	[ ]	[ ]	[ ]	[ ]	[ ]
Mobile Phone	[ ]	[ ]	[ ]	[ ]	[ ]
Voice Mail	[ ]	[ ]	[ ]	[ ]	[ ]
Video conferencing	[ ]	[ ]	[ ]	[ ]	[ ]
Electronic Information Services eg news/tenders	[ ]	[ ]	[ ]	[ ]	[ ]
Telephone	[ ]	[ ]	[ ]	[ ]	[ ]

How would you rate the following statements (1 strongly agree - 5 strongly disagree):

	Strongly agree 1	2	3	4	Strongly disagree 5
1. Electronic Commerce Technologies will be the norm for the exchange of business transaction within the next 5 years	[ ]	[ ]	[ ]	[ ]	[ ]
2. EDI would be used more widely if one document standard was used	[ ]	[ ]	[ ]	[ ]	[ ]
3. EDI is too intrusive and complicated for small business	[ ]	[ ]	[ ]	[ ]	[ ]
4. EDI is not an appropriate technology for small business	[ ]	[ ]	[ ]	[ ]	[ ]
5. EDI will never be as widely used in small business as FAX, phone or Australia post	[ ]	[ ]	[ ]	[ ]	[ ]
6. EDI delivers more benefits to large companies than small companies	[ ]	[ ]	[ ]	[ ]	[ ]

Tick whether EDI caused any of the following problems within your business?

1. a lack of understanding of equipment   [ ]

2. intransigence when dealing with
       business partners   [ ]

3. negative impacts to the inventory of the
       business   [ ]
4. a lowering of staff satisfaction   [ ]

5. a reduction in efficiency in the business   [ ]

6. reluctance of the staff to change their work
       habits   [ ]
7. lack of awareness by staff of the 'bigger
       picture'   [ ]
8. lack of impartial advice   [ ]

9. few willing partners who utilise the
       technology   [ ]
10. low volume of transactions using
       the technology   [ ]
11. frequent revision to meet the partners
       data requirements   [ ]
12. duplication of tasks within the
       business   [ ]
13. cost of the technology outweighing the
       benefits   [ ]
14. lack of available standards   [ ]

15. too many standards   ]

14. the need for the business to go through
   a process of re-engineering   [ ]

15. difficulty in integrating the data into
   day-to-day business processes   [ ]

16. difficulty in integrating the data into
   existing computer systems   [ ]

17. reduction of control of the business [ ]

18. frequent upgrades of technology   [ ]

19. enforced priorities by business partners [ ]

20. too many networks   [ ]

Do you use any of these technologies when dealing with other companies in the following areas

	Internet	Mobile Phone	Voice Mail	DIP	Electronic Catalogues	EDI	FAX	Elecronic Mail	
1. Precontractual (finding potential customers)	[ ]	[ ]		[ ]	[ ]	[ ]	[ ]	[ ]	[ ]
2. Contractual (request for tenders, submitting tenders)	[ ]	[ ]		[ ]	[ ]	[ ]	[ ]	[ ]	[ ]
3. Ordering (purchase orders, acknowledgements etc.)	[ ]	[ ]		[ ]	[ ]	[ ]	[ ]	[ ]	[ ]
4. Transport Related Transactions	[ ]	[ ]		[ ]	[ ]	[ ]	[ ]	[ ]	[ ]
5. Settlement (invoices, payments, remittances)	[ ]	[ ]		[ ]	[ ]	[ ]	[ ]	[ ]	[ ]
6. Post Settlement (statistical reporting	[ ]	[ ]		[ ]	[ ]	[ ]	[ ]	[ ]	[ ]

244

Appendix 6
Goal 3 Sweden

This section is subdivided into 5 subsections:
- Subsection A6.1 examines the adoption factors (criteria for adoption, barriers to adoption, benefits from adoption and disadvantages from adoption of E-commerce) across the 6 business age categories.
- Subsection A6.2 examines the adoption factors across the 4 business size categories.
- Subsection A6.3 examines the adoption factors across the 4 business sector categories
- Subsection A6.4 examines the adoption factors across the 4 market focus categories
- Subsection A6.5 examines the adoption factors across the 5 IT skill categories

It should be noted that in an effort to improve readability, only those tables that demonstrate statistical significance are shown. All other tables appear in Appendix 3.

A6.1 Comparison of the adoption factors (members versus non-members of a small business strategic alliance) across the 6 business age categories

The complete data from the study was subdivided into 6 groups, one for each of the business age categories. These were:
- Less than 1 year in business
- 1 – 2 years in business
- 3 – 5 years in business
- 6 – 10 years in business
- 11 – 20 years in business
- more than 20 years in business

A comparison of means of ratings (using two-tailed t-tests) between those respondents that were members of a small business strategic alliance and those that were not was carried out to determine whether there were any significant differences in the perceptions of criteria, barriers, benefits or disadvantages between members and non-members for particular business ages.

A6.1.1 A comparison of ratings of criteria (between those respondents that were members of a small business strategic alliance and those that were not) within the six business age categories.

Based on an examination of the literature and case studies carried out in Australia, 14 criteria for adoption of E-commerce by SMEs were identified. A set of frequency analyses was carried out to determine their applicability to the regional Swedish study (see section 4.2.1). Three criteria:
Demand or pressure from customers
Demand or Pressure from suppliers
The availability of External technical support

were determined to be not applicable to the Swedish study and were eliminated. A series of two-tailed t-tests was applied to the remaining 11 criteria to determine whether, within each of the six business age group categories, the means of perception of importance for the criteria were significantly different between those respondents that were members of a small business strategic alliance and those that were not. As there was no comparable data for the first of these business age groups (< 1 year in business), data is presented for the remaining 5 business age groups only. Tables A3.19 – A3.22 show the data for the 5 remaining age groups, 3-5 years, 6-10 years, 11-20 years, >20 years. An examination of the data in those tables shows that there are no significant differences in the rating of criteria between those respondents that were members of a small business strategic alliance and those that were not.

A6.1.2 Summary of comparison of criteria across the 6 business age categories

As can be seen, there are no significant differences in the rating of applicability of the criteria for any of the business age categories for the Swedish sample.

A6.1.3 A comparison of ratings of barriers (between those respondents that were members of a small business strategic alliance and those that were not) within the six business age categories.

Based on an examination of the literature and case studies carried out in Australia, 8 barriers for adoption of E-commerce by SMEs were identified. A set of frequency analyses was carried out to determine their applicability to the Swedish study (see section 4.2.2). All barriers were determined to be applicable. A series of two-tailed t-tests was applied to barriers to determine whether, within each of the six business age group categories the means of perception of importance for the barrier was significantly different between those respondents that were members of a small business strategic alliance and those that were not. As there was no comparable data for the first two of these business age groups (< 1 year in business, 1 – 2 years in business), data is presented for the remaining 4 business age groups only.

The minimum sample size (at 99.9% degree of confidence) was determined to be 37 (see Section 3.5.1) An examination of the sample sizes for 3 – 5years and 6 – 10 years shows that these fall well short of that minimum size. As such no t-tests were carried out.

Table A6.1 shows the comparison of ratings of barriers between those respondents that were members of a small business strategic alliance and those that were not, for the business age category, 11 - 20 years.

Table A6.1

A comparison of the means of rating of <u>barriers</u> to adoption of E-commerce between those respondents that were members of a small business strategic alliance and those that were not, for the business age category, 11 - 20 years

Barriers	Mean Members	N Members	Mean Non-members	N Non-members	t-value	Sig.
A	3.94	18	4.00	5	.091	.929
B	3.71	17	3.57	7	-.209	.837
C	3.50	16	4.17	6	.975	.341
D	3.50	18	3.50	6	.000	1.000
E	2.88	16	4.29	7	2.641	.015*
F	2.94	16	3.50	6	.952	.352
G	2.81	16	3.33	6	.863	.398
H	2.33	15	3.20	5	1.256	.225

* p<.05
** p<.01
*** p<.001

Legend

A	*E-commerce doesn't fit with products/services*
B	*E-commerce doesn't fit with the way we do business*
C	*E-commerce doesn't fit the way our customers work*
D	*We don't see the advantage of using E-commerce*
E	*Lack of technical know how*
F	*Security risks*
G	*Cost too high*
H	*Not sure what to choose*

An examination of the data in Table A6.1 shows that the means of ratings of one <u>barrier</u> *lack of technical know how* is significantly different (at the .05 level) for the business age group 11 – 20 years. The data shows that those respondents that were not part of a small business strategic alliance rated this <u>barrier</u> higher (mean 4.29) when compared to the mean rating (2.88) for those respondents that were part of a small business strategic alliance. No other <u>barriers</u> showed any significant difference between those respondents that were members of a small business strategic alliance and those that were not, for the business age category, 11 - 20 years.

Table A6.2 shows the comparison of ratings of <u>barriers</u> between those respondents that were members of a small business strategic alliance and those that were not, for the business age category, > 20 years.

Table A6.2
A comparison of the means of rating of <u>barriers</u> to adoption of E-commerce between those respondents that were members of a small business strategic alliance and those that were not, for the business age category, > 20 years

Barriers	Mean Members	N Members	Mean Non-members	N Non-members	t-value	Sig.
A	3.56	18	3.07	15	-.949	.350
B	3.11	18	3.13	15	.042	.966
C	3.00	18	3.93	15	2.323	.027*
D	3.00	18	2.50	14	-1.032	.311
E	3.37	19	2.73	15	-1.231	.227
F	2.50	18	2.33	15	-.401	.691
G	2.67	18	2.67	15	.000	1.000
H	3.39	18	3.25	16	-.271	.788

* p<.05
** p<.01
*** p<.001

Legend

A	*E-commerce doesn't fit with products/services*
B	*E-commerce doesn't fit with the way we do business*
C	*E-commerce doesn't fit the way our customers work*
D	*We don't see the advantage of using E-commerce*
E	*Lack of technical know how*
F	*Security risks*
G	*Cost too high*
H	*Not sure what to choose*

An examination of the data in Table A6.2 shows that the means of ratings of one <u>barrier</u> *E-commerce doesn't fit the way our customers work* is significantly different (at the .05 level), for the business age category, > 20 years. Those respondents who were not part of a small business strategic alliance showed a mean rating of 3.93, compared to 3.00 for those that were part of a small business strategic alliance. No other <u>barriers</u> showed any significant difference between those respondents that were members of a small business strategic alliance and those that were not, for the business age category, > 20 years.

A number of authors have suggested that barriers such as *E-commerce doesn't fit with products/services*, *E-commerce doesn't fit with the way we do business* and *E-commerce doesn't fit the way our customers work* are often more prevalent in 'older' SMEs that have long-standing day-to-day procedures. While not rigorously tested, these authors suggested that membership of a small business strategic alliance may reduce the impact of these barriers in these 'older' SMEs.

While two of the barriers show no significant differences in the means of ratings, one barrier, and *E-commerce doesn't fit the way our customers work,* does support these suggestions in the Karlstad study, for regional SMEs that have been in business for more than 20 years.

Perhaps even more interesting is the fact that there were no significant differences in the means of ratings of any of the barriers for SMEs under 10 years of age.

A6.1.4 A comparison of ratings of <u>benefits</u> (between those respondents that were members of a small business strategic alliance and those that were not) within the six business age categories.

Based on an examination of the literature and case studies carried out in Australia, 11 <u>benefits</u> derived from the adoption of E-commerce by SMEs were identified. A set of frequency analyses was carried out to determine their applicability to the Swedish study (see section 4.2.3). Two <u>benefits</u>:

> *Reduced stock*
>
> *Improved marketing*

were deemed as not applicable to the study and were eliminated. A series of two-tailed t-tests was carried out on the <u>benefits</u> to determine whether, within each of the 6 business age groups, the means of perception of <u>benefits</u> was significantly different between those respondents that were members of a small business strategic alliance and those that were not. As there was no comparable data for the first of these business age groups (< 1 year in business), data is presented for the remaining 5 business age groups only.

The minimum sample size (at 99.9% degree of confidence) was determined to be 37 (see Section 3.5.1) An examination of the sample sizes for 1 – 2 years and 3 – 5 years shows that these fall well short of that minimum size. As such no t-tests were carried out. Tables A3.23 – A3.25 present the data for regional SMEs in the 5 age groups, 6 - 10 years, 11 – 20 years, > 20 years. An examination of the data shows that there are no significant differences in the rating of <u>benefits</u> between those respondents that were members of a small business strategic alliance and those that were not.

The disadvantages for the Karlstad study were eliminated (see section 4.3).

A6.1.5 Conclusions concerning the appropriateness of small business strategic alliances with regards business age

Section A6.1 has provided detail comparisons of the means of ratings of <u>criteria</u>, <u>barriers</u> and <u>benefits</u> of E-commerce adoption between regional SMEs that are members of a small business strategic alliance and regional SMEs that are not (across the 6 business age categories). The data shows that there are no significant differences in the means of ratings of either <u>criteria</u> for adoption of E-commerce or <u>benefits</u> from having adopted E-commerce, between SMEs that are members of a small business strategic alliance and SMEs that are not.

Two <u>barriers</u>, *lack of technical know-how* and *E-commerce doesn't fit the way our customers work* were significantly higher for respondents that were not part of a small business strategic alliance for the business age categories, 11 – 20 years and > 20 years respectively. No other barriers, or business age category showed any significant differences in the means of ratings

A6.2 Comparison of the adoption factors (members versus non-members of a small business strategic alliance) across the 4 business size categories

The complete set of data from the study was subdivided into 4 groups, one for each of the business size categories. These were:
- 0 employees
- 1 – 9 employees
- 10 – 19 employees
- 20 – 49 employees

A comparison of the means of ratings between regional SMEs that are members of a small business strategic alliance and regional SMEs that are not was carried out within each of the business size categories to determine whether membership of a small business strategic alliance altered the perception of importance of criteria, barriers, benefits or disadvantages within particular business size categories.

A6.2.1 Comparison of the means of rating of criteria between SMEs that are members of a small business strategic alliance and SMEs that are not, within the 4 business size categories

Based on an examination of the literature and case studies carried out in Australia, 14 criteria for adoption of E-commerce by SMEs were identified. A set of frequency analyses was carried out to determine their applicability to the regional Swedish study (see section 4.2.1). Three criteria:

Demand or pressure from customers
Demand or Pressure from suppliers
The availability of External technical support

were determined to be not applicable to the Swedish study and were eliminated. A series of two-tailed t-tests was applied to the remaining 11 criteria to determine whether, within each of the four business size categories, the means of perception of importance for the criteria were significantly different between those respondents that were members of a small business strategic alliance and those that were not.

The minimum sample size (at 99.9% degree of confidence) was determined to be 37 (see Section 3.5.1) An examination of the sample sizes for sole traders shows that these fall well short of that minimum size. As such no t-tests were carried out.

Table A3.26 present the data for those businesses that have between 1 and 9 employees. An examination of the data shows that there are no significant differences in the mean ratings of any of the criteria between those respondents that were members of a small business strategic alliance and those that were not.

Table A6.3 presents the data for those businesses that have between 10 and 19 employees.

Table A6.3

A comparison of the means of rating of <u>criteria</u> for adoption of E-commerce between those respondents that were members of a small business strategic alliance and those that were not, that had 10 - 19 employees

Criteria	Mean Members	N Members	Mean Non-members	N Non-members	t-value	Sig.
B	1.60	5	2.95	22	2.489	.020*
D	3.20	5	4.05	22	1.620	.118
E	4.80	5	4.41	22	-1.240	.226
F	2.00	5	3.10	22	1.559	.132
G	3.60	5	3.77	22	.399	.693
H	4.40	5	4.27	22	-.415	.681
I	3.80	5	3.18	22	-1.393	.176
J	4.40	5	3.50	22	-1.906	.068
K	4.80	5	4.15	22	-2.196	.038*
M	4.60	5	3.77	22	-1.668	.108
N	2.40	5	3.18	22	1.595	.123

* $p<.05$
** $p<.01$
*** $p<.001$

Legend

A	*Demand/pressure from customers*
B	*Pressure of competition*
C	*Demand/Pressure from suppliers*
D	*Reduction of costs*
E	*Improvement to customer service*
F	*Improvement in lead time*
G	*Increased sales*
H	*Improvement to internal efficiency*
I	*Strengthen relations with business partners*
J	*Reach new customers/markets*
K	*Improvement in competitiveness*
L	*External technical support*
M	*Improvement in marketing*
N	*Improvement in control and follow-up*

An examination of the data in Table A6.3 shows that the means of ratings of two of the <u>criteria</u> (*pressure of competition, improvement in competitiveness*) showed a significant difference (at the .01 level) between those respondents that were members of a small business strategic alliance and those that were not. The mean rating for the criterion *pressure from competition* for respondents that were members of a small business strategic alliance was 1.60, compared to 2.95 for non-members. By comparison, the mean rating for the criterion *improvement in competitiveness* was higher (4.80) for respondents that were members of a small business strategic alliance than for non-members (4.18). No other criteria showed any significant differences between those respondents that were members of a small business strategic alliance and those that were not.

A6.2.2 A comparison of ratings of <u>barriers</u> (between those respondents that were members of a small business strategic alliance and those that were not) within the four business size categories.

Based on an examination of the literature and case studies carried out in Australia, 8 barriers for adoption of E-commerce by SMEs were identified. A set of frequency analyses was carried out to determine their applicability to the regional Swedish study (see section 4.2.2). All barriers were determined to be applicable. A series of two-tailed t-tests was applied to barriers to determine whether, within each of the four business size group categories the means of perception of importance for the barrier was significantly different between those respondents that were members of a small business strategic alliance and those that were not.
The minimum sample size (at 99.9% degree of confidence) was determined to be 37 (see Section 3.5.1) An examination of the sample sizes for sole traders shows that these fall well short of that minimum size. As such no t-tests were carried out.

A6.2.3 A comparison of ratings of <u>benefits</u> (between those respondents that were members of a small business strategic alliance and those that were not) within the four business size categories.

Based on an examination of the literature and case studies carried out in Australia, 11 benefits derived from the adoption of E-commerce by SMEs were identified. A set of frequency analyses was carried out to determine their applicability to the regional Swedish study (see section 4.2.3). Two benefits:
> *Reduced stock*
> *Improved marketing*

were deemed as not applicable to the study and were eliminated. A series of two-tailed t-tests was carried out on the benefits to determine whether, within each of the 4 business size groups, the means of perception of benefits was significantly different between those respondents that were members of a small business strategic alliance and those that were not.
The minimum sample size (at 99.9% degree of confidence) was determined to be 37 (see Section 3.5.1) An examination of the sample sizes for sole traders shows that these fall well short of that minimum size. As such no t-tests were carried out.
Table A3.29 presents the data for businesses that had 1 - 9 employees.
Table A6.4 presents the data for businesses that had 10 - 19 employees.

A comparison of the means of rating of <u>benefits</u> from adoption of E-commerce between those respondents that were members of a small business strategic alliance and those that were not, that had 10 - 19 employees

Benefit	Mean Members	N Members	Mean Non-members	N Non-Members	t-value	Sig.
A	2.40	5	3.61	23	2.185	.038*
B	2.60	5	3.42	22	1.432	.165
C	2.20	5	3.48	23	2.128	.043*
E	3.60	5	2.87	23	-1.547	.134
F	2.60	5	3.43	23	1.665	.108
G	3.40	5	3.22	23	-.423	.670
H	3.80	5	2.91	23	-1.776	.087
I	3.80	5	3.57	23	-.536	.596
K	4.20	5	3.42	23	-1.275	.214

* p<.05
** p<.01
*** p<.001

Legend

A	*Lower administration costs*
B	*Lower production costs*
C	*Reduced lead-time*
D	*Reduced stock*
E	*Increased sales*
F	*Increased internal efficiency*
G	*Improved relations with business partners*
H	*New customers and markets*
I	*Improved competitiveness*
J	*Improved marketing*
K	*Improved quality of information*

Despite the differences in the N values (5 and 23) standard deviation were shown to be sufficiently similar (F = 2.505 and .296) to accept the differences in the t values.

An examination of the data in Table A6.4 shows that the means of ratings of two <u>benefits</u>, *lower administration costs*, and *reduced lead time*, showed significant differences (at the .05 level) between those respondents that were members of a small business strategic alliance and those that were not. The mean rating of those respondents that were not part of a small business strategic alliance to *lower admin costs* was 3.61, compared to 2.40 for respondents that were part

of a small business strategic alliance. A similar comparison was seen for the benefit *reduced lead-time*. The mean rating of those respondents that were not part of a small business strategic alliance to *reduced lead time* was 3.48, compared to 2.20 for respondents that were part of a small business strategic alliance. No other benefits showed any significant differences.
Table A6.5 presents the data for businesses that had 20 - 49 employees.

Table A6.5
A comparison of the means of rating of benefits from adoption of E-commerce between those respondents that were members of a small business strategic alliance and those that were not, that had 20 - 49 employees

Benefit	Mean Members	N Members	Mean Non-members	N Non-Members	t-value	Sig.
A	2.88	8	2.95	19	.148	.884
B	3.00	8	2.67	19	-.671	.508
C	3.13	8	2.95	19	-.326	.747
E	3.25	8	2.47	19	-1.798	.084
F	3.25	8	3.53	19	.493	.626
G	3.25	8	3.16	19	-.199	.844
H	3.50	8	2.61	19	-2.080	.048*
I	3.50	8	3.37	19	-1.057	.300
K	3.50	8	3.37	19	-.259	.798

* $p<.05$
** $p<.01$
*** $p<.001$

Legend

A	*Lower administration costs*
B	*Lower production costs*
C	*Reduced lead-time*
D	*Reduced stock*
E	*Increased sales*
F	*Increased internal efficiency*
G	*Improved relations with business partners*
H	*New customers and markets*
I	*Improved competitiveness*
J	*Improved marketing*
K	*Improved quality of information*

An examination of the data in Table A6.5 shows that the means of rating of one benefit, *new customers and markets*, showed significant differences (at the .05 level) between those respondents that were members of a small business strategic alliance and those that were not. The mean rating of those respondents that were not part of a small business strategic alliance to *new customers and markets* was 2.61, compared to 3.50 for respondents that were part of a small business strategic alliance. No other benefits showed any significant differences.

A6.2.4 Conclusions concerning the appropriateness of small business strategic alliances with regards business size

Section A6.2 has provided detailed comparisons of the means of ratings of criteria, barriers and benefits of E-commerce adoption between those respondents that were members of a small business strategic alliance and those that were not. The data has shown that several criteria are significantly different for particular business sizes. These are:

- *Pressure from competition*   (11 – 19 employees)
- *Improved competitiveness*   (11 – 19 employees)

No significant differences were found in any of the barriers for any business size category.
The ratings of several benefits showed significant differences for particular business size categories. These are:

- *Lower administration costs*   (11 – 19 employees)
- *Reduced lead time*   (11 – 19 employees)
- *New customers and markets*   (20 – 49 employees)

As previously stated (see section A6.1.5), all disadvantages were found to be inapplicable to the study and were eliminated from further consideration.

A6.3 Comparison of the adoption factors (members versus non-members of a small business strategic alliance) across the 4 business sector categories

The complete set of data from the study was subdivided into 4 groups, one for each of the business sector categories. These were:

- Industrial
- Service
- Retail
- Financial

A comparison of the means of rating between regional SMEs that are members of a small business strategic alliance and regional SMEs that are not was carried out within each of the sector categories to determine whether membership of a small business strategic alliance altered the perception of importance of criteria, barriers, benefits or disadvantages within particular sector categories.

A6.3.1 Comparison of the means of rating of <u>criteria</u> between SMEs that are members of a small business strategic alliance and SMEs that are not within the 4 business sector categories

Based on an examination of the literature and case studies carried out in Australia, 14 <u>criteria</u> for adoption of E-commerce by SMEs were identified. A set of frequency analyses was carried out to determine their applicability to the regional Swedish study (see section 4.2.1). Three <u>criteria</u>:

Demand or pressure from customers
Demand or Pressure from suppliers
The availability of External technical support

were determined to be not applicable to the Swedish study and were eliminated. A series of two-tailed t-tests was applied to the remaining 11 <u>criteria</u> to determine whether, within each of the four business sector categories, the means of perception of importance for the <u>criteria</u> were significantly different between those respondents that were members of a small business strategic alliance and those that were not.

Tables A3.30 – A3.31 presents that data for the categories industrial and retail. An examination of data in these tables shows that there are no significant differences in the mean ratings of any of the <u>criteria</u> between those respondents that were members of a small business strategic alliance and those that were not.

Table A6.6 presents the data for those businesses that are from the service sector.

Table A6.6

A comparison of the means of rating of <u>criteria</u> for adoption of E-commerce between those respondents that were members of a small business strategic alliance and those that were not, and were from the service sector

<u>Criteria</u>	Mean Members	N Members	Mean Non-members	N Non-members	t-value	Sig.
B	2.67	15	2.39	36	-.736	.465
D	3.27	15	3.31	36	.093	.926
E	3.73	15	4.08	36	.984	.330
F	2.87	15	2.74	35	-.260	.796
G	2.36	14	3.00	36	1.465	.150
H	3.53	15	3.95	37	1.126	.265
I	3.13	15	3.06	36	-.201	.841
J	2.50	14	3.42	36	2.171	.035*
K	3.33	15	3.69	36	.835	.398
M	2.47	15	3.69	36	2.958	.005**
N	2.07	14	2.81	36	1.777	.082

* $p<.05$
** $p<.01$
*** $p<.001$

Legend

A	*Demand/pressure from customers*
B	*Pressure of competition*
C	*Demand/Pressure from suppliers*
D	*Reduction of costs*
E	*Improvement to customer service*
F	*Improvement in lead-time*
G	*Increased sales*
H	*Improvement to internal efficiency*
I	*Strengthen relations with business partners*
J	*Reach new customers/markets*
K	*Improvement in competitiveness*
L	*External technical support*
M	*Improvement in marketing*
N	*Improvement in control and follow-up*

An examination of the data in Table A6.6 shows that the means of ratings of two of the criteria were significantly different between respondents that were members of a small business strategic alliance and respondents that were not. The criterion *reaching new customers and markets* showed a significant difference in the means of ratings (at the .05 level). The mean rating of respondents that were not members of a small business strategic alliance was 3.42, compared to 2.50 for respondents that were members of a small business strategic alliance. The criterion *improvement to marketing* showed a significant difference in the means of ratings (at the .01 level) with the mean rating for non-members being 3.67, compared to alliance members 2.47. No other criteria showed any significant difference.

A6.3.2 A comparison of ratings of barriers (between those respondents that were members of a small business strategic alliance and those that were not) within the four business sector categories.

Based on an examination of the literature and case studies carried out in Australia, 8 barriers for adoption of E-commerce by SMEs were identified. A set of frequency analyses was carried out to determine their applicability to the regional Swedish study (see section 4.2.2). All barriers were determined to be applicable. A series of two-tailed t-tests was applied to barriers to determine whether, within each of the four sector group categories the means of perception of importance for the barrier was significantly different between those respondents that were members of a small business strategic alliance and those that were not.

The minimum sample size (at 99.9% degree of confidence) was determined to be 37 (see Section 3.5.1) An examination of the sample sizes for the industrial shows that these fall well short of that minimum size. As such no t-tests were carried out.

Table A3.32 presents the data the category service.

An examination of data in the tables shows that there are no significant differences in the mean ratings of any of the barriers between those respondents that were members of a small business strategic alliance and those that were not.

As all of the respondents from the financial sector had adopted E-commerce, there was no barriers data to report.

A6.3.3 A comparison of ratings of benefits (between those respondents that were members of a small business strategic alliance and those that were not) within the four business sector categories.

Based on an examination of the literature and case studies carried out in Australia, 11 benefits derived from the adoption of E-commerce by SMEs were identified. A set of frequency analyses was carried out to determine their applicability to the Swedish study (see section 4.2.3). Two benefits:

Reduced stock

Improved marketing

were deemed as not applicable to the study and were eliminated. A series of two-tailed t-tests was carried out on the benefits to determine whether, within each of the 4 sector groups, the means of perception of benefits was significantly different between those respondents that were members of a small business strategic alliance and those that were not.

Table A6.7 presents the data for businesses that from the industrial sector.

Table A6.7

A comparison of the means of rating of benefits from adoption of E-commerce between those respondents that were members of a small business strategic alliance and those that were not, for businesses from the industrial sector

Benefit	Mean Members	N Members	Mean Non-members	N Non-Members	t-value	Sig.
A	2.85	13	2.88	16	.083	.935
B	3.00	13	2.50	16	-1.160	.256
C	3.31	13	2.94	16	-.798	.432
E	3.46	13	2.94	16	-1.1483	.150
F	3.31	13	2.94	16	-.839	.409
G	3.62	13	3.06	17	-1.765	.088
H	3.79	14	3.06	17	-2.156	.039*
I	3.46	13	3.22	18	-.623	.538
K	4.00	14	3.63	16	-.933	.359

* $p<.05$
** $p<.01$
*** $p<.001$

Legend

258

A	Lower administration costs
B	Lower production costs
C	Reduced lead-time
D	Reduced stock
E	Increased sales
F	Increased internal efficiency
G	Improved relations with business partners
H	New customers and markets
I	Improved competitiveness
J	Improved marketing
K	Improved quality of information

An examination of Table A6.7 shows that the means of ratings for one benefit *new customers and markets* was significantly different between those respondents that were part of a small business strategic alliance and those that were not. The mean rating for those respondents that were part of a small business strategic alliance was 3.79, compared to 3.06 for those that were not part of a small business strategic alliance. No other benefit showed any significant difference. Table A6.8 presents the data for businesses that from the service sector.

Table A6.8
A comparison of the means of rating of benefits from adoption of E-commerce between those respondents that were members of a small business strategic alliance and those that were not, for businesses from the service sector

Benefit	Mean Members	N Members	Mean Non-members	N Non-Members	t-value	Sig.
A	3.36	14	3.00	35	-.859	.395
B	2.93	14	2.94	35	.029	.977
C	3.64	14	3.15	35	-1.173	.247
E	2.14	14	2.79	33	1.763	.085
F	2.71	14	3.06	34	.840	.405
G	2.64	13	2.94	32	.853	.398
H	2.15	13	3.09	32	2.372	.022*
I	2.93	14	3.31	35	1.113	.271
K	2.57	14	3.53	34	2.134	.038*

* $p < .05$
** $p < .01$
*** $p < .001$

Legend

259

A	Lower administration costs
B	Lower production costs
C	Reduced lead-time
D	Reduced stock
E	Increased sales
F	Increased internal efficiency
G	Improved relations with business partners
H	New customers and markets
I	Improved competitiveness
J	Improved marketing
K	Improved quality of information

An examination of Table A6.8 shows that the means of ratings of two of the benefits, *new customers and markets* and *improved quality of information* show a significant difference (at the .05 level) between respondents that were part of a small business strategic alliance and those that were not. The mean rating of the benefit, *new customers and markets* was 3.09 for those respondents that were part of a small business strategic alliance, compared to 2.15 for those that were not. The mean rating of the benefit, *improved quality of information* also rated higher (3.53) for those respondents that were part of a small business strategic alliance, when compared to the mean rating for those that were not part of a small business strategic alliance (2.57). No other benefits showed a significant difference in the means of the rating.

Table A6.9 presents the data for businesses that from the retail sector.

Table A6.9

A comparison of the means of rating of benefits from adoption of E-commerce between those respondents that were members of a small business strategic alliance and those that were not, for businesses from the retail sector

Benefit	Mean Members	N Members	Mean Non-members	N Non-Members	t-value	Sig.
A	2.89	9	3.28	18	.623	.539
B	2.22	9	3.28	18	1.681	.205
C	2.33	9	3.56	18	2.108	.045*
E	2.44	9	2.94	18	.911	.371
F	2.70	10	3.56	18	1.498	.146
G	2.56	9	3.83	18	2.582	.016*
H	2.78	9	2.83	18	.094	.926
I	2.88	8	3.78	18	1.535	.138
K	3.44	9	3.44	18	.000	1.000

* p<.05
** p<.01
*** p<.001
Legend

A	*Lower administration costs*
B	*Lower production costs*
C	*Reduced lead-time*
D	*Reduced stock*
E	*Increased sales*
F	*Increased internal efficiency*
G	*Improved relations with business partners*
H	*New customers and markets*
I	*Improved competitiveness*
J	*Improved marketing*
K	*Improved quality of information*

An examination of Table A6.9 shows that the means of ratings of two of the benefits, *reduced lead time* and *improved relations with business partners* show a significant difference (at the .05 level) between respondents that were part of a small business strategic alliance and those that were not. The mean rating of the benefit, *reduced lead-time* was 3.56 for those respondents that were part of a small business strategic alliance, compared to 2.33 for those that were not. The mean rating of the benefit, *improved relations with business partners* also rated higher (3.83) for those respondents that were part of a small business strategic alliance, when compared to the mean rating for those that were not part of a small business strategic alliance (2.56). No other benefits showed a significant difference in the means of the rating.

The minimum sample size (at 99.9% degree of confidence) was determined to be 37 (see Section 3.5.1) An examination of the sample sizes for the financial sector shows that these fall well short of that minimum size. As such no t-tests were carried out.

A6.3.4 Conclusions concerning the appropriateness of small business strategic alliances with regards business sector

Section A6.3 has provided detailed comparisons of the means of ratings of criteria, barriers and benefits of E-commerce adoption between those respondents that were members of a small business strategic alliance and those that were not. The data has shown that several criteria are significantly different for particular business sectors. These are:

- *Reaching New customers and markets*   (Service sector)
- *Improvement to marketing*   (Service sector)

Finally the mean ratings of several benefits showed significant differences between those respondents that were members of a small business strategic alliance and those that were not for particular business sectors. These were:

- *New customers and markets*   (industrial sector)
- *New customers and markets*   (service sector)
- *Improved quality of information*   (service sector)

- *Reduced lead time*   (retail sector)
- *Improved relations with business partners* (retail sector)

As previously stated (see section 4.2.4), all disadvantages were found to be inapplicable to the study and were eliminated from further consideration.

A6.4 Comparison of the adoption factors (members versus non-members of a small business strategic alliance) across the 4 market focus categories

The complete set of data from the study was subdivided into 4 groups, one for each of the market focus categories. These were:
- Local
- Regional
- National
- International

A comparison of the means of rating between SMEs that are members of a small business strategic alliance and SMEs that are not was carried out within each of the sector categories to determine whether membership of a small business strategic alliance altered the perception of importance of criteria, barriers, benefits or disadvantages within particular market focus categories.

A6.4.1 Comparison of the means of rating of criteria between SMEs that are members of a small business strategic alliance and SMEs that are not within the 4 market focus categories

Based on an examination of the literature and case studies carried out in Australia, 14 criteria for adoption of E-commerce by SMEs were identified. A set of frequency analyses was carried out to determine their applicability to the regional Swedish study (see section 4.2.1). Three criteria:

Demand or pressure from customers

Demand or Pressure from suppliers

The availability of External technical support

were determined to be not applicable to the Swedish study and were eliminated. A series of two-tailed t-tests was applied to the remaining 11 criteria to determine whether, within each of the four business sector categories, the means of perception of importance for the criteria were significantly different between those respondents that were members of a small business strategic alliance and those that were not.

Table A6.10 presents the data for the local market focus respondents.

Table A6.10

A comparison of the means of rating of <u>criteria</u> for adoption of E-commerce between those respondents that were members of a small business strategic alliance and those that were not, and were local market respondents

Criteria	Mean Members	N Members	Mean Non-members	N Non-members	t-value	Sig.
B	2.65	20	2.47	36	-.460	.647
D	3.80	20	3.44	36	-.966	.338
E	4.15	20	3.89	36	-.859	.394
F	3.00	19	2.86	36	-.315	.754
G	3.21	19	3.17	36	-.109	.913
H	3.70	20	4.03	37	1.156	.253
I	2.80	20	3.22	36	1.176	.245
J	3.25	20	3.22	36	-.068	.946
K	3.40	20	4.00	36	1.624	.110
M	3.11	19	3.31	36	.459	.648
N	2.20	20	3.14	36	2.707	.009**

* p<.05
** p<.01
*** p<.001

Legend

A	*Demand/pressure from customers*
B	*Pressure of competition*
C	*Demand/Pressure from suppliers*
D	*Reduction of costs*
E	*Improvement to customer service*
F	*Improvement in lead-time*
G	*Increased sales*
H	*Improvement to internal efficiency*
I	*Strengthen relations with business partners*
J	*Reach new customers/markets*
K	*Improvement in competitiveness*
L	*External technical support*
M	*Improvement in marketing*
N	*Improvement in control and follow-up*

An examination of the data in Table A6.10 shows that the means of ratings of one criterion, *improvement in control and follow-up* was a significantly different (at the .01 level) between those respondents that were members of a small business strategic alliance and those that were not. The mean rating of this <u>criterion</u> was 3.14 for those respondents that were members of a small business strategic alliance, compared to 2.20 for those that were not. No other criteria showed any significant differences.

Due to the low number of respondents for regionally focused SMEs, no comparison was possible for this group. Table A3.34 presents the data for the national market focus respondents.

An examination of Table A3.34 shows that there were no significant differences in the means of the ratings of any of the criteria between those respondents that were members of a small business strategic alliance and those that were not for the national market focus group of respondents.

A6.4.2 A comparison of ratings of barriers (between those respondents that were members of a small business strategic alliance and those that were not) within the four market focus categories.

Based on an examination of the literature and case studies carried out in Australia, 8 barriers for adoption of E-commerce by SMEs were identified. A set of frequency analyses was carried out to determine their applicability to the regional Swedish study (see section 4.2.2). All barriers were determined to be applicable. A series of two-tailed t-tests was applied to barriers to determine whether, within each of the four market focus group categories the means of perception of importance for the barrier was significantly different between those respondents that were members of a small business strategic alliance and those that were not.

Table A6.11 presents the data for businesses that indicated that they were locally market focused.

Table A6.11
A comparison of the means of rating of barriers to adoption of E-commerce between those respondents that were members of a small business strategic alliance and those that were not, that indicated that they were locally market focused

Barriers	Mean Members	N Members	Mean Non-members	N Non-members	t-value	Sig.
A	3.72	36	3.50	22	-.589	.558
B	3.56	34	3.05	22	-1.307	.197
C	3.18	34	3.50	20	.812	.420
D	3.46	35	2.65	20	-2.219	.031*
E	3.41	34	3.10	20	-.806	.424
F	2.85	33	2.84	19	-.019	.985
G	3.03	33	3.22	18	.473	.639
H	3.13	31	3.17	18	.091	.928

* p<.05
** p<.01
*** p<.001

Legend

A	E-commerce doesn't fit with products/services
B	E-commerce doesn't fit with the way we do business
C	E-commerce doesn't fit the way our customers work
D	We don't see the advantage of using E-commerce
E	Lack of technical know how
F	Security risks
G	Cost too high
H	Not sure what to choose

An examination of the data in Table A6.11 shows that the means of ratings of one barrier, *we don't see the advantage of using E-commerce* was significantly different (at the .05 level) between those respondents that were members of a small business strategic alliance and those that were not. The mean rating for respondents that were members of a small business strategic alliance was 3.46, compared to 2.65 for those that were not. No other barriers showed any significant differences.

The minimum sample size (at 99.9% degree of confidence) was determined to be 37 (see Section 3.5.1) An examination of the sample sizes for the regional and national sector shows that these fall well short of that minimum size. As such no t-tests were carried out.

As there was insufficient data for respondents that had an international market focus, no comparisons could be made.

A6.4.3 A comparison of ratings of <u>benefits</u> (between those respondents that were members of a small business strategic alliance and those that were not) within the four market focus categories.

Based on an examination of the literature and case studies carried out in Australia, 11 benefits derived from the adoption of E-commerce by SMEs were identified. A set of frequency analyses was carried out to determine their applicability to the regional Swedish study (see section 4.2.3). Two benefits:

    Reduced stock
    Improved marketing

were deemed as not applicable to the study and were eliminated. A series of two-tailed t-tests was carried out on the benefits to determine whether, within each of the 4 market focus groups, the means of perception of benefits was significantly different between those respondents that were members of a small business strategic alliance and those that were not.

Table A6.12 presents the data for businesses that from the locally focused respondents.

Table A6.12

A comparison of the means of rating of <u>benefits</u> from adoption of E-commerce between those respondents that were members of a small business strategic alliance and those that were not, for businesses that are locally focused

<u>Benefit</u>	Mean Members	N Members	Mean Non-members	N Non-Members	t-value	Sig.
A	2.90	20	3.16	37	.691	.493
B	2.85	20	3.05	37	.514	.609
C	2.80	20	3.14	37	.848	.400
E	2.50	20	2.61	36	.309	.758
F	2.70	20	3.46	37	2.123	.038*
G	2.55	20	3.17	36	1.695	.096
H	2.60	20	2.69	36	.237	.814
I	2.89	19	3.49	37	1.651	.104
K	3.35	20	3.19	37	-.402	.627

* $p<.05$
** $p<.01$
*** $p<.001$

Legend

A	*Lower administration costs*
B	*Lower production costs*
C	*Reduced lead-time*
D	*Reduced stock*
E	*Increased sales*
F	*Increased internal efficiency*
G	*Improved relations with business partners*
H	*New customers and markets*
I	*Improved competitiveness*
J	*Improved marketing*
K	*Improved quality of information*

An examination of the data in Table A6.12 shows that the means of ratings of one <u>benefit</u> *increased internal efficiency* were significantly different (at the .05 level). The mean rating for respondents that were members of a small business strategic alliance was 2.70, compared to 3.46 for those that were not. No other <u>benefits</u> showed any significant differences.

Table A3.34 shows the data for the national respondents. An examination of the table shows that there were no significant differences in the means of the ratings of any of the <u>benefits</u>.

A6.4.4 Conclusions concerning the appropriateness of small business strategic alliances with regards market focus

Section A6.4 has provided detailed comparisons of the means of ratings of criteria, barriers and benefits of E-commerce adoption between those respondents that were members of a small business strategic alliance and those that were not.
The data has shown that several criteria are significantly different for particular market focus respondents. These are:

- *Improvement in control and follow-up* (Local)

The ratings of several barriers showed significant differences for particular business sector categories. These are:

- *Don't see any advantage in using E-commerce* (Local)

Finally the mean ratings of several benefits showed significant differences between those respondents that were members of a small business strategic alliance and those that were not for particular business sectors. These were:

- *Increased internal efficiency* (Local)

As previously stated (see section 4.2.4), all disadvantages were found to be inapplicable to the study and were eliminated from further consideration.

A6.5 Comparison of the adoption factors (members versus non-members of a small business strategic alliance) across the 5 levels of IT skill

The complete set of data from the study was subdivided into 5 groups, one for each of the levels of IT skills. These were:

- no skill
- low skill
- normal skill
- high skill
- expert skill

A comparison of the means of rating between regional SMEs that are members of a small business strategic alliance and regional SMEs that are not was carried out within the 5 groups to determine whether membership of a small business strategic alliance altered the perception of importance of criteria, barriers, benefits or disadvantages within either of the groups.

A6.5.1 Comparison of the means of rating of criteria between SMEs that are members of a small business strategic alliance and SMEs that are not, across the 5 levels of IT skill

Based on an examination of the literature and case studies carried out in Australia, 14 criteria for adoption of E-commerce by SMEs were identified. A set of frequency analyses was carried out to determine their applicability to the regional Swedish study (see section 4.2.1). Three criteria:

Demand or pressure from customers
Demand or Pressure from suppliers
The availability of External technical support

were determined to be not applicable to the Swedish study and were eliminated. A series of two-tailed t-tests was applied to the remaining 11 <u>criteria</u> to determine whether, within the 5 groups, the means of perception of importance for the <u>criteria</u> were significantly different between those respondents that were members of a small business strategic alliance and those that were not. As there was insufficient data for the no-skill and low skill groups, they were not analysed.

Table A6.13 provides the data for respondents that indicated their levels of IT skills were normal.

Table A6.13
A comparison of the means of rating of <u>criteria</u> for adoption of E-commerce between those respondents that were members of a small business strategic alliance and those that were not, where respondents indicated their company levels of IT skill was normal

<u>Criteria</u>	Mean Members	N Members	Mean Non-members	N Non-members	t-value	Sig.
B	2.43	21	2.61	44	.539	.592
D	3.32	22	3.30	44	-.068	.946
E	4.14	21	4.16	44	.056	.955
F	2.62	21	2.42	43	-.517	.607
G	2.95	21	3.48	44	1.411	.163
H	3.83	23	3.93	45	.412	.682
I	3.27	22	3.34	44	.209	.835
J	3.14	21	3.82	44	1.807	.076
K	3.55	22	3.89	44	.987	.327
M	3.10	21	4.00	44	2.561	.013*
N	2.33	21	2.77	43	1.398	.167

* $p < .05$
** $p < .01$
*** $p < .001$

Legend

A	*Demand/pressure from customers*
B	*Pressure of competition*
C	*Demand/Pressure from suppliers*
D	*Reduction of costs*
E	*Improvement to customer service*
F	*Improvement in lead-time*
G	*Increased sales*

H	*Improvement to internal efficiency*
I	*Strengthen relations with business partners*
J	*Reach new customers/markets*
K	*Improvement in competitiveness*
L	*External technical support*
M	*Improvement in marketing*
N	*Improvement in control and follow-up*

An examination of the data in Table A6.13 shows that the means of ratings of one criterion, *improvement to marketing* were significantly different (at the .05 level). The mean rating for respondents that were part of a small business strategic alliance was 3.10, compared to 4.00 for those respondents that were not part of a small business strategic alliance. No other criteria showed any significant differences.

Table A6.14 provides the data for those respondents that indicated that they had high levels of IT skill in their business.

Table A6.14

A comparison of the means of rating of criteria for adoption of E-commerce between those respondents that were members of a small business strategic alliance and those that were not, where respondents indicated their company levels of IT skill was high

Criteria	Mean Members	N Members	Mean Non-members	N Non-members	t-value	Sig.
B	2.50	12	2.52	21	.052	.959
D	3.67	12	3.00	21	-1.502	.143
E	4.54	13	3.71	21	-2.157	.039*
F	2.83	12	3.33	21	1.025	.313
G	3.31	13	3.24	21	-.157	.876
H	3.83	12	4.14	22	.899	.376
I	3.17	12	3.14	21	-.053	.958
J	3.85	13	2.95	21	-2.247	.032*
K	3.58	12	3.81	21	.491	.627
M	3.54	13	3.52	21	-.032	.975
N	3.00	12	3.05	21	.109	.914

* $p < .05$
** $p < .01$
*** $p < .001$

Legend

A	*Demand/pressure from customers*
B	*Pressure of competition*

C	*Demand/Pressure from suppliers*
D	*Reduction of costs*
E	*Improvement to customer service*
F	*Improvement in lead-time*
G	*Increased sales*
H	*Improvement to internal efficiency*
I	*Strengthen relations with business partners*
J	*Reach new customers/markets*
K	*Improvement in competitiveness*
L	*External technical support*
M	*Improvement in marketing*
N	*Improvement in control and follow-up*

An examination of the data in Table A6.14 shows that the means of ratings for two criteria, *improvement to customer service*s and *reaching new customers and markets* were significantly different (at the .05 level). In both cases, the respondents that were part of a small business strategic alliance rated these criteria higher (4.54 and 3.85 respectively), than those that were not part of a small business strategic alliance (3.71 and 2.95 respectively). No other criteria showed any significant differences in the means of the ratings.

A6.5.2 A comparison of ratings of <u>barriers</u> (between those respondents that were members of a small business strategic alliance and those that were not) across the 5 levels of IT skill

Based on an examination of the literature and case studies carried out in Australia, 8 barriers for adoption of E-commerce by SMEs were identified. A set of frequency analyses was carried out to determine their applicability to the regional Swedish study (see section 4.2.2). All barriers were determined to be applicable. A series of two-tailed t-tests was applied to barriers to determine whether, within the 5 groups, the means of perception of importance for the barrier was significantly different between those respondents that were members of a small business strategic alliance and those that were not. As there was insufficient data for the no-skill category no analysis took place.

Table A6.15 presents the data for the respondents that indicated their levels of IT skills were low.

Table A6.15
A comparison of the means of rating of <u>barriers</u> to adoption of E-commerce between those respondents that were members of a small business strategic alliance and those that were not, where respondents indicated their company levels of IT skill was low

Barriers	Mean Members	N Members	Mean Non-members	N Non-members	t-value	Sig.
A	4.00	15	2.91	11	-1.817	.082
B	4.06	16	2.83	12	-2.108	.045*
C	3.50	14	3.36	11	-.234	.817
D	4.00	16	2.27	11	-3.395	.002**
E	4.27	15	3.60	10	-1.190	.246
F	3.36	14	3.00	10	-.615	.545
G	3.36	14	3.40	10	.077	.939
H	3.79	14	4.00	11	.367	.717

* p<.05
** p<.01
*** p<.001

Legend

A	*E-commerce doesn't fit with products/services*
B	*E-commerce doesn't fit with the way we do business*
C	*E-commerce doesn't fit the way our customers work*
D	*We don't see the advantage of using E-commerce*
E	*Lack of technical know how*
F	*Security risks*
G	*Cost too high*
H	*Not sure what to choose*

An examination of the data in Table A6.15 shows that the means of ratings for one <u>barrier</u>, *E-commerce doesn't fit the way we do business* were significantly different (at the .05 level). The mean rating of respondents that were members of a small business strategic alliance was 4.06, compared to 2.83 for those that were not members of a small business strategic alliance. The table also shows that the means of ratings for one <u>barrier</u>, *We don't see any advantage of using E-commerce* were significantly different (at the .01 level). Respondents that were members of a small business strategic alliance rated this <u>barrier</u> higher (4.00) than those that were not members of a small business strategic alliance (2.27). No other <u>barriers</u> showed any significant difference. Table A6.16 provides the data for those that indicated their business's levels of IT skill was normal.

271

Table A6.16
A comparison of the means of rating of <u>barriers</u> to adoption of E-commerce between those respondents that were members of a small business strategic alliance and those that were not, where respondents indicated their company levels of IT skill was normal

Barriers	Mean Members	N Members	Mean Non-members	N Non-members	t-value	Sig.
A	3.50	30	3.59	22	.238	.813
B	3.25	28	3.46	24	.526	.601
C	3.10	29	4.00	22	2.412	.020*
D	3.17	30	3.29	21	.295	.769
E	3.17	29	3.13	24	-.123	.902
F	2.68	28	2.67	21	-.034	.973
G	2.76	29	3.10	21	.862	.393
H	2.88	26	2.95	20	.170	.866

* $p < .05$
** $p < .01$
*** $p < .001$

Legend

A	*E-commerce doesn't fit with products/services*
B	*E-commerce doesn't fit with the way we do business*
C	*E-commerce doesn't fit the way our customers work*
D	*We don't see the advantage of using E-commerce*
E	*Lack of technical know how*
F	*Security risks*
G	*Cost too high*
H	*Not sure what to choose*

An examination of the data in Table A6.16 shows that the means of ratings for one <u>barrier</u>, *E-commerce doesn't fit the way our customers work* was significantly different (at the .05 level). The mean rating for respondents that were members of a small business strategic alliance was 3.10, compared to 4.00 for those respondents that were not members of a small business strategic alliance. No other <u>barrier</u> provided any significant differences. Table A3.36 provides the data for those respondents that indicated that their business's levels of IT skills were high.

There was insufficient data to carry out an examination of the high or expert skill level respondents.

A6.5.3 A comparison of ratings of benefits (between those respondents that were members of a small business strategic alliance and those that were not) across the 5 levels of IT skill

Based on an examination of the literature and case studies carried out in Australia, 11 benefits derived from the adoption of E-commerce by SMEs were identified. A set of frequency analyses was carried out to determine their applicability to the regional Swedish study (see section 4.2.3). Two benefits:

> *Reduced stock*
> *Improved marketing*

were deemed as not applicable to the study and were eliminated. A series of two-tailed t-tests was carried out on the benefits to determine whether, across the five levels of IT skill, the means of perception of importance for the benefit was significantly different between those respondents that were members of a small business strategic alliance and those that were not. There was insufficient data to examine the respondents that had no levels of IT skill in their business.
Tables A3.35 - A3.36 show the data for the categories, normal and high. An examination of the data in the tables shows that there were no significant differences in the means of rating of the barriers between those respondents that were part of a small business strategic alliance and those that were not.

A6.5.4 Conclusions concerning the appropriateness of small business strategic alliances with regards levels of IT skill

Section A6.5 has provided detailed comparisons of the means of ratings of criteria, barriers and benefits of E-commerce adoption between those respondents that were members of a small business strategic alliance and those that were not. The data has shown that several criteria are significantly different for particular levels of IT skill. These are:

- *Improvement to marketing*   (Normal skill)
- *Improvement to customer service*   (High skill)
- *Reach New customers and markets*   (high skill)

The ratings of several barriers showed significant differences for particular business sector categories. These are:

- *Don't see any advantage in using E-commerce*   (Low skill)
- *E-commerce doesn't fit the way we do business*   (Low skill)
- *E-commerce doesn't fit the way we do business*   (Normal skill)

As previously stated (see section 4.2.4), all disadvantages were found to be inapplicable to the study and were eliminated from further consideration.

A6.6 Conclusion concerning the various subsets of the Swedish study

The third goal of the study was:

To determine whether differences in the perceptions of <u>barriers</u> to adoption, <u>criteria</u> for adoption, <u>benefits</u> of adoption or <u>disadvantages</u> of adoption of E-commerce technologies (membership versus non-membership of a small business strategic alliance) are specific to SMEs of a certain business age, business size, business sector or market focus or whether these perceptions are specific to the level of IT skill.

Section 4.5 shows that for particular subsets of the study, the mean ratings of some of the <u>criteria</u>, <u>barriers</u> and <u>benefits</u> of E-commerce adoption are significantly different between respondents that were part of a small business strategic alliance and respondents that were not. The data shows however, that there are no underlying patterns across any of the business characteristics for any of the adoption patterns.

Criteria

- *Pressure from competition*   (11-19 employees)
- *Improved competitiveness*   (11-19 employees)
- *Reaching new customers/markets*   (service sector)
- *Reaching new customers/markets*   (high levels of IT skills)
- *Improvement to marketing*   (service sector)
- *Improvement to marketing*   (normal levels of IT skill)
- *Improvement to customer services*   (high levels of IT skill)
- *Improvement in control and follow-up* (local focus)

Five of the eleven <u>criteria</u> showed no significant difference between respondents that were part of a small business strategic alliance and respondents that were not. These were:

- *Reduction of cost*
- *Increased sales*
- *Improvement in lead-time*
- *Improved internal efficiency*
- *Strengthening of relations with business partners*

Barriers

- *E-commerce doesn't fit the way our customers work*   (>20yrs in bus.)
- *E-commerce doesn't fit the way our customers work*   (normal skill)
- *E-commerce doesn't fit the way we do business*   (low skill)
- *Don't see any advantage to using E-commerce*   (low skill)
- *Don't see any advantage to using E-commerce*   (local)

Five of the eight <u>barriers</u> showed no significant differences between respondents that were part of a small business strategic alliance and respondents that were not. These were:

- *Security risks*
- *Lack of Technical know-how*
- *E-commerce doesn't fit with our products and services*
- *Cost too high*

- *Not sure what to choose*

Benefits
- *New customers/markets*   (20-50 employees)
- *New customers/markets*   (industrial)
- *New customers/markets*   (service)
- *Reduced lead time*   (11-19 employees)
- *Improved quality of information*   (service)
- *Lower admin. costs*   (11-19 employees)
- *Improved relations with business partners*   (retail)
- *Increased internal efficiency*   (local)

Three of the nine <u>benefits</u> showed no significant differences between respondents that were part of a small business strategic alliance and respondents that were not. These were
- *Increased sales*
- *Lower production costs*
- *Improved competitiveness*

A6.6.1 Business age
A study by Donckels & Lambrecht (1997) that examined small business strategic alliances in SME decision making found that the business age of the SME was significant with both the choice of small business strategic alliance as well as its ongoing role in the decision making process.

11 <u>criteria</u>, 8 <u>barriers</u> and 9 <u>benefits</u> of E-commerce adoption by SMEs were examined across each of the 6 business age groupings. The results (see Tables A6.1 and A6.2) showed that only 2 <u>barriers</u> demonstrated a significant difference in applicability between respondents that were members of a small business strategic alliance and respondents that were not. The <u>barrier</u>, *lack of technical know how* was significantly more applicable to respondents that were not members of a small business strategic alliance for the 11-20 business age group. The <u>barrier</u> *E-commerce doesn't fit the way our customers work* was also significantly more applicable to respondents that were not members of a small business strategic alliance for the > 20 years group.

While it may be argued that membership of a small business strategic alliance has reduced the perception of two barriers, *lack of technical know how* and *E-commerce doesn't fit the way our customers work* for two of the age groupings (11-20 years, > 20 years), respectively, it may equally be argued that there are no real differences between members and non-members across any of the other age groupings or any of the other barriers. This raises questions as to the applicability of the findings of Donckels & Lambrecht to the regional Karlstad study.

A6.6.2 Business size

In a study of 591 SMEs, Smith et al (2002) found that business size, in terms of numbers of employees, appeared to significantly affect the involvement and role of small business strategic alliances in decision-making.

11 criteria, 8 barriers and 9 benefits of E-commerce adoption by SMEs were examined across each of the 4 business size groupings.

Three criteria showed a significant difference between respondents that were members of a small business strategic alliance and respondents that were not. For SMEs that had 0 employees, the criterion, *improvement in lead-time* was considered significantly more applicable to respondents that were members of a small business strategic alliance than it was for non-members. For the business size 11 – 20 employees, two criteria, *pressure from competition* and *improvement in competitiveness* were significantly more applicable to respondents that were members of a small business strategic alliance than they were for non-members.

There were no significant differences for any of the barriers for any of the business size categories.

The data in Tables A6.3 and A6.4 shows that contrary to expectations and the findings of Dennis (2000) and Achrol & Kotler (1999) it is the non-member respondents that indicated greater benefits through E-commerce adoption than member respondents. One possible explanation is that the benefits new customers/markets had already been achieved through membership of a small business strategic alliance.

A6.6.3 Business Sector

Two recent studies (Schindehutte & Morris 2001, BarNir & Smith 2002) focusing on the role of small business strategic alliances in SME decision making, found that the business sector in which an SME operates, influenced decisions both in the type of small business strategic alliance as well as the role played by that alliance. This, coupled with the findings of Riquelme (2002), that concluded that the service sector was more likely to benefit through adoption of E-commerce, suggested a closer examination of each of the business sectors. 11 criteria, 8 barriers and 9 benefits of E-commerce adoption by SMEs were examined across each of the 4 business sector categories.

Only one business sector, the service sector (see Table A6.6) showed any significant differences between respondents that were members of a small business strategic alliance and respondents that were not. Two criteria, *reaching new customers/markets* and *improvement to marketing*, were rated as more applicable by respondents that were not members of a small business strategic alliance than they were by respondents that were members of a small business strategic alliance. One possible explanation is that those respondents that were members of a small business strategic alliance had, in part, achieved their marketing 'needs' through membership of the small business strategic alliance and thus had adopted E-commerce for other reasons.

While the results do support the findings of Riquelme (2002), at least for two criteria, *reaching new customers/markets* and *improvement to marketing*, the majority of results show no significant differences in the ratings of criteria, barriers or benefits of E-commerce adoption. This would suggest that Riquelme's view, viz., that the service sector was more likely to benefit through adoption of E-commerce is, at best, questionable for the regional Karlstad study.

An examination of Tables A6.7, A6.8, A6.9 shows that three of the four business sectors demonstrated significant differences in applicability of benefits between respondents that were members of a small business strategic alliance and respondents that were not. For the industrial sector (see Table A6.7), there was a significant difference in the rating of one benefit, *new customers and markets*. Respondents that were members of a small business strategic alliance rated this benefit more applicable than respondents that were not members of a small business strategic alliance.

For the service sector, two benefits, *new customers and markets* and *improved quality of information* showed a significant difference in applicability of benefits between respondents that were members of a small business strategic alliance and respondents that were not (see Table A6.8). In both cases, respondents that were not members of a small business strategic alliance rated this benefit more applicable than respondents that were members of a small business strategic alliance. These results are contrary to earlier results of Riquelme (2002) and Marchewka & Towell (2000).

For the retail sector, two benefits, *reduced lead time* and *improved relations with business partners* showed a significant difference in applicability of benefits between respondents that were members of a small business strategic alliance and respondents that were not (see Table A6.9). In both cases, respondents that were not members of a small business strategic alliance rated this benefit more applicable than respondents that were members of a small business strategic alliance.

A number of authors, Jorde & Teece (1989), Marchewka & Towell (2000) and Achrol & Kotler (1999) have suggested that membership of a small business strategic alliance produces greater benefits for members, where E-commerce adoption is concerned. The results of the Karlstad study would suggest that for the retail respondents, the reverse is the case.

It is interesting to compare the three sectors. For the industrial sector, benefits are more applicable to respondents that were members of a small business strategic alliance. For the service and retail sectors benefits are more applicable to respondents that were not members of a small business strategic alliance. These differences in findings would tend to support the findings of Schindehutte & Morris 2001 and BarNir & Smith 2002 that business sector appears to dictate the role of the small business strategic alliance.

However, the results from the service and retail sectors contradict the suggestions of Overby & Min (2000), Marchewka & Towell (2000) and Achrol & Kotler (1999) that membership of a small business strategic alliance provides greater benefits to members where E-commerce adoption is concerned.

A6.6.4 Market Focus

Studies carried out by Schindehutte & Morris 2001 and BarNir & Smith 2002 concluded that, among other business characteristics, market focus dictates decisions concerning the structure and role of small business strategic alliances. Blackburn & Athayde (2000) also noted that market focus, particularly international market focus, was associated with decisions concerning E-commerce adoption by SMEs. 11 criteria, 8 barriers and 9 benefits of E-commerce adoption by SMEs were examined across each of the 4 market focus groupings to determine whether there were any significant differences in applicability between respondents that were members of a small business strategic alliance and respondents that were not.

Two market focus groups, local and international provided criteria that showed a significant difference in applicability between respondents that were members of a small business strategic alliance and respondents that were not. One criterion, *improvement in control and follow up* showed a significant difference for local respondents (see Table A6.10). The data in Table A6.10 shows that respondents that were not members of a small business strategic alliance rated this criterion more applicable than respondents that were members of a small business strategic alliance.

Only one market focus group, the locally focused respondents provided any significant differences in the applicability of barriers. Table A6.11 shows that one barrier, *we don't see any advantage to using E-commerce* was significantly more applicable to respondents that were members of a small business strategic alliance than respondents that were not.

While the result does support the views of Schindehutte & Morris (2000) and BarNir & Smith (2002), for locally focused respondents from Karlstad, the lack of any significant differences for the other market focus categories raises questions as to whether, for the Karlstad respondents, market focus, other than local focus, has any real association with membership/non-membership of a small business strategic alliance, in terms of barriers to E-commerce adoption. Interestingly, the results in Table A6.11, that members of a small business strategic alliance rated the barrier, *we don't see any advantage to using E-commerce* higher than non-members is contrary to earlier findings of Overby & Min (2000) and Marchewka & Towell (2000) in the literature.

A number of authors (Gulledge & Sommer 1998, Vescovi 2000, Ritchie & Brindley 2001) have suggested that E-commerce is more applicable to SMEs that have an international market focus. A number of government publications have taken this a stage further and suggested that this is achievable through the development of a small business strategic alliance. An examination of Table A6.12 shows that for the Swedish study these assertions are incorrect, it is the locally and regionally focused respondents that showed differences in applicability between respondents that were members of a small business strategic alliance and respondents that were not.

Table A6.12 shows that one benefit, *increased internal efficiency* showed a significant difference in the rating of applicability between respondents that were members of a small business strategic alliance and respondents that were not. Respondents that were not members of a small business strategic alliance rated this as more applicable than respondents that were members. Again, this is contrary to earlier suggestions of Overby & Min (2000) and Marchewka & Towell (2000) who suggest that members would achieve greater benefits than non-members.

A6.6.5 Level of IT skill

A number of studies (Yap et al 1992, Thong et al 1996, MacGregor & Bunker 1996, MacGregor et al 1998) have shown that the adoption and use of any form of technology is significantly associated with the levels of IT skill in the organization. Studies carried out by Dennis (2000) and Marchewka & Towell (2000) have further concluded that many SMEs make use of small business strategic alliances to make up for the shortfall of IT skill in their own business. 11 criteria, 8 barriers and 9 benefits of E-commerce adoption by SMEs were examined across each of the 5 IT skill level groupings to determine whether there were any significant differences in applicability between respondents that were members of a small business strategic alliance and respondents that were not.

Three skill levels, normal, high and expert (see Tables A6.13 and A6.14) provided criteria that showed a significant difference between respondents that were members of a small business strategic alliance and respondents that were not.

278

Table A6.13 shows that one criterion, *improvement in marketing* provided a significant difference between respondents that were members of a small business strategic alliance and respondents that were not, for respondents that indicated their IT skill level was normal. Respondents that were not members of a small business strategic alliance rated this criterion as significantly more applicable than respondents that were members of a small business strategic alliance. One possible explanation is that enhanced marketing may have been achievable through membership of the members of a small business strategic alliance and thus was not as important a criterion for E-commerce adoption.

Table A6.14 provides the data for respondents that indicated their IT level as high. An examination of the data in Table A6.14 shows that 2 criteria, *improvement to customer service* and *reaching new customers/markets* were significantly more applicable to respondents that were members of a small business strategic alliance.

If, as suggested by Yap et al 1992, Thong et al 1996, MacGregor & Bunker 1996 and MacGregor et al 1998, the level of IT skill is significantly associated with the adoption of technology, the data comparing the means of ratings of barriers to E-commerce adoption should provide significant differences, particularly with the no and low skill categories.

Two IT skill level groups, low and normal, produced significant differences in the applicability of barriers between respondents that were members of a small business strategic alliance and respondents that were not (see Table A6.15 and A6.16).

Table A6.15 provides the data for respondents that indicated that their IT skill level was low. Two barriers, *E-commerce doesn't fit the way we do business* and *we don't see any advantage to using E-commerce* showed significant differences in applicability between respondents that were members of a small business strategic alliance and respondents that were not. In both cases, respondents that were part of a small business strategic alliance rated these as more applicable than respondents that were not part of a small business strategic alliance. This would suggest that for this group, the findings of Dennis (2000) that small business strategic alliances dissipate technical barriers must be questioned.

While the data in Table A6.15 does support the notion that differences in the ratings of barriers to E-commerce adoption would be expected at the low skill level, the results are contrary to suggestions of Marchewka & Towell (2000) and Achrol & Kotler (1999) who predicted that membership of a small business strategic alliance would tend to dissipate perceived barriers to E-commerce in respondent SMEs.

Table A6.16 shows that one barrier, *E-commerce doesn't fit the way our customers do business* showed a significant difference in applicability between respondents that were members of a small business strategic alliance and respondents that were not, for the normal IT skill respondents. Respondents that were not part of a small business strategic alliance rated this barrier as more applicable than respondents that were part of a small business strategic alliance.

279

Appendix 7
Goal 3 Australia

This section is subdivided into 5 subsections:
- Subsection A7.1 examines the adoption factors (<u>criteria</u> for adoption, <u>barriers</u> to adoption, <u>benefits</u> from adoption and <u>disadvantages</u> from adoption) of E-commerce across the 6 business age categories.
- Subsection A7.2 examines the adoption factors across the 4 business size categories.
- Subsection A7.3 examines the adoption factors across the 4 business sector categories
- Subsection A7.4 examines the adoption factors across the 4 market focus categories
- Subsection A7.5 examines the adoption factors across the 5 IT skill categories

It should be noted that in an effort to improve readability, only those tables that demonstrate statistical significance are shown. All other tables appear in Appendix 4.

A7.1 Comparison of the adoption factors (members versus non-members of a small business strategic alliance) across the 6 business age categories

The complete data from the study was subdivided into 6 groups, one for each of the business age categories. These were:
- Less than 1 year in business
- 1 – 2 years in business
- 3 – 5 years in business
- 6 – 10 years in business
- 11 – 20 years in business
- more than 20 years in business

A comparison of means of ratings (using two-tailed t-tests) between those respondent SMEs that were members of a small business strategic alliance and those that were not was carried out to determine whether there were any significant differences in the perceptions of <u>criteria</u>, <u>barriers</u>, <u>benefits</u> or <u>disadvantages</u> between members and non-members of a small business strategic alliance for particular business ages of business.

A7.1.1 A comparison of ratings of <u>criteria</u> (between those respondent SMEs that were members of a small business strategic alliance and those that were not) within the six business age categories.

Based on an examination of the literature and case studies carried out in Australia, 14 <u>criteria</u> for adoption of E-commerce by SMEs were identified. A set of frequency analyses was carried out to determine their applicability to the regional Australian study (see section 5.2.1). Three <u>criteria</u>:

Demand or pressure from suppliers
Strengthen relations with business partners
The availability of external technical support

280

were determined to be not applicable to the study and were eliminated. A series of two-tailed t-tests was applied to the remaining 11 criteria to determine whether, within each of the six business age group categories, the means of perception of importance for the criteria were significantly different between those respondent SMEs that were members of a small business strategic alliance and those that were not. An examination of the data showed that no business age category had sufficient data to carry out the two-tailed t-tests.

A7.1.2 A comparison of ratings of <u>barriers</u> (between those respondent SMEs that were members of a small business strategic alliance and those that were not) within the six business age categories

Based on an examination of the literature and case studies carried out in Australia, 8 barriers for adoption of E-commerce by SMEs were identified. A set of frequency analyses was carried out to determine their applicability to the Australian study (see section 5.2.2). All barriers were determined to be applicable. A series of two-tailed t-tests was applied to barriers to determine whether, within each of the six business age group categories the means of perception of importance for the barrier was significantly different between those respondent SMEs that were members of a small business strategic alliance and those that were not. As there was no comparable data for three of these business age groups (< 1 year in business, 1 – 2 years in business, > 20 years in business), data is presented for the remaining 3 business age groups only. Table A7.1 provides the data for SMEs that have been in operation for between 10 and 20 years.

Table A7.1

Comparison of means of rating of <u>barriers</u> to the E-commerce adoption (between respondent SMEs that were members of a small business strategic alliance and respondent SMEs that were not) – 10 to 20 years group

Barriers	Mean Members	N Members	Mean Non-members	N Non-members	t-value	Sig.
A	3.19	21	3.13	48	.151	.881
B	3.14	21	3.46	48	.810	.421
C	3.24	21	3.10	48	.329	.743
D	2.86	21	3.38	48	-1.351	.181
E	2.48	21	3.33	48	-1.936	.059
F	2.86	21	2.96	48	.241	.810
G	2.00	21	3.23	48	-2.816	.006**
H	2.38	21	2.79	48	-.945	.348

* p<.05
** p<.01
*** p<.001
Legend

A	*E-commerce doesn't fit with products/services*
B	*E-commerce doesn't fit with the way we do business*

C	*E-commerce doesn't fit the way our customers work*
D	*We don't see the advantage of using E-commerce*
E	*Lack of technical know how*
F	*Security risks*
G	*Cost too high*
H	*Not sure what to choose*

An examination of the data in Table A7.1 shows that the means of ratings of one <u>barrier</u>, *cost too high*, showed a significant difference between respondent SMEs that were members of a small business strategic alliance and respondent SMEs that were not (at the .01 level). . Those that were members of a small business strategic alliance rated this <u>barrier</u> more applicable than those that were not.

A number of authors have suggested that membership of a small business strategic alliance 'softens' the impact of barriers to E-commerce adoption. The data from Wollongong supports this view for the barrier, *cost too high*. It is interesting to note, however, that membership of a small business strategic alliance appears to have had little effect on any of the other barriers to E-commerce adoption in the regional Wollongong study.

A7.1.3 A comparison of ratings of <u>benefits</u> (between those respondent SMEs that were members of a small business strategic alliance and those that were not) within the six business age categories.

Based on an examination of the literature and case studies carried out in Australia, 11 <u>benefits</u> derived from the adoption of E-commerce by SMEs were identified. A set of frequency analyses was carried out to determine their applicability to the Australian study (see section 4.2.3). Two <u>benefits</u>:
> *Reduced stock*
> *Improvement in relations with business partners*

were deemed as not applicable to the study and were eliminated. A series of two-tailed t-tests was carried out on the <u>benefits</u> to determine whether, within each of the 6 business age groups, the means of perception of <u>benefits</u> was significantly different between those respondent SMEs that were members of a small business strategic alliance and those that were not. The data showed that only 2 business age groups had sufficient data to provide comparisons, these were the 3 – 5 years and 10 – 20 years groups.

The minimum sample size (at 99.9% degree of confidence) was determined to be 37 (for 95% it was 21). The sample size is below both of these.

A7.1.4 A comparison of ratings of <u>disadvantages</u> (between those respondent SMEs that were members of a small business strategic alliance and those that were not) within the six business age categories.

Based on previous studies in the literature and the two pilot studies in Australia, 7 <u>disadvantages</u> found from the adoption of E-commerce in SMEs were identified. A series of frequency tests was applied to the data (see section 5.2.4) to determine the applicability of the <u>disadvantages</u> to the Australian study. Four <u>disadvantages</u>:

Deterioration of relations with business partners
Higher costs
Doubling of work
Reduction in flexibility of work

were deemed as not applicable to this study and were eliminated. A series of two-tailed t-tests was carried out on the remaining <u>disadvantages</u> to determine whether there was any significant difference in the ratings of the <u>disadvantages</u> between those respondent SMEs that were members of a small business strategic alliance and those that were not.

The minimum sample size (at 99.9% degree of confidence) was determined to be 37 (for 95% it was 21). The sample size is below both of these for all sub-groups.

A7.1.5 Conclusions concerning the appropriateness of small business strategic alliances with regards business age

Section A7.1 has provided detailed comparisons of the means of rating of <u>criteria</u>, <u>barriers</u>, <u>benefits</u> and <u>disadvantages</u> between those respondent SMEs that were members of a small business strategic alliance and those that were not. The data showed that three <u>criteria</u>, *pressure from competition, reaching new customers and markets, improvement in competitiveness* all showed a significant difference in rating between those respondent SMEs that were members of a small business strategic alliance and those that were not for the business age group 10 – 20 years.

The data showed that one <u>barrier</u>, *cost too high*, showed significant differences between those respondent SMEs that were members of a small business strategic alliance and those that were not for both the 3 – 5 years group as well as the 10 – 20 years group.

A7.2 Comparison of the adoption factors (members versus non-members of a small business strategic alliance) across the 4 business size categories

The complete set of data from the study was subdivided into 4 groups, one for each of the business size categories. These were:

- 0 employees
- 1 – 9 employees
- 10 – 19 employees
- 20 – 49 employees

A comparison of the means of rating between SMEs that are members of a small business strategic alliance and SMEs that are not was carried out within each of the business size categories to determine whether membership of a small business strategic alliance altered the perception of importance of <u>criteria</u>, <u>barriers</u>, <u>benefits</u> or <u>disadvantages</u> within particular business size categories.

283

A7.2.1 Comparison of the means of rating of <u>criteria</u> between SMEs that are members of a small business strategic alliance and SMEs that are not, within the 4 business size categories

Based on an examination of the literature and case studies carried out in Australia, 14 <u>criteria</u> for adoption of E-commerce by SMEs were identified. A set of frequency analyses was carried out to determine their applicability to the Australian study (see section 5.2.1). Three <u>criteria</u>:

> *Demand or pressure from suppliers*
> *Strengthen relations with business partners*
> *The availability of external technical support*

were determined to be not applicable to the study and were eliminated. A series of two-tailed t-tests was applied to the remaining 11 <u>criteria</u> to determine whether, within each of the six business age group categories, the means of perception of importance for the <u>criteria</u> were significantly different between those respondent SMEs that were members of a small business strategic alliance and those that were not. There was only sufficient data to examine the business size group 1 – 9 employees.

Table A7.2 presents the data for business size 1 – 9 employees.

Table A7.2

Comparison of means of rating of <u>criteria</u> for E-commerce adoption, between respondent SMEs that were members of a small business strategic alliance and respondent SMEs that were not (1 – 9 employees)

<u>Criteria</u>	Mean Members	N Members	Mean Non-members	N Non-members	t-value	Sig.
A	2.13	8	3.14	14	-1.365	.187
B	1.50	8	3.71	14	-4.311	.000***
D	3.75	8	3.36	14	.509	.616
E	3.00	8	3.93	14	-1.430	.168
F	2.50	8	2.79	14	-.398	.695
G	2.63	8	4.07	14	-2.231	.037*
H	3.25	8	4.07	14	-1.337	.196
J	2.38	8	4.07	14	-2.680	.014*
K	2.50	8	4.21	14	-2.658	.015*
M	2.63	8	3.64	14	-1.446	.158
N	2.88	8	3.64	14	-1.224	.235

* p<.05
** p<.01
*** p<.001

Legend

A	*Demand/pressure from customers*
B	*Pressure of competition*

284

C	Demand/Pressure from suppliers
D	Reduction of costs
E	Improvement to customer service
F	Improvement in lead-time
G	Increased sales
H	Improvement to internal efficiency
I	Strengthen relations with business partners
J	Reach new customers/markets
K	Improvement in competitiveness
L	External technical support
M	Improvement in marketing
N	Improvement in control and follow-up

An examination of the data in Table A7.2 shows that the means of ratings for one criterion, *pressure from competition*, showed a significant difference (at the .001 level). The data also shows that the means of ratings for three criteria, *improvement in lead time, improvement in internal efficiency, reaching new customers and markets*, showed significant differences (at the .05 level). In all cases those respondent SMEs that were not members of a small business strategic alliance rated the criteria as more applicable than those that were members of a small business strategic alliance.

A number of recent studies have suggested that small business strategic alliances support member SMEs through improvement in sales, marketing, competitiveness and strengthening relationships with business partners. As such, it would be expected that SMEs that are members of a small business strategic alliance would rate these criteria as more important than non-member SMEs. The data from the Wollongong study shows that the reverse is the case, with non-member respondents rating these criteria as more applicable than member respondents.

A7.2.2 A comparison of ratings of barriers (between those respondent SMEs that were members of a small business strategic alliance and those that were not) within the four business size categories.

Based on an examination of the literature and case studies carried out in Australia, 8 barriers for adoption of E-commerce by SMEs were identified. A set of frequency analyses was carried out to determine their applicability to the Australian study (see section 5.2.2). All barriers were determined to be applicable. A series of two-tailed t-tests was applied to barriers to determine whether, within each of the four business size group categories the means of perception of importance for the barrier was significantly different between those respondent SMEs that were members of a small business strategic alliance and those that were not.

Table A7.3 presents the data for the sole traders.

Table A7.3
Comparison of means of rating of <u>barriers</u> to the E-commerce adoption (between respondent SMEs that were members of a small business strategic alliance and respondent SMEs that were not) –sole traders group

<u>Barriers</u>	Mean Members	N Members	Mean Non-members	N Non-members	t-value	Sig.
A	4.14	7	3.05	20	1.511	.143
B	4.14	7	3.05	20	1.558	.132
C	4.00	7	2.55	20	2.115	.045*
D	3.43	7	3.15	20	.384	.704
E	3.14	7	3.20	20	-.075	.941
F	2.29	7	2.75	20	-.645	.525
G	3.43	7	3.75	20	-.467	.645
H	2.14	7	2.45	20	-.431	.670

* p<.05
** p<.01
*** p<.001

Legend

A	*E-commerce doesn't fit with products/services*
B	*E-commerce doesn't fit with the way we do business*
C	*E-commerce doesn't fit the way our customers work*
D	*We don't see the advantage of using E-commerce*
E	*Lack of technical know how*
F	*Security risks*
G	*Cost too high*
H	*Not sure what to choose*

An examination of the data in Table A7.3 shows that the means of ratings for one <u>barrier</u>, *E-commerce doesn't fit the way our customers work*, showed significant differences (at the .05 level). The data shows that the <u>barriers</u> was more applicable to respondent SMEs that are members of a small business strategic alliance.

A major premise, upon which many authors (Marchewka & Towell 2000, Jorde & Teece 1989) advocate small business strategic alliances, is the notion that they reduce the impact of barriers to adoption of E-commerce in SMEs. An examination of the data from the Wollongong study shows that not only are there no significant differences for 7 of the 8 barriers, but one barrier, *E-commerce doesn't fit the way our customers work*, has shown the reverse, that members rated it more applicable to their situation than did non-members.

Table A7.4 provides the data for SMEs that had 1 – 9 employees.

Table A7.4
Comparison of means of rating of <u>barriers</u> to the E-commerce adoption (between respondent SMEs that were members of a small business strategic alliance and respondent SMEs that were not) –1 – 9 employees group

Barriers	Mean Members	N Members	Mean Non-members	N Non-members	t-value	Sig.
A	3.29	24	3.36	66	-.187	.852
B	3.48	24	3.55	66	-.186	.853
C	4.46	24	3.47	66	1.601	.113
D	2.88	24	3.55	66	-1.899	.061
E	2.83	24	3.45	66	-1.553	.124
F	2.96	24	2.94	66	.052	.959
G	1.92	24	3.12	66	-3.564	.001***
H	2.54	24	2.94	66	-1.037	.302

* p<.05
** p<.01
*** p<.001

Legend

A	*E-commerce doesn't fit with products/services*
B	*E-commerce doesn't fit with the way we do business*
C	*E-commerce doesn't fit the way our customers work*
D	*We don't see the advantage of using E-commerce*
E	*Lack of technical know how*
F	*Security risks*
G	*Cost too high*
H	*Not sure what to choose*

An examination of the data in Table A7.4 shows that the means of ratings for one <u>barrier</u>, *cost too high*, showed a significant difference (at the .001 level). The data shows that non-members rated this <u>barrier</u> as more applicable to their situation than members.

A7.2.3 A comparison of ratings of <u>benefits</u> (between those respondent SMEs that were members of a small business strategic alliance and those that were not) within the four business size categories.

Based on an examination of the literature and case studies carried out in Australia, 11 <u>benefits</u> derived from the adoption of E-commerce by SMEs were identified. A set of frequency analyses was carried out to determine their applicability to the Australian study (see section 5.2.3). Two <u>benefits</u>:
    Reduced stock

Improvement to relations with business partners

were deemed as not applicable to the study and were eliminated. A series of two-tailed t-tests was carried out on the benefits to determine whether, within each of the 4 business size groups, the means of perception of benefits was significantly different between those respondent SMEs that were members of a small business strategic alliance and those that were not. As there is insufficient data for sole traders, 10-19 employees, 20 –50 employees, Table A7.5 presents the data for the 1 – 9 employee group.

Table A7.5
Comparison of means of rating of benefits to the E-commerce adoption (between respondent SMEs that were members of a small business alliance and respondent SMEs that were not) – 1 to 9 employees

	Mean Members	N Members	Mean Non-members	N Non-Members	t-value	Sig.
A	3.13	8	3.00	14	.173	.864
B	1.63	8	2.36	14	-.916	.371
C	2.00	8	2.50	14	-.605	.552
E	1.88	8	3.21	14	-2.215	.039*
F	3.50	8	3.79	14	-.454	.655
H	2.13	8	3.21	14	-1.405	.175
I	2.25	8	3.86	14	-2.360	.029*
J	2.38	8	3.71	14	-1.897	.072
K	3.13	8	3.64	14	-.787	.441

* $p<.05$
** $p<.01$
*** $p<.001$

Legend

A	*Lower administration costs*
B	*Lower production costs*
C	*Reduced lead-time*
D	*Reduced stock*
E	*Increased sales*
F	*Increased internal efficiency*
G	*Improved relations with business partners*
H	*New customers and markets*
I	*Improved competitiveness*
J	*Improved marketing*
K	*Improved quality of information*

An examination of the data in Table A7.5 shows that the means of ratings of two underlined benefits, *increased sales, improved competitiveness* showed a significant difference (at the .05 level). In both cases non-members rated this benefit as more applicable to their situation than members.

An examination of the government initiatives concerned with membership of a small business strategic alliance, suggests that greater benefits are achievable, for SMEs, through the alliance, when adopting E-commerce. The Wollongong data shows that it is the non-member respondents, not the member respondents that have reported a greater benefit from E-commerce adoption.

A7.2.4 A comparison of ratings of disadvantages (between those respondent SMEs that were members of a small business strategic alliance and those that were not) within the four business size categories.

Based on previous studies in the literature and the two pilot studies in Australia, 7 disadvantages found from the adoption of E-commerce in SMEs were identified. A series of frequency tests was applied to the data (see section 5.2.4) to determine the applicability of the disadvantages to the Australian study. Four disadvantages were deemed not applicable to the study. These were:

Deterioration of relations with business partners
Higher costs
Doubling of work
Reduction in flexibility of work

A series of two-tailed t-tests was carried out on the disadvantages to determine whether there was any significant difference in the ratings of the disadvantages between those respondent SMEs that were members of a small business strategic alliance and those that were not. There was insufficient data to examine any of the business size groups except 1 – 9 employees.

Table A7.6 provides the details of the two-tailed t-tests for the 1 – 9 employee group.

Table A7.6

Comparison of means of rating of disadvantages to the E-commerce adoption (between respondent SMEs that were members of a small business alliance and respondent SMEs that were not) 1 to 9 employees

	Mean Members	N Members	Mean Non-members	N Non-Members	t-value	Sig.
C	2.13	8	4.21	14	-3.206	.004**
F	2.25	8	2.93	14	-1.202	.243
G	2.25	8	3.43	14	-1.576	.131

* p<.05
** p<.01
*** p<.001

Legend

A	*Deterioration of relations with business partners*
B	*Higher costs*
C	*Computer maintenance*

289

D	*Doubling of work*
E	*Reduced flexibility of work*
F	*Security*
G	*Dependence on E-commerce*

An examination of the data in Table A7.6 shows that the means of ratings of one disadvantage, *computer maintenance* showed a significant difference (at the .01 level). Respondent SMEs that were not part of a small business strategic alliance rated this disadvantage as more applicable than members of a small business strategic alliance.

A7.2.5 Conclusions concerning the appropriateness of small business strategic alliances with regards business size

Section A7.2 has provided detailed comparisons of the means of ratings of <u>criteria</u>, <u>barriers</u>, <u>benefits</u> and <u>disadvantages</u> of E-commerce adoption between those respondent SMEs that were members of a small business strategic alliance and those that were not.
The data has shown that several <u>criteria</u> are significantly different for particular business sizes. These are:

- *Pressure of competition*   (1 – 9 employees)
- *Increased sales*   (1 – 9 employees)
- *Reach new customers/markets*   (1 – 9 employees)
- *Improvement in competitiveness*   (1 – 9 employees)

The data showed that several <u>barriers</u> showed significant differences for particular business sizes. These are:

- *E-commerce doesn't fit the way our customers work*
        (0 employees)
- *Cost too high*   (1 – 9 employees)

The data showed that several <u>benefits</u> showed significant differences for particular business sizes. These are:

- *Increased sales*   (1 – 9 employees)
- *Improved competitiveness*   (1 – 9 employees)

The data showed that one disadvantage showed significant differences for particular business sizes. This was:

- *Computer maintenance*   (1 – 9 employees)

A7.3 Comparison of the adoption factors (members versus non-members of a small business strategic alliance) across the 4 business sector categories

The complete set of data from the study was subdivided into 4 groups, one for each of the business sector categories. These were:

- Industrial
- Service

- Retail
- Financial

A comparison of the means of rating between regional SMEs that are members of a small business strategic alliance and regional SMEs that are not was carried out within each of the sector categories to determine whether membership of a small business strategic alliance altered the perception of importance of criteria, barriers, benefits or disadvantages within particular sector categories.

A7.3.1 Comparison of the means of rating of criteria between SMEs that are members of a small business strategic alliance and SMEs that are not within the 4 sector categories

Based on an examination of the literature and case studies carried out in Australia, 14 criteria for adoption of E-commerce by SMEs were identified. A set of frequency analyses was carried out to determine their applicability to the regional Australian study (see section 5.2.1). Three criteria:

Demand or pressure from suppliers
Strengthen relations with business partners
The availability of external technical support

were determined to be not applicable to the study and were eliminated. A series of two-tailed t-tests was applied to the remaining 11 criteria to determine whether, within each of the four business sector categories, the means of perception of importance for the criteria were significantly different between those respondent SMEs that were members of a small business strategic alliance and those that were not. Insufficient data was available to carry out t-tests on the industrial or financial respondent SMEs.

A7.3.2 A comparison of ratings of barriers (between those respondent SMEs that were members of a small business strategic alliance and those that were not) within the four business sector categories.

Based on an examination of the literature and case studies carried out in Australia, 8 barriers for adoption of E-commerce by SMEs were identified. A set of frequency analyses was carried out to determine their applicability to the regional Australian study (see section 5.2.2). All barriers were determined to be applicable. A series of two-tailed t-tests was applied to barriers to determine whether, within each of the four sector group categories the means of perception of importance for the barrier was significantly different between those respondent SMEs that were members of a small business strategic alliance and those that were not. There was insufficient data to examine the financial respondent SMEs.

Table A4.19 presents the data for the retail sectors. An examination of the data in the table shows that there were no significant differences for the ratings of any of the criteria.

Table A7.7 presents the data for the service sector.

Table A7.7
Comparison of means of rating of <u>barriers</u> to the E-commerce adoption (between respondent SMEs that were members of a small business strategic alliance and respondent SMEs that were not) – service sector

<u>Barriers</u>	Mean Members	N Members	Mean Non-members	N Non-members	t-value	Sig.
A	3.55	22	3.19	43	.860	.393
B	3.52	22	3.30	43	.534	.595
C	4.73	22	2.95	43	2.306	.024*
D	3.18	22	3.35	43	-.414	.680
E	2.82	22	2.86	43	-.093	.926
F	3.00	22	2.49	43	1.345	.184
G	2.09	22	2.86	43	-1.935	.057
H	2.32	22	2.49	43	-.411	.683

* $p<.05$
** $p<.01$
*** $p<.001$
Legend

A	*E-commerce doesn't fit with products/services*
B	*E-commerce doesn't fit with the way we do business*
C	*E-commerce doesn't fit the way our customers work*
D	*We don't see the advantage of using E-commerce*
E	*Lack of technical know how*
F	*Security risks*
G	*Cost too high*
H	*Not sure what to choose*

An examination of the data in Table A7.7 shows that the means of ratings of one <u>barrier</u>, *E-commerce doesn't fit the way our customers work* showed a significant difference (at the .05 level). Respondent SMEs that were part of a small business strategic alliance rated this <u>barrier</u> as more applicable than respondent SMEs that were not.

Again, a major premise, upon which many authors advocate small business strategic alliances, is the notion that they reduce the impact of barriers to adoption of E-commerce in SMEs. An examination of the data from the Wollongong study shows that not only are there no significant differences for 7 of the 8 barriers, but one barrier, *E-commerce doesn't fit the way our customers work*, has shown the reverse, that members rated it more applicable to their situation than did non-members.

A7.3.3 A comparison of ratings of <u>benefits</u> (between those respondent SMEs that were members of a small business strategic alliance and those that were not) within the four business sector categories.

Based on an examination of the literature and case studies carried out in Australia, 11 <u>benefits</u> derived from the adoption of E-commerce by SMEs were identified. A set of frequency analyses was carried out to determine their applicability to the Australian study (see section 5.2.3). Two <u>benefits</u>:

Reduced stock
Improvement of relations with business partners

were deemed as not applicable to the study and were eliminated. A series of two-tailed t-tests was carried out on the <u>benefits</u> to determine whether, within each of the 4 sector groups, the means of perception of <u>benefits</u> was significantly different between those respondent SMEs that were members of a small business strategic alliance and those that were not. There was insufficient data to carry out two-tailed t-tests on the industrial or financial sectors.

A7.3.4 A comparison of ratings of <u>disadvantages</u> (between those respondent SMEs that were members of a small business strategic alliance and those that were not) within the four business sector categories.

Based on previous studies in the literature and the two pilot studies in Australia, 7 <u>disadvantages</u> found from the adoption of E-commerce in SMEs were identified. A series of frequency analyses was applied to the data (see section 5.2.4) to determine the applicability of the <u>disadvantages</u> to the Australian study. Four <u>disadvantages</u> were deemed not applicable to the study. These were:

Deterioration of relations with business partners
Higher costs
Doubling of work
Reduction in flexibility of work

A series of two-tailed t-tests was carried out on the <u>disadvantages</u> to determine whether there was any significant difference in the ratings of the <u>disadvantages</u> between those respondent SMEs that were members of a small business strategic alliance and those that were not. As there was insufficient data to examine the financial or industrial respondent SMEs, only the service and retail sectors are shown.

A7.3.5 Conclusions concerning the appropriateness of small business strategic alliances with regards business sector

Section A7.3 has provided detailed comparisons of the means of ratings of <u>criteria</u>, <u>barriers</u> and <u>benefits</u> of E-commerce adoption between those respondent SMEs that were members of a small business strategic alliance and those that were not.

The data showed that one <u>barrier</u> showed a significant difference for particular sectors. This was:

- *E-commerce doesn't fit the way our customers work*
  (service sector)

A7.4 Comparison of the adoption factors (members versus non-members of a small business strategic alliance) across the 4 market focus categories

The complete set of data from the study was subdivided into 4 groups, one for each of the market focus categories. These were:
- Local
- Regional
- National
- International

A comparison of the means of rating between SMEs that are members of a small business strategic alliance and SMEs that are not was carried out within each of the sector categories to determine whether membership of a small business strategic alliance altered the perception of importance of criteria, barriers, benefits or disadvantages within particular market focus categories.

A7.4.1 Comparison of the means of rating of criteria between SMEs that are members of a small business strategic alliance and SMEs that are not within the 4 market focus categories

Based on an examination of the literature and case studies carried out in Australia, 14 criteria for adoption of E-commerce by SMEs were identified. A set of frequency analyses was carried out to determine their applicability to the regional Australian study (see section 5.2.1). Three criteria:

Demand or pressure from suppliers
Strengthen relations with business partners
The availability of external technical support

were determined to be not applicable to the study and were eliminated. A series of two-tailed t-tests was applied to the remaining 11 criteria to determine whether, within each of the four market focus categories, the means of perception of importance for the criteria were significantly different between those respondent SMEs that were members of a small business strategic alliance and those that were not. There was insufficient data to examine the local, national or international market focus groups.

A7.4.2 A comparison of ratings of barriers (between those respondent SMEs that were members of a small business strategic alliance and those that were not) within the four market focus categories.

Based on an examination of the literature and case studies carried out in Australia, 8 barriers for adoption of E-commerce by SMEs were identified. A set of frequency analyses was carried out to determine their applicability to the regional Australian study (see section 5.2.2). All barriers were determined to be applicable. A series of two-tailed t-tests was applied to barriers to determine whether, within each of the four market focus group categories the means of perception of importance for the barrier was significantly different between those respondent SMEs that were members of a small business strategic alliance and those that were not. There was insufficient data to examine the international respondent SMEs.

Table A7.8 presents the data for the regionally focused respondent SMEs.

Table A7.8
Comparison of means of rating of <u>barriers</u> to the E-commerce adoption (between respondent SMEs that were members of a small business strategic alliance and respondent SMEs that were not) – regional focus

Barriers	Mean Members	N Members	Mean Non-members	N Non-members	t-value	Sig.
A	3.00	19	3.05	59	-.117	.907
B	3.39	19	3.30	59	.116	.868
C	4.58	19	3.12	59	2.010	.048*
D	2.89	19	3.37	59	-1.259	.212
E	2.58	19	3.20	59	-1.391	.168
F	2.79	19	2.71	59	.201	.841
G	2.21	19	2.95	59	-1.780	.079
H	2.32	19	2.71	59	-.954	.343

* p<.05
** p<.01
*** p<.001

Legend

A	*E-commerce doesn't fit with products/services*
B	*E-commerce doesn't fit with the way we do business*
C	*E-commerce doesn't fit the way our customers work*
D	*We don't see the advantage of using E-commerce*
E	*Lack of technical know how*
F	*Security risks*
G	*Cost too high*
H	*Not sure what to choose*

An examination of the data in Table A7.8 shows that the means of ratings of one <u>barrier</u>, *E-commerce doesn't fit the way our customers work*, showed a significant difference (at the .05 level). Respondent SMEs that were part of a small business strategic alliance rated this <u>barrier</u> as more applicable than respondent SMEs that were not.

Advocates of small business strategic alliances point to a reduction of the impact of barriers to adoption of E-commerce in SMEs. An examination of the data from the Wollongong study shows that not only are there no significant differences for 7 of the 8 barriers, but one barrier, *E-commerce doesn't fit the way our customers work*, has shown the reverse, that members rated it more applicable to their situation than did non-members.

A7.4.3 A comparison of ratings of <u>benefits</u> (between those respondent SMEs that were members of a small business strategic alliance and those that were not) within the four market focus categories.

Based on an examination of the literature and case studies carried out in Australia, 11 <u>benefits</u> derived from the adoption of E-commerce by SMEs were identified. A set of frequency analyses was carried out to determine their applicability to the Australian study (see section 5.2.3). Two <u>benefits</u>:

> *Reduced stock*
> *Improvement of relations with business partners*

were deemed as not applicable to the study and were eliminated. A series of two-tailed t-tests was carried out on the <u>benefits</u> to determine whether, within each of the 4 market focus groups, the means of perception of <u>benefits</u> was significantly different between those respondent SMEs that were members of a small business strategic alliance and those that were not. There was insufficient data to carry out two-tailed t-tests on the local, national or international groups.

A7.4.4 A comparison of ratings of <u>disadvantages</u> (between those respondent SMEs that were members of a small business strategic alliance and those that were not) within the four market focus categories.

Based on previous studies in the literature and the two pilot studies in Australia, 7 <u>disadvantages</u> found from the adoption of E-commerce in SMEs were identified. A series of frequency tests was applied to the data (see section 5.2.4) to determine the applicability of the <u>disadvantages</u> to the Australian study. Four <u>disadvantages</u> were deemed not applicable to the study. These were:

> *Deterioration of relations with business partners*
> *Higher costs*
> *Doubling of work*
> *Reduction in flexibility of work*

A series of two-tailed t-tests was carried out on the <u>disadvantages</u> to determine whether there was any significant difference in the ratings of the <u>disadvantages</u> between those respondent SMEs that were members of a small business strategic alliance and those that were not. As there was insufficient data to examine the local, national, international respondent SMEs, only the regional group is shown.

A7.4.5 Conclusions concerning the appropriateness of small business strategic alliances with regards market focus

Section A7.4 has provided detailed comparisons of the means of ratings of <u>criteria</u>, <u>barriers</u> and <u>benefits</u> of E-commerce adoption between those respondent SMEs that were members of a small business strategic alliance and those that were not.

The data showed that one <u>barrier</u> is significantly different for particular market focus respondent SMEs. This is:

> • *E-commerce doesn't fit the way our customers work* (regional)

There were no significant differences for any of the <u>benefits</u>.

296

A7.5 Comparison of the adoption factors (members versus non-members of a small business strategic alliance) across the 5 levels of IT skill

The complete set of data from the study was subdivided into 5 groups, one for each of the levels of IT skills. These were:

- no skill
- low skill
- normal skill
- high skill
- expert skill

A comparison of the means of rating between regional SMEs that are members of a small business strategic alliance and regional SMEs that are not was carried out within the 5 groups to determine whether membership of a small business strategic alliance altered the perception of importance of <u>criteria</u>, <u>barriers</u>, <u>benefits</u> or <u>disadvantages</u> within either of the groups.

A7.5.1 Comparison of the means of rating of <u>criteria</u> between SMEs that are members of a small business strategic alliance and SMEs that are not within the 5 levels of IT skills categories

Based on an examination of the literature and case studies carried out in Australia, 14 <u>criteria</u> for adoption of E-commerce by SMEs were identified. A set of frequency analyses was carried out to determine their applicability to the Australian study (see section 5.2.1). Three <u>criteria</u>:

Demand or pressure from suppliers
Strengthen relations with business partners
The availability of external technical support

were determined to be not applicable to the study and were eliminated. A series of two-tailed t-tests was applied to the remaining 11 <u>criteria</u> to determine whether, within each of the four market focus categories, the means of perception of importance for the <u>criteria</u> were significantly different between those respondent SMEs that were members of a small business strategic alliance and those that were not. There was insufficient data to examine any of the skill groups, with the exception of the average skills.

A7.5.2 A comparison of ratings of <u>barriers</u> (between those respondent SMEs that were members of a small business strategic alliance and those that were not) across the 5 levels of IT skill

Based on an examination of the literature and case studies carried out in Australia, 8 <u>barriers</u> for adoption of E-commerce by SMEs were identified. A set of frequency analyses was carried out to determine their applicability to the Australian study (see section 5.2.2). All <u>barriers</u> were determined to be applicable. A series of two-tailed t-tests was applied to <u>barriers</u> to determine whether, within the 5 groups, the means of perception of importance for the <u>barrier</u> was significantly different between those respondent SMEs that were members of a small business strategic alliance and those that were not. There was insufficient data to examine the data for the no skill respondent SMEs. Table A4.20 presents the data for the low skill respondent SMEs.

An examination of the data in Table A4.20 shows that there were no significant differences in the ratings of any of the barriers.

Table A7.9 presents the data for the average skill respondent SMEs.

Table A7.9

Comparison of means of rating of barriers to the E-commerce adoption (between respondent SMEs that were members of a small business strategic alliance and respondent SMEs that were not) – average levels of IT skill

Barriers	Mean Members	N Members	Mean Non-members	N Non-members	t-value	Sig.
A	3.33	18	3.10	42	.516	.608
B	3.71	18	3.31	42	.933	.355
C	4.94	18	3.14	42	2.152	.036*
D	2.72	18	3.14	42	-1.018	.313
E	3.17	18	3.07	42	.200	.842
F	3.28	18	2.50	42	1.903	.062
G	2.33	18	2.86	42	-1.200	.235
H	2.28	18	2.45	42	-.383	.703

* $p<.05$
** $p<.01$
*** $p<.001$

Legend

A	*E-commerce doesn't fit with products/services*
B	*E-commerce doesn't fit with the way we do business*
C	*E-commerce doesn't fit the way our customers work*
D	*We don't see the advantage of using E-commerce*
E	*Lack of technical know how*
F	*Security risks*
G	*Cost too high*
H	*Not sure what to choose*

An examination of the data in Table A7.9 shows that the means of ratings of one barrier *E-commerce doesn't fit the way our customers work*, showed a significant difference (at the .05 level). Respondent SMEs that were part of a small business strategic alliance rated this barrier as more applicable than respondent SMEs that were not.

Table A4.21 presents the data for respondent SMEs that had a high level of skill.

An examination of the data in Table A4.21 shows that there were no significant differences for any of the barriers.

There was insufficient data to examine the expert skill respondent SMEs.

A7.5.3 A comparison of ratings of <u>benefits</u> (between those respondent SMEs that were members of a small business strategic alliance and those that were not) within the five levels of IT skill categories.

Based on an examination of the literature and case studies carried out in Australia, 11 <u>benefits</u> derived from the adoption of E-commerce by SMEs were identified. A set of frequency analyses was carried out to determine their applicability to the Australian study (see section 5.2.3). Two <u>benefits</u>:

  Reduced stock
  Improvement of relations with business partners

were deemed as not applicable to the study and were eliminated. A series of two-tailed t-tests was carried out on the <u>benefits</u> to determine whether, within each of the 5 levels of IT skill groups, the means of perception of <u>benefits</u> was significantly different between those respondent SMEs that were members of a small business strategic alliance and those that were not. There was insufficient data to examine any of the categories except the average skill group.

A7.5.4 A comparison of ratings of <u>disadvantages</u> (between those respondent SMEs that were members of a small business strategic alliance and those that were not) within the five levels of IT skill categories

Based on previous studies in the literature and the two pilot studies in Australia, 7 <u>disadvantages</u> found from the adoption of E-commerce in SMEs were identified. A series of frequency tests was applied to the data (see section 5.2.4) to determine the applicability of the <u>disadvantages</u> to the Australian study. Four <u>disadvantages</u> were deemed not applicable to the study. These were:

  Deterioration of relations with business partners
  Higher costs
  Doubling of work
  Reduction in flexibility of work

A series of two-tailed t-tests was carried out on the <u>disadvantages</u> to determine whether there was any significant difference in the ratings of the <u>disadvantages</u> between those respondent SMEs that were members of a small business strategic alliance and those that were not. There was insufficient data to examine any of the categories with the exception of the average group.

A7.5.5 Conclusions concerning the appropriateness of small business strategic   alliances with regards levels of IT skill

Section 4.5.5 has provided detailed comparisons of the means of ratings of <u>criteria</u>, <u>barriers</u> and <u>benefits</u> of E-commerce adoption between those respondent SMEs that were members of a small business strategic alliance and those that were not.

The data showed that one <u>barrier</u> is significantly different for particular levels of IT skill. This is:

 • *E-commerce doesn't fit the way our customers work* (average)

299

A7.6 Conclusion concerning the various subsets of the Australian study

The third goal of the study was:
- To determine whether the membership of small business strategic alliances alters perceptions of any of the adoption factors (barriers to adoption, criteria for adoption, benefits of adoption or disadvantages of adoption) of E-commerce technologies for specific sectors of the SME population (certain business ages, business sizes, business sectors, market focuses, particular levels of IT skill).

Section 5.5 shows that for particular subsets of the Australian study, the mean ratings of some of the criteria, barriers, benefits and disadvantages of E-commerce adoption are significantly different between respondent SMEs that were part of a small business strategic alliance and respondent SMEs that were not. The following is an overall summary:

Criteria
- *Pressure of competition*　　　　　(1 – 9 employees)
- *Increased sales*　　　　　　　　　(1 – 9 employees)
- *Reach new customers/markets*　　(1 – 9 employees)
- *Improvement in competitiveness*　(1 – 9 employees)

Five of the eleven criteria showed no significant differences between respondent SMEs that were part of a small business strategic alliance and respondent SMEs that were not. These were:
- *Reduction of costs*
- *Improvement to customer services*
- *Demand/Pressure from Customers*
- *Improvement in Lead-time*
- *Improvement to internal efficiency*
- *Improvement in marketing*
- *Improvement in control and follow up*

Barriers
- *Cost too high*　　　　　　　　　　　　　(10 – 20 years)
- *E-commerce doesn't fit the way our customers work*
　　　　　　　　　　　　　　　　　　　　　　(0 employees)
- *Cost too high*　　　　　　　　　　　　　(1 – 9 employees)
- *E-commerce doesn't fit with the way we do business*
　　　　　　　　　　　　　　　　　　　　　　(service sector)
- *E-commerce doesn't fit the way our customers work*
　　　　　　　　　　　　　　　　　　　　　　(service sector)
- *E-commerce doesn't fit the way our customers work* (regional)
- *E-commerce doesn't fit the way our customers work* (average)

Five of the eight barriers showed no significant differences between respondent SMEs that were part of a small business strategic alliance and respondent SMEs that were not. These were:
- *E-commerce doesn't fit with our products and services*
- *We don't see any advantage in using E-commerce*

- *Lack of technical know how*
- *Security*
- *No sure what to choose*

Benefits

- *Increased sales*   (1 – 9 employees)
- *Improved competitiveness*   (1 – 9 employees)

Seven of the nine <u>benefits</u> showed no significant differences between respondent SMEs that were part of a small business strategic alliance and respondent SMEs that were not. These were

- *Lower administration costs*
- *Lower production cost*
- *Improved quality of information*
- *Reduced lead time*
- *Increased internal efficiency*
- *Improved competitiveness*
- *Improved marketing*

Disadvantages

- *Computer maintenance*   (1 – 9 employees)

Two of the three <u>disadvantages</u> showed no significant difference between respondent SMEs that were part of a small business strategic alliance and respondent SMEs that were not. This was:

- *Security*
- *Dependence on E-commerce*

This is quite an unexpected finding from the study. An examination of the literature concerned with E-commerce adoption in SMEs would show that the disadvantage most often cited is security. Conventional wisdom would suggest, then, that differences in ratings would occur between members and non-members of a small business strategic alliance. The results show, however, that this was the only disadvantage that did not show any difference in ratings between members and non-members.

A7.6.5 Goal 3

The third goal of the present study was

- To determine whether the membership of small business   strategic alliances alters perceptions of any of the adoption factors (barriers to adoption, criteria for adoption, benefits of adoption or disadvantages of adoption) of E-commerce technologies for specific sectors of the SME population (certain business ages, business sizes, business sectors, market focuses, particular levels of IT skill).

A7.6.5.1 Business age

A number of studies (Keeley & Knapp 1995, Reuber & Fischer 1999, Donckels & Lambrecht 1997) have concluded that the business age of the SME is a business characteristic that is associated with E-commerce adoption in SMEs as well as decisions to become involved in some for of small business strategic alliance. These studies suggest that while 'younger' SMEs are more likely to seek out a small business strategic alliance, these same younger SMEs are often the ones more likely to avoid adopting E-commerce.

11 criteria, 8 barriers, 9 benefits and 3 disadvantages of E-commerce adoption were examined across the 6 business age groupings. Only one business age group, 11-20 years showed any significant differences in the ratings of applicability of criteria between respondents that were members of a small business strategic alliance and respondents that were not. Three criteria, *pressure from competition, reach new customers/markets* and *improvement in competitiveness* showed any significant differences in the ratings of applicability of criteria between respondents that were members of a small business strategic alliance and respondents that were not. In all cases, respondents that were not members of a small business strategic alliance rated these as more applicable to their situation than did member respondents. While the number of respondents that had adopted E-commerce was smaller than expected in the Wollongong study, the data concerned with significant differences in the ratings of criteria (members/non-members) would tend to support the findings of Keeley & Knapp (1995), Reuber & Fischer (1999), Donckels & Lambrecht (1997) that small business strategic alliances are associated with decisions concerning E-commerce for certain age categories. It is interesting to note, however, that much of the government literature, concerned with the development of small business strategic alliances, tends to suggest that these changes in priorities would result in members rating criteria as more important than non-members. This is not the case in the Wollongong study. One possible explanation, suggested from earlier studies (see Dennis 2000, Achrol & Kotler 1999) is that respondents may have gained a measure of these criteria through membership of a small business strategic alliance and thus did not rate it so critical a criteria in E-commerce adoption.

One business age group, 11 – 20 years provided barriers that showed significant differences in the ratings of applicability between respondents that were members of a small business strategic alliance and respondents that were not. Table A7.1 show that data.

An examination of the data in A7.1 shows that one barrier, *cost too high* showed a significant difference in the rating of applicability between respondents that were members of a small business strategic alliance and respondents that were not for the two business age groupings. Non-member respondents rated this barrier as more applicable to their situation compared to member respondents. This supports early findings by Jorde & Teece (1989) who suggest that, among other functions, small business strategic alliances reduce the cost burden on members.

Despite the suggestions of Marchewka & Towell (2000), Datta (1988) and Achrol & Kotler (1999), that membership of a small business strategic alliance can enhance both technical and marketing know how and can reduce the potential for these to be barriers, no significant differences were found in any of the benefits or disadvantages.

A7.6.5.2 Business size

In a study of 591 SMEs, Smith et al (2002) found that business size, in terms of numbers of employees, appeared to significantly affect the involvement and role of small business strategic alliances in decision-making. 11 criteria, 8 barriers, 9 benefits and 3 disadvantages of E-commerce adoption by SMEs were examined across each of the 4 business size groupings.

One business size group (1 – 9 employees) showed significant differences in the applicability of criteria between respondents that were members of a small business strategic alliance and respondents that were not. An examination of Table A7.2 shows that for the 1 – 9 employee group four criteria pressure from competition, *reach new customers/markets, increased sales, improvement to competitiveness* showed a significant difference in the applicability of criteria between respondents that were members of a small business strategic alliance and respondents that were not. In all cases, respondents that were not members of a small business strategic alliance rated these as more applicable to their situation than did member respondents. While the number of respondents that had adopted E-commerce was smaller than expected in the Wollongong study, the data concerned with significant differences in the ratings of criteria (members/non-members) would tend to support the findings of Smith et al (2002) that small business strategic alliances are associated with decisions concerning E-commerce for certain size categories. It is interesting to note, however, that much of the government literature, concerned with the development of small business strategic alliances, tends to suggest that these changes in priorities would result in members rating criteria as more important than non-members. This is not the case in the Wollongong study. Again, one possible explanation, suggested from earlier studies (see Dennis 2000, Achrol & Kotler 1999) is that respondents may have gained a measure of these criteria through membership of a small business strategic alliance and thus did not rate them as important in E-commerce adoption.

Table A7.3 show that three business size group, 10 – 19 employees showed significant differences in the applicability of barriers between respondents that were members of a small business strategic alliance and respondents that were not.

For the sole traders (see Table A7.3) one barrier, *E-commerce doesn't fit the way our customers work* was significantly more applicable to respondents that were members of a small business strategic alliance. A number of authors, Eccles & Crane (1998 cited Dennis 2000) and Achrol & Kotler (1999) suggested that small business strategic alliances reduce the barriers to technology, particularly in E-commerce adoption, to their SME members. The data for sole traders in the Wollongong study does not support these earlier findings.

An examination of Table A7.4 shows that for the 1 – 9 employee group, one barrier, *cost too high* was significantly more applicable to respondents that were not members of a small business strategic alliance. Again, this supports early findings by Jorde & Teece (1989) who suggest that, among other functions, small business strategic alliances reduce the cost burden on members.

Table A7.5 shows that one business size group, 1 – 9 employees provided benefits that showed a significant difference in rating between respondents that were members of a small business strategic alliance and respondents that were not. The data shows that two benefits, *increased sales* and *improvement to competitiveness* rated significantly more applicable to respondents that were not members of a small business strategic alliance than members. A number of authors, Marchewka & Towell (2000), Schindehutte & Morris (2001) and Achrol & Kotler (1999) have

303

suggested that SMEs achieve greater benefits from E-commerce adoption, through membership of a small business strategic alliance. The Wollongong results show the reverse of these earlier studies, with non-membership indicating higher perceived benefits when compared to member respondents.

Again, one possible explanation, suggested from earlier studies (see Dennis 2000, Achrol & Kotler 1999) is that respondents may have gained a measure of these criteria through membership of a small business strategic alliance and thus did not rate it so critical a criteria in E-commerce adoption.

Table A7.6 shows that one business size, 1 – 9 employees showed a significant difference in the rating of applicability of one disadvantage, *computer maintenance*, between respondents that were members of a small business strategic alliance and respondents that were not. An examination of the data in Table A7.6 shows that respondents that were not members of a small business strategic alliance rated this disadvantage as more applicable to their situation than did member respondents. This results supports the findings of Marchewka & Towell (2000) that membership of a small business strategic alliance provides, amongst other things, technical knowledge.

A study by Smith et al (2002) found that business size significantly affects the role of small business strategic alliances in decision-making concerned with E-commerce adoption. The data in Tables A7.1 – A7.6 supports these views. However, the results from the Wollongong study show that the effect of business size is not as would normally be expected. For the business size, 1 – 9 employees, four criteria, 1 barrier, 2 benefits and 1 disadvantage were more applicable to non-member respondents. Thus members of a small business strategic alliance found less benefits than non-members, but also had less barriers to E-commerce adoption than non-members. This must raise the question as to the nature of the effect of business size where membership/non-membership of a small business strategic alliance is concerned.

A7.6.5.3 Business Sector

Two recent studies (Schindehutte & Morris 2001, BarNir & Smith 2002) focusing on the role of small business strategic alliances in SME decision making, found that the sector in which an SME operates, dictated decisions both in the type of small business strategic alliance as well as the role played by that alliance. This, coupled with the findings of Riquelme (2002), that concluded that the service sector was more likely to benefit through adoption of E-commerce, suggested a closer examination of each of the business sectors. 11 criteria, 8 barriers, 9 benefits and 3 disadvantages of E-commerce adoption by SMEs were examined across each of the 4 business sector groupings.

A number of studies (Dennis 2000, Achrol & Kotler 1999) have concluded that membership of a small business strategic alliance reduces financial, technical and marketing barriers to its members more than an SME is able to achieve in isolation. An examination of the data in Table A7.7 shows that for the service sector of the Australian study, this appears to be the case. Table A7.7 shows that one barrier, *E-commerce doesn't fit the way our customers work* was significantly more applicable to respondents that were members of a small business strategic alliance than respondents that were not. A number of authors, Eccles & Crane (1998 cited Dennis 2000) and Achrol & Kotler (1999) suggested that small business strategic alliances reduce the barriers to technology, particularly in E-commerce adoption, to their SME members. The data for the service sector in the Wollongong study does not support these earlier findings.

A7.6.5.4 Market Focus

Studies carried out by Schindehutte & Morris (2001) and BarNir & Smith (2002) concluded that, among other business characteristics, market focus dictates decisions concerning the structure and role of small business strategic alliances. Blackburn & Athayde (2000) also noted that market focus, particularly international market focus, was associated with decisions concerning E-commerce adoption by SMEs. 11 criteria, 8 barriers, 9 benefits and 3 disadvantages of E-commerce adoption by SMEs were examined across each of the 4 market focus groupings to determine whether there were any significant differences in applicability between respondents that were members of a small business strategic alliance and respondents that were not.
Again, only the regional market focus group produced a barrier, *E-commerce doesn't fit the way our customers work* that showed a significant difference between respondents that were members of a small business strategic alliance and respondents that were not. An examination of Table A7.8 shows that respondents that were members of a small business strategic alliance rated this barrier as more applicable to their situation than non-member respondents. Thus while earlier studies (Achrol & Kotler 1999 and Dennis 2000) have concluded that membership of a small business strategic alliance reduces technical, financial and marketing barriers to it members, the data shows that, at least for the Australian study, this is not the case.

A7.6.5.5 Level of IT skill

Studies have shown that the adoption and use of any form of technology is significantly associated with the levels of IT skill in the organization (see Yap et al 1992, Thong et al 1996, MacGregor & Bunker 1996, MacGregor et al 1998). Studies carried out by Dennis (2000) and Marchewka & Towell (2000) have further concluded that many SMEs make use of small business strategic alliances to make up for the shortfall in their own business. 11 criteria, 8 barriers and 9 benefits of E-commerce adoption by SMEs were examined across each of the 5 IT skill level groupings to determine whether there were any significant differences in applicability between respondents that were members of a small business strategic alliance and respondents that were not.
Only one skill category, average skill, provided significant differences in the applicability of criteria, barriers, benefits and disadvantages between respondents that were members of a small business strategic alliance and respondents that were not.
A number of studies (Dennis 2000, Achrol & Kotler 1999) have concluded that membership of a small business strategic alliance reduces financial, technical and marketing barriers to its members more than an SME is able to achieve in isolation. An examination of the data in Table A7.9 shows that for the average levels of IT skill group of the Australian study, this appears to be the case. Table A7.9 shows that one barrier, *E-commerce doesn't fit the way our customers work* was significantly more applicable to respondents that were members of a small business strategic alliance than respondents that were not. A number of authors, Eccles & Crane (1998 cited Dennis 2000) and Achrol & Kotler (1999) suggested that small business strategic alliances

reduce the barriers to technology, particularly in E-commerce adoption, to their SME members. The data for the levels of IT skill, in the Wollongong study, does not support these earlier findings.

The following section contains 4 published articles derived from the interviews carried out in the pilot study. The interviews have not been included because they are extremely lengthy and the articles give a better representation of the findings of those interviews. It should also be noted that interviews were designed and carried out by the author and all articles derived from the interviews were substantially written by the author.

MacGregor R.C., Bunker D.J., Pierson J.K. & Forcht K.A A (1997) Pilot study of Small Business's Perception of Vendor Services: Are These Associated with Small Business IT Educational Requirements Australian Journal of Information Systems vol 5, no. 1, pp 45 - 54

A Pilot Study of Small Business's Perception of Vendor Provided Services: Are These Associated with Small Business's IT Educational Requirements?

R.C. MacGregor
Department of Business Systems
University of Wollongong

D.J. Bunker
Department of Business Systems
University of Wollongong

J.K. Pierson
Department of Information and Decision Sciences
James Madison University

K.A. Forcht
Department of Information and Decision Sciences
James Madison University

Introduction

Since the microcomputer became readily available in the early 1980's, more and more small firms have adopted them into their day-to-day operations. Initially, most small businesses acquired computer technology for the purposes of accounting (Baker 1987, Heikkila, Saarinan & Saaksjarvi 1991). More recently, computer technology has been acquired for a variety of uses (Raymond & Paré 1992, Raymond 1990, Raymond & Bergeron 1992). With increase in sophistication of information systems used in small business, there has been a growing need to provide adequate training for personnel (Cragg & Zinatelli 1995).

Originally training was minimal, usually being provided by the vendor from whom the technology was purchased. Today, however, more and more training is being provided by service organisations and, in some cases, universities and colleges. A number of reasons have been suggested. Raymond et al (1993) suggest that the use of technology by small business tends to affect the structure of the business often resulting in a more complex organisation, with the increase of technology. Chan & Huff (1993) suggest that technology allows the organisation to focus on strategic decisions rather than simply maintaining the operational status quo. With this change of emphasis, there is a requirement to examine training curricula such that these address the needs of the small business client.

When considering curriculum design, Nelson (1991) suggests that a curriculum which merely addresses the technical issues only provides half the requisite knowledge and skills necessary to adequately adopt and maintain information technology in an organisation. This is supported in the literature by the many studies which point to the problem incurred when organisational issues are not adequately considered at the inception of technology (Turner & Karasek 1984, MacGregor & Clarke 1988, Raymond 1988, Sharp & Lewis 1992, Kahn & Robertson 1992, Williams 1992, Bergeron et al 1992, Hedberg & Harper 1992).

A number of studies (Wattenberger & Scaggs 1979, Rislov 1979, Hansen 1985, El-Khawas 1985, Dawkins 1988, Beeson et al 1992) have suggested that in order to include organisational issues into curriculum design, it is necessary to involve employer groups into the development of university/college IT training programs. While many of these studies focus on larger businesses, recent studies (Neergaard 1992, Holzinger & Hotch 1993, MacGregor & Cocks 1994, DelVecchio 1994) have suggested that there is no less a need to involve employer groups at the small business level.

A number of factors have been found to impinge upon both the use of computer technology as well as the training requirements deemed necessary in the small business environment. Some of these factors may be termed 'intrinsic', ie. they are part of the structure and function of the firm. These would include the size of the firm, the level of management involvement, the level of skill of the workforce (Cragg & Zinatelli 1995, MacGregor & Bunker 1995). Other factors such as complexity of the software acquired, changes to structure of the workplace after the implementation of IT, criteria for determination of success are more 'extrinsic' factors which impinge upon use as well as training requirements.

This paper begins by briefly considering the findings of several studies examining the acquisition and subsequent use of computer technology in the medical professions which provides the research background for the study. The nature of small business is briefly considered. The paper then examines small business's IT curricula needs. Finally, it is hypothesised that, in line with the background study findings, the level of satisfaction with pre-installation vendor service will affect those curricular inclusions deemed most important by the small business community, while the level of satisfaction with vendor post-installation services will affect those curricular inclusions less important to the small business community.

Research Background

Several studies were carried out in Australia examining the various branches of the medical profession and their use and training need following the acquisition of computer technology

(MacGregor & Cocks 1994, MacGregor et al 1997). These studies found that amongst other factors associated with use and training requirements of IT was the level of satisfaction with vendor services. The study found that the level of satisfaction / dissatisfaction with those vendor services normally provided prior to purchase and installation was strongly associated with the rating of curricular inclusions deemed important inclusions in training programs. These pre-installation services included delivery of equipment, vendor supplied information concerning the suitability of equipment and software to the business as well as overall equipment suitability.

By comparison, the study found that no such association was evidenced when post-installation services were examined. These post installation services included training, vendor supplied manuals and documentation as well as vendor after sales service. Indeed, the study found that the level of satisfaction / dissatisfaction with vendor post-installation service was only associated with curricular inclusions deemed less important in a training program.

Based on the finding within the medical profession, this study aims to determine whether these associations (satisfaction with vendor services & rating of importance of potential curricular inclusions in an IT training program) are unique to the medical profession or whether they apply to small business in general.

The Nature of Small Business

There have been many studies, both in terms of research initiatives as well as governmental studies on the nature of small business. Many of these studies have opted for the approach which identifies the differences, small to large business and it is this approach which best summarises the nature of small business. Studies by Brigham & Smith (1967), Walker (1975), Delone (1988) found that small businesses are more risky than their larger counterparts. Rotch (1987) found the amount of record keeping is minimal compared to larger businesses. Reynolds et al (1994), in an extensive study, suggest that, among other factors, small businesses tended to be centralised with informal and inadequate planning and control, concentrated more on product than customers and used limited process or product technology.

This is accentuated when computer technology is introduced into the small business environment. Studies (Cragg & King 1993, Holzinger & Hotch 1993, Chen 1993, DelVecchio 1994) showed that small businesses lacked the relevant technical expertise to identify and acquire computer technology, very often relying on vendor/consultant groups to perform these tasks. Indeed, one of the more pertinent studies examining this phenomenon was carried out in Singapore (see Yap et al 1992). Among other findings, the study showed that where larger businesses used a resident IT department, smaller businesses viewed the vendor/consultant as a surrogate of that IT department. The study showed that the level and type of service provided by the vendor very often permeated all facets of continued use with the technology including upgrading decisions, company structuring around the newly acquired technology, level of use of the technology. This has been supported in subsequent studies (Cragg & Zinatelli 1995, MacGregor & Bunker 1995). In all these studies the vendor was a small business consisting of a sales force with some technical support. Most were retailers of technology rather than branches of manufacturers.

Decisions Taken Prior to Data Gathering

The definition of what constitutes a small business varies both across research initiatives as well as governmental guidelines. A number of researchers (Delone 1988, Chen 1993) have avoided these questions by using governmental guidelines and employing mailing lists prepared by these government agencies. The current study has adopted a similar approach by developing a mailing list through the Small Business component of the Illawarra Chamber of Commerce Directory, known as the Illawarra Business Directory. The geographic area covered by this directory includes southern suburbs of Sydney, as well as the cities of Nowra and Wollongong (a population of approximately half a million).

As with the definition of small business, decisions concerning inclusions in IT training programs offered through university/colleges vary widely. Two internationally regarded models have been provided by the ACM and the DPMA groups. Lo (1991) suggested that in order to fully examine all possible curricular inclusions a composite subset of those provided by ACM and DPMA needed to be established. Lo's study arrived at 51 subjects.

The current study began with the set suggested by LO. These were examined in the light of small business needs. A number were discarded, being considered more relevant to computing professionals than small business. These included areas such as Data Communications, Advanced Programming and Algorithm Development, Expert Systems, Human Computer Interaction. Those that remained were further analysed for content to determine whether they could be 'collapsed' into a smaller group. This approach is in line with the views expressed by Seeborg & Ma (1989) that when non-computing groups were considered, the potential offerings should be significantly reduced. As such, Lo's original 51 subjects has been reduced to 15 (see Table 1).

310

Table 1
Curriculum Subject Groups

Subjects	Brief Description
Structure and function of computer hardware	study of the major components of the microcomputer
Programming	problem solving and program development
Database/Spreadsheets	the use of databases and spreadsheets in common business problems
Business Analysis	analysis of the major functions and data in the business
Information Analysis	data modeling techniques
Office Automation	integration of the microcomputer into the office
Business Accounting Systems	design and use of accounting software
Computer Evaluation Techniques	techniques for testing and comparing potential hardware and software purchase options
Accountancy	introductory principles of accounting
Finance	introduction to corporate valuations and financial markets
Marketing	market segments, buyer behaviour etc.
Business Law	partnerships, liabilities, contracts etc.
Statistics	descriptive and inferential statistics
Management Principles	goal determination, implementation etc.
Interpersonal Skills	verbal, written, formal and informal communication

In line with the studies carried out by MacGregor & Cocks (1994) two hypotheses were tested. For clarity these will be phrased in the affirmative, rather than the null.

H_1 The level of satisfaction with vendor pre-installation service (delivery of   equipment, vendor supplied information, equipment suitability) is positively associated with the perception of importance of those curricular inclusions deemed important. In other words, high levels of satisfaction with vendor services will be accompanied by a higher rating of those curricular inclusions   deemed most important.

H_2 The level of satisfaction with vendor post-installation service (Manuals,   training, after sales   service) is positively associated with the perception of importance of those curricular inclusions deemed less important. In other   words, high level of satisfaction with vendor post-installation service will not be accompanied with a higher rating of those curricular inclusions deemed most important but will be accompanied with a higher rating of those curricular inclusions deemed less important.

It should be noted that the determination of which curricular inclusions are most important and which are less important are based on the responses to the questionnaire. In line with previous studies (Seeborg & Ma 1989, Lo 1991, Ang & Lo 1991, Ang 1992), only the top six rated curricular inclusions will be considered most important. All others will be considered less important.

Method

As already noted, a mailing list was developed from a government supplied list known as the Illawarra Business Directory. The definition used within this document for small business was that the company had 50 or less employees and was not a subsidiary of any other firm. As the study was examining the association between vendor supplied services and the rating of curricular inclusions in an IT training program, vendor companies fitting the profile of small business were removed from the mailing list.

A questionnaire was developed to be sent to small business managers. Respondents were asked to rate the curricular inclusion areas (see Table 1) in terms of their importance (1 not very important - 5 very important) as an inclusion in a college/university provided IT training program directed towards small business. Additionally respondents were asked to rate their perception of vendor services (1 very poor - 5 very good) in the following:
- delivery and installation of computer equipment
- availability of information concerning computer technology
- satisfaction with equipment and software
- after sales service
- computer systems training
- computer systems documentation

Analysis of Results

A total of 600 questionnaires were distributed. Responses were obtained from 131 business representing a 21.8% response. Of interest, this is substantially higher than the 10% and 7% responses achieved by MacGregor & Cocks in their examination of the medical profession.

58% of respondents indicated that they had previously undertaken some form of college/university training in their particular field. Less than 20% had undertaken any college/university based IT training.

Of particular interest was the fact that all respondents indicated the regular use of IT in their day-to-day business, with only 7% of respondents indicating they had been using computer technology for less than a year.

Prior to examining the hypotheses, it was necessary to gain an overall opinion as to the general interest in college/university based IT program directed to small business. As such, the following approach was adopted. If any one of the 15 curricular inclusion areas (see Table 1) was rated 5 (very important) by a respondent, the respondent was categorised as seeing the development of a college/university IT training program for small business as very important. If no curricular inclusions was rated at 5 but at least one was rated at 4 (important), the respondent was categorised as seeing some importance to the development of such a program. All other respondents were categorised as seeing no importance in such a program. Table 2 provides the responses.

Table 2
The importance of developing a college/university based IT training program for small business

Very Important	(at least one curricular inclusion rated 5)	109
Important	(at least one curricular inclusion rated 4)	12
Not Important		10

The results in Table 2 suggest that there is a perception by the small business managers who responded to the survey of the importance of a university/college based IT training program specifically directed to small business. 83% of the respondents considered the development of a training program to be important, with a further 9% giving some support to such a development. Of interest is the fact that while only 58% of the respondents indicated some form of university/college education, the results are almost identical to those carried out on the medical profession (MacGregor & Cocks 1994). In those studies, 84.5% of respondents indicated their support for a university/college based IT training course directed towards their specific needs, with a further 10.4% seeing some importance to the development.

Respondents were asked to rate vendor performance (on a scale 1 - very poor to 5 - very good) across six categories. These were:
- delivery and installation of computer equipment
- availability of information concerning computer technology
- satisfaction with equipment and software
- after sales service
- computer systems training

- computer systems documentation

Table 3 indicates the overall responses.

Table 3
Overall Rating of Vendor Provided Services by Small Business managers

Service	Rating				
	1	2	3	4	5
	Very Poor				Very Good
delivery and installation of computer equipment	9	16	31	50	25
availability of information concerning computer technology	6	25	44	32	24
satisfaction with equipment and software	7	11	34	51	28
after sales service	13	22	49	28	19
computer systems training	28	26	51	17	9
computer systems documentation	26	24	42	24	15

A study carried out by MacGregor & Cocks (1994) on the computer usage of the Australian Veterinary profession showed that by far the greatest dissatisfaction with vendor services appeared to be in the areas of vendor documentation and manuals, vendor after sales problem rectification and vendor training. An examination of table 4 would suggest that this trend is not isolated to the area of veterinary software but appears to affect all areas of small business. While 63% of small business respondents rated the equipment as above average, only 19.6% rated the training in the same manner. An examination of the figures pertaining to manuals and documentation, as well as after sales problem rectification, show that vendor after sales service is, for the most part not rated highly. Only 28% of the respondents considered the manuals and documentation above average, while 37% rated problem rectification by the vendor as above average. Indeed, it would seem that in all areas of after sales service (changes to system, training, documentation and problem rectification) vendor support and services was significantly less than those areas which might be designated 'pre-sales support'.

Respondents were asked to rate the 15 curricular inclusions in terms of their importance for a university/college IT training course for small business. Table 4 shows the means and ranking of responses.

314

Table 4
Relative Importance of each of the curricular inclusions

Topic	mean	rank
Struct/funct of hardware	3.16	10.5
Programming	3.09	13
Database/S'sheet	4.18	2
Business Analysis	4.04	4
Info. Analysis	4.08	3
Office Autom.	3.75	6
Bus/Acc't Systs	4.28	1
Eval. Techniques	3.39	8
Accounting	4.01	5
Finance	3.65	7
Marketing	3.10	12
Business Law	2.66	15
Statistics	2.99	14
Mgt Principles	3.16	10.5
Interpersonal Skills	3.19	9

The results in Table 4 show that the most preferred inclusions (deemed to be the top six) in a university/college IT training program for small business are: Business and Accounting Systems, Database and Spreadsheets, Information Analysis, Business Analysis, Accounting, and Office Automation. It is interesting to note that a previous study of the medical profession (MacGregor & Cocks 1994) showed that five of the six were also considered very important. Indeed, the only difference between the two respondent groups was that the medical profession indicated a need for Marketing in preference to Office Automation.

The results in Table 4 highlight several other important issues. Firstly, there appears to be a perception by small business respondents of the need to fully understand the nature of their business and the data that business utilises. This is borne out in the high ratings of Business Analysis and Information Analysis. Secondly, there is a perception that knowledge of hardware and software is of less importance to the business than the understanding of the proper use of the software. Finally, there appears a perception that in order to use database, spreadsheets and accounting software correctly, there is a need to complete some study in the area of Accounting.

A series of chi-square tests were applied to the data to determine whether the ratings of the curricular inclusions were associated with the ratings of the six vendor services. Table 5 indicates those curricular inclusions whose rating was associated with the rating of vendor services. To simplify the data, those respondents who rated vendor services as 1 or 2 (very poor, poor) were considered dissatisfied. All others were considered satisfied.

Table 5
The Rating of Potential Curricular Inclusions in a College/University IT Training Course for Small Business which were Associated with the Ratings of Vendor Services

Vendor Service	Subject Service	Rating of Service	Rating of Importance of Curricular Inclusions				
			1 not impt.	2	3	4	5 very impt.
Delivery of Equipment	Database/ Spreadsheet significant (p<0.05)	Satisfied Dissatisfied	0 2	3 2	7 1	26 6	70 14
	Information Analysis significant (p<0.05)	Satisfied Dissatisfied	0 2	3 1	20 5	28 9	55 8
	Business Acct Systems significant (p<0.005)	Satisfied Dissatisfied	0 3	1 1	8 3	38 7	59 11
Vendor Provided Info.	Business Acct. Systems significant (p<0.05)	Satisfied Dissatisfied	2 1	0 2	11 1	29 13	58 14
	Management Principles significant (p<0.05)	Satisfied Dissatisfied	7 0	5 7	32 6	38 13	18 5
Equipment	Database/ Spreadsheet significant (p<0.005)	Satisfied Dissatisfied	0 2	6 0	8 0	28 4	71 12
	Information Analysis significant (p<0.05)	Satisfied Dissatisfied	1 2	5 0	24 1	29 8	53 7
After Sales Service	Statistics significant (p<0.05)	Satisfied Dissatisfied	6 6	14 7	26 15	33 4	17 3
Training	Marketing significant (p<0.05)	Satisfied Dissatisfied	11 3	7 6	25 19	27 10	7 16
Manuals	Statistics significant (p<0.05)	Satisfied Dissatisfied	6 6	16 6	21 21	29 7	9 10

Table 5 provides a number of results. Firstly, satisfaction in terms of vendor delivery of equipment appears to be associated with the rating of several curricular inclusions - Database and

316

Spreadsheets, Information Analysis, Business Accounting Systems. In all cases, dissatisfaction with vendor provided services is associated with a lower rating of these curricular inclusions in terms of their importance.

Satisfaction with vendor provided information was examined to determine if it was associated with the rating of any of the 15 curricular inclusions. Table 5 shows that the rating of two curricular inclusions - Business Accounting Systems, Management Principles were associated with the level of satisfaction of the respondents. Those who were satisfied with vendor provided information rated the curricular inclusion Business Accounting Systems higher than those who expressed dissatisfaction. This was reversed for the curricular inclusion Management Principles, with those who were dissatisfied rating it higher than those who expressed satisfaction.

The results in Table 5 show that the level of satisfaction with the equipment is associated with two curricular inclusions - DataBase and Spreadsheets, Information Analysis. In both cases those who were satisfied rated the curricular inclusions higher than those who were dissatisfied.

Satisfaction with after sales service is associated with the rating of one curricular inclusion - Statistics. Those who were satisfied with the after sales service rated this inclusion higher than those who were not.

The results in Table 5 show that the level of satisfaction with vendor provided training is associated with the curricular inclusion Marketing. Unlike the rating of after sales service, those who rated the training as satisfactory tended to rate the inclusion Marketing lower than those who were dissatisfied.

Finally Satisfaction in terms of vendor provided manuals was compared to the 15 curricular inclusions. The results in Table 5 show that satisfaction with vendor provided manuals is associated with the rating of the inclusion Statistics. While those who were dissatisfied with the vendor provided service could see some merit in the inclusion, those who were satisfied, at best, tended to be equivocal concerning its importance.

Discussion

Before discussing the issues raised by the data and examining the hypotheses posited, the limitations of the study need to be emphasised. The first obvious limitation of this pilot study is the geographic spread of the respondent small businesses. All respondents were located in one urban region of Australia. All businesses are within easy commuting distance of a large university campus and a high percentage of managers have had some university experience. The second limitation of this study centres around the concepts of satisfaction and perception of importance. The literature suggests that very often these concepts are viewed comparatively rather than singly. For example, it may be argued that dissatisfaction with vendor provided training may be a measure of it being less effective than vendor supplied after sales service. Thus while training may have, of itself, been successful, it was judged comparatively with other measures. Finally, the comparison of curricular inclusions, rated across a five point scale and satisfaction rated across a two point scale does not necessarily provide a linear basis for discussion. The reduction, however, of satisfaction to a two point scale was deliberate such that comparative issues were reduced.

Despite the limitations, a number of insights are provided by the data. Firstly, there appears to be an overwhelming desire by the respondents for some form of university/college IT training program specifically directed towards small business. The study confirmed earlier findings by Cragg & Zinatelli (1995) and Chen (1993), that computer technology in the small business arena is still primarily aimed at accounting type functions. This is further borne out in the data with accounting centred curricular inclusions being rated higher than other less accounting centred ones. Indeed, the data suggests that technical inclusions - Structure and Function of Hardware and Software, Programming are of little interest to the small business manager.

Of particular interest is the rating by respondents of vendor supplied services. It would seem that vendor companies are primarily sales directed and provide far better pre-sales service than their after sales. In particular, vendor provided training and manuals appear to be inadequate to the need of the small business.

Two hypotheses were posited. The first suggested that satisfaction with vendor provided pre-sales service would be associated with a higher rating of those curricular inclusions deemed important. The results showed that three of the top inclusions - Database and Spreadsheets, Information Analysis, Business Accounting Systems were rated higher by those who expressed satisfaction as compared to those who expressed dissatisfaction. Interestingly, one inclusion not within the top six, Management Principles, was also associated with the level of satisfaction of vendor provided pre-sales service and actually showed a reversal of rating association, with those who were dissatisfied rating it higher than those who expressed satisfaction. As such, the first hypothesis is rejected.

A number of reasons for the associations are possible. It may be argued that those who rate inclusions such as Database and Spreadsheets, Information Analysis, Business Accounting Systems were better planned in their acquisition of IT. In such cases more attention was paid to vendor provided information, delivery schedules and actual equipment. Conversely it may be argued that satisfaction with the vendor has allowed the small business more scope to investigate training and training requirements than a less satisfied customer.

The second hypothesis suggested that higher levels of satisfaction with vendor provided post-sales service would be associated with higher ratings of those inclusions deemed less important. Unlike the studies carried out by MacGregor & Cocks (1994), this study does not support the hypothesis. While it is true to say that post-sales satisfaction is only associated with the rating of less important inclusions, the nature of the association varies both with the particular vendor service as well as the inclusion.

Conclusion

This pilot study of 131 small businesses in Australia has examined both the perception of vendor services as well as the perception of training needs. The results suggest that there is an overwhelming need for the development of a university/college IT trainig program directed specifically towards small business. These programs should avoid the more technical aspects of IT and concentrate on areas which invlove the analysis and use of software in the small business.

The results further show that there is a perception by small business that vendor post-sales service, particularly in the areas of training and manuals are not adequate.

Finally the study has shown that a number of vendor provided service appear to be associated with the rating of importance of potential curricular inclusions in IT training programs.

Although the results have important implications, additional research is required in a number of areas. Firstly, the reasons why certain measures of satisfaction only appear to be associated with certain curricular inclusions. In order to pursue this, these factors need to be refined and followed up by extensive interviewing. Perhaps more importantly, a more intensive examination needs to be carried out to examine how small businesses communicate with vendors, such that the effect of various measures of satisfaction may be better explained.

References

Ang A.Y. (1992) Information Systems Curricula: A Southeast Asian Perspective **Journal of Computer Information Systems** pp. 7 - 15

Ang A.Y. & Lo B.W.N. (1991) Changing emphasis in information systems curriculum: An Australian Industrial **Perception Proceedings of the Second Conference on Information   Systems and Database Special Interest Group** pp. 339 - 355

Baker W.H. (1987) Status of Information Management in Small Businesses **Journal of Systems Management** vol 38, No. 4, pp 10 - 15

Beeson G.W., Stokes D.M. & Symmonds H.C. (1992) An Innovative Higher Education   Course to Meet Industry's Needs **Journal of Higher Education Research and Development** vol 11,   no. 1, pp 21 - 38

Bergeron F., Raymond L. & Rivard S. (1992) Organisational Benefits of Electronic Data   Interchange   **Proceedings of the Third Australian Conference on Information Systems** Wollongong,   Australia pp 563 - 578

Brigham E.F. & Smith K.V. (1967) The cost of capital to the small **firm The Engineering Economist** vol. 13, no. 1, pp. 1 - 26

Chan Y.E. & Huff S.L. (1993) Investigating Information Systems Strategic Alignment **Proceeding of   the 14th Annual Conference on Information Systems** Orlando, Fl, pp 345 - 363

Chen J.C. (1993) The impact of microcomputers on small businesses: England 10 years later **Journal   of Small Business Management** vol. 31, no. 3, pp. 96 - 102

Cragg P.B. & Zinatelli N. (1995) The Evolution of Information Systems in Small Firms **Information &   Management** vol 29, pp 1- 8

Cragg P.B. & King M. (1993) Small Firm Computing: Motivators and Inhibitors **MIS Quarterly** vol.   17, no. 1, pp. 47 - 60

Dawkins J.S. (1988) **Higher Education: A Policy Statement** Canberra, Australian Government Printing   Office

Delone W.H. (1988) Determinants for Success for Computer Usage in Small Business **MIS Quarterly**   pp. 51 - 61

DelVecchio M. (1994) Retooling the Staff along with the system **Bests Review** vol. 94, no. 11, pp. 82   - 83

El-Khawas E. (1985) Campuses Weld the Corporate Link **Educational Record** Spring pp 37 - 39

Hansen L.A. (1985) A More or Less Happy Relationship: Industry University Co-Operation in Denmark **European Journal of Education** 10, pp 197 - 208

Hedberg J & Harper B. (1992) Information Systems Strategy in the Small Education
Organisation **Proceedings of the Third Australian Conference on Information
Systems** Wollongong, Australia

Heikkila J., Saarinen T. & Saaksjarvi M. (1991) Success of Software Packages in Small
Business: An Exploratory Study **European Journal of Information Systems** Vol 1,
No. 3, pp 159 - 169

Holzinger A.G. & Hotch R. (1993) Small Firms Usage Patterns **Nations Business** vol. 81, no. 8,
pp. 39 - 42

Kahn H. & Robertson I.T. (1992) Training and Experience as Predictors of Job Satisfaction
and Work Motivation When Using Computers **Journal of Behaviour and Information
Technology** vol. 11, pp 53 - 60

Lo B.W.N. (1991) Australian Information Systems Curricula **The Journal of Computer
Information Systems** vol. 31, pp. 20 - 33

MacGregor R.C. & Clarke R.J. (1988) The Loss of the 'Informal' in Systems Design in Bullinger
H.J., Protonotarios E.N., Bouwhuis D. & Relm F. (eds.) **Proceedings of Eurinfo '88**
Athens, Greece

MacGregor R.C. & Cocks R.S. (1994) Computer Usage and Satisfaction in the Australian
Veterinary Industry **Australian Veterinary Practitioner** vol 25 no 1 pp 43 - 48

MacGregor R.C. & Bunker D.J. (1997) The Effect of Criteria Used in the Acquisition of
Computer Technology on the Ongoing Success with Information Technology in Small
Business, forthcoming

MacGregor R.C., Bunker D.J., Cocks R.S., Pierson J.K. & Forcht K.A. (1997) A Comparison of
Two Studies Examining Computer Education Requirements in Small Business,
forthcoming

Meredith G.G. (1994) **Small Business Management in Australia** McGraw Hill, 4th Edition

Neergaard P. (1992) Microcomputers in Small and Medium Sized Companies: Benefits
Achieved and Problems Encountered **Proceedings of the Third Australian Conference
on Information Systems** Wollongong, Australia

Nelson R.R. (1991) Education Needs as Perceived by IS and End-User Personnel: A Survey of
Knowledge and Skill Requirements **MIS Quarterly** December pp 503 - 521

Raymond L. (1988) The Impact of Computer Training on Attitudes and Usage Behaviour of
Small Business Managers **Journal of Small Business Management** vol. 26, pp. 8 - 13

Raymond L. (1990) End User Computing in the Small Business Context: Foundations and
Directions for Research **Data Base** vol 20, no. 3, pp 20 - 28

Raymond L. & Paré G. (1992) Measurement of Information Technology Sophistication in Small
Manufacturing Businesses **Information Resource Management Journal** vol 5, no. 2, pp
1- 13

Raymond L. & Bergeron F. (1992) Personal DSS Success in Small Enterprises **Information &
Management** vol 22, no. 5, pp 301 - 308

Raymond L., Paré G. & Bergeron F. (1993) Information Technology and Organisational
Structure Revisited: Implications for Performance **Proceeding of the 14th Annual
Conference on Information Systems** Orlando, Fl, pp 129 - 143

Reynolds W., Savage W. & Williams A. (1994) **Your Own Business: A Practical Guide to
Success** ITP

320

Rislov S. (1979) Speaking with Employers in Cohen A.M. (ed.) **Shaping the Curriculum** Josey Bass, San Francisco, pp 51 - 54

Rotch W. (1967) **Management of Small Enterprises: Cases and Readings** University of Virginia   Press

Seeborg I.S. & Ma C. (1989) MIS Program Meets Reality: A Survey of Alumni from an Undergraduate Program **Interface** vol. 10, pp. 51 - 60

Sharp C. & Lewis N. (1992) Corporate Memory and Management Information Systems **Proceedings**   of the Third Australian Conference on Information Systems Wollongong, pp 149 - 160

Turner J.A. & Karasek R.A. jr (1984) Software Ergonomics: Effects of Computer Application Design   Parameters on Operator Task Performance and Health **Ergonomics** vol. 27, no. 6, pp 663 -   690

Walker E.W. (1975) Investment and Capital Structure Decision Making in Small Business in Walker   E.W. (ed.) **The Dynamic Small Firm: Selected Readings** Austin Press, Texas

Wattenberger J.I & Scaggs (1979) Curriculum Revision and the Process of Change in Cohen A.M.   (ed.)   **Shaping the Curriculum** Josey Bass, San Francisco, pp 1 - 10

Williams T.A. (1992) Information Technology and Interorganisation **Change Proceedings of the**   **Third Australian Conference on Information Systems** Wollongong, Australia pp 295 -   308

Yap C.S., Soh C.P.P. & Raman K.S. (1992) Information Systems Success Factors in Small Business   **International Journal of Management Science** 20, pp. 597 - 609

MacGregor R.C., Waugh P. & Bunker D.J. (1996) ELECTRONIC DATA INTERCHANGE
AND SMALL BUSINESS: ARE THE VIEWS PUSHED BY THE EDI ADVOCATES THE
SAME AS THOSE USED WHEN SMALL BUSINESS IS CONSIDERING ADOPTING
COMPUTER TECHNOLOGY 14th International Conference for the Association of
Management pp 53 - 58

ELECTRONIC DATA INTERCHANGE AND SMALL BUSINESS: ARE THE VIEWS PUSHED BY THE EDI ADVOCATES THE SAME AS THOSE USED WHEN SMALL BUSINESS IS CONSIDERING ADOPTING COMPUTER TECHNOLOGY

R.C. MacGregor
P. Waugh
D.Bunker
Department of Business Systems
University of Wollongong
Northfields Avenue
Wollongong 2522
Australia
Email Correspondence p.waugh@uow.edu.au

ABSTRACT

A study carried out by the EDI World Institute in Canada suggested that a variety of benefits
could be realised by small-medium sized enterprises if they were to adopt electronic commerce
techniques. Several survey-based studies have been carried out on the small business community
in Australia. The data gathered from these studies suggests that many of the premises upon
which Electronic Commerce is both designed and disseminated to small businesses are based on
incorrect assumptions. This paper examines the reasons behind, and approaches used by small
businesses in their adoption of information technology. It will be argued that for EDI to be viable
in the small business environment, there needs to be a far greater understanding of this
environment and the mechanisms by which it adopts and utilises computer technologies and
techniques.

INTRODUCTION

Like so many technologies used in the world of small business, Electronic Data Interchange
(EDI) has both its advocates as well as its critics. Advocates (Zack 1994, Pletsch 1994, Huttig
1994, Evans-Correia 1994, Udo & Pickett 1994, Britt 1995) suggest, among other advantages,
the ability for EDI to:

- elimination of re-keying of errors
- faster trading cycles
- better customer response
- reduced inventory levels

- reduced information and storage
- more efficient use of information

More recently there has been a 'push' to expand the role of EDI in the area of small business. Pletsch (1994) suggests that the movement of small businesses to EDI is becoming a business necessity. This view is supported by Huttig (1994) who suggests the use of pooled microcomputers in an EDI environment increases the purchasing power of those organisations within the pool.

Hinge (1989) suggests that EDI allows both intra and interorganisational functions to be carried out more effectively and efficiently. Rockart & Short (1989) suggest that the use of EDI allows the organisation to respond more quickly to global competition, risk, service and costs, while Kavan & Van Over (1990) suggest that EDI allows better cash management throughout the organisation.

In most instances, these authors tend to point to specific organisations who have adopted EDI and have shown specific improvement. Fallon (1988), for example, utilised General Motors as the example where design and manufacturing time were significantly reduced, while Sehr (1989) has identified the Levi Strauss company as one which has benefited through the analysis of market trends using EDI techniques.

In a recent study examining the use of EDI in small business, The EDI World Institute (1995) suggested that the benefits of EDI to small business would include:

- improving the bottom line
- working faster and better within the organisation
- strengthening customer relations
- preparing for the future in business

This paper begins by briefly examining the nature of small business, in particular the use of IT by such organisations. Using the data gathered from a recent survey of small business's uptake and use of IT in Australia, it will be hypothesised that the benefits suggested by the EDI world institute are not viewed as paramount when IT uptake is considered in the small business environment. Finally the paper will present data from a pilot study of EDI in small business in Australia. While the data cannot at this stage be considered representative of the entire small business community, it does appear to further invalidate some of the claims made by the EDI World Institute, as far as EDI use in small business is concerned.

THE NATURE OF SMALL BUSINESS

The nature of small business has been the topic of both governmental committee findings as well as research initiatives. Brigham & Smith (1967) found that small businesses tended to be more risky than their larger counterparts. This view is supported by later studies (Walker 1975, Delone 1988). Cochran (1981) found that small businesses tended to be subject to higher failure rates while Rotch (1987) suggested that small businesses tended not to maintain adequate records of transactions. Perhaps most important in any discussion concerning small business is the view given by Barnett & Mackness (1983), that small businesses are not miniature versions of larger businesses, but quite unique in their own right.

Perhaps the most detailed definition of a small business was provided by Reynolds et al (1994). They suggested that the following characteristics make up the organisational environment in which a small business operates:

- small management team
- strong owner influence
- centralised power and control
- lack of specialist staff
- multi-functional management
- a close and loyal work team
- informal and inadequate planning and control systems
- lack of promotable staff
- lack of control over business environment
- limited ability to obtain finance
- labor intensive work
- limited process and product technology
- narrow product/service range
- limited market share
- heavy reliance on few customers
- decisions - intuitive instead of rational
- leadership - personal but not task oriented
- education experience and skill - practical but narrow
- low employee turnover
- product dedication rather than customer orientation
- reluctance to take risks
- management swayed by personal idiosyncrasies
- strong desire to be independent
- intrusion of family interests

When the introduction of IT into small business is considered, there are marked differences between small businesses and their larger counterparts (Barnett & Mackness 1983). Khan & Khan (1992) suggest that most small businesses avoid sophisticated software or applications. This view is supported by studies carried out in the United Kingdom by Chen (1993). Cragg & King (1993) suggest that small businesses often lack the necessary expertise to fully utilise IT. This view is supported by the findings of Holzinger & Hotch (1993) and Delvecchio (1994). Indeed, Yap et al (1992) have shown that many small businesses use consultant or vendor expertise in the identification of hardware and software as their first critical step towards computerisation. They conclude that ongoing success with IT is positively associated with vendor support, vendor training, vendor after sales service and vendor expertise. This is supported in recent studies (MacGregor & Cocks 1994, Wood & Nosek 1994, MacGregor & Bunker 1995).

Added to the views and findings concerning small business, are the variety of definitions of what actually constitutes a small business. Some definitions tend to be based purely on a quantitative perspective, either amount of staff, or amount of turnover, while others attempt to utilise a qualitative definition, similar to those provided by Reynolds et al (1994). Meredith (1994) suggests that any definition of a small business must include a qualitative as well as a quantitative component. The quantitative component should examine staff, turnover, assets as well as any other financial measure, while the qualitative component should reflect mode of operation as well as organisational procedures.

Not only are there a myriad of views concerning the nature of small business, but from a governmental standpoint, there are a variety of definitions of small business. In the United Kingdom a small business is defined as:

'having fewer than 50 employees and was not a subsidiary to any other company'

In the United States:

'a small business concern shall be deemed to be one which is independently owned and operated and which is not dominant in its field of operation' (United States Small Business Administration - based on section 3 of the Small Business Act 1953)

While in Australia, a small business is defined as:

'small business is one in which one or two persons are required to make all the critical decisions (such as finance, accounting personnel, inventory, production, servicing, marketing and selling decisions) without the aid of internal (employed) specialists and with the owners having knowledge in one or two functional areas of management' (Meredith 1994, p 31)

As indicated, a study has been carried out primarily to examine the nature of the adoption of information technology by small business. While it is not the province of this paper to examine that question, it is relevant to examine some of the findings which impact upon the level of adoption of EDI in Australian small businesses.

HYPOTHESES TESTED

A number of hypotheses are tested. To avoid ambiguity, these will be phrased in the affirmative rather than the null.

H_1 Small Businesses do not acquire computer technology with the primary intention of improving the bottom line.

H_2 Small Businesses are more likely to decide to acquire computer technology such that work can be carried out faster and better in the organisation.

H_3 Small Business is not likely to acquire computer technology with the primary intention of improving customer relations

325

H₄ Small Business is not likely to acquire computer technology with the prime objective to enhance the business in the future.

SURVEY INSTRUMENT

General Acquisition and Use of IT in small Business

A questionnaire was developed. The questionnaire sought information concerning number of employees, suitability of the computer technology being used, the rationale for computerisation, the practices adopted by the business with the acquisition of the computer as well as the education level and requirements of the organisation.

A mailing list was developed by the Illawarra Chamber of Commerce. The geographic area covered included the southern suburbs of Sydney, the cities of Wollongong and Nowra (Population approx. 500,000). The sampling frame developed was companies with a work force less than 50, where the company was not a subsidiary of a larger company.

Respondents were asked the amount of time (in hours per week) were devoted by the organisation to develop new projects for the computer. Respondents were also asked the importance (not important/ of some importance/ very important) as well as their own business's ability (poor/ passable/ good) placed on:

- using technology to meet business requirements
- implementing new hardware and software
- knowing what information was needed to run the business
- designing new systems
- Evaluating the benefits of computer technology
- implementing new systems for specific applications

Finally respondents were asked which of the following criteria was the major reason for the acquisition of computer technology:

- improving the bottom line
- working faster and better within the organisation
- strengthening customer relations
- preparing for the future in business

Use of EDI in Small Business

As already stated, this questionnaire was a pilot which sought information concerning the number of years IT as well as EDI had been used in the small business. Respondents were asked to indicate the percentage of companies with which their own business communicated using EDI as well as the percentage of revenue attributable to EDI technology use. The questionnaire asked whether EDI was freely chosen or forced and whether, given the choice again, EDI would be adopted. Finally the questionnaire sought information as to whether any of the following problems had occurred in the use of EDI:

326

- Number of transaction too low to warrant EDI
- Tasks often needed to be duplicated since the installation of EDI technology
- There were few willing partners to warrant the use of EDI
- The cost of EDI outweighed the benefits
- There were problems attributable to standards incurred when EDI was being used

As the distribution was a pilot study to evaluate the survey instrument, the mailing list was restricted to those small businesses who utilised EDI when trading with Australia's largest company BHP.

ANALYSIS OF RESULTS

General Acquisition and Use of IT in small Business

A total of 600 questionnaires were distributed. Responses were obtained from 131 businesses, representing a response rate of 21.8%. All respondents indicated that they were using IT in their day-to-day work.
Table 1 indicates the number of hours spent on developing new projects.

Table 1
Number of Hours Spent by Small business on New Projects Using the Computer

Number of Hours	Number of Respondents	Percentage
0 - 1	67	51.1
1 - 2	19	14.5
2 - 5	27	20.6
> 5	18	13.7

As can be seen from Table 1, most small businesses do not spend many hours developing new applications. Indeed, over 65% of respondents indicated that less than two person-hours per week are spent on this task.
Table 2 indicates small business rating of the importance of: using technology to meet business requirements, implementing new hardware and software, knowing what information was needed to run the business, designing new systems, evaluating the benefits of computer technology, implementing new systems for specific applications.

327

Table 2
Small Business Rating in Importance of Various Day-to-day Activities Connected with Computer Technology

Activity	Not Important	Some Importance	Very Important
using technology to meet business requirements	12	63	36
implementing new hardware and software	15	75	20
knowing what information was needed to run the business	9	65	41
designing new systems	20	62	27
Evaluating the benefits of computer technology	13	71	27
implementing new systems for specific applications	18	68	21

An examination of table 2 suggests that while there is some expression of importance for the factors: using technology to meet business requirements, implementing new hardware and software, knowing what information was needed to run the business, designing new systems, evaluating the benefits of computer technology, implementing new systems for specific applications, with the exception of the factors 'using technology to meet business requirements' and 'knowing what information was needed to run the business', most small business respondents are, at best, equivocal concerning future enhancement to their current computer usage. Indeed, if the factors 'implementing new hardware and software' and 'implementing new systems for specific applications' are considered, less than 16% of respondents considered them of great importance to the on-going success of the small business.

Respondents were asked which was the major criteria used in the acquisition of IT. Table 3 indicates the findings.

Table 3
Major Criteria Considered with Acquisition of IT in the Small Business

Criteria	Percentage
Improvement of the Company's Bottom Line	14.5%
Working faster and better within the organisation	54%
Strengthening customer relations	16.7%
Preparing for the future in business	9%
Not Sure	3.8%

The results in Table 3 would tend to support the view of Reynolds et al (1994) and MacGregor & Bunker (1995) which suggest that for the most part small businesses are not customer oriented, nor are they interested in gaining larger market shares, but rather they are intent on improving efficiency and effectiveness of their day-to-day procedures.

The Use of EDI in Small Business

A total of 60 questionnaires were distributed. Responses were obtained from 16 (26.7%) small businesses. As already indicated, the purpose of the distribution was to test the survey instrument and thus figures presented cannot be considered typical of the small business community as a whole. Th results, however, do suggest that the use of EDI by small business does not entirely match the claims made by the EDI World Institute.

Respondents were asked the number of years they had been using IT and EDI techniques within their company. Table 4 indicates the findings.

Table 4
Number of years IT and EDI techniques have been operational within the small business

	< 2 years	2 - 5 years	> 5 years
Use of IT in business	0	2	14
Use of EDI in business	0	3	13

An examination of Table 4 indicates that the respondents have had sufficient experience with both IT and EDI to make value judgements on both.

Respondents were asked the percentage of companies they dealt with using EDI as well as the percentage of revenue attributable to EDI. Table 5 indicates the findings.

Table 5
The Percentage of the Number of Companies dealt with using EDI as well as the Percentage of Revenue Attributable to using EDI

	<1%	1 - 5%	5 - 10%	10 - 15%	>15%
Number of Companies	4	5	4	3	0
Revenue	0	1	0	0	15

An examination of Table 5 shows that while 15 of the 16 respondents indicated that an important percentage of their revenue comes from the use of EDI, this revenue does not constitute a major proportion of their business in terms of the number of companies with which they deal.

Respondents were asked if they chose to use EDI or it was forced on them. 75% of respondents indicated that EDI was forced by trading partners. Respondents were also asked if, given free choice again whether they would choose to use EDI techniques. 56% indicated that they would not use EDI again if they had the choice.

Finally respondents were asked whether any of the following difficulties had to be regularly dealt with since the inception of EDI:

- Number of transaction too low to warrant EDI

- Tasks often needed to be duplicated since the installation of EDI technology
- There were few willing partners to warrant the use of EDI
- The cost of EDI outweighed the benefits
- There were problems attributable to standards incurred when EDI was being used

Table 6 indicates the findings.

Table 6
Difficulties Encountered with the use of EDI

Difficulty	Percentage of Respondents Reporting the Difficulty
Number of transactions too low to warrant use of EDI	62.5%
Tasks need to be Duplicated	43.7%
Few willing partners	62.5%
Cost of EDI outweighs the benefit	37.5%
Problems with the imposed standards of EDI	31.2%

While over 60% of respondents indicated that they had few willing partners and thus the number of transactions utilising EDI was too low to fully justify the technology, perhaps more alarming are the finding which indicate that over 43% of the respondents indicated that work utilising EDI technology needed to be re-done to fit their normal day-to-day operations. It would seem that rather than EDI being an assistance to small business by reducing the workload, as suggested by the EDI World Institute, it actually duplicates effort whenever exchanges are carried out using EDI techniques.

DISCUSSION

Hypothesis 1 (H_1) posited that small business do not acquire computer technology with the primary intention of improving the bottom line. An examination of Table 3 would tend to support this hypothesis. Only 14.5% of respondents indicated that computer technology had been acquired with the view of improving the bottom line of the company. This result tends to support the views of Reynolds et al (1994) and recent studies carried out on the Australian Veterinary profession (MacGregor & Cocks 1994). If we examine this question with the view to the acquisition of EDI, results seem to suggest that even with the low number of willing partners and resulting transaction, 37.5% of respondents indicated that indeed EDI was more costly than alternate methods.

Hypothesis 2 (H_2) posited that small businesses are more likely to decide to acquire computer technology such that work can be carried out faster and better in the organisation. An examination of Table 3 would again tend to support this view with 54% of respondents indicating that their primary reason for acquiring IT was to carry out work more efficiently.

Hypothesis 3 (H_3) posited that a small business is not likely to acquire computer technology with the primary intention of improving customer relations. An examination of Table 3 would suggest that only about 16% of small businesses have customer relations uppermost as a criterion for the acquisition of IT. This again tend to support the views of Reynolds et al (1994) who suggest that small businesses are often more product oriented than customer oriented.

Hypothesis 4 (H_4) posited that a small business is not likely to acquire computer technology with the prime objective to enhance the business in the future. Again this hypothesis is accepted based on the data found in Table 3.

CONCLUSION

Most advocates of EDI in small business tend to suggest that the benefits of EDI to small business manager include:
- improving the bottom line
- working faster and better within the organisation
- strengthening customer relations
- preparing for the future in business

However, studies carried out by Rotch (1987), Reynolds et al (1994), Delvecchio (1994), and supported by the current study would suggest that not all of these factors are paramount when small business managers are considering the adoption of IT or EDI.

Many advocates of EDI in small business tend to utilise data from larger organisations and then re-apply the findings to the small business environment. The data in this study would tend to support the view of Barnett and Mackness (1983) that small businesses are not small larger businesses but quite unique and intrinsically different in their own right.

It would seem, then, that for EDI to be applicable to small business, designers and advocates alike need to examine the nature of small business far more closely. They need to realise that many are product rather than customer based, that most small businesses are interested in maintaining a stability rather than attempting to increase market share and that most small businesses need to maintain a position of independence.

The current thrust of EDI use tends to be pivotal upon gaining a strategic edge and improving the bottom line through changes to the business structure and function. The current study suggests that these factors are lost on most small business managers.

REFERENCES

Barnett R.R. & Mackness J.R. (1983) An Action Research Study of Small Firm   Management **Journal of Applied Systems** 10, pp. 63 - 83

Britt P. (1995) EDI/EFT Moves Forward **America's Community Banker** vol 4, No 8, pp 7 - 8

Brigham E.F. & Smith K.V. (1967) The cost of capital to the small **firm The Engineering Economist** vol. 13, no. 1, pp. 1 - 26

Chen J.C. (1993) The impact of microcomputers on small businesses: England 10 years later **Journal of Small Business Management** vol. 31, no. 3, pp. 96 - 102

Cochran A.B. (1981) Small Business Mortality Rates: A Review of the Literature **Journal of Small Business Management** vol. 19, no. 4, pp. 50 - 59

Cragg P.B. & King M. (1993) Small Firm Computing: Motivators and Inhibitors **MIS Quarterly** vol. 17, no. 1, pp. 47 - 60

Delone W.H. (1988) Determinants for Success for Computer Usage in Small Business **MIS Quarterly** pp. 51 - 61

DelVecchio M. (1994) Retooling the Staff along with the system **Bests Review** vol. 94, no. 11, pp. 82 - 83

EDI World Institute (1995) **The WHY EDI Guide for Small and Medium-Sized Enterprises** EDI World Institute, Canada

Evans-Correia K. (1994) New company lets small suppliers in on EDI **Purchasing** vol 116, no 4, pp 76

Fallon J. (1988) GM Europe Blaze EDI Trail: Will Link 200 Suppliers in Seven Countries **MIS Week** Dec 19

Hinge K.C. (1989) **Electronic Data Interchange: From Understanding to Implementation** American Management Association, New York

Holzinger A.G. & Hotch R. (1993) Small Firms Usage Patterns **Nations Business** vol. 81, no. 8, pp. 39 - 42

Huttig J.W. (1994) Big Lessons for Small Business **Secured Lender** Vol 50, No 5, pp 44 - 49

Kavan B.C. & Van Over D. (1990) Electronic Data Interchange: A Research Agenda **Proceedings of the Twenty-Third Annual Hawaii International Conference on Systems Science** pp 192 - 197

Khan E.H. & Khan G.M. (1992) Microcomputers and Small Businesses in Bahrain **Industrial Management and Data Systems** vol. 92, no. 6, pp. 24 - 28

MacGregor R.C. & Cocks R.S. (1994) Computer Usage and Satisfaction in the Australian Veterinary Industry **Australian Veterinary Practitioner** vol 25 no 1 pp 43 - 48

MacGregor R.C. & Bunker D.J. (1995) The Effect of Criteria Used in the Acquisition of Computer Technology on the Ongoing Success with Information Technology in Small Business, forthcoming

Meredith G.G. (1994) **Small Business Management in Australia** McGraw Hill, 4th Edition

Pletsch A. (1994) Study showing EDI Acceptance Level on the Rise **Computing Canada** vol 20, no 19, pp 13

Reynolds W., Savage W. & Williams A. (1994) **Your Own Business: A Practical Guide to Success** ITP

Rockart J.F. & Short J.E. (1989) IT in the 1990's: Managing Organisational Interdependence **Sloan Management Review** vol 30, no 2, pp 7 - 17

Rotch W. (1967) **Management of Small Enterprises: Cases and Readings** University of Virginia Press

Sehr B. (1989) Levi Strauss Strengthens Customer Ties with Electronic Data Interchange: Levilink Network Carries Order and Shipment Information **Computerworld** vol 30, Jan '89

Udo G.J. & Pickett G.C. (1994) EDI Conversion Mandate: The Big Problem for Small Businesses **Industrial Management** vol 36, no 2, pp 6 - 9

Walker E.W. (1975) Investment and Capital Structure Decision Making in Small Business in Walker E.W. (ed.) **The Dynamic Small Firm: Selected Readings** Austin Press, Texas

Wood J.G. & Nosek J.T. (1994) Discrimination of Structure and Technology in a Group Support System: The Role of Process Complexity **ICIS** Vancouver, pp. 187 - 199

Yap C.S., Soh C.P.P. & Raman K.S. (1992) Information Systems Success Factors in Small Business **International Journal of Management Science** 20, pp. 597 - 609

Zack M.H. (1994) The State of EDI in the U.S. Housewares Manufacturing Industry **Journal of Systems Management** vol 45, no 12, pp 6 - 10

MacGregor R.C., Bunker D.J. & Waugh P. (1998) Electronic Commerce and Small/Medium Enterprises (SME's) in Australia: An Electronic Data Interchange (EDI) Pilot Study, Proceedings of the 11th International Bled Electronic Commerce Conference, Slovenia, June

Electronic Commerce and Small/Medium Enterprises (SME's) in Australia: An Electronic Data

Interchange (EDI) Pilot Study

R.C. MacGregor
P. Waugh
D.J. Bunker

Introduction

The use of Electronic Data Interchange (EDI) in small business is by no means a new phenomenon (Gaedeke & Tooelian 1991, Dixon & Hodgetts 1991, Martin et al 1994, Reepers and Smithson 1994, Kalakota & Whinston 1996, MacGregor et al 1996). When considering the benefits of EDI adoption, Massetti & Zmud (1996) suggest that these can be categorised into two types - operational benefits and strategic benefits.

Operationally, EDI has been shown to reduce cycle times and costs through the standardisation and improved speed of exchanged documents (Metzgen 1990, Banerjee & Golhar 1992). At a strategic level, EDI has allowed organisations to change their approach to business dealings, ultimately enhancing their competitiveness (Sokol 1989, Wrigley et al 1994, EDI World Institute 1995).

Like many technologies, much has been written in both scholarly journals as well as practitioner publications about the success of EDI within companies or groups of companies. In many cases these articles have been accompanied by calls for management and trading partner involvement in the planning and design of the EDI effort (Swatman & Swatman 1991, Galliers 1991, Galliers et al 1993). A closer examination of these claims, however, would suggest that many are highly theoretical (Hinterhuber & Levin 1994, O'Callaghan & Turner 1995) or are more anecdotal accounts of EDI implementation and benefits (Dix & Naze 1993, Paper & Rai 1994, Sokol 1995, EDI World Institute 1995).

When the literature surrounding the design and use of EDI in small business is concerned, it appears that few studies have been carried out. When the involvement of trading partners, management, staff or vendors and their effect upon ongoing success are considered, little useful data is available.

In an effort to examine the roles of management, trading partners, vendors and staff on the ongoing success of EDI implementation in small business this paper reports the findings of a pilot study recently carried out on small businesses in Australia. The pilot study examined the association of involvement by management, staff, trading partners and vendors upon various criteria for ongoing EDI success in the small business environment. The paper begins by considering the nature of small business, in particular the use of IT and EDI in small business.

334

Data from the pilot study is presented to determine whether associations between involvement and criteria for perceived success can be determined. Finally the paper concludes by suggesting more stringent studies which should be carried out in the area of ongoing success with EDI and small business.

The Nature of Small Business

The nature of small business has been the topic of both governmental committee findings as well as research initiatives. Brigham & Smith (1967) found that small businesses tended to be more risky than their larger counterparts. This view is supported by later studies (Walker 1975, Delone 1988). Cochran (1981) found that small businesses tended to be subject to higher failure rates while Rotch (1987) suggested that small businesses tended not to maintain adequate records of transactions. Perhaps most important in any discussion concerning small business is the view given by Barnett & Mackness (1983), that small businesses are not miniature versions of larger businesses, but quite unique in their own right.

Perhaps the most detailed definition of a small business was provided by Reynolds et al (1994). They suggested that among the many characteristics which make up the organisational environment in which a small business operates are the following:

- small management team
- centralised power and control
- lack of specialist staff
- multi-functional management
- informal and inadequate planning and control systems
- lack of control over business environment
- limited market share

When the introduction of IT into small business is considered, there are marked differences between small businesses and their larger counterparts (Barnett & Mackness 1983). Khan & Khan (1992) suggest that most small businesses avoid sophisticated software or applications. This view is supported by studies carried out in the United Kingdom by Chen (1993). Cragg & King (1993) suggest that small businesses often lack the necessary expertise to fully utilise IT.

Despite the belief by many that EDI is becoming a business necessity (Pletsch 1994, Huttig 1994), small business has been slow to move towards the technology. A number of reasons have been given for this. Evans-Correia (1994) suggests that most small businesses lack the technical, financial and administrative resources to implement EDI. Buchanan (1995) considers the high set up cost a disincentive while Aruanchalam (1995) suggests that lack of awareness of EDI benefits is the major cause for non adoption. This view is supported by Massetti & Zmud (1996) who suggest that while 'success stories' abound there are few practical links for the business practitioner to hold onto.

Decisions Taken Prior to the Survey

As this study primarily intended to examine the association of management, trading partners, vendor and staff involvement with the planning and design of EDI systems and the ongoing success of the business utilising that EDI system, only small businesses with at least two years experience with EDI were targeted. The decision as to what constituted a small business needed to be considered.

In line with previous studies examining IT in small business in Australia (MacGregor & Cocks 1994, MacGregor & Bunker 1996, MacGregor et al 1997) a small business was defined as:

'having fewer than 50 employees and was not a subsidiary to any other   company'

Finally the concept of ongoing success needed to be considered.

An examination of the literature suggests that ongoing success must include financial results, business operations, market share and customer relationships. In line with studies carried out by the EDI World Institute (1995), these were subdivided as follows:

Financial Results
- financial
- profits
- inventory levels
- employee related expenses
- revenue

Business Operations
- quality of transactions exchanged
- efficiency of the business
- IS development
- document cycle time
- time spent on the manual functions of the business
- employee satisfaction

Market share
- company specialisation
- company market share
- company strategic position in the marketplace

Customer relationships
- delivery times
- benefits to customers
- quality of exchanged information with the customer
- shipping costs
- strategic alliances with customers
- implementation of strategic programs with customers

Initially a five point Lickert scale (large improvement/ improvement/ no change/ deterioration/ large deterioration) was considered, however the distinction between large improvement and improvement as well as large deterioration and deterioration were not considered sufficiently clear. As such a three point scale (deterioration/ no change/ improvement) was used.

Survey Instrument

A questionnaire was developed. Then questionnaire sought information as to whether staff, management, trading partners or vendors were involved in the planning and design of the EDI system The questionnaire further sought information as to whether financial,
profits,
inventory levels,
employee related expenses,
revenue,
quality of transactions exchanged,
efficiency of the business,
 IS development,
document cycle time,
time spent on the manual functions of the business,
employee satisfaction,
company specialisation,
company market share,
company strategic position in the marketplace,
delivery times,
benefits to customers,
quality of exchanged information with the customer,
shipping costs,
strategic alliances with customers or
implementation of strategic programs with customers
were improved, remained the same or deteriorated with the advent of EDI.

Analysis of Results

80 questionnaires were distributed to small businesses known to have at least two years background in EDI use. These businesses were within the Wollongong and southern Sydney area. Responses were obtained from 20 businesses representing a 25% return rate.
Table 1 indicates the overall responses to the implementation of EDI.

Table 1
Ongoing Success Following the Implementation of EDI

Criteria	Improved	No Change	Deterioration
financial	10	10	
profits	9	10	1
inventory levels	8	10	2
employee related expenses	5	12	3
revenue	11	7	1
quality of transactions exchanged	10	8	2

efficiency of the business	12	7	1
IS development	9	11	
document cycle time	11	8	1
time spent on the manual functions of the business	10	9	1
employee satisfaction	10	8	2
company specialisation	5	15	
company market share	4	16	
company strategic position in the marketplace	6	14	
delivery times	10	10	
benefits to customers	14	6	
quality of exchanged information with the customer	9	9	2
shipping costs	2	18	
strategic alliances with customers	9	11	
implementation of strategic programs with customers	4	16	

As can be seen in Table 1, the introduction of EDI has provided a mixed result to those respondent small businesses. Of particular interest are those factors which might be termed strategic in nature, company specialisation, market share, strategic position in the marketplace, strategic programs with customers. IN all cases most respondents report no change to the position of the company after the implementation of EDI. It would appear that for the most part EDI tends only to affect the operational level of the small business rather than have any dramatic effect on the strategic level.

The data was examined to determine whether the involvement of staff, trading partners, management or vendors in the planning and design was associated with ongoing success. A series of Chi-Square tests were carried out.

Table 2 indicates the factors of ongoing success associated with the involvement/non involvement of staff in the planning and design of the EDI system.

Table 2
Factors of Ongoing Success Associated with Staff Involvement in the Planning and Design of EDI Systems

Quality of exchanged information with the customer

	Improved	No Change	Deterioration
Staff Involved	5		
Staff not Involved	4	9	2

(p<.05)

Implementation of Strategic programs with customers

	Improved	No Change	Deterioration
Staff Involved	3	2	
Staff not Involved	1	14	

(p<.05)

The results in table 2 show that both the quality of information and the implementation of strategic programs with customers was associated with the involvement of staff in the planning and design of EDI systems. 100% of those respondents who involved their staff in the planning and design of the Edi systems indicated that the quality of information was improved. This compares to only 27% improvement by those companies who did not involve their staff. A similarly dramatic comparison (60% vs 13%) can be seen in terms of strategic programs with customers.

The data was examined to determine whether management involvement was associated with any of the ongoing success factors. The data showed no significant association between management involvement and any of the factors.

A series of Chi-Square tests were carried out to determine whether vendor involvement was associated with any of the factors of ongoing success. Table 3 indicates the findings.

Table 3
Factors of Ongoing Success Associated with Vendor Involvement in the Planning and Design of EDI Systems

Efficiency of the Business

	Improved	No Change	Deterioration
Vendor Involved	6		
Vendor not Involved	6	7	1

(p<.05)

IS Development

	Improved	No Change	Deterioration
Staff Involved	5		
Staff not Involved	4	11	

(p<.05)

Delivery Times

	Improved	No Change	Deterioration
Staff Involved	5		
Staff not Involved	5	10	

(p<.05)

Benefits to the customers

	Improved	No Change	Deterioration
Staff Involved	6		
Staff not Involved	8	6	

(p<.05)

Implementation of Strategic programs with customers

	Improved	No Change	Deterioration
Staff Involved	3	2	
Staff not Involved	1	14	

(p<.05)

An examination of Table 3 shows that in all cases the involvement of the vendor is associated with improvement after the implementation of EDI. In the areas of Efficiency of the Business, IS Development, Delivery Times and Benefits to the Customer, vendor involvement led to 100 reported improvement by the respondents. This is substantially reduced to 43% (efficiency of the business), 26% (IS development), 33% (delivery times), 57% (benefit to the customers) where vendors were not involved in the planning and design of the EDI system.

Finally the data was examined to determine whether the involvement of trading partners in the planning and design of EDI systems is associated with any of the factors of ongoing success. While 50 respondents indicated that trading partners were involved in the planning and design there was no significant association between the involvement of trading partners and any of the factors of ongoing success.

Discussion

The results provided above show a number of important considerations for small business. Firstly it would appear that in the small business environment EDI tends, at best, to improve the operational level while having little impact on the strategic level. A number of explanations are possible. Several studies (Khan & Khan 1992, Cragg & King 1993, MacGregor & Bunker 1996) have suggested that when using IT, small businesses tend merely to use those functions which impact upon the operational level of the business rather than the strategic level. These results support the findings of Reynolds et al (1994) who suggest that small businesses not only lack the technical expertise of larger businesses but have a limited desire to improve market share. The results in table 1 would tend to reinforce these earlier findings. When EDI is considered alone, Massetti & Zmud (1996) suggest that very often the tactical link is omitted making it difficult for small/medium businesses to strategically alter their business approach. While this may be an explanation of the findings, clearly further research need to be undertaken.

Of interest is the finding that despite the many studies which call for management and trading partner involvement in planning and design of EDI systems, neither group was significantly associated with improvement in any of the factors of ongoing success. This raises a number of questions which require further research: Is the involvement of management and trading partners only associated with the more strategic areas of ongoing success? And if so does the reluctance of small business to undertake strategic alteration negate this association?

An examination of tables 2 and 3 show that both staff and vendor group involvement is associated with some factors of ongoing success of EDI in small business. In all cases there is a far greater perceived improvement by those respondents who did involve vendor and staff in the planning and design. Of interest, however, is the fact that no group appear to be associated with those factors deemed financial.

Conclusion

A pilot study has been undertaken to determine to role of management, vendors, staff and trading partners in the ongoing success of EDI in small business.

As a pilot study a number of shortcomings can be pinpointed. Firstly the nature of the involvement of the different groups needs further clarification. In particular whether the role was operational or strategic in nature. Likewise the reason for EDI implementation into the small business needs to be taken into account. Finally a more effective measure of the criteria for ongoing success need to be established.

This study has shown that in the respondent group examined there is more likely to be improvement in those areas deemed operational rather than those considered strategic. Furthermore it appears that management and trading partners have no significant association with any of the criteria for ongoing success. By comparison some of the factors are associated with the involvement of staff and vendors.

Clearly further research needs to be undertaken to determine whether such findings apply to the larger community or community subcategories. Further examination need to be made as to why only some of the criteria for success are associated with specific involved groups and not all.

References

Aranuchulam V. (1995) EDI: Analysis and Adoption, Uses, Benefits and Barriers **Journal of Systems Management** vol 46, pp 60 - 64

Banerjee S. & Golhar D.Y. (1992) Impact of Electronic Data Interchange on the JIT Environment **Proceeding of the Decision Sciences Institute** pp 943 - 945

Barnett R.R. & Mackness J.R. (1983) An Action Research Study of Small Firm Management **Journal of Applied Systems** 10 pp. 63 - 83

Buchanan L (1995) The Business Outlook **CIO Webmaster Supplement** pp 52 - 57

Brigham E.F. & Smith K.V. (1967) The cost of capital to the small **firm The Engineering Economist** vol. 13 no. 1 pp. 1 - 26

Chen J.C. (1993) The impact of microcomputers on small businesses: England 10 years later **Journal of Small Business Management** vol. 31 no. 3 pp. 96 - 102

Cochran A.B. (1981) Small Business Mortality Rates: A Review of the Literature **Journal of Small Business Management** vol. 19 no. 4 pp. 50 - 59

Cragg P.B. & King M. (1993) Small Firm Computing: Motivators and Inhibitors **MIS Quarterly** vol. 17 no. 1 pp. 47 - 60

Delone W.H. (1988) Determinants for Success for Computer Usage in Small Business **MIS Quarterly** pp. 51 - 61

DelVecchio M. (1994) Retooling the Staff along with the system **Bests Review** vol. 94 no. 11 pp. 82   - 83

Dix L.Z. & Naze J. (1993) Talk to your Plants **Computerworld** pp 35

Dixon B.R & Hodgetts R.M. (1991) **Effective Small Business management** Harcourt Brace Jovanovich, Sydney

EDI World Institute (1995) **The WHY EDI Guide for Small and Medium-Sized Enterprises** EDI World Institute Canada

Evans-Correia K. (1994) New company lets small suppliers in on EDI **Purchasing** vol 116 no 4 pp 76

Gaedeke R.M. & Tootelian D.H. (1991) **Small Business Management** Ally & Bacon, Boston

Galliers R.D. (1991) Strategic Information Systems Planning: Myths Realities and Guidelines for Successful Implementation **European Journal of Information Systems** vol 1, no 1, pp 55 -   64

Galliers R.D., Swatman P.M.C. & Swatman P.A. (1993) Strategic Information Systems Planning: Deriving Comparative Advantage from EDI **The Sixth International EDI Conference** Bled, pp 197 - 206

Hinterhuber H.H. & Levin B.M. (1994) Strategic Networks - The Organisation of the Future **Long   Range Planning** vol 27, no 3, pp 43 - 53

Kalakota R. & Whinston A.B. (1996) **Frontiers of Electronic Commerce** Addison-Wesley Mass.

Khan E.H. & Khan G.M. (1992) Microcomputers and Small Businesses in Bahrain **Industrial Management and Data Systems** vol. 92 no. 6 pp. 24 - 28

MacGregor R.C. & Cocks R.S. (1994) Computer Usage and Satisfaction in the Australian Veterinary Industry **Australian Veterinary Practitioner** vol 25 no 1 pp 43 - 48

MacGregor R.C. & Bunker D.J. (1996) The Effect of Priorities Introduced During Computer Acquisition on Continuing Success with It in Small Business Environments **Information Resource Management Association International Conference** Washington pp 271 - 277

MacGregor R.C., Waugh P. & Bunker D.J. (1996) Attitudes of Small Business to the Implementation and Use of IT: Are We Basing EDI Design Initiatives for Small Business on Myths **Ninth International Conference on EDI-IOS**, Slovenia, pp 377 - 388

MacGregor R.C., Bunker D.J., Pierson J. & Forcht K. (1997) A Pilot Study of Small Business's Perception of Vendor Provided Services: Are these Associated with Small Business IT Educational Requirements **Australian Journal of Information Systems** vol 5, no 1, pp 44 -   53

Martin E.W., Dettayes D.W, Hoffer J.A & Perkins W.C. (1994) **Management Information Technology: What Managers Need to Know** MacMillan, New York

Massetti B. & Zmud R. (1996) Measuring the Extent of EDI Use in Complex Organisations: Strategies and Illustrative Examples **MIS Quarterly** vol 20, n0 3, pp 331 - 345

Meztgen F. (1990) **Killing the Paper Dragon: EDI in Business** Heinemann, UK

O'Callaghan R. & Turner J. Electronic Data Interchange - Concepts and Issues in Krcmar H., Bjorn-Anderson N., & O'Callaghan R. (eds) **EDI in Europe** Wiley and Sons UK

Paper D. & Rai A. (1994) The Impact of Industrial, Organisational and Technological Factors of EDI Diffusion **Proceeding of the Decision Sciences Institute** pp 843 -845

Reepers N. & Smithson S. (1994) EDI in Germany and the UK: Strategic and Operational Use **European Journal of Information Systems** vol 3, no 3, pp 169 - 178

Reynolds W. Savage W. & Williams A. (1994) **Your Own Business: A Practical Guide to Success** ITP

Rotch W. (1967) **Management of Small Enterprises: Cases and Readings** University of Virginia Press

Sokol P.K. (1989) **EDI: The Competitive Edge** McGranth Hill, New York

Swatman P.M.C. & Swatman P.A. (1991) Integrating EDI into the Organisation's Systems: A Model of the Stages of Integration **ICIS**

Walker E.W. (1975) Investment and Capital Structure Decision Making in Small Business in Walker E.W. (ed.) **The Dynamic Small Firm: Selected Readings** Austin Press Texas

Wrigley C.D., Wagenaar R.W. & Clarke R.A. (1994) Electronic Data Interchange in International Trade: Frameworks for the Strategic Analysis of Ocean Port Communities **Journal of Strategic Information Systems** vol 3, no 3, pp 211 - 234

MacGregor R.C., Waugh P., Bunker D. & Courtney J.F. (1997) Adoption of EDI by Small
Business: Are the Advocates in Tune with the Views of Small Business? – A Pilot Study
Proceedings of 30th Hawaiian International Conference on System Sciences Big Island of
Hawaii, pp 42 - 48

Adoption of EDI by Small Business: Are the Advocates in Tune with the Views of Small Business - A Pilot Study

R.C.MacGregor*
P.Waugh*
D.J.Bunker*
* Department of Business Systems
University of Wollongong
Northfields Avenue
Wollongong Australia 2500
email Correspondence p.waugh@uow.edu.au
J.F. Courtney
Texas A & M

Abstract

*Several recent studies have attempted to provide mechanisms to assist small businesses to adopt
EDI into their organizations. These appear to be based on the premise that small business
acquire and use computer technology to increase market share, gain strategic advantage and
promote customer and interorganisational relationships. Several surveys have been carried out
on the small business community in Australia and these suggest that these premises are not
uppermost in the minds of small business managers. This paper examines the reasons behind,
and approaches used by small businesses in their adoption of information technology. It will be
argued that for EDI to be viable in the small business environment, there needs to be a far
greater understanding of this environment and the mechanisms by which it adopts and utilizes
computer technologies and techniques.*

1. Introduction

Despite the ability, today, for companies to replace inefficient and costly paper-based
processes with computer-based communication, recent studies [1], [2], [3], [4], [5] suggest that
small firms are often reluctant to adopt these alternatives. Electronic Data Interchange (EDI) is
one such computer-based technology whose adoption by small firms has been slower than
anticipated [6], [7].

A number of studies have attempted to provide mechanisms through which small firms can
more easily embrace EDI technologies in their day-to-day running. [2] and [8] have stressed the
need to reduce the appearance of EDI as a highly technical issue and to replace it with a strategic
approach. Parker and Swatman [4] have incorporated this into and educative approach where
organizational support and preparedness are stressed as mechanisms through which EDI can
provide strategic advantage. Iacovou et al [5] take this a step further by suggesting that for EDI

344

to be successful in small business there is a need to view the information technology as integrated towards strategic advantage. Indeed, in all cases, the mechanisms are based upon the desire, by small business management, to increase market share and strategic advantage through IT acquisition and use.

While this paper does not dispute the findings and approaches, it will be argued that most small business managers do not adopt computer technology for the purpose of gaining an increase in the market share, or strategic advantage.

The paper begins with a brief examination of the nature of small business. It will then provide results of a survey which examined the motivation behind the acquisition of computer technology by small businesses. Finally, the paper will present data from a small pilot study of small business EDI users in Australia. While the data of this pilot study cannot be considered representative of the entire small business EDI community, it does appear to support the notion that factors such as strategic advantage and larger market share are not uppermost when EDI or IT, in general, are being acquired.

The paper concludes by suggesting that while the approaches to EDI adoption suggested in the literature may be valid for those firms motivated by increases in market share and strategic advantage over competitors, the majority of small businesses do not fall into this category.

2. The Nature of Small Business

The nature of small business has been the topic of both government committee as well as research initiatives. From a government standpoint there are a variety of definitions of small business:

'having fewer than 50 employees and was not a   subsidiary to any other company' UK [25]

In the United States:
'a small business concern shall be deemed to be   one which is independently owned and operated   and which is not dominant in its field of   operation' (United States Small Business   Administration - based on   section 3 of the Small Business Act 1953)

While in Australia, a small business is defined as:
'small business is one in which one or two   persons are required to make all the critical   decisions (such as finance, accounting personnel,   inventory, production, servicing, marketing and selling decisions) without the aid of internal (employed) specialists and   with the   owners   having knowledge in one or two   functional areas of management' [9]

From a research standpoint, a number of studies have attempted to examine the nature of small business. Brigham & Smith [10] found that small businesses tended to be more risky than their larger counterparts. This view is supported by later studies [11], [12]. Cochran [13] found that small businesses tended to be subject to higher failure rates while Rotch [14] suggested that small businesses tended not to maintain adequate records of transactions. Perhaps most important in any discussion concerning small business is the view given by Barnett & Mackness [15], that small businesses are not miniature versions of larger businesses, but quite unique in their own right.

3. IT and Small Business: Implications for Strategies to Incorporate EDI

An examination of the literature surrounding the strategies for the adoption of EDI in small business nominates three motivational variables which impact upon successful implementation of EDI and should form the basis for any implementation strategy. These are (1) the desire of the small business manager to improve market share through the use of IT, (2) the primary intentions of improving customer and interorganisational relations through the acquisition of IT, and (3) the desire of the small business manager to increase strategic advantage through the use of IT.

These factors will be examined briefly.

3.1 Improvement of Market Share

A number of authors [16], [17] suggest that an advantage of EDI is the ability of the organization to respond to global competition and risk and to plan for market fluctuations. Galliers [18] and Parker & Swatman [4] consider that for EDI to be attractive, a manager needs to view the technology as supporting wider market share over competitors.

However, an examination of small business acquisition and use of IT would suggest that, for the most part, increasing market share is not considered a prime motivating factor. Reynolds et al [19] suggest that small businesses tend to maintain, rather than increase a narrow product service range and limited market share. Studies examining motivation for the acquisition of computer technology in small business, carried out in Greece, Denmark and Ireland [20], [21], and more recently in Australia [22] have concluded that few small businesses place high priority on the use of computer technology to increase market share.

3.2 Improvement of Customer and Interorganisational Relationships

Swatman & Swatman [23], Udo & Pickett [24] and Parker & Swatman [4] suggest that a very important benefit of EDI usage by an organization is the increase in customer satisfaction as well as the strengthening of interorganisational relationships. Indeed, Iacovou et al [5] suggest that this is one mechanism where external pressure is able to be absorbed by the organization.

An examination of the small business community, however, would suggest that by and large small businesses tend to be more dedicated to product rather than to customers [19], often relying on a small customer base for their survival. Studies [21], [22], [25] suggest that the major emphasis, by small business when considering computerization is to improve the intraorganizational (day-to-day) efficiency.

3.3 Increased Strategic Advantage

Most advocates of EDI [26], [27], [28], [29] consider that one important outcome of the use of EDI is the increase to the user of strategic advantage over non-EDI competitors. The EDI World

Institute [30] suggest that not only is strategic advantage an obvious result of implementing the technology, but organizations who remain outside of the EDI trading circle will ultimately be forced to utilize EDI or face financial ruin.

A study by Neergaard [21] of Danish businesses showed that only 4% based their decisions or expectations of computer technology resulting in an increase in financial viability. This view is supported by Reynolds et al [19] who argue that most small businesses tend to maintain a limited share of the market rather than attempting to increase this.

4. Hypotheses

Based on the literature survey presented above, three hypotheses are tested:

H_1 Small Businesses do not acquire computer technology with the primary intention of improving market share.

H_2 Small Business is not likely to acquire computer technology with the primary intention of improving customer and interorganisational relations

H_3 Small Businesses are not likely to acquire computer technology with the prime objective to gain strategic advantage.

5. General IT Acquisition Survey

A number of authors [31], [32] suggest that when attitudes to EDI are being considered, these must be taken in the context to attitudes to IT in general. Based on this view, a questionnaire was developed which sought small business attitudes to the implementation of IT within their organizations. In particular, the questionnaire sought information concerning number of employees, suitability of the computer technology being used, the rationale for computerization, the practices adopted by the business with the acquisition of the computer as well as the education level and requirements of the organization.

A mailing list was developed by the Illawarra Chamber of Commerce. The geographic area covered included the southern suburbs of Sydney, the cities of Wollongong and Nowra (Population approx. 500,000). The sampling frame developed was companies with a work force less than 50, where the company was not a subsidiary of a larger company.

Respondents were asked which one of the following criteria was the major reason for acquisition of computer technology:
- improving market share
- working faster and better within the organization
- strengthening customer and interorganisational relations
- gaining strategic advantage

Respondents were asked to rate the importance (not important / of some importance / very important) that their organization placed on the following:
- using technology to meet business requirements
- implementing new hardware and software
- knowing what information was needed to run the business

347

- designing new systems
- evaluating the benefits of computer technology
- implementing new systems for specific applications

6. Analysis of Results

A total of 600 questionnaires were distributed. Responses were obtained from 131 businesses, representing a response rate of 21.8%. All respondents indicated that they were using IT in their day-to-day work.

Respondents were asked which was the major criteria used in the acquisition of IT. Table 1 indicates the findings.

Table 1
Major Criteria Considered with Acquisition of IT in the Small Business

Criteria	Percentage
1. Improvement of the Company's Market share	14.5%
2. Working faster and better within the organization	54%
3. Strengthening customer and interorganisational relations	16.7%
4. Gaining Strategic Advantage	9%
5. Not Sure	3.8%

The results in table 1 support the views of Neergaard [21] and MacGregor & Bunker [25] that small business is not oriented towards strategic advantage or gaining larger amounts of market share. The results also support the finding of Reynolds et al [19] who found that most small businesses are product rather than customer oriented. Overwhelmingly the main motivation for the acquisition of IT is the need to improve the day-to-day efficiency of the organization.

Table 2 indicates small business rating of the importance of: using technology to meet business requirements, implementing new hardware and software, knowing what information was needed to run the business, designing new systems, evaluating the benefits of computer technology, implementing new systems for specific applications.

Table 2
Small Business Rating in Importance of Various Day-to-Day Activities Connected with Computer Technology

Activity	Not Imp'tant	Some Imp'ance	Very Imp'tant
using technology to meet business requirements	12	63	36
implementing new hardware and software	15	75	20
knowing what information was needed to run the business	9	65	41
designing new systems	20	62	27
evaluating the benefits of computer technology	13	71	27
implementing new systems for specific applications	18	68	21

Table 2 provides some interesting findings. Of least importance to small business is the implementation of new hardware or software or applications (only 19% of respondents indicated these functions to be very important. Overwhelmingly the major importance of IT within small business is the use of it to meet day-to-day needs. This supports the findings of [33] who found that most small businesses opted for the simplest software, their only criteria being that it will carry out day-to-day tasks of the business.

7. Pilot EDI Study

As already stated, while this study cannot be considered indicative of the general population, the small number of results still provide an interesting adjunct to the findings of the general IT survey findings.

Respondents were asked to indicate the percentage of companies with which they communicated using EDI. The questionnaire asked whether EDI was freely chosen or forced. Finally the questionnaire sought information as to whether any of the following problems had occurred in the use of EDI:
- number of transaction too low to warrant EDI
- tasks often needed to be duplicated since the installation of EDI technology

- there were few willing partners to warrant the use of EDI
- the cost of EDI outweighed the benefits
- there were problems attributable to standards incurred when EDI was being used

A mailing list was supplied by Australia's largest company, Broken Hill Pty Ltd (BHP). Sixty small businesses were targeted, the main aim to test the survey instrument. Responses were obtained from 16.

Table 3 indicates the percentage of businesses dealt with using EDI technology.

Table 3
Percentage of Companies Dealt with Using EDI Technology

0 - 5% of customers dealt with using EDI	9
5 - 15% of customers dealt with using EDI	7
> 15% of customers dealt with using EDI	0

Clearly the results in table 3 support the views of [24] that small business tend not to adopt EDI because of lack of trading partners.

Respondents were asked to indicate if they had chosen EDI or were forced by larger trading partners. 75% of the respondents indicated that they had been forced by larger trading partners to adopt EDI.

Finally respondents were asked about the type of problems they encountered when using EDI. Table 4 indicates the problems encountered by respondents together with the percentage of respondents who expressed the problem.

Table 4
Difficulties Encountered with the Use of EDI

Difficulty	Percentage of Respondents Reporting the Difficulty
Number of transactions too low to warrant use of EDI	62.5%
Tasks need to be Duplicated	43.7%
Few willing partners	62.5%
Cost of EDI outweighs the benefit	37.5%
Problems with the imposed standards of EDI	31.2%

350

While over 60% of respondents indicated that they had few willing partners and thus the number of transactions utilizing EDI was too low to fully justify the technology, perhaps more alarming is the findings which indicate that over 43% of the respondents indicated that work utilizing EDI technology needed to be re-done to fit their normal day-to-day operations. Almost one third of the respondents indicated that they had problems dealing with enforced standards. While a number of mechanisms to overcome this problem have been examined in the literature, the combination of high percentage indicating they were forced to adopt EDI, together with the low percentage of actual business transacted using EDI would suggest that such a problem will be ongoing and may actually lead to increases in the duplication of work already experienced by respondents.

8. Discussion

Hypothesis 1 (H_1) posited that small business do not acquire computer technology with the primary intention of improving the market share. An examination of Table 1 would tend to support this hypothesis. Only 14.5% of respondents indicated that computer technology had been acquired with the view of improving the market share of the company. This result tends to support the views of Reynolds et al (1994) and recent studies carried out on the Australian Veterinary profession [22].

Hypothesis 2 (H_2) posited that a small business is not likely to acquire computer technology with the primary intention of improving customer and interorganisational relations. An examination of Table 1 would suggest that only about 16% of small businesses have customer or interorganisational relations uppermost as a criterion for the acquisition of IT. This again tend to support the views of [19] who suggest that small businesses are often more product oriented than customer oriented.

Hypothesis 3 (H_3) posited that small business is not likely to acquire computer technology with the primary objective of gaining strategic advantage. An examination of table 1 shows that only 9% of small businesses acquired IT for the reason of gaining strategic advantage.

An examination of table 2 would suggest that most small businesses tend to acquire and use computer technology with the aim of improving the day-to-day running of the business. 39% thought it was more important to know how to use the computer to run the business than implement new technologies for specific applications (19%).

9. Conclusion

Most strategies aimed at promoting EDI acquisition and use in small business are premised upon the assumptions that small business managers acquire and use IT for the purposes of improving customer and interorganisational relationships and to assist in the gaining of larger market share and strategic advantage within the business. Previous studies have suggested that, for the most part, these premises do not apply to small business. The first of the studies, examined in this paper would support that view. Overwhelmingly most respondents were more interested in acquiring and using IT to enhance the day-to-day running of their business. The data further suggests that most small businesses are content to maintain the status quo rather than implement new technologies for specific applications.

An examination of the results of the second study shows that most EDI small business users are forced to use the technology by larger trading partners. Most have few other trading partners with whom they deal using the technology. This mismatch of customers to technology appears to be resulting in difficulties with implied standards as well as duplication of workload.

It would seem, then, that for EDI to be applicable to small business, designers and advocates alike need to examine the nature of small business far more closely. They need to realize that many are product rather than customer based, that most small businesses are interested in maintaining a stability rather than attempting to increase market share or strategic advantage.

Clearly, the current studies need to be widened considerably such that a more representative view of small business attitude to EDI can be established. It is intended that this be approached firstly by a series of case studies, to be followed by a more nationally representative survey.

Further research also needs to be carried out to determine whether the views of managers are based upon a real desire to maintain status quo or whether other factors such as fear of technology is affecting these views.

10. References

[1] Lalonde R. "EDI, Part of a Larger Paradigm Shift" in Gricar J. & Novak J (eds.) *EDI: Strategic Systems in the Global Economy of the 90's - Proceedings of the 6th International EDI-IOS Conference* Bled, Slovenia, 1993, pp. 368 - 376

[2] McCubbrey D.J. "The Benefits of Partnership: The Real Payoff from EDI" in Gricar J. & Novak J (eds.) *EDI: Strategic Systems in the Global Economy of the 90's - Proceedings of the 6th International EDI-IOS Conference* Bled, Slovenia, 1993, pp. 76 - 81

[3] Swatman P.M.C. "Business Process Redesign Using EDI: The BHP Steel Experience" *Australian Journal of Information Systems* vol. 1, no 2, (1994), pp. 55 - 73

[4] Parker C. & Swatman P.M.C. "Educating Tomorrow's Managers for Telecommunications and EDI: A Cross Cultural Experience" Faculty of Computing, Monash University, 1995

[5] Iacovou C.L., Benbasat I. & Dexter A.S. "Electronic Data Interchange and small organizations: Adoption and impact of technology" *MIS Quarterly* vol. 19, no 4, 1995, pp. 465 - 485

[6] Pfeiffer H.K.C. *The Diffusion of Electronic Data Interchange* Springer-Verlag, NY, 1992

[7] Nilson A. "EDI - Building the Business Case for the SME" in Harris B.M., Parfet & Sarson R. (eds.) *The EDI Yearbook 1993. Electronic Trader: The European EDI Magazine* NCC Blackwell, Oxford, 1993, pp. 24 - 25

[8] Valocic T. *Corporate Networks: The Strategic Use of Telecommunications* Artech House, Boston, 1993

[9] Meredith G.G. *Small Business Management in Australia* McGraw Hill, 4th Edition, 1994

[10] Brigham E.F. & Smith K.V. "The cost of capital to the small firm" *The Engineering Economist* vol. 13, no. 1, 1967, pp. 1 - 26

[11] Walker E.W. "Investment and Capital Structure Decision Making in Small Business" in Walker E.W. (ed.) *The Dynamic Small Firm: Selected Readings* Austin Press, Texas 1975

[12] Delone W.H. "Determinants for Success for Computer Usage in Small Business" *MIS Quarterly* 1988 pp. 51 - 61

[13] Cochran A.B. "Small Business Mortality Rates: A Review of the Literature" *Journal of Small Business Management* vol. 19, no. 4, 1981 pp. 50 - 59

[14] Rotch W. *Management of Small Enterprises: Cases and Readings* University of Virginia Press 1967

[15] Barnett R.R. & Mackness J.R. "An Action Research Study of Small Firm Management" *Journal   of Applied Systems* 10, 1983 pp. 63 - 83

[16] Rockart J.F. & Short J.E. "IT in the 1990's: Managing Organizational Interdependence" *Sloan Management Review* vol. 30, no 2, 1989 pp. 7 - 17

[17] Sehr B. "Levi Strauss Strengthens Customer Ties with Electronic Data Interchange: Levilink Network Carries Order and Shipment Information" *Computerworld* vol. 30, 1989

[18] Galliers R.D "Information Systems, Operational Research and Business Reenginering" *International Transactions on Operational Research* vol. 1, no 2

[19] Reynolds W., Savage W. & Williams A. *Your Own Business: A Practical Guide to Success* ITP 1994

[20] Doukidis G.I., Smithson S. & Naoum G. "Information systems management in Greece: Issues and perceptions" *Journal of Strategic Information Systems* 1: 1992 pp. 139 - 148

[21] Neergaard P. "Microcomputers in small and medium-size companies: benefits achieved and problems encountered" *Proceedings of the Third Australian Conference on Information Systems*, Wollongong 1992 pp. 579 - 604

[22] MacGregor R.C. & Cocks R.S. "Computer Usage and Satisfaction in the Australian Veterinary Industry" *Australian Veterinary Practitioner* vol. 25 no 1 1994 pp. 43 - 48

[23] Swatman P.M.C. & Swatman P.A. "EDI and its Implications for Industry" in Clarke R. & Cameron J. (eds.) *Managing Information Technology's Organizational Impact* North Holland, Amsterdam 1991

[24] Udo G.J. & Pickett G.C. "EDI Conversion Mandate: The Big Problem for Small Businesses" *Industrial Management* vol. 36, no 2, 1994, pp. 6 - 9

[25] MacGregor R.C. & Bunker D.J. "The Effect of Criteria Used in the Acquisition of Computer Technology on the Ongoing Success with Information Technology in Small Business", 1995 forthcoming

[26] Huttig J.W. "Big Lessons for Small Business" *Secured Lender* Vol. 50, No 5, 1994 pp. 44 - 49

[27] Pletsch A. "Study showing EDI Acceptance Level on the Rise" *Computing Canada* vol. 20, no 19, 1994 pp. 13

[28] Zack M.H. "The State of EDI in the U.S. Housewares Manufacturing Industry" *Journal of Systems Management* vol. 45, no 12, 1994 pp. 6 - 10

[29] Britt P. "EDI/EFT Moves Forward" *America's Community Banker* vol. 4, No 8, 1995 pp. 7 - 8

[30] EDI World Institute *The WHY EDI Guide for Small and Medium-Sized Enterprises* EDI World Institute, Canada 1995

[31] Harvey D. "A Discussion of the Organizational Impacts of EDI" *Proceedings of the Third Australian Conference on Information Systems* Wollongong, Australia 1992 pp. 609 - 620

[32] Mackay D. "The Contribution of EDI to the Structural Change of the Australian Automotive Industry" *Proceedings of the Third Australian Conference on Information Systems* Wollongong, Australia 1992 pp. 633 - 652

[33] Khan E.H. & Khan G.M. "Microcomputers and Small Businesses in Bahrain" *Industrial Management and Data Systems* vol. 92, no. 6, 1992 pp. 24 - 28

www.ingramcontent.com/pod-product-compliance
Lightning Source LLC
Chambersburg PA
CBHW071401050326
40689CB00010B/1711